PROGRESS IN LYMPHOLOGY – XX

Proceedings of the
20th International Congress of Lymphology
September 26-October 1st, 2005
Salvador, Brazil

Editors:

Mauro Figueiredo C. Andrade, M.D.
President, International Society of Lymphology
Department of Surgery
University of São Paulo
São Paulo, Brazil

Marlys H. Witte, M.D.
Secretary-General, International Society of Lymphology
Executive Editor, *Lymphology*
Professor of Surgery
The University of Arizona College of Medicine
Tucson, Arizona, USA

Dados Internacionais de Catalogação na Publicação (CIP)
(Câmara Brasileira do Livro, SP, Brasil)

International Congress of Lymphology (20. : 2005 :
Salvador, BA)
Progress in lymphology - XX : Proceedings of
the 20th International Congress of Lymphology /
Organization Mauro Figueiredo C. Andrade. —
1. ed. — São Paulo : Ícone, 2007.

ISBN 978-85-274-0919-3

1. Linfedema - Tratamento 2. Sistema linfático -
Congressos 3. Sistema linfático - Doenças -
Diagnóstico - Congressos 4. Sistema linfático -
Doenças - Tratamento - Congressos I. Andrade,
Mauro Figueiredo C..

CDD-616.42006
06-9178 NLM-WH 700

Índices para catálogo sistemático:

1. Congressos : Linfologia : Diagnóstico e
tratamento : Medicina 616.42006
2. Linfologia : Diagnóstico e tratamento :
Congressos : Medicina 616.42006

PROGRESS IN LYMPHOLOGY – XX

Proceedings of the
20th International Congress of Lymphology
September 26-October 1st, 2005
Salvador, Brazil

Icone
editora

Revised by
Rosa Maria Cury Cardoso
Mauro Andrade

Lay out
Nelson Mengue Surian

ÍCONE EDITORA LTDA.
Rua Anhanguera, 56
CEP 01135-000 – São Paulo – SP
Tel./Fax.: (5511) 3392-7771
www.iconeeditora.com.br
e-mail: iconevendas@iconeeditora.com.br

20TH INTERNATIONAL CONGRESS OF LYMPHOLOGY
ORGANIZING COMMITTEE

President: Mauro Andrade
Vice-President: Henrique Jorge Guedes Neto
General Secretary: Alfredo Jacomo

Scientific Committee:
Ester Azoubel – President
Solange Gomes
Henrique Jorge Guedes Neto
José Luiz Cataldo
Eliud Garcia Duarte Junior
Claudia Stein Gomes
Andrea Kafejian Haddad
José Maria Godoy
Eneida Couto
Anacleto de Carvalho
Maria Del Carmen Perez
Cleusa Belczak

Social Committee:
Marlise Andrade
Yumiko Jacomo
Ana Paula Rodrigues
Walkíria Hueb
Walter Ferreira de Azevedo

BOARD OF DIRECTORS
Sociedade Brasileira de Linfologia

Alfredo Luiz Jacomo
Andrea Paula Kafejian-Haddad
Claudia Stein Gomes
Eliud Garcia Duarte Junior
Esther Azoubel
Henrique Jorge Guedes Neto
José Luiz Cataldo
José Maria Pereira de Godoy
Marlise Aparecida Carvalho de Andrade
Solange do Carmo Gomes Neto
Walkíria Ciappina Hueb
Walter Ferreira de Azevedo Júnior
Yumiko Asada Jacomo

TABLE OF CONTENTS

Editorial

Chapter 1
Basic, Molecular Lymphology and Genetics

Chapter 5
Clinics in Lymphology

Chapter 8
Adipose tissue and Lymphedema

Chapter 9
Oriental Medicine and Lymphatics

Editorial

TREATMENT OF PERIPHERAL LYMPHEDEMA (LO): A DIFFICULT JOB

R. V. Cluzan

Since many years during the congresses of the International Society of Lymphology some recommendations (1-2) are revisited trying to summarize the techniques for LO treatment: Physical Therapy (mainly CDT) and Surgery (derivative or reconstructive). But since some years criticisms and doubts on the efficacy of these treatments or on some part of them appeared in the literature underlining the difficulties the lymphologists are facing with.

1 Difficulties: Therapeutic means facing the tissue changes into a LO: techniques and results

1-1 Physiotherapy and Therapy

All the specialists insist on the importance of Hygienic measures (Skin care) and treatment of any infections. The lymphatic function failure is responsible for the so frequent infections. Probably more than half of the patients experiments at least one infectious crisis in their life.

1-1-1 Physiotherapy must be performed following the classical recommendations in 2 phases:

Phase 1: decongestive phase in intensive course (between 3 to 4 weeks) with every day: skin care, manual lymph drainage (MLD) starting at the root of the limb and extended progressively to the distal part of the affected limb plus multilayer non-elastic bandages and exercises.

Phase 2: stability: skin care, exercises and elastic compression.

The superiority of such techniques versus elastic compression alone has been demonstrated. (3)

In some conditions these intensive courses of treatment must be repeated. There is a large consensus on this strategy in our world of lymphology supported by the most famous experts in this field.

But since some years some authors expressed some doubts on the utility of the MLD in the strategy of treatment compared to bandaging

In some papers we find very strange views like:

A *Lyn Kliman, et al:" There is insufficient evidence to support an evidence based recommendations which to base a practice guideline for treatment LO"*!!! (4).

B The analysis of literature by C. Badger et al:

"Crossover study MLD followed by auto massage versus no treatment. Improvements in both groups were attributable to the use of compression sleeves, MLD provided no extra benefit at any point during the trial".

C Andersen : No efficacy of MLD + bandaging in the swelling reduction versus bandaging alone (5)

All these publications must be taken with prudence for two main reasons:

-First we would like to be sure that they talk on true MLD. To often we meet patients treated by physiotherapists who believe practicing DLM but in fact it is not at all correct MLD.

-The swelling reduction is not the alone end point of the treatment. We can have a swelling reduction of the limb with an increase of the adjacent part of the trunk (Fig. 1) Or without improvement of the quality of life.

1-1-2 Results

Nevertheless there is a large consensus on the efficacy of Physiotherapy on the swelling reduction even if some patients do not respond or even can have a deterioration of their conditions at the end of the first treatment.

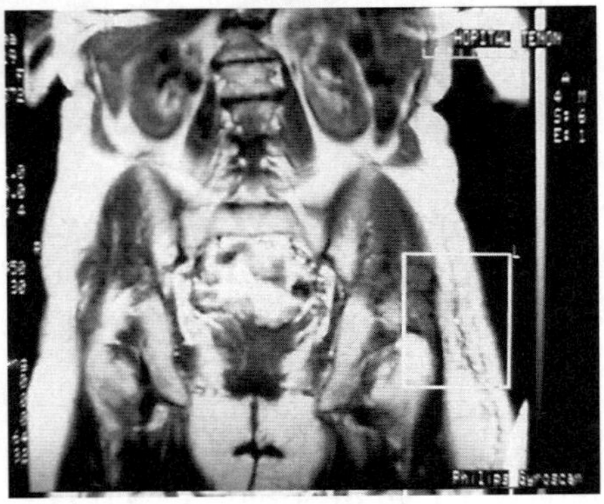

Fig. 1.

In 1985 Pr M. Földi (6) published the results of 399 upper limb LO post cancer of the breast treatment treated by Combined Decongestive Physiotherapy (patients without any Cancer recurrence): 56% of the patients had a swelling reduction superior to 50% but 5 % had no improvement and even an increase of the

Table 1 treatment to the end of first course (CDP) and 5 years later

Volume Changes	End 1 st Course UL (2)	End 1 st Course LL (1)	5 years later UL (2)	5 years later LL(1)
Number	260	126	64	40
Increasing	6%	8%	16%	23%
Decreasing 2-20%	16%	32%	17%	24%
Decreasing 21-39%	39%	31%	31%	22%
Decreasing 40-100%	39%	39%	36%	31%
Total	100%	100%	100%	100%

Inpatients ± 1 CDT / year + elastic Support +MLD 1 to 2 /week - Hôpital Cognacq-Jay Unité de Lymphologie - R.V.Cluzan, Personal data- 1999.
(1 : LL Lower limb - 2 UL :Upper limb)

volume and 3 years later the situation was worse with 47% of the patients having an increase of the volume

We have had the same type of results (table 1)

1-2 Surgery. 1-2-1 Debulking surgery reduce the swelling and we can understand that in some conditions (hot countries or no possibility to have locally some physiotherapy) these procedures could be proposed but we cannot support that in the countries where physiotherapy is available.

S.S Ogunbiyi et al (7) consider as good results a patients happy with surgery + limb size reduction.

Based on 218 operations these authors believe to have 65 to 75 % of such good results . But when we see on these patients, several years after this surgery, the "impact" on the psychology can be considerable and very bad. (Fig. 2)

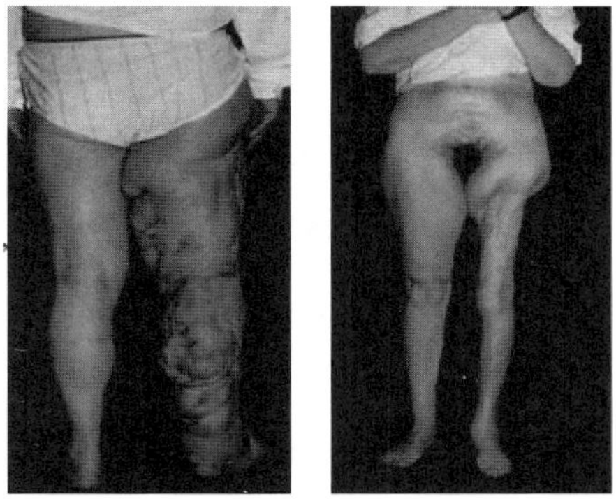

Fig. 2.

1-2-2 Lymphatic microsurgery in the hands of experimented surgeons seems to give positive results.

C.Campisi (8) et al have published in 2004 the results of 25 years of experience with the following results

	patients	%
swelling reduction		
> 75%	616	73%
> 50%	202	24%
up to 25%	25	3%

The difficulty with such surgery is to appreciate the role of the physiotherapy which is always associated. What is the part of each technique? It is difficult to decide what is the role of surgery alone? Some authors underlined that even without any swelling reduction some patients failed better.

(softening without swelling reduction or psychological impact?).

1-2-3 An interesting proposal has been made by W.L.Olzewski (9) concerning the role of fibrotic nodes removal of at the root of the limbs. Even if the improvement remains limited the mode of action of this technique must be taken in consideration and maybe introduced into the therapeutic means.

1-2-4 Baumeister technique (10) is also able to bring some patient's improvement.

1-2-5 When positive results on the swelling can be obtained with these techniques of microsurgery this means that the lymphatic tree below the area of the obstacle is functional. Beltramino in 2003 (11) underlined the difficulties that the derivative or reconstructive surgery is facing with (what about the function of the initial tissue channels, the initial lymphatics, the anchoring filaments, the valves, etc; and how to detect these difficulties before surgery).

The difficult point is to make a choice between these different techniques. The decision is not clear and varies according to the author's opinion

1-2-6 Liposuction as proposed by H. Brorson (12) could be useful for patients where the fat component of their swelling limb is superior to the liquid phase (mobile part). But when looking to the results we must be prudent when we see over 100% volume reduction several years after surgery. What doe it means: atrophic changes?

1-3 The drugs. The means for infections treatment (Antibiotics and Fungicides) are fundamental

The actual drugs which have been proposed for lymphedema treatment (it is to say for reducing the swelling) can bring some positive results but their activity remains very limited when compared with the decongestive techniques (more or less 10 to 15% swelling reduction during the available DB control studies versus placebo) The well known benzopyrones seem to have a much better activity on animal than on man.!!! The number of patients which have to be included in a controlled trial comparing drugs + decongestive therapy versus decongestive therapy alone cannot be done according to the much number of patients to be included. It is not realistic.

Specific drugs for treating LO have to be discovered.

1-4 whatever the treatments, when improving the patients, it is exceptional to recover physical normality for anatomical reasons. In a LO the excess of volume comes from the epifascial area where we find:

1-4-1 Oedema (mobile part)

1-4-2 Fibrosis at several stage or aging (Figs. 3 and 4 Histological section Lower Limb LO).

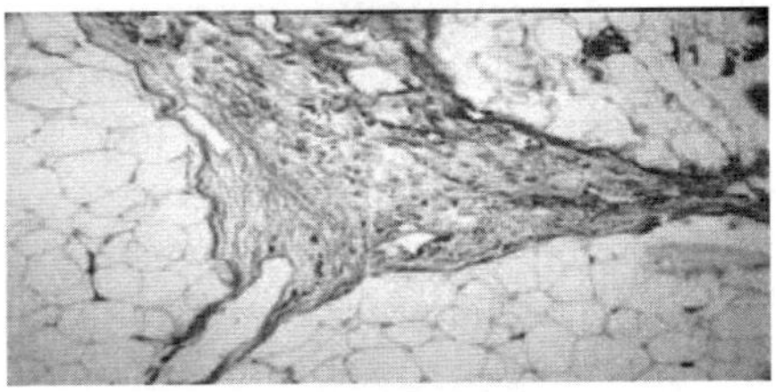

Fig 3. Young fibrosis which can be lightly improved: from firm to smooth (decrease liquid around the collagen fibers but not any disappearance of these fibers).

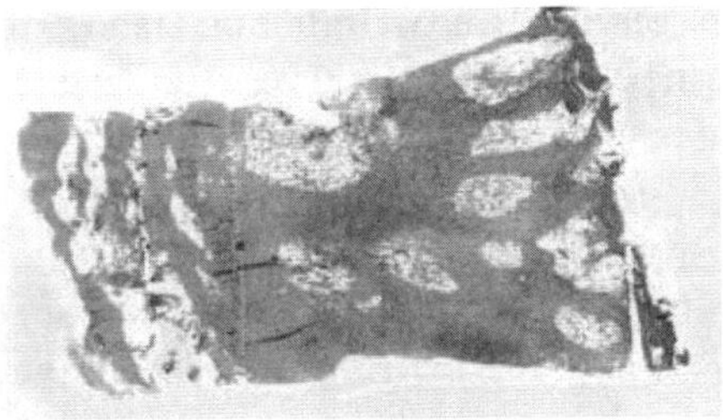

Fig 4. Old fibrosis where the quantity of collagen fibres cannot be changed.

This fibrosis is variable and without any relation to the lasting time of the LO and Huth underlined in 1983 (13) that if there are *«Fragmentation and separation of elastic fibres of the cutis» «Progressive fibrosis of the cutis*

and subcutis. Nevertheless we have to point out that ***a rather high amount of cases with long persisting lymphostatic oedema do not lead to these alterations***». Relation between stagnation of hirgh proteins and fibrosis must be review probably for explaining such differences.

1-4-3 Fat excess: Already underlined with Magnetic Nuclear Resonance imaging, some more specific evaluations have pointed out the importance of this phenomenon:

-High resolution magnetic resonance imaging specific coil (70 microns resolution) shows a considerable increase of the fats component of the fat mass at the level of the calf in unilateral Lower limb LO (Fig. 6) (14) Increased size of subcutaneous superficial lobules by 80% and deep area by 60%.

- Analysis with Dual X rays Absorptiometry can demonstrate in upper limb secondary LO an increase of the fat component which can reach + 19.19% for the fat mass compared to the normal

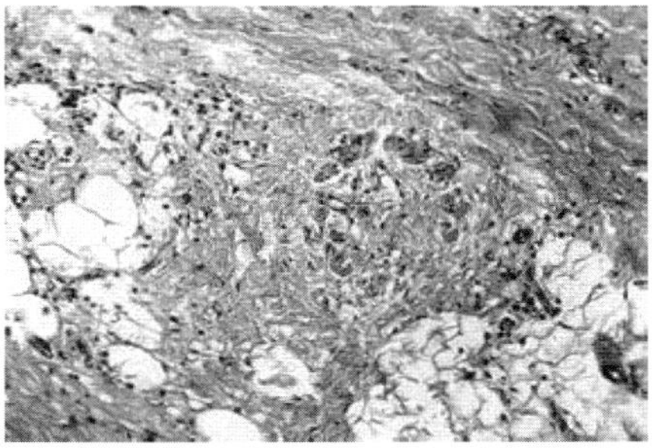

Fig. 5. Fibrosis destroying the vessel from the exterior part of the vessel.

contralateral limb (range +0. 07 to + 48.69%) (15).

1-4-4 Some lymphatic tree **abnormalities** can explained also the difficulties to swelling reduction.

Fibrosis around the lymphatic vessels wall or destroying the wall completely from the exterior of the wall (Figs. 5 and 6) or in primary LO abnormalities of the initial part of the lymphatic tree (Fig. 6)

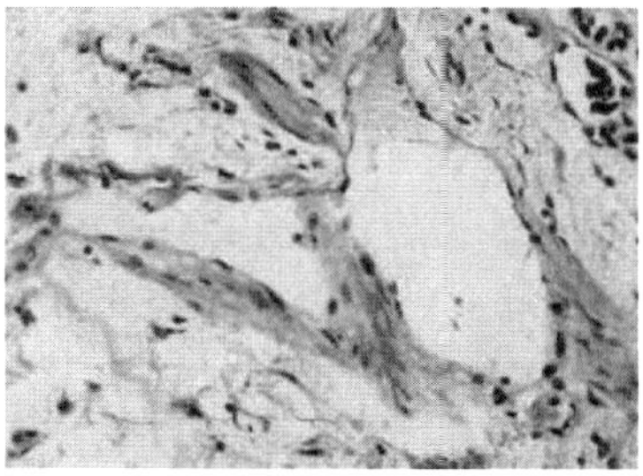

Fig. 6. Atypical smooth muscular fibers around a small collector.

Examining systematically histological surgical specimen of lymphangiectomies for Primary LO we found on 25 Surgical specimen (16) 15 / 25 smooth muscular **atypical fibers.**

7 / 25 abnormal collectors and in the deep, 3 / 25 very small lymphangioma.

All these abnormalities could be a consequence of the LO or a causal factor (Altorfer et al Folia. Folia angiologica, 1977, and Dellscha, Lymphology, 1999).

1-4-5 The last tissue changes (we cannot appreciate clinically to day) are the **changes** into the **proteoglycans** (at least hyaluronan retention) which could play a very important role into the difficulties for swelling reduction and stability.

1-4-6 when we get a swelling reduction after any treatment we can ask our self the question: which percentage of the tissue changes we have been able to obtain (Mobile substances, Fibrosis, Fat excess, Changes into the fundamental ground substance).

2 Difficulties in relations to the human comportment.

2 – 1 The compliance from the patient to the treatment is fundamental for stability

Elastic compression is fundamental after swelling reduction according to the destruction of elastic fibbers but the acceptance of this method is not so easy to get from the patients.

Lasinski in 2002 underlined this point (17) With a good compliance the patients can get a stability of 93.9% for upper limb and 84.9% for the lower limb after decongestive therapy 5 years later.

If not, the results are worse: 53.1% for upper limb and 12.3 % for the lower limb.

2 – 2 With aging the functional capacity of the lymphatic vessels decreases. This has been described for the first time by X. Bichat and confirm latter by Huth (18) who underlined the phenomenon of age dependant lymphangiosclerosis. More recently A.P. Pecking pointed out the decrease of the lymphatic function with aging by using the lymphoscintigraphic kinetic test confirming the view of Bichat.

2 – 3 the therapeutic results must take into consideration much more than the swelling reduction. To often in the published papers the main end point is practically only this swelling reduction!!!

- We must pay much more attention to the associated pathologies like in Secondary Upper Limb LO post cancer of the breast treatment where the patient are suffering more from limitation of range motion, fibrous cord, brachial nerve trauma, nerve entrapment etc. (19).

2 **Body image changes.** Looking to this point we underlined in1998 after analysis of 480 patients (upper Limb LO) with the Bonhomme test and 33 with Rorschach Test. that these patients had some difficulties to draw a specific feminine characteristic and to draw a coherent image with inhibition, frustration, and poor emotional ability. (20).

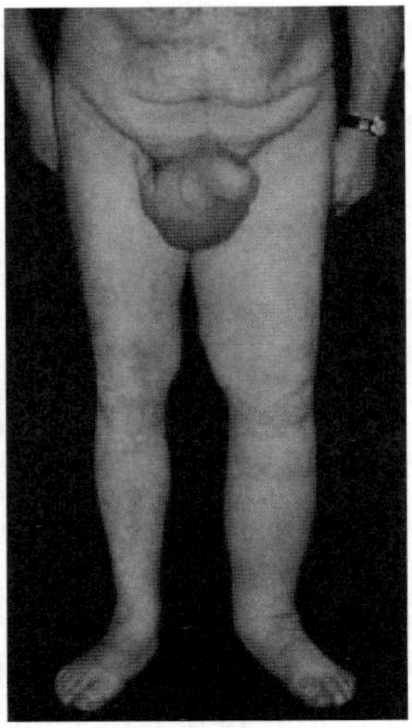

Fig. 7.

As an example this 75 years old man (Fig. 8): LO of the left Lower Limb + Penoscrotal LO Post treatment of Cancer of the Prostate. Fellow of Artist school he draw himself (Bomhomme test) as a young man without any LO and he has no sex!!!

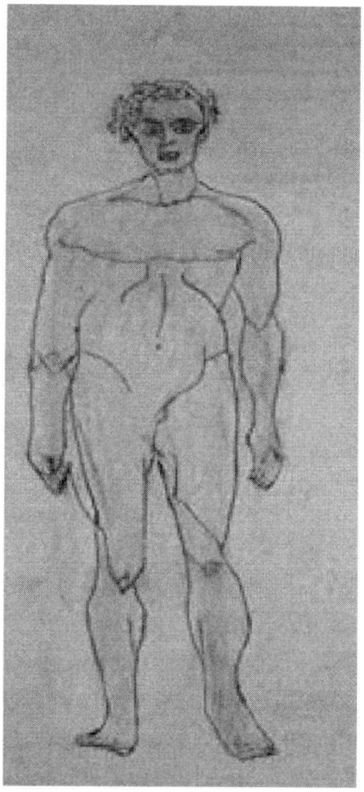

Fig. 8.

- **Interesting 2 papers in 2002** underlined the lack of direct relation between the quality of life improvement and the swelling reduction (21 and 22). More recently it has been pointed out by using special device for evaluation of manual dexterity after vascular brain attack that in upper limb secondary LO the changes concerning the function seemed to impair the quality of life much more than the swelling (23)

Conclusion

For anatomical (tissue changes) and human reasons the come back to normality is not realistic when looking to LO treatment even if in some cases the anatomical improvement seems good.

The need to be treated, to follow hygienic measures, to wear elastic support with regularity, the changes into the functional ability of the affected limb and the body image the chronic character of this disease, the deterioration of the quality of life explain why LO treatment is a difficult job.

We must pay much more attention to the results we can get with our techniques by analysing the balance positive and negative of our results looking much more to the global disagreement of this disease for the patient. The last difficulty if for the patient to discover over the world at least one lymphologist + one physiotherapist well trained in diagnosis and treatment. Waiting for fundamental progresses in the management of LO (discovery to come in lymphangiogenesis and remodelling process) we must make all our efforts to diffuse the available techniques everywhere in the world and to try to include in our standard evaluation all the aspects of this very complicated disease.

Bibliography

1. The Diagnosis and Treatment of Peripheral Lymphedema, Consensus document Lymphology, 28, N° 3, 1995, 113-117
2. The Diagnosis and Treatment of Peripheral Lymphedema, Consensus Document, Lymphology,36, N° 2, 2003, 84 -91.
3. Boris M, S.Weindorf, B.Lasinski, Persistence of lymphedema reduction after non invasive complex lymphedema therapy, Oncology 11, 1997,99.
4. Lyn Kliman, Rebecca KS. Wong, Nancy S. Laetsch Members of supportive care Guidelines group of cancer care Ontario's Program in evidence base The treatment of lymphedema related to breast cancer: a systematic review and evidence summary Support care cancer (2004) 12, 421-431
5. Andersen L et al Treatment of Breast Cancer related Lymphedema with or without manual lymphatic drainage Acta Oncol 2000, 39 (3), 399-405
6. Földi M, Complex decongestive physiotherapy, Progress in Lymphology X, Ed : J.R.Casley-Smith, N.B.Piller, University of Adelaide Press, 1985, 165-167.
7. Ogunbiyi S.O., K.G. Burnand The role of Surgery in Lymphedema. The role of surgery in Lymphedema. Progress in Lymphology XIX Ed E.Földi, M.Földi, M.H.Witte, Lymphology 37, suppl, 1-717, 2004, 423-431.
8. Campisi C, et al. Lymphatic Microsurgery: clinical outcome of over 25 years Progress in Lymphology XIX, Lymphology 37 suppl, 2004, 443-451
9. W.L.Olszewski, Excision of fibrotic inguinal lymph nodes is indicated in lymphedema patients with no-lymph-flow in the groin, Progress in lymphology XVIII, ed: C.Campisi, M.H.Witte,C.L.Witte, Lymphology 35 (suppl)1-760, 2002, 430-432
10. G.H.Baumeister et al, Autogenous lymphvessels Transplantation; The Euro.J.of Lymphology, Vol V,N) 17-18, 1995, 19-22
11. R., Beltramino Operations for lymphedema, Lymphology, Vol 36, N° 3 Sept. 2003 107-109
12. H.Brorson et al Complete Reduction of Arm Lymphedema With Liposuction 7 Years Results, Progress in Lymphology XVIII, ed C.Campisi , M.H.Witte, C.L.Witte, Lymphology 35 (suppl) 1-2002, 436-439
13. F.Huth : Lymphostatic disease , general pathology of the lymphovascular system, in Lymphangiology, Ed: M.Földi and J.R.Casley Smith, Schattauer, 1983, 314-33
14. Idy Pereti Iliana et al, Lymphoedematous skin and subcutis: In vivo High resolution imaging resonance imaging evaluation, The journal of Investigative Dermatology, Vol 110, N° 5, 1998, 782-786
15. Cluzan R.V, A.P.Pecking, J.C.Ruiz, et al Biphotonic Absorbtiometry of the Secondary Upper Limb Lymphedema, R.V Progress in Lymphology XVI, Ed J.A.Jimenez Cossio, A. Farrajota, E.Samaniego; M.H.Witte and C.L.Witte, Lymphology 31 (suppl) 1-621, 1998, 296-298
16. Cluzan, R. R.Levillain L'Hyperplasie musculaire lisse dans les lymphoedèmes,

Ergebniss der Angiologie, F.K.Schattauer Verlag, 1975,71-77.

17. B.Lasinski, M.Boris, Comprehensive lymphedema management : results of a five year follow upProgress in Lymphology XVIII,ed C.Campisi, M.H/Wittte C.L.Witte, Lymphology 35 (suppl)1-760, 2002, 301-304.
18. Huth F, General Pathology of the Lymphovascular system, in Lymphangiology, ed M.Földi and J.R.Casley Smith. Schattauer, 1983,232-235
19. Brennan J., Pain in the lymphedematous arm following treatment of breast cancer, Evaluation and treatment National Lymphedema Network Newsletter March 1999.
20. Alliot F., M.A.Georger, R.V.Cluzan et al Body Image and the Rorschach test in secondary uppe Limb LO, Progress in Lymphology XVI Ed J.A.Jimenez Cossio, M.D.Farrajota, E.Samaniego, M.H.Witte, C.L.Witte, Lymphology 31 (suppl) 1-621, 1998, 427-429.
21. Weiss J.M., et al The effect of complete decongestive therapy on the quality of life of patients with peripheral lymphedema, , Lymphology, Vol 35, N°2,2002 , 45-58.
22. Launois R.et al, specific quality of life scale in upper limb lymphedema: The ULL – 27 Questionnaire, Progress in Lymphology XVIII, Ed C.Campisi, M.H.Witte, C.L.Witte, 2002 , 181-187.
23. S.J.Pain, S.L.Vowler, A.D. Purushotham, Is physical function a more appropriate measure than volume excess in the assessment of breast cancer related lymphoedema Europ. J. of Cancer, 19, 2003, 2168-2172.

Chapter 1
Basic, Molecular Lymphology and Genetics

THE GENERALIZED HYPO-DYSPLASTIC LYMPHATIC-LYMPHEDEMA PHENOTYPE OF ANGIOPOIETIN-2 KNOCKOUT MICE PERSISTS THROUGHOUT ADULTHOOD AND IS FULLY RESCUED BY ANGIOPOIETIN-1 KNOCK-IN

R. Hunter[1], M. Witte[1], M. Dellinger[1], B. Kriederman[1], R. Zeigler[1], C. Suri[3], N. Gale[2], G. Yancopoulos[2]

[1]Department of Surgery, University of Arizona, Tucson, AZ and [2]Regeneron Pharmaceuticals, Inc., Tarrytown, NY[3]

Introduction

Angiopoietins 1 and 2 (Ang1 and Ang2) are potent hemangiogenic/lymphangiogenic factors that bind to the endothelial cell-specific Tie2 receptor tyrosine kinase. Ang1 has been shown to promote hemangiogenic maturation and stabilization via recruitment of perivascular cells by activation of Tie2 (1). But Ang2, depending on the activity of VEGF, can activate either blood vessel sprouting or regression by blocking the Tie2 receptor (2). According to our collaborative study (3), Ang2 knockout (Ang2 KO) mice exhibited aplastic and/or hypoplastic lymphatic channels and nodes, as well as severe chylous ascites shortly after nursing. Lymphatic evaluations were generally performed within the first two weeks of life due to an extremely high mortality rate (95%-99%). Surprisingly, when Ang1 cDNA was knocked into the Ang2 gene (Ang1 KI), the aberrant lymphatic phenotype was rescued in the intestine. In this comprehensive study, we examined Ang2KO and Ang1KI mice (including adult survivors up to 15 months of age) clinically using Evans blue dye and immunohistologically using Lyve-1 and anti-α smooth muscle antibody staining.

Materials and Methods

Evans Blue Dye Visualization

To clinically evaluate the structure and function of the lymphatics, Evans blue dye (EBD) was injected intradermally, under ketamine/xylazine anesthesia, into the dorsum of the paws and into the snout. Under a dissecting microscope, EBD-stained lymphatic vessels and lymph nodes were examined from the hind limbs to the cisterna chyli and thoracic duct; from the forelimbs to the axilla; and from the snout to the jugular lymph nodes.

Whole-Mount LYVE-1 and SMA Antibody Staining

The ear whole mount immunohistochemistry protocol was adapted from previous published methods (4). Whole ears were collected and gently peeled apart to separate the dorsal and ventral layers. Cartilage was removed from the dermal layer by peeling and/or scraping with medium fine forceps. Tissues were fixed with 1% paraformaldehyde (in PBS, pH7.4) for 60 minutes at RT, permeabilized for 1 hour in PBS + 0.3% Triton X-100 buffer, and blocked with 3% goat serum in buffer overnight. Lymphatic staining was accomplished with Lyve-1 (Upstate Biotech 07-538) antibody diluted 1:1000 in buffer for 24 hours, followed by washing and incubation with Alexa flour 488 (Molecular Probes) at 1:500 for 24 hours. Smooth muscle and pericyte staining utilized Cy3 conjugated monoclonal anti-SMA (Sigma C-6198) 1:800 for 24 hours. Tissues were mounted using Citiflour with dermal aspect placed toward the coverslip.

Results

In the Ang2 KO mice, lymphedema of the hind paws was uniformly prominent at birth and persisted throughout adulthood. Peritoneal and/or pleural fluid was present in 25% of adults examined. Also, 30% of Ang2 KO adults had some degree of organ tissue adhesions (Fig. 1). Using Lyve-1 antibody staining, the Ang2 KO ear exhibited a disorganized hypo-dysplastic lymphatic phenotype. Unlike the wild type and heterozygous littermates, these Ang2 KO mice completely lacked functional lymphatics below the cisterna chyli, exhibiting no EBD transport from the hindlimb injection sites. Axillary and cervical lymph nodes and vessels were usually present but hypo-dysplastic. In contrast, the Ang1 KI mice exhibited neither lymphedema nor accumulation of

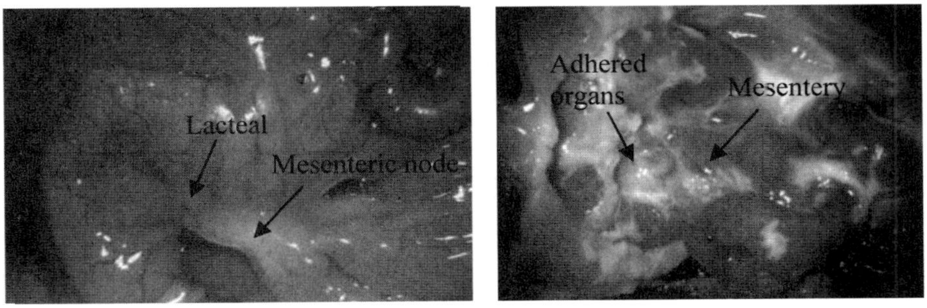

Fig. 1. (A) Normal intestines and mesentery of wild-type mouse. (B) Chronic chylous ascites and organ tissue adhesions in Ang2 KO mouse.

peritoneal/pleural fluid. They also displayed well-visualized and functional ear, hind limb, retroperitoneal, central, cervical, axillary, as well as intestinal lymphatics.

Conclusion

Ang2 has been shown to be required for postnatal vascular and lymphatic remodeling, yet the serious defects in the Ang2 KO mice are survivable. The Ang1 KI cDNA can totally correct the lymphatic defect (but not the hyaloid blood vascular defect in the eye) by activating the Tie2 receptor, which indicates that Ang2 is an agonist of Tie2 during postnatal lymphatic remodeling. These two murine genetic variants thereby provide useful models to dissect the antagonistic and cooperative roles and signaling pathways of the Angiopoietins and VEGF families in lymphangiogenesis and hemangiogenesis.

References

1. Suri C, Jones P, Patan S, et al: Requisite role of angiopoietin-1, a ligand for the TIE2 receptor, during embryonic angiogenesis. *Cell.* 87:1171-1180, 1996.
2. Lobov I, Brooks P and Lang R: Angiopoietin-2 displays VEGF-dependent modulation of capillary structure and endothelial cell survival in vivo. *PNAS.* 99:11205-11210, 2002.
3. Gale N, Thurston G, Hackett S, et al: Angiopoietin-2 is required for postnatal angiogenesis and lymphatic patterning, and only the latter is rescued by angiopoietin-1. *Developmental Cell.* 3:411-423, 2002.
4. Augustin H (Ed): *Methods in Endothelial Cell Biology*: Springer Lab Manuals, Chapter 30, 2004. ISBN# 3-540-21397-X

Acknowledgments

Supported by Arizona Disease Control Research Commission Contract #6011(MW)

FOXC2 GENE INSUFFICIENCY AND IMBALANCE IN THE GENESIS OF THE DISTINCTIVE LYMPHATIC AND OCULAR PHENOTYPE OF LYMPHEDEMA-DISTICHIASIS SYNDROME

A Noon[1], R Hunter[1], B Kriederman[1], M Witte[1], M Bernas[1], M Rennels[2], S Enerback[4], N Miura[5], R Erickson[3], C Witte[1]

[1]Surgery, [2]Pathology & [3]Pediatrics, University of Arizona, Tucson, AZ; [4]Medicinal Chemistry, Göteborg University, Göteborg, Sweden; [5]Biochemistry, Hamamatsu University, Japan

Background

Lymphedema-distichiasis (L-D) syndrome is a rare autosomal dominant disorder manifesting as lower limb lymphedema of pubertal onset and distichiasis, an aberrant second row of eyelashes arising from the meibomian glands. Other associated features may include: cardiovascular anomalies (including Tetralogy of Fallot), cleft palate, hydrops fetalis, cystic hygroma, and bone defects. In contrast with Milroy lymphedema syndrome, the lymphatic channels have been reported to be *hyper*plastic rather than *hypo*plastic.

In previous studies, affected members of L-D families were identified to have inactivating, nonsense and frameshift mutations in the winged helix transcription factor *FOXC2*, a master gene implicated in head and neck development and energy metabolism, on chromosome 16q24.3. These families were then reviewed for the spectrum and severity of their lymphatic and ocular phenotypes. The most common phenotypic features were distichiasis and age-dependent lymphedema, along with variable associated findings such as Tetralogy of Fallot and cleft palate, in addition to a variety of ocular features that included: photophobia, periorbital edema, corneal abrasions, exotropia, ectropion, cataract, blepharospasm, optic nerve hypoplasia, and ptosis. Truncating *FOXC2* mutations were found in all families.

To delineate how *FOXC2* gene dosage might contribute to the L-D lymphatic and ocular abnormalities, we examined lymphatic and ocular tissues in mice heterozygous for a targeted disruption of *Foxc2* (+/-), transgenic for *Foxc2* with an adipocyte promoter (+/+,+Tg), and with the combined transgenic heterozygous genotype (+/-,+Tg), comparing our findings to wildtype controls (+/+).

Material and Methods

Foxc2 haploinsufficient mice (*Foxc2* +/-) on the C57BL6

strain were acquired from N. Miura (Akita University, Japan). *Foxc2* transgenic mice (+/+,+Tg) with an adipocyte promoter were acquired from S. Enerback (Göteborg University, Sweden). *Foxc2* +/- and +/+,+Tg mice were bred at the University of Arizona to obtain *Foxc2* transgenic-haploinsufficient (+/-,+Tg) mice. Littermate and non-littermate wildtype C57BL6 mice served as controls. Mice of both sexes and ages ranging from 5 to 53 weeks were included.

Prior to phenotypic observations all mice received an intramuscular injection of a ketamine:xylazine:sterile NaCl (20:1:79) mixture in the ratio of ~0.1ml/10g body weight. Once anesthetized, all mice received an intradermal injection of Evans Blue dye (1% w/v) in the left ear, distally in all four limbs, and in the snout. All mice were observed using a Weck dissecting microscope with 15-25X magnification. All ocular and lymphatic phenotypes were examined with and without the dissecting microscope.

A lymphatic vessel/node score was devised to quantify the severity of these phenotypic findings. Numerical values for the scores were based upon vessel and node observations. Lymphatic vessel observations included the number of Evans Blue dye-stained efferent and afferent vessels and branching vessels. Lymph node observations included: extra number of blue-stained nodes, presence of non-blue-stained nodes and nodes with extra lobes. These abnormalities were examined in five regions: iliac, popliteal, sacral, axillary, and jugular. After phenotypic examinations, animals were then sacrificed and tissues were harvested for histological studies.

Results

Lymphatic observations in *Foxc2* (+/-), (+/+,+Tg), and (+/-,+Tg) animals, with variable penetrance, revealed L-D's distinctive *hyperplastic* lymphatic phenotype score characterized by an increased number of lymphatic channels and lymph nodes as well as retrograde lymph reflux, when compared to the wildtype controls. In addition, the presence of abnormal ocular findings mimicking L-D were always observed in *Foxc2* (+/-) and (+/-,+Tg) mice, but never in (+/+,+Tg) or (+/+) mice, in the form of distichiasis with the variable addition of ocular edema, dysplasia, cataracts, corneal abrasions, or ptosis. Furthermore, *Foxc2* knockouts (-/-) were previously reported to exhibit cleft palate, bony abnormalities, and aortic arch and interventricular septal defects resembling Tetralogy of Fallot as do some L-D patients.

Discussion

Our prior study showed that the phenotypic spectrum of human L-D syndrome is mirrored in the genetically engineered *Foxc2* murine models both in features of high penetrance (distichiasis and lymphatic hyperplasia/dysplasia) as well as those of lower, more variable expressivity. The findings from our current study suggest that *FOXC2* imbalance rather than insufficiency underlies the L-D *hyperplastic* lymphatic phenotype but only insufficiency can produce the L-D ocular maldevelopment, and further, that *FOXC2* gene dosage/expression level crucially influences the spectrum, penetrance, and severity of L-D phenotypes.

References

1. J Kinmonth, The Lymphatics: Diseases, Lymphography, and Surgery. Williams & Wilkins Press, London, 1972.
2. Traboulsi EI, K Al-Khayer, M Matsumoto, MA Kimak, S Crowe, SE Wilson, DN Finegold, RE Ferrell, DM Meisler: Lymphedema–Distichiasis Syndrome and *FOXC2* Gene Mutation. *American Journal of Ophthalmology, 134:592-596, 2002.*
3. J Fang, SL Dagenais, RP Erickson, MF Arlt, MW Glynn, JL Gorski, LH Seaver, TW Glover: Mutations in *FOXC2* (MFH-1), a forkhead family transcription factor, are responsible for the hereditary lymphedema-distichiasis syndrome. *American Journal of Human Genetics. 67:1382-1388, 2000.*
4. RP Erickson, SL Dagenais, MS Caulder, CA Downs, G Herman, MC Jones, WS Kerstjens-Frederikse, AC Lidral, M McDonald, CC Nelson, M Witte, TW Glover: Clinical heterogeneity in lymphoedema-distichiasis with *FOXC2* truncating mutations. *Journal of Medical Genetics. 38:761-766, 2001.*
5. Witte MH, MJ Bernas, KA Northup, CL Witte: Molecular lymphology and genetics of lymphedema-angiodysplasia syndromes. In: Textbook of Lymphology. M Foldi, E Foldi, S Kubik (Eds), Urban & Fisher Verlag, Munchen, Germany, 2003, pp. 471-493.
6. K Iida, H Koseki, H Kakinuma, N Kato, Y Mizutani-Koseki, H Ohuchi,H Yoshioka, S Noji, K Kawamura, Y Kataoka, F Ueno, M Taniguchi, N Yoshida, T Sugiyama, N Miura: Essential roles of the winged helix transcription factor MFH-1 in aortic arch patterning and skeletogenesis. *Development 124: 4627-4638, 1997.*
7. Cederberg A, LM Gronning, B Ahren, K Tasken, P Carlsson, S Enerback: *FOXC2* Is a winged helix gene that counteracts obesity, hypertriglyceridemia, and diet-induced insulin resistance. *Cell 106:563-573, 2001.*
8. Kriederman BM, TL Myloyde, MH Witte, SL Dagenais, CL Witte, M Rennels, MJ Bernas, MT Lynch, RP Erickson, MS Caulder, N Miura, D Jackson, BP Brooks, TW Glover: *Foxc2* haploinsufficient mice are a model for human autosomal dominant lymphedema-distichiasis syndrome. *Human Molecular Genetics 12:1179-1185, 2003.*

Acknowledgments

1. NIH HL71206 (PI T. Glover, and University of Arizona subcontract (PI M. Witte)
2. Arizona Disease Control Research Commission (ADCRC) Contract # I-103, (PI M. Witte)
3. Western Alliance to Expand Student Opportunities (WAESO) KMD52761136F03UR002 (A. Noon)
4. NIH NCRR R2515670 Science Education Partnership Award (A. Noon)

DETECTION OF TRPV CHANNEL EXPRESSION IN RAT LYMPHATIC VESSELS

Eric A. Bridenbaugh, B.S.,[1] Wei Wang, M.D.,[1] Pierre-Yves von der Weid, Ph.D.,[2] David C. Zawieja, Ph.D.[1]

[1]Department of Medical Physiology, College of Medicine, Division of Lymphatic Biology, Cardiovascular Research Institute, Texas A&M University System Health Science Center, College Station, TX 77843-1114
[2]Mucosal Inflammation and Smooth Muscle Research Groups, Department of Physiology & Biophysics, Faculty of Medicine, University of Calgary, Calgary, Alberta, Canada T2N 4N1

INTRODUCTION

The lymphatic system plays a necessary role in interstitial fluid and macromolecule homeostasis, immune cell transport, and dietary lipid absorption. While blood vessels contain muscular walls that undergo tonic contractions to alter vascular resistance and, thus, control blood flow, lymphatics at the level of the collecting vessels and higher contain muscular walls capable of both rapid/phasic and slow/tonic contractions that both generate and regulate lymph flow. While the unique capability of lymphatics to undergo rapid phasic contractions has been known for several centuries, the mechanical and biochemical elements governing this phenomenon still remain largely under-investigated (1,2). Because lymphatic contraction is crucial to lymphatic function, a solid understanding of the mechanisms regulating the lymphatic contractile process is necessary to gain a comprehensive understanding of lymphatic biology.

The transient receptor potential (TRP) cation channel superfamily consists of seven protein families based on amino acid homology (3). The TRPV subfamily (ion channels structurally related to the vanilloid/capsaicin receptor) are thermosensitive, nonselective cation channels that have been reported to "sense" physical stimuli such as stretch/pressure, osmolarity, and temperature changes (4), all of which are potent modulators of lymphatic pumping, making TRPV channels of great interest with respect to lymphatic contractile function. It is not known if lymphatic vessels possess these channels. As a first step to understanding how lymphatic vessels respond to physical stimuli, we investigated the mRNA expression of TRPV channel subtypes 1-6 in rat thoracic ducts, cervical lymphatics, and mesenteric lymphatics using quantitative, real-time PCR (qPCR). For comparison to the vascular system, we also evaluated TRPV mRNA expression in rat arteries, veins, arterioles, and venules. Additionally, we confirmed the protein expression of TRPV1, 2, & 4 in lymphatic vessels using confocal fluorescence microscopy.

MATERIALS AND METHODS

Animals – Male Sprague-Dawley rats (~300-350 g) were anaesthetized with a combination of a fentanyl/ droperidol solution (0.3 mL/kg IM) and diazepam (2.5 mg/kg IM).

RNA isolation – Blood and lymphatic vessels (5-9 of each vessel type) were isolated as rapidly as possible, placed directly into RNA*later* (Ambion), and cleaned of extraneous material. Total vessel RNA was isolated using a rotor-stator homogenizer and TRIzol Reagent (Invitrogen) according to the manufacturer's instructions. The RNA was subsequently DNase-treated with DNA-*free* (Ambion) and analyzed for integrity and quantity using the Agilent 2100 bioanalyzer and RNA6000 Pico LabChip Kit (Agilent Technologies).

Quantitative, real-time polymerase chain reaction (qPCR) – Total RNA samples were reverse transcribed to cDNA using the iScript cDNA Synthesis Kit (Bio-Rad). 18s rRNA and TRPV1-6 mRNA quantities were assessed using specific primers and fluorogenic probes on an ABI PRISM 7700 Sequence Detector System. Relative quantitation was performed using the $\Delta\Delta$Ct method in which the quantity of mRNA in each sample relative to 18s rRNA is normalized to an arbitrary reference sample. Statistics were performed using the JMP IN v5 software package. Significance was assessed using a one-way ANOVA with a Student's t post hoc test ($p < 0.05$).

Immunohistochemistry – 1.0-1.5 cm long segments of lymphatic vessels were gently isolated from the mesentery. The vessel segments were cannulated onto glass pipettes, pressurized, fixed for 1 hr in 2% paraformidahyde-PBS, and permeabilized for 5 min in -20°C methanol. The vessels were incubated overnight at 4ºC with rabbit anti-TRPV1 (Abcam), TRPV2 (Abcam), or TRPV4 (Alomone Labs) primary antibodies and 1 hr with a goat/anti-rabbit secondary antibody conjugated to Oregon Green 488. The vessels were imaged on a Leica TCS SP2 AOBS confocal microscope using a 50x objective. Image reconstruction was performed using the Leica Confocal Software package.

RESULTS

Utilizing qPCR, we detected mRNA for TRPV subtypes 1-4 in rat lymphatic and blood vessels. We were unable to detect TRPV5 and TRPV6 in rat thoracic ducts and cervical lymphatics (other vessel types were not tested for TRPV5 & 6 mRNA content). Thoracic duct, cervical, and mesenteric lymphatic vessels expressed significantly more TRPV2 mRNA than subclavian arteries and veins as well as mesenteric arterioles and venules ($p<0.05$). Additionally, the three lymphatic vessels expressed significantly more TRPV1 & 3 mRNA than all blood vessels tested other than the subclavian artery (Fig.1).

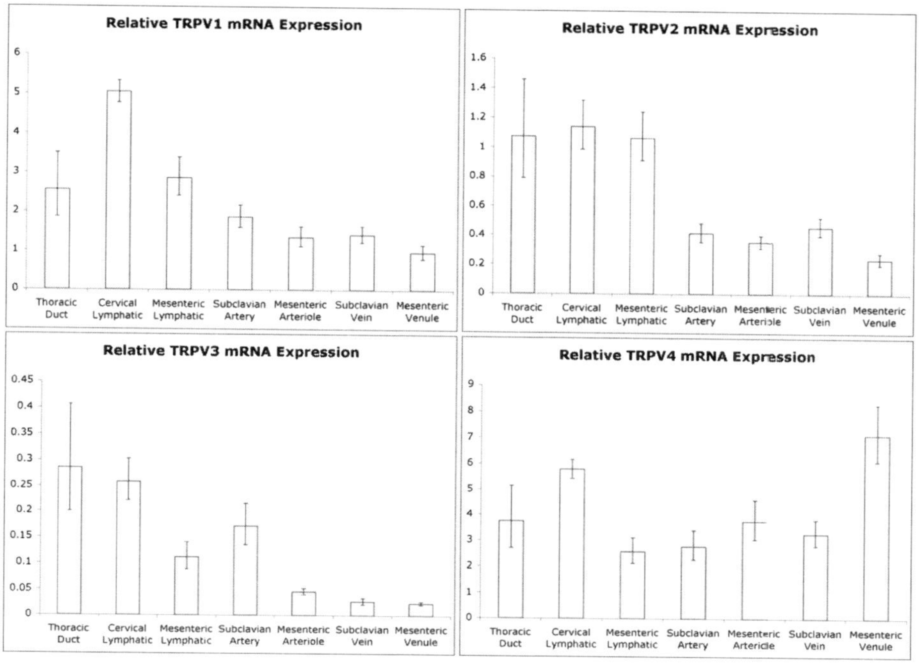

Fig. 1. Relative TRPV1-4 mRNA expression levels in rat thoracic ducts, cervical lymphatics, mesenteric lymphatics, subclavian arteries, subclavian veins, mesenteric arterioles, and mesenteric venules as detected using quantitative, real-time PCR. Error bars represent ±1 SEM.

Utilizing confocal fluorescence microscopy, we confirmed the expression of TRPV1, TRPV2, and TRPV4 protein in rat mesenteric lymphatics (Fig. 2). TRPV1 and TRPV2 appeared to be expressed primarily in the smooth muscle layer of the lymphatic vessels while TRPV4 appeared to be expressed in both the smooth muscle and the endothelium.

DISCUSSION

For TRPV subtypes 1-3, the three lymphatic vessels tested consistently expressed greater quantities of mRNA compared to nearly all of the blood vessel types tested. This elevated TRPV mRNA expression in lymphatic vessels is consistent with the potent contractile response to both distention and temperature observed in these vessels. The presence of these channels on lymphatic vessels could provide a mechanism by which physical stimuli could lead to an influx of calcium into the lymphatic smooth muscle leading to membrane depolarization and contraction.

While TRPV1 is often expressed on C-sensory nerve fibers associated with the vasculature, the authors have been unable to locate any published reports of TRPV1

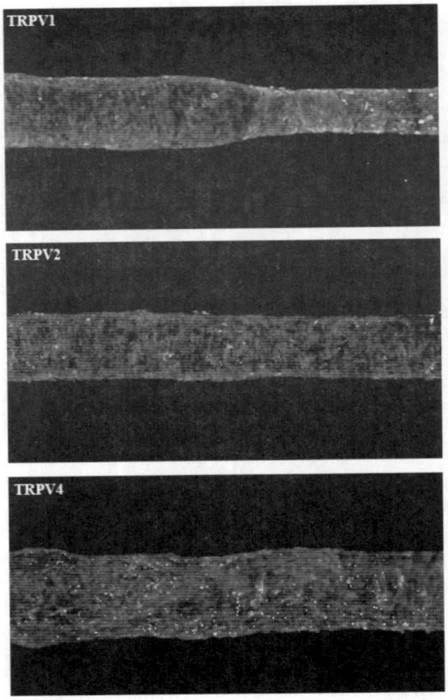

Fig. 2. TRPV1, 2, & 4 protein expression in rat mesenteric lymphatic vessels as detected by confocal fluorescence microscopy. Vessels are approximately 80-120 μm in diameter.

protein expression directly on vascular smooth muscle cells. The detection of TRPV1 protein in lymphatic smooth muscle is a novel finding and suggests that TRPV1 may play a role in the unique physiology of lymphatic vessels. TRPV1 activation is often associated with the release of substance P from C-sensory fibers (5); rat mesenteric lymphatic vessels exhibit a profound increase in contractility following treatment with substance P, which presumably allows them to increase lymph output during the periods of increased fluid extravasation associated with inflammation (6). It is possible that lymphatic vessels may respond both indirectly through substance P and directly through TRPV1 channels to a TRPV1 stimulus thus facilitating a coordinated participation of lymphatic vessels in an inflammatory response.

ACKNOWLEDGMENTS

This work was funded by grants from the NIH (R01 HL075199).

REFERENCES

1. Gnepp, DR: Lymphatics. In: *Edema*, NC Staub, AE Taylor (eds.), Raven Press, New York, 1984, 263-298.
2. Bridenbaugh, EA, AA Gashev, DC Zawieja: Lymphatic muscle: a review of contractile function. Lymphatic Research & Biology 1 (2003), 147-158.
3. Clapham, DE: TRP channels as cellular sensors. Nature 426 (2003), 517-524.
4. O'Neil, RG, RC Brown: The vanilloid receptor family of calcium-permeable channels: molecular integrators of microenvironmental stimuli. News in Physiological Sciences 18 (2003), 226-231.
5. Szallasi, A, PM Blumberg: Vanilloid (capsaicin) receptors and mechanisms. Pharmacological Reviews 51 (1999), 159-211.
6. Amerini, S, M Ziche, ST Greiner, DC Zawieja: Effects of substance P on mesenteric lymphatic contractility in the rat. Lymphatic Research & Biology 2 (2004), 2-10.

IMMUNOHISTOPATHOLOGY OF HUMAN LEG LYMPHATICS IN LYMPHEDEMA– SKIN PLEXUS AND COLLECTORS

Olszewski W.L., Zaleska M., Cakala M., Zolich D.

Department of Surgical Research & Transplantology, Medical Research Center, Polish Academy of Sciences, Warsaw, Poland

Recent progress in immunohistopathology and development of new biological markers of lymphatic endothelium allow to assess the morphological and functional status of human limb lymphatics. We studied normal skin and collecting lymphatics of lower legs in healthy non-lymphedema subjects and in obstructive lymphedema patients. **Aim**. To investigate lymphatic endothelium in skin superficial and deep system and collecting trunks in lower legs. **Material**. Skin fragments and superficial lymphatics were harvested from 10 patients with obstructive lymphedema stage IV of lower limbs undergoing debulking surgery and 6 healthy (ischemic) legs amputated because of irreversible arterial changes. **Methods.** Immunohistochemical staining of specimens was performed using monoclonal antibodies agains LYVE1, prox1, podoplanin, chemokines CCL19 and CCL21, receptor CCR7, VEGF C and VEGF C R. **Results. Control limbs.** LYVE1 was detected in small skin lymphatics. In lymphatic trunks staining was very weak. Neither prox1 nor podoplanin were identifiable in skin and collectors. Slight staining for CCL19 and CCL21 was seen both in skin and collecting lymph vessels. No presence of receptor CCR7 was detected. VEGF C and its receptor flt4 were present in skin lymphatics but not in collecting vessels. **Lymphedematous skin and collectors.** Neither LYVE nor podoplanin and prox 1 could be identified in lymphatic structures. Also there was no chemokine CCL19 and 21 or CCL9. No VEGF C and its receptor were identified in skin and large lymphatics. **Conclusions.** Normal lymphatics stain very weakly for LYVE1 and contain little of CCL19 and 21 as well as VEGF compared with embryonic vessels. Differentiated lymphatics probably contain less receptors, chemokines and growth factors. In long-lasting lymphedema lymphatic endothelium undergoes major degenerative changes.

LYMPHANGIOGENESIS???

Are the structures budding off from dermal vessels "new lymphatics"?

Lymphatic endothelial cells of these structure do not in vivo incorporate bromdeoxyuridine (BrdU) into DNA, a marker of dividing cells.

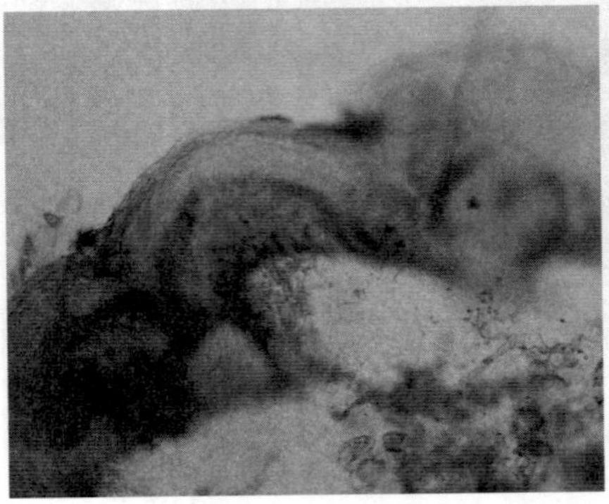

Dilatation of skin superficial lymphatics

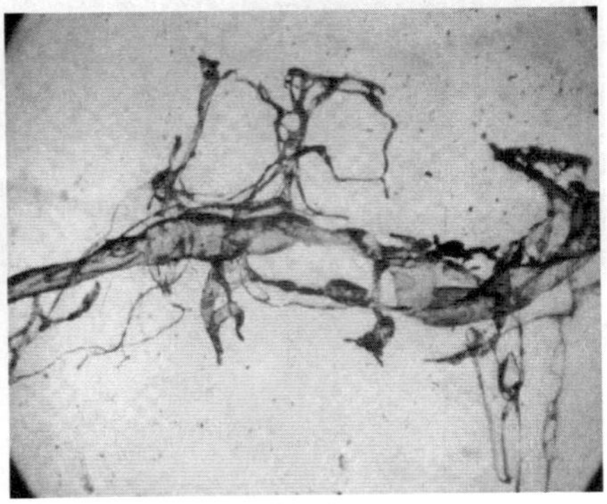

Dilatation of collector

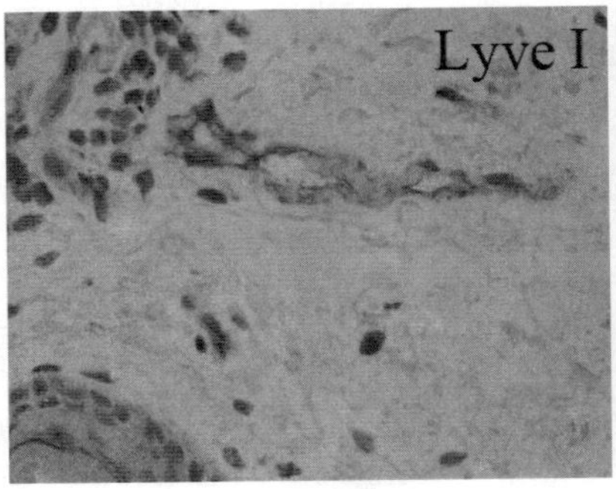

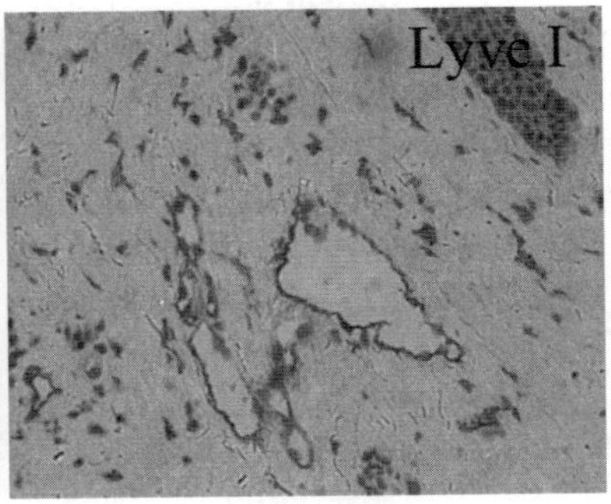

normal dilated
lymphatics

DEGENERATIVE BUT NOT REGENERATIVE CHANGES IN LYMPH NODES

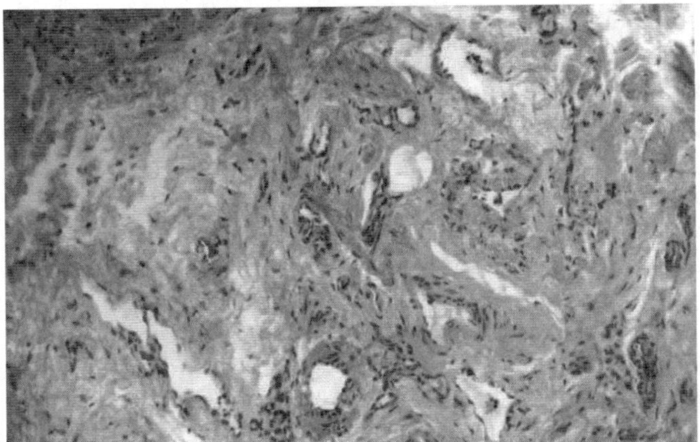

Fibrosis of lymph node

EXPRESSION OF GROWTH FACTORS, CHEMOKINES AND RECEPTORS IN HUMAN LEG TISSUES

	Tissues		Collectors		Lymph nodes	
	N	L	N	L	N	L
LYVE1	+	+	-	-	+	±
Prox1	-	-	-	-	-	-
Podoplanin	-	-	-	-	-	-
VEGF- C	±	±	±	±	-	-
VEGF- CR	-	-	-	-	-	-
CCL21	±	-	-	-	+	-
CCL19	±	-	-	-	+	-
CCR7	-	-	-	-	-	-
CXCL13	-	-	-	-	-	-
CXCR5	-	-	-	-	++	+

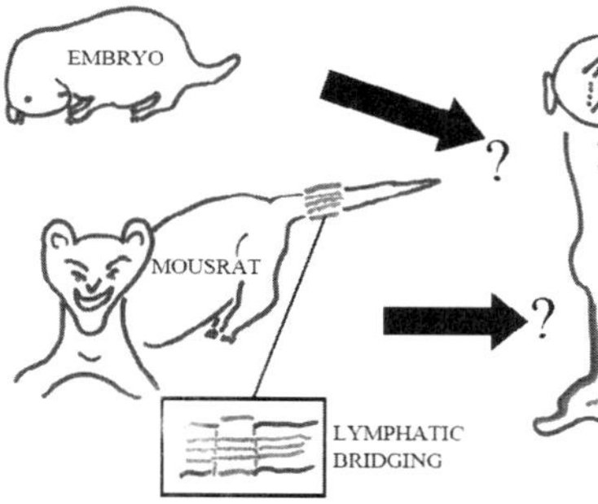

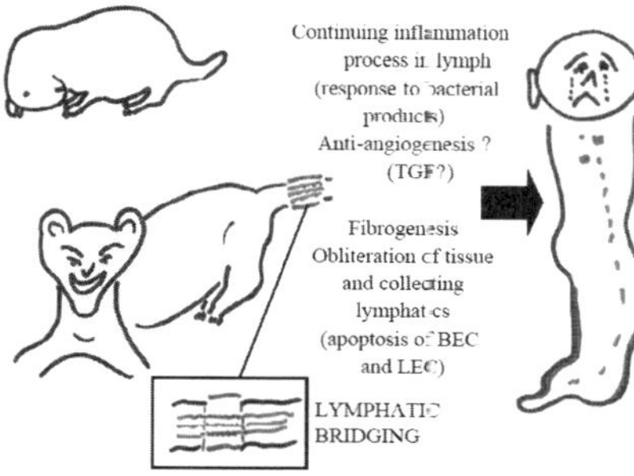

1 Results of studies on lymphangiogenesis and lymphonodogenesis on healthy animals should cautiously be extrapolated to human lymphedema.

2 No evident lymphangiogenesis and lymphonodogenesis observed in human tissues with damaged lymphatics and nodes.

THE RATIO OF LYMPHATIC AND BLOOD ENDOTHELIAL CELLS IN A MEDIUM CONDITIONED WITH PREADIPOCYTES

A. M. Boos[1/2], U. Fiedler[2], E. Földi[3], G.B. Stark[1], G. Felmerer[1]

[1] Department of Plastic and Hand Surgery, University of Freiburg Medical Center, Freiburg / Germany

[2] Department of Vascular Biology and Angiogenesis Research, Tumor Biology Center, Freiburg, Germany

[3] Földiklinik, Clinic for Lymphology, Hinterzarten, Germany

Introduction

Lymphatic vessels consist of a single layer of lymphatic endothelial cells. In contrary to blood vessels, lymphatic capillaries are not covered by smooth muscle cells or pericytes and a basal membrane is missing. During physiological conditions the lymphatic system plays an important role in maintaining homoeostasis, in transporting tissue fluid, biological macromolecules and inflammatory cells from peripheral tissues back to the blood vascular network (Witte et al., 2001). Imbalance between lymph formation and absorption leads to edema for example caused by inflammation or neoplastic obstruction. Even after complex physical treatment of lymphedemas extended limbs remain (Földi et al., 1981). A characteristic feature of chronic lymphedema is the increase of adipose tissue (Fig.1).

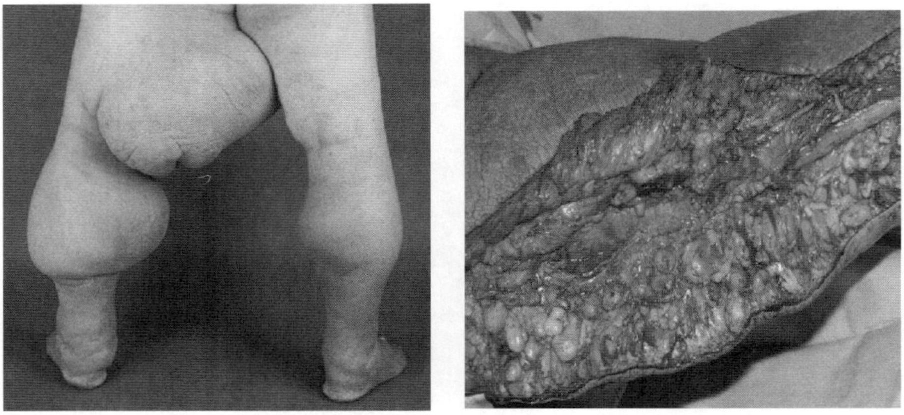

Fig. 1. The increase of adipose tissue is a characteristic feature of chronic lymphedema. On the left picture a forty year old man with a primary chronic lymphedema can be seen. The right picture was taken during surgery while reducing hypertrophy tissue.

Interactions between blood capillary endothelial cells and preadipocytes are well known to exist (Bjorntorp et al., 1983). But there are a lot of questions which are not answered up to now. It is not known how the adipose hypertrophy arises, if there are interactions between adipocytes and LEC and if adipocytes produce mediators which lead to an increase of LEC. Therefore the ratio of lymph and blood capillary endothelial cells was examined in a medium conditioned to preadipocytes by focusing on secreted mediators.

It has to be clarified if the ratio of LEC to BEC can be influenced by addition of one of the known growth factors like VEGF-A and C or by mediators in a conditioned preadipocyt medium, proposing that preadipocytes secret potent mediators like: VEGF – A / B / C / D / E or ang 1 / 2.

The VEGF family is the best characterised group of endothelial specific growth factors (Fig.2). VEGF – A stimulates endothelial cell migration and proliferation by binding and activation of VEGFR-1 and VEGFR-2 (Gale NW, Yancopoulos GD,1999). VEGF-B binds exclusively to VEGFR-1 and mediates extra cellular matrix degradation and promotes migration and adhesion. In contrast VEGF-E binds exclusively to VEGFR-2. (Shibuya M. 2003) VEGF-3 binds both VEGFR-2 and VEGFR-3. Upon binding to VEGFR-3 VEGF-C regulates lymphangiogenesis. VEGFR-3 primarily expressed by lymphatic endothelial cells and some hematopoietic cells in adults. VEGF-C stimulates migration and proliferation of endothelial cells and increases vascular permeability (Lohela et al.,

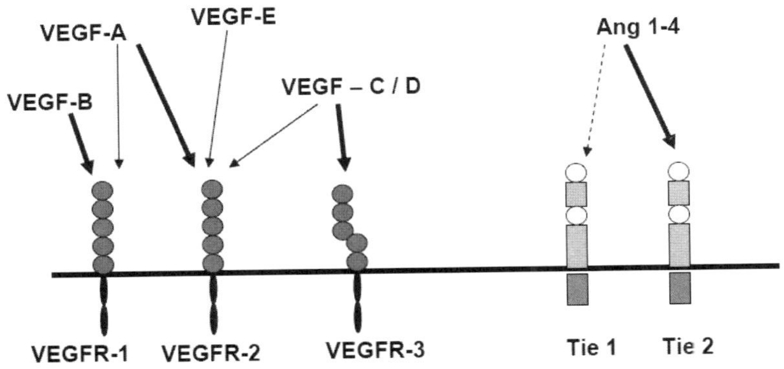

Fig. 2. Short overview of involved growth factors: The VEGF family is the best characterised group of endothelial specific growth factors. The second important family is the Angiopoietin-tie family. (For further details see description)

2003). It has recently been shown that an excess of VEGF-C causes lymphatic hyperplasia in developmental models and adult tissues (Saaristo et al., 2002). VEGF-C therapy holds potential for augmenting the growth of lymphatics in situations requiring increased lymphatic drainage, such as in lymphedema. It has been shown that VEGF-C overexpressing tumors induce the growth of immature and malfunctional lymphatics in the periphery.

A second doss of receptor protein involved in angiogenesis is the Ang / Tie System. The system controls remodelling, maturation and stability of the vascular bed (Fachinger et al. 1999). The Angiopoietins act on both the blood and the lymphatic system. However their exact role is not clarified yet (Yuan et al., 2002).

Lyve-1 is a transmembrane glycoprotein, which contains a hyaluronan binding domain and is involved in the uptake of hyaluronic acid. Besides sinusoidal endothelial cells of the spleen and liver as well as placental syncytiotrophoblasts it is exclusively expressed on LEC. Collecting vessels can be negative for Lyve-1. In cultured HDMEC Lyve-1 seems to detect a subpopulation of LEC, which are also positive for Podoplanin and Prox 1.

Material and Methods

All experiments were conducted using human dermal microvascular endothelial cells (HDMEC), which are a mixture of blood endothelial cells (BEC) and lymphatic endothelial cells (LEC), rather then pure LEC. HDMEC were extracted from human skin, which was removed by dermolipektomie–surgery like abdomino plastic or face lifts. After mechanical and enzymatic treatment a mixture of dermal cells was obtained. This mixture was sorted using magnetic beads (Dynal Biotech) and an antibody against CD31 (DAKO). The received HDMEC were cultivated in endothelial cell growth medium MV (Promo Cell).

Preadipocyes were obtained from human subcutaneous fat which was removed by dermolipektomie–surgery. This fat was cut in small pieces and incubated 4 h at 37°C in a mixture of collagenase, glucose and albumin. After that the fat was homegenized and the cells were be harvested by centrifugation. Cells were cultivated in endothelial cell growth medium MV (Promo Cell).

Cells were cultivated for 3 days under 7 different conditions in endothelial cell basal medium (Promo Cell) containing 10 % FCS (fetal calf serum, Sigma) (Tab. 1). Cells were stimulated with 25 ng / ml VEGF–A (R&D), 150 ng / ml VEGF–C (R&D) and10% conditioned preadipocyte medium (2days old). In blocking experiments soluble VEGFR-1/2 Tie 2 were added. Cells were observed 3 days and stained for CD 31 (DAKO) and LYVE 1 (relia tech).As secondary antibodys

HDMEC	EBM	10% FCS		1:10 PAC	VEGFs	inhibitor
+	+	+		---------	-----------	-----------
+	+	+		+	-----------	-----------
+	+	+		---------	VEGF-A	-----------
+	+	+		---------	VEGF-C	-----------
+	+	+		+	-----------	VEGFR 1
+	+	+		+	-----------	VEGFR 2
+	+	+		+	-----------	Tie 2

Tab. 1: Experimental design: By using endothelial cell basal medium cells were cultivated for 3 days under 8 different conditions.To this 10 % fetal calf serum was added and in addition as controls 25 ng / ml VEGF–A, 150 ng / ml VEGF–C and 10 % medium, which were conditioned 2 days by pre-adipocytes. In another 4 preparations the endothelial cell basal medium with 10 % FCS and 10 % medium from a pre-adipocytes culture were used and in every preparation one of the following growth factor receptor was inhibited: VEGFR- 1/2 or Tie 2 receptor.

a donkey anti goat Alexa 488 and a donkey anti rabbit Cy 3 (both molecular probes) were used. Every day 3 fields of vision were counted and the ratio of BECs to LECs was determined.

Results

HDMEC were cultivated 3 days under 7 different conditions. The number of LEC increases upon growth in preadipocyte conditioned media (Figs. 3/4). No variance of the ratio between LEC and BEC was observed when VEGF-A or VEGF-C was added. Moreover none of the soluble VEGFR and soluble Tie 2 was able to block enhanced LEC growth by preadipocyte supernatant. We observed that the amount of LEC that were stimulated with conditioned pre-adipocytes–medium was augmented in comparison to BEC. This effect was obvious on the first observation day; (Fig. 5) but longer incubation times did not increase the effect. On the 2nd and 3rd day a decrease of the effect was observed, which can be explained by administration of growth factors which were in the preadipocytes –medium.

The blocking of the factors VEGFR-1 / 2 and Tie2 has no effect. The growth factor receptors VEGF-A / B / E and Ang 1 /2 are not involved in the observed effects suggesting that VEGF-A / B / E and Ang 1 /2 are not mediating LEC proliferation induced by preadipocyte supernatant.

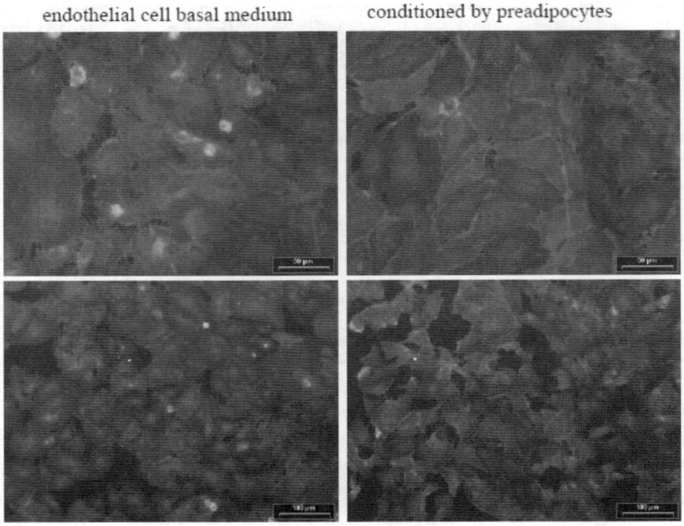

Fig. 3. After 1/ 2 and 3 days a CD 31 / LYVE 1 double staining was conducted, CD 31 is shown in green, lyve 1 in red and blue are all cell nuclei. Here are two pictures from the second day. In the controll picture with endothelial cell basal medium only few LEC can be found. But on the picture conditioned by preadipocytes there are much more LEC.

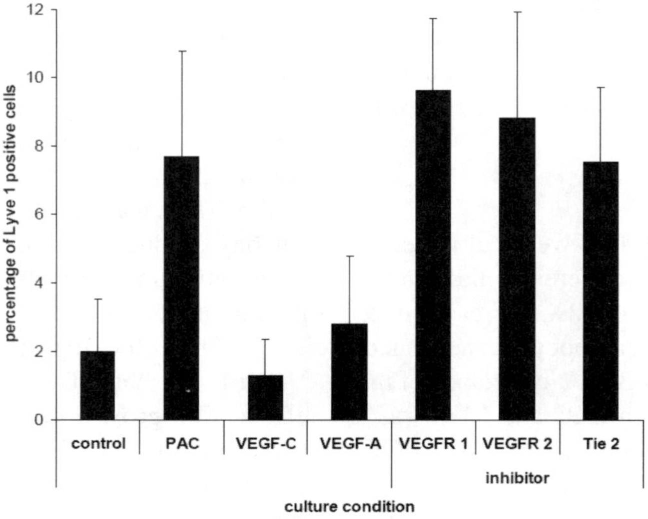

Fig. 4. Percentage of LEC after one day is shown. The number of LEC increases under influence of preadipocyte conditioned media. Blocking of VEGFR-1 / 2 and tie2 has no effect compared to the conditon only with preadipocyte prepared media. Under VEGF-C or VEGF- A no difference to the control is noted.

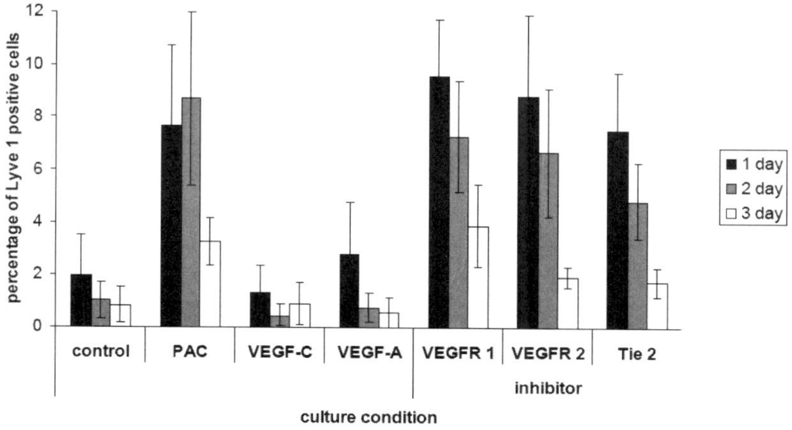

Fig. 5. Development of LEC ratio in a three day follow up: The amount of the LEC that are stimulated with conditioned pre- adipocytes–medium increases more in comparison to the BEC. On 2nd and 3nd day a decrease of the effect was observed, which could be explained by usage of growth factors. No variance of the ratio were seen when VEGF-A or VEGF-C was added. In the conditions with inhibition of receptor VEGFR 1, 2 and Tie 2 a similar stimulation effect on the LEC compared to pure conditioned medium is noted.

Conclusion

It has been shown that the ratio of LEC increases by stimulation with preadipocyte conditioned medium. Longer incubation does not increase the effect. On day 2 / 3 a decrease of the influence can be observed possibly due to wastage of growth factors. There is no effect by addition of soluble VEGF-C / A, and by blocking VEGFR 1/ 2. Therefore VEGF-A / B / E can not be the prominent factors in these events. The blocking of the Angiopoietins has also no effect, that means Ang 1 /2 are not the major players.

It seems that LEC and preadipocytes are in multifactorial interaction which can not be reduced to a single vascular growth factor.

Further studies will be necessary to identify the factor or allele component of preadipocytes stimulating LEC growth or differentiation. These analyses will provide important information on the development and therapy of adipose hypertrophy and chronic lymphedema.

References

1. Bjorntorp, P., (1983) Interactions of adipocytes and their precursor cells with endothelial cells in culture, Cell Res
2. Fachinger, G., Deutsch, U., Risau, W. (1999). Functional interaction of

vascular endothelial-protein-tyrosine phosphate with the Angiopoietin receptor Tie-2, Oncogene

3. Fiedler, U., Krissl, T., Koidl, S., Weiss,C., Koblizek,T., Deutsch,U., Martiny- Baron, G., Marmé, D., Augustin, .G. (2003). Angiopoietin-1 and Angiopoietin-2 Share the Same Binding Domains in the Tie-2 Receptor Involving the First Ig-like Loop and the Epidermal Growth Factor-like Repeats, J. of Biological Chemistry
4. Földi, E., Földi, M., (1981), Komplexe physikalische Entstauungstherapie des chronischen Gliedmassenlymphödems, Physikalische Therapie
5. Hamada, K., Oike, Y., Takakura, N., Ito, Y., Jussila, L., Dumont, D.J., Alitalo, K., Suda, T., (2000), VEGF-C signalling pathways through VEGFR-2 and VEGFR-3 in vasculoangiogenesis and haematopoiesis, Blood
6. Lohela, M., Saaristo, A., Veikkola, T., Aitali, K., (2003), Lymphangiogenic growth factors, receptors and therapies, Thromb Haemost
7. Saaristo, A., Veikkola, T., Enholm, B., Hytonen, M., Arola, J., Pajusola, K., Turunen, P., Jeltsch, M., Karkkainen, M.J., Kerjaschki ,D., et al., (2002), Adenoviral VEGF-C overexpression induces blood vessel enlargement, tortuosity, and leakiness but no sprouting angiogenesis in the skin or mucous membranes, FASEB
8. Witte, M. H., Bernas, M.J., Martin, C.P., Witte, C. L., (2001), Lymphangiogenesis and lymphangiodysplasia: from molecular to clinical lymphology, Microsc Res Tech
9. Yuan, L., Moyon, D., Pardanaud, L., Breant, C., Karkkainem, M.J., Alitalo, K., Eichmann, A., (2002), Abnormal lymphatic vessel development in neuropilin2 mutant mice, Development
10. Gale NW, Yancopoulos GD (1999), Growth factors acting via endothelial cell-specific receptor tyrosine kinases: VEGFs, angiopoietins, and ephrins in vascular development., Genes Development
11. Shibuya M. (2003), Vascular endothelial growth factor receptor-2: its unique signaling and specific ligand, VEGF-E., Cancer Science

WALDEYER'S RING: ANATOMICAL REVIEW

Alfredo Luiz Jácomo, Ph.D.; Silvio Antonio Monteiro Marone, MD, Ph.D.; Mauro Figueiredo Carvalho de Andrade, MD, PhD; Guilherme Zanutto Cardillo

Assistant Professor – Disciplina de Topografia Estrutural Humana, Surgery Department – Medicine School, University of São Paulo.
Assistant Professor of Otorhinolaryngology. Department of Ophthalmology and Otorhinolaryngology. Medicine School, University of São Paulo.
Disciplina de Topografia Estrutural Humana, Surgery Department – Medicine School, University of São Paulo.
Internship of sixth year, Medicine School, University of São Paulo.

Abstract

The tonsils form part of a circular band of adenoid tissue which guards the opening into the digestive and respiratory tubes, known as Waldeyer's ring. The anterior part of the ring is formed by the submucous adenoid collections (lingual tonsil) on the posterior part of the tongue; the lateral portions consist of the palatine tonsils and the adenoid collections in the vicinity of the auditory tubes, while the ring is completed behind by the pharyngeal tonsil on the posterior wall of the pharynx. In the intervals between these main masses are found smaller collections of adenoid tissue. This paper intends to give to the clinician an anatomical review about the subject.

Introduction

The lymphatics vessels and the lymphnodes, as the same in the others body parts, have in the head and neck an important clinical application. Even with the large connections among the lymphatics vessels, the lymph flows through specifically and determinate regions.

Despite of the frequent variations between the lymphatics vessels and lymphnodes, the knowledge of the disposure of the lymphatics structures, markedly the lymphnodes, is very important in the diagnosis and treatment of the infections and neoplasm from this region.

The lower part of oral cavity and the adjacent walls of the pharynx have an accumulated lymphatic tissue which forms some isolated lymphatic organs. So, we have the palatine tonsil (or faucial), the pharyngeal tonsil, the lingualtonsil and an accumulus of lymphatic tissue posterior of the ostium pharingeum tubae auditivae known as tonsil of torus tubarius. Yet, at the pillars and adjacent parts of pharyngeal mucosa there are a lot of lymphatic follicules.

These lymphatic structures protect the entrance of the respiratory and digestive tract. They are named as pharynx lymphatic ring or Waldeyer's ring. The Waldeyer's ring is very developed in the first years of live passing through important transformations, becoming regressive and atrophied with age.

Anatomical Description

1. Pharyngeal tonsil

The pharyngeal tonsil is localized at the mucous of the roof and posterior wall of nasopharynx. It has a rounded shape, having some degrees and sulcus. It is marked of narrow sulcus, deeper and irregular, known as crypta tonsilaris. Sometimes, the pharyngeal tonsila has a deeper sulcus at the center, which follows through the connective tissue surrounding. This deeper depression is known as pharyngeal bursa.

Vascularization

The *arterial irrigation* starts from the branches of external carotid, the ascending pharyngeal artery and the maxillary artery, in its terminal branch, sphenopalatine artery.

Lymphatic Drainage

The lymphatics collectors are divided into medial and lateral, corresponding the lymphatics collectors of the superior part of the pharynx.

The medial lymphatic collectors are the most numerous, about 8 to 12. It begins on the roof and the posterior wall of the pharynx, particularly at the pharyngeal tonsil, passing though the anterior wall of the pharynx to the posterior wall, perforating the constrictor pharyngis superior muscle and the buccopharyngeal fascia, reaching a space between this fascia and the pre-vertebralis fascia, called retropharyngeal space. Afterwards, the lymph flow is directed for the retropharyngeal lateral lymphnodes and, in some cases, going straight to the lymphatic channel of the internal jugulary vein or deeper cervical lymphnodes.

The lateral lymphatic collectors also pass thought the constrictor pharyngis superior muscle and the buccopharyngeal fascia, directing to retropharyngeal lateral lymphnodes or either going straight to the lymphnodes of the internal jugulary vein lymphatic channel or to the deeper cervical lymphnodes.

2. Tubarius Tonsil

The tubarius tonsil is a lymphoid tissue localized at submucous in the nasopharynx, posteriorly at the pharyngeal ostium of the auditory tube.

Vascularization

The *arterial irrigation* becomes from branches of the sphenopalatine artery and the ascending pharyngeal artery, direct branches of external carotid artery.

The *lymphatic vessels* of these tonsil also go towards to the retropharyngeal space, reaching the lateral retropharyngeal lymphnodes or, without passing in this lymphnodes, going straight to the deeper cervical lymphnodes.

3. Palatine Tonsil

The palatine tonsil is a huge lymphoid mass located in the lateral part of the fauces, between the glossopalatine and pharyngopalatine arches. This lymphoid tissue, however, doesn't fill all the space between the arcs. So, a small depression, know as supratonsillar fossa, fills this region. The mucous plica which pass trough supratonsillar fossa, between the two arches, is called plica semilunaris and the continuation of this plica is called plica triangularis. Between the plica triangularis and the surface of the tonsil is a space known as the tonsillar sinus. This sinus may be obliterated by its walls becoming adherent.

The palatine tonsil has two faces: medial and lateral.

The medial surface of the tonsil is free, except anteriorly, where it is covered by the plica triangularis. According to Gray, it presents from twelve to fifteen orifices leading into small crypts or recesses from which numerous follicles branch out into the tonsillar substance.

The lateral or deep surface is adherent to a fibrous capsule which is continued into the plica triangularis. It is separated from the inner surface of the constrictor pharyngis superior muscle usually by some loose connective tissue. This muscle intervenes between the tonsil and the external maxillary artery with its tonsillar and ascending palatine branches. The internal carotid artery lies behind and lateral to the tonsil at a distance of 20 to 25 mm. from it.

At childhood, the tonsils are relatively (and frequently absolutely) larger than in the adult, and about one-third of the tonsil is imbedded. After puberty the imbedded portion diminishes considerably in size and the tonsil assumes a disk-like form, flattened from side to side. The shape and size of the tonsil, however, vary considerably in different individuals.

Vascularization

Arterial irrigation: the arterial supplying the tonsil are:

- tonsillar artery, branch from the external maxillary, which passs trought the superior constrictor muscle and reach the inferior pole of the tonsil.
- the ascending palatine artery, facial artery branch;
- the ascending pharyngeal artery, branch from the external carotid;
- the descending palatine branch of the internal maxillary;
- the lingual artery, branch from the external carotid and
- a twig from the small meningeal.

Venous drainage: occurs mainly by the external palatine vein, which directs to the pharyngeal plexus and then to the facial vein.

The *lymphatic vessels* of the palatine tonsil, usually three to five in number, emerge from the pharynx walls, posterior, superior and inferior of the styloglossus muscle and directs posteriorly to the stylohyoideus and posterior belly of digastricus muscle, reaching the deeper cervical lymphnodes, mostly the jugularis-digastricus lymphnode. Another and smaller lymphatic vessels follow the ascending palatine artery until its origin in the facial artery, in a deeper cervical lymphnode, togheter the origin of facial artery.

4. Lingual Tonsil

The mucous of the dorsum of the tongue, posterior of the foramen cecum and the sulcus terminalis is rough and freely mobile over the nearby parts. It has numerous lymph follicles which form the lingual tonsil.

Each lymph follicles form a rounded salience which center has a perforated small orifice that leads into a cavity or recess. Around this cavity lots of nodules of lymphoid tissue are grouped.

Vascularization

The *arterial vascularization* becomes of lingual artery, branch of the external carotid.

The *lymphatic drainage*: in this region, the embryology knowledgement of the development of the tonge is very important, because the anterior two thirds and the posterior third differ, not only in the development, but also in the lymphatic drainage.

So, in the tongue, it has a submucous net or a lymphatic vessel plexus, where the lymph of the posterior third drains for the deeper cervical lymphnodes, located nearby the posterior digastric belly, for the

Jugularis digastricus lymphnode of the same side and the opposite side and also drains to the deeper cervical lymphnodes, localizated inferiorly, called jugularis-omohyoideus lymphnode.

Conclusion

The Waldeyer's ring has an important clinical application. General practitioners and specialists must know these structures in order to think about differential diagnosis and apply the adequate treatment for the particular patient, surgical or not.

If surgery is needed, specifically for cancer, knowing the patterns of lymphatic drainage and the vascular pedicles are very important in order to proceed the complete surgery.

Bibliography

1. Gray, H. Anatomy of the Human Body - Revised e Re-edited by Warren H. Lewis. 20ª Ed., New York, Ed.Bartebly.com, 2000. Avaliuable on: http://www.bartleby.com/107/
2. Llorca, F.O. Anatomia Humana. 2ª. Ed. Barcelona, Spain. Editorial Científico-Médica, 1960.

3. Moore, K.L.; Dalley, A.E. Anatomia Orientada para a Clínica. 4ª Ed. 2001. Rio de Janeiro, Guanabara-Koogan.
4. Rouvière, H. Anatomia Humana Descriptiva y Topográfica. Tomo I, II e III. 3ª Ed. Espanha. Casa Editorial Bailly-Bailliere.
5. Testut, L.; Jacob, O. Tratado de Anatomia Topográfica. 8ª Ed. Espanha, Salvat Editores, 1950.

LIPID-LOADEN MACROPHAGES AND FOAM CELLS LEAVE ARTERIAL WALL VIA LYMPHATIC SYSTEM

Andrzej Szuba[1], Piotr Dziegiel[2], Marzena Podhorska[2], Maciej Zabel[2], Dariusz Janczak[3], Pawel Chudoba[3], Wojciech Polak[3], Dariusz Patrzalek[3]

[1]Wroclaw School of Medicine, Department of Internal and Occupational Medicine and Hypertension
[2]Wroclaw School of Medicine, Department of Histology
[3]Wroclaw School of Medicine, Department of Vascular Surgery and Transplantology, Wroclaw, Poland

ABSTRACT

AIM: Accumulation of lipids in macrophages in arterial intima is a key step in developement of atherosclerosis. It was suggested that lipid loaden macrophages have decreased mobility and usually do not leave arterial wall contributing to formation of atherosclerotic plaque. We hypothesized that lipid loaden macrophages and foam cells may leave arterial wall via advential lymphatic system and may play important role in regression of atherosclerosis and normal metabolism of arterial wall.

METHOD

Segments of large arteries with adventitia (abdominal aorta, iliac and femoral artery) and adjacent lymphnodes were obtained from organ donors (victims of accidents, sudden brain death). Fragments of arterial wall and lymphnodes were embeded in paraffin or prepared for electron microscopy studies. Lymphatics of arterial adventitia were visualized with immunohistochemistry using LYVE-1 and Prox-1 antibodies. Anti ApoB antibodies were used to detect LDL lipoproteins within arterial wall and macrophages. Electron microscopy studies of adventitia and lymphnodes were also performed. RESULTS: Lipid loaden macrophages and foam cells were found in adventitia and paraaortic lymphnodes. Macrophage phagosom content stained positively with ApoB antibodies confirming presence of digested LDL lipoproteins within macrophages.

CONCLUSION

Our findings suggest that migration of lipid loaden macrophages from arterial wall through adventitial lymphatics is a physiological process present also in persons without significant atherosclerosis. This process may represent important mechanism of physiological regression of atherosclerosis.

KEY WORDS: atherosclerosis, adventia, lymph nodes

INTRODUCTION

Arterial atherosclerosis is the major killer of human population. Pathogenesis of arterial atherosclerosis continues to be focus of researchers around the world. Infiltration of lipids in arterial intima is a key step in development of atherosclerosis. In response to lipid deposition an inflammatory process develops with migration of macrophages into arterial intima. Accumulation of lipids in macrophages leads to formation of foam cells, which eventually undergo apoptosis contributing to formation of atherosclerotic plaque [1,2]. Lymphatic vessels are abundant in arterial adventitia and lymphatic system plays a major role in HDL metabolism and reverse cholesterol transport [2,3,4]. We hypothesize that lymphatic system may play an important role in regression of atherosclerosis and normal metabolism of arterial wall. Lipid loaden macrophages and foam cells may leave arterial wall via advential lymphatic system and migrate to regional lymphnodes as a part of physiological function of lymphatic system.

MATERIAL AND METHODS

Segments of large arteries with adventitia (abdominal aorta, iliac and femoral artery) and adjacent lymphnodes were obtained from organ donors (victims of accidents, sudden brain death) and patients undergoing vascular surgery. Samples from 40 patients in different stage of atherosclerotic process were examined [age 20 – 70]

Fragments of arterial wall and lymphnodes were embedded in paraffin or prepared for electron microscopy studies. Lymphatics of arterial adventitia were visualized with immunohistochemistry using anti-LYVE-1, anti- Prox-1 and anti-podoplanin antibodies (Reliatech, Germany). Anti ApoB antibodies (Novocastra) were used to detect LDL lipoproteins within arterial wall and macrophages. Macrophages were identified with anti-CD-68 antibodies (DAKO). Transmission electron microscopy studies of adventitia and lymphnodes were also performed for identification of foam cells.

The study was approved by the Bioethics Committee of the Wroclaw University of Medicine.

RESULTS

Lymphatic vessels are present in arterial adventitia but are also detected in media and within atherosclerotic plaque. CD68+, ApoB+ macrophages are present in intima, media and adventitia of the large arteries in different stages of atherosclerosis. CD68+, ApoB+

macrophages are found in pararterial lymphnodes and are more abundant in advanced athero-sclerosis.

DISCUSSION

Presence of lipid loaden macrophages and foam cells in media, adventitia and paraarterial lymphnodes may reflect migration of macrophages from arterial wall through adventitial lymphatics. These findings may support hypothesis of lipid transport from the arterial wall via adventitial lymphatics in response to lipid infiltration [4,6]. It may represent and important mechanism of regression of atherosclerosis. These are preliminary findings and further studies are necessary to confirm our hypothesis.

REFERENCES

1. Ross, R., Atherosclerosis–an inflammatory di*sease.* N Engl J Med, 1999. **340**(2): pp. 115-26.
2. Ball, R.Y., et al., Evidence that the death of macrophage foam cells contributes to the lipid core of atheroma. Atherosclerosis, 1995. **114**(1): pp. 45-54.
3. Eliska O, Eliskova M, Miller AJ.The morphology of the lym-phatics of the coronary arteries in the dog. Lymphology, 1999 Jun;32(2):45-57.
4. Nanjee MN, Cooke CJ, Wong JS, Hamilton RL, Olszewski WL, Miller NE.: Composition and ultrastructure of size subclasses of normal human peripheral lymph lipoproteins: quantification of cholesterol uptake by HDL in tissue fluids. J Lipid Res. 2001 Apr;42(4):639-48.
5. Nanjee MN, Cooke CJ, Garvin R, Semeria F, Lewis G, Olszewski WL, Miller NE. Intravenous apoA-I/ lecithin discs increase pre-beta-HDL concentration in tissue fluid and stimulate reverse cholesterol transport in humans. J Lipid Res. 2001 Oct;42(10):1586-93
6. Nordestgaard BG, Hjelms E, Stender S, Kjeldsen K: Different efflux pathways for high and low density lipoproteins from porcine aortic intima. Arteriosclerosis. 1990 May-Jun;10(3):477-85.

THREE DIMENSIONAL IMAGING OF LYMPHANGIOGENESIS USING SPECIFIC MARKERS FOR BOTH LYMPHATIC AND BLOOD VESSELS

T. Ezaki*, S. Morikawa and K. Shimizu

Department of Anatomy & Developmental Biology, Tokyo Women's Medical University, Tokyo 162-8666, Japan

INTRODUCTION

It is very important to understand the structures and functions of local microcirculatory system including lymphatics under both physiological and pathological conditions. During the development or regeneration of tissues, the three dimensional (3D) imaging of the microvessels is an essential strategy for studies on the local microcirculation. Recent technologies have enabled us to discover several specific markers for vascular endothelial cells. The markers should represent highly reliable characteristics of the structure and function of endothelial cells. Previously, a benign murine lymphangioma with some endothelial specific markers was established for studies on the roles of lymphatic vessels in the local microcirculation [**1**]. Therefore, we produced rat monoclonal antibodies (mAbs) against the tumor cells to identify murine lymphatic vessels and blood vessels [**2, 3**]. We also used a tomato lectin to label directly the blood vessels. In this report, our recent approaches using these specific endothelial markers to studies on the local microcirculatory system by the three dimensional (3D) imaging are introduced.

MATERIALS AND METHODS

Benign lymphangiomas were induced in C57BL/6 mice by the intraperitoneal injection of Freund's incomplete adjuvant as described elsewhere [**1**]. Monoclonal antibodies reactive to mouse lymphatic endothelium and blood endothelium (LA102 and LA5, respectively) were obtained by the rapid differential immunization of DA rats with the lymphangioma cells as previously reported [**2, 3**]. To discriminate blood vessels from lymphatic vessels, we used intravascular perfusion of tomato lectin as reported previously [**4**]. Briefly, under anesthesia, mice were injected intravenously (i.v.) with FITC-conjugated tomato lectin (*Lycopersicon esculentum* lectin; Vector Laboratories, Inc., Burlingame, USA, 100 μg lectin per 100 μl of buffered saline). The tomato lectin binds uniformly to the luminal surface of endothelial cells, thus can label all blood vessels that have a patent blood supply. For the immunostaining of lymphatics in the diaphragm as whole mount preparations, purified LA102 mAb (100 μg/100 μl in PBS) was injected intraperitoneally 30 min prior to the lectin injection. After 5 min, the chest was opened and the aorta was perfused via the left ventricle with 2% paraformaldehyde (PFA) in 0.1 M phosphate buffer (PB; pH7.2) for 5 min followed by PBS for 5 min at a pressure of 120 mmHg. Various tissues were excised, cut into small pieces and further immersed in 20% sucrose in PBS at 4°C for overnight. The tissues were then snap-frozen in liquid nitrogen. Cryosections of 10-50 μm thickness were made and immunostained with various antibodies. Some tissues, such as the mesentery and the diaphragm, were also directly mounted onto slide-glasses as whole-mount spreads and immunostained. For the immunofluorescent staining, a Cy-3 conjugated goat anti-rat Ig antibody (Jackson ImmunoResearch, West Grove, PN, USA) was used as a secondary reagent. The proper concentration of each antibody was predetermined beforehand. Three-dimensional images were obtained using a Leica TCS-SL confocal laser-scanning microscope.

RESULTS

LA102 mAb reacts with an about 25-27 kDa molecule expressed on mouse lymphatic vessels but not with any types of blood vessels. Namely, LA102 mAb strongly recognized endothelial cells of almost all mouse lymphatic vessels except for large lymphatic trunks, such as the thoracic duct. In contrast, LA5 mAb reacts with an about 12-13 kDa molecule on most of the blood vessels, but not with lymphatics. Interestingly, however, LA5mAb did not react with the endothelial cells of large blood vessels, the liver sinusoids and splenic sinuses. The specificity of LA5 mAb was confirmed by the antigen co-localization with the tomato lectin labeled blood vessels.

In this study, we have developed the simultaneous imaging technique of both lymphatic and blood vessels using these monoclonal antibodies in combination with the FITC-labeled tomato lectin. In cryosections of various tissues, such as the small intestine, the pancreas and the tongue, the LA102 positive lymphatic sinus networks are clearly distinguished from the lectin-positive blood capillary networks. In cryosections of the diaphragm from a mouse bearing adjuvant-induced benign lymphangiomas, we found that the original lymphangiomas did not entirely have typical lymphatic endothelial phenotypes, and that some of the tubular structures are

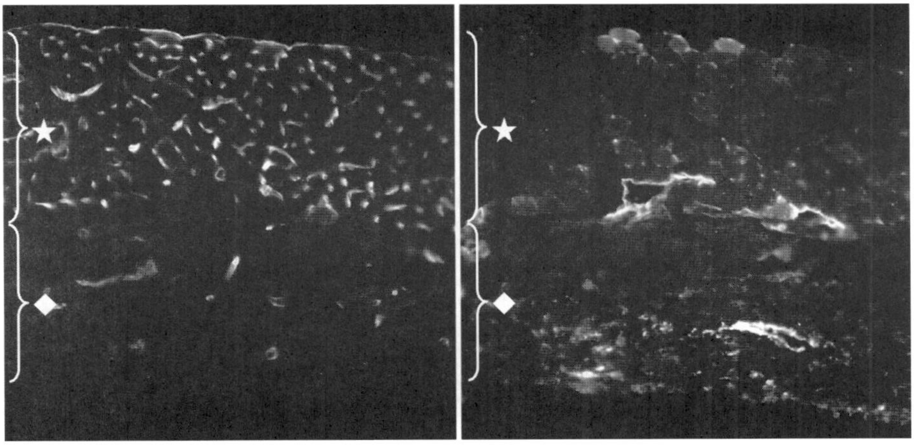

Fig.1. Double immunofluorescent confocal scanning images of a diaphragm with lymphangioma with tomato lectin (left) and LA102 mAb (right). The lymphangioma (**diamond**) was developed on the abdominal surface of the diaphragm (**star**) as described above.

also positive for the tomato lectin as a blood vessel marker (Fig.1).

The antigen distribution pattern of LA102 in the diaphragm as a whole mount preparation was further analyzed three-dimensionally by the confocal laser-scanning microscopy. The lymphatic vessels of both surfaces of the diaphragm were clearly distinguished from the local blood vessels. The lymphatic vessels distributed in the diaphragm from the abdominal side to the thoracic side were stained without any co-localization of antigen as compared with the local blood vessels. Fig. 2 shows the LA102-positive lymphatic networks (as a single-color image) distributed from the abdominal surface to the thoracic surface of the diaphragm as a 3D image.

DISCUSSION

The main aim of this study was to identify a novel lineage-specific marker for mouse lymphatic vessels and differentiate them from blood vessels in local tissues for the 3D analysis of lymphangiogenesis under both physiological and pathological conditions. We produced a rat mAb, LA102 that only recognized lymphatic endothelial cells but not any types of blood vessel endothelium. LA102 antigen may reflect the typical phenotype of lymphatic vessels distinct from blood vessels. We also obtained another mAb, LA5 that reacted with most blood vascular endothelial cells, but not with lymphatic endothelium. Various markers of both lymphatic and

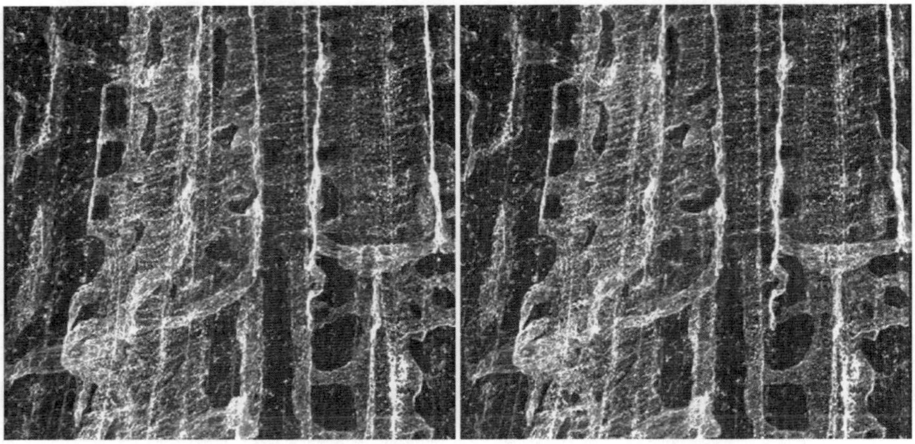

Fig. 2. Stereo-pair micrograph of a mouse diaphragm obtained by the confocal laser-scanning microscopy. The 3D image of LA102 positive lymphatic vessel networks distributed throughout a diaphragm is observed as black and white figures. The back image represents the lymphatic vessels on the thoracic side, whereas the front image represents those on the abdominal side.

blood vascular endothelial cells have been reported and used for the identification of local microcirculatory system as listed previously [**3**].

In the present study, we demonstrated our recent approach using these specific endothelial markers to studies on the local microcirculatory system by the 3D imaging using a confocal laser-scanning microscope. The immunostaining of lymphatic networks with LA102 mAb in combination with the fluorescent tomato lectin labeling of blood vascular networks has successfully revealed the whole 3D image of both vascular systems in a mouse diaphragm. This technique may be very useful for the investigations of spatial relationship of the two vascular systems, particularly in lymphangiogenesis and angiogenesis in development or under various pathological conditions [**5**]. The simultaneous observation of the two vascular systems will provide accurate and reliable estimation of the local microcirculation. In the usual immunostaining of cryosections, we found that the original lymphangiomas did not entirely have typical lymphatic endothelial phenotypes, and that some of the tubular structures are also positive for blood vessel markers. This may suggest that the original benign lymphangiomas consist of heterogeneous cellular origins. They may be a good cell source for both lymphatic and blood vascular endothelial cell lines in culture after the positive selection by the specific mAbs.

In conclusion, the new markers for both lymphatic and blood vessel endothelial cells are very reliable and useful tools to analyze the spatial relationship in the local microcirculation during lymphangiogenesis and angiogenesis by the 3D imaging technique.

ACKNOWLEDGMENTS

The authors are grateful to Mrs. Y. Yamazaki, Ms. K. Nakata, Ms. H. Kasahara and Ms. K. Moriya for their devoted technical help. This work was mainly supported by a Grant-in-Aid for Scientific Research in 2004-2005 from the Ministry of Education, Culture, Sports, Science and Technology of Japan.

REFERENCES

1. T. Ezaki, K. Kuwahara, S. Morikawa, K. Matsuno and N. Sakaguchi. Characterization of adjuvant-induced rat lymphangiomas as a model to study the lymph drainage from abdominal cavity. Jap. J. Lymphol. **27** (2004), 1-10.
2. S. Morikawa, K. Kuwahara, N. Sakaguchi, M. K. and T. Ezaki. A new marker for lymphatic endothelial cells recognized by a monoclonal antibody. Lymphology **37 Suppl.** (2004), 105-108.
3. T. Ezaki, K. Kuwahara, S. Morikawa, K. Shimizu, N. Sakaguchi, K. Matsushima and K. Matsuno. Production of two novel monoclonal antibodies that distinguish mouse lymphatic and blood vascular endothelial cells. Anat. Embryol. **in press** (2006).
4. T. Ezaki, P. Baluk, G. Thurston, A. La Barbara, C. Woo and D. M. McDonald. Time course of endothelial cell proliferation and microvascular remodeling in chronic inflammation. Am. J. Pathol. **158** (2001), 2043-2055.
5. K. Alitalo, T. Tammela and T. V. Petrova. Lymphangiogenesis in development and human disease, Nature **438** (2005), 946-953.

LYMPHATIC PHENOTYPE OF CHY-3 MICE

Michael T. Dellinger,[1] Robert J. Hunter,[2] Michael J. Bernas,[2] Robert P. Erickson[3] and Marlys H. Witte[2]

Departments of [1]Molecular and Cellular Biology, [2]Surgery and [3]Pediatrics, The University of Arizona, Tucson, USA

INTRODUCTION

The lymph vasculature is a hierarchal network of vessels whose development is dependent on the coordinate interaction of numerous growth factors and their respective receptors and signaling pathways. The growth factor Vascular Endothelial Growth Factor C (VEGF-C) and the receptor tyrosine kinase VEGFR-3 are intimately involved in regulating the development of the lymph vasculature. Transgenic mouse models have shown that overexpression of VEGF-C can result in lymphatic vessel hyperplasia and that signaling via VEGFR-3 is sufficient to stimulate this hyperplasia (Jeltsch et al., 1997; Veikkola et al, 2001). Targeted inactivation of *Vegfc* in mouse has shown that *Vegfc* is indispensable for the development of a functional network of lymphatic vessels. *Vegfc*$^{+/-}$ mice exhibit chylous ascites, lymphedema and cutaneous lymphatic hypoplasia thus indicating that two copies of *Vegfc* are needed for the proper development of the lymph vasculature (Karkkainen et al., 2004).

Chylous ascites 3 (*Chy-3*) mice are a mutant line of mice with one copy of *Vegfc* and the lymphatic phenotype of these mice has not been fully characterized. *Chy-3* mice were previously generated by X-ray mutagenesis and were reported to have milky abdomens at birth and edema of the limbs and tail. Cytogenetic analysis of the chromosomes of *Chy-3* mice revealed chromosomal breakpoints at cytogenetic bands 8A4 and 8B3 (Cattanach et al, 1993). The gene for *Vegfc* is within this deleted region and accordingly we further explored the lymphatic phenotype of *Chy-3* mice.

MATERIALS AND METHODS

Recovery of live mice from frozen embryos

Chy-3 frozen embryos were purchased from MRC Harwell. We followed the suggested MGU Harwell protocol for the recovery of live mice from frozen embryos and generated a colony.

Real time PCR

The protocol developed for genotyping the trisomic mouse model for Down syndrome was modified to genotype *Chy-3* mice for the deletion of chromosome 8 (Liu et al., 2003). Genomic DNA was extracted from mouse tail tips and used in the real-time PCR reaction. The Ct of *Vegfc* was compared to the Ct of *Apob* to determine if one or two copies of *Vegfc* were present. The *Apob* gene is located on chromosome 12 and should always be present as two copies. The sequences for primers and probe for *Vegfc* are: forward primer 5'-CCAGTCACAATCAGTTTTGCCA-3', reverse primer 5'-GTGGTAATGTTGCTGGCAGAGA-3', and probe 5'-FAM-CACACTTCCTGCCGGTGCATGTCT-TAMRA-3'. The sequences for primers and probe for *Apob* are: forward 5'-CACGTGGGCTCCAGCATT-3', 5'-TCACCAGTCATTTCTGCCTTTG-3', and probe 5'-VIC-CCAATGGTCGGGCACTGCTCAA-TAMRA. The PCR set-up, reaction conditions and data analysis were the same as those used to genotype the mouse model of Down syndrome (Liu et al., 2003).

Evans blue dye injections

Evans blue dye was injected intradermally into the hindlimbs, forelimbs, ear, and snout of anesthetized *Chy-3* mice and wild-type littermates. Following the injections, the popliteal, sacral, axillary, and jugular regions were dissected and visualized under a dissecting microscope.

Whole mount immunofluorescence

The whole mount immunofluorescence protocol followed the methods of Augustin (2005). Whole mount immunofluorescence was performed on 1% paraformaldehyde fixed tissues. Tissues were blocked overnight with 3% goat serum in 0.3% Triton-X 100 in PBS. Vascular smooth muscle cells and pericytes were detected by incubating tissues for 24 hours with a Cy3 conjugated anti-a-Smooth Muscle Actin (Sigma C-6198) antibody. Lymphatic vessels were detected by incubating tissues for 24 hours with an antibody against Lyve-1 (Upstate Cell Signaling Solutions #07-538) then incubating for 24 hours with an Alexa Fluor488 secondary antibody (Molecular Probes 84B2-1). All samples were mounted with citifluor and analyzed using a fluorescent microscope.

RESULTS

Real time PCR should produce a fold difference of *Vegfc* to *Apob* of approximately 0.5 in mice that have one genomic copy of *Vegfc* and two genomic copies of *Apob*. The fold difference of *Vegfc* to *Apob* should be approximately 1.0 in mice that have two genomic copies of *Vegfc* and two genomic copies of *Apob*. PCR results yielded two populations of mice, one with a mean fold difference of *Vegfc* to *Apob* of 0.513 (95% CI: 0.467-0.561) and another with a mean fold difference of *Vegfc* to *Apob* of 1.33 (95% CI: 1.25-1.40). The mice in the population with the reduced mean fold difference uniformly displayed hindlimb edema and were determined to be *Chy-3* mice.

Evans blue dye hind limb injections produced no visualization of the popliteal nodes, sacral nodes, nor iliac lymph nodes and vessels in *Chy-3* mice. In contrast, the afferent lymphatic vessels leading to the axillary and jugular lymph nodes effectively transported Evans blue dye in *Chy-3* mice. Evans blue dye injections in the ear showed that EBD is transported from the injection site, but the pattern of EBD filled lymphatic vessels is different in *Chy-3* mice compared to wild-type mice.

Whole mount immunofluorescence of *Chy-3* and wild-type adult ears demonstrated that *Chy-3* mice exhibit hypoplasia of lymphatic vessels.

DISCUSSION

The complete lymphatic phenotypic description of mutant lines of mice is crucial to gain an understanding of the role the gene product serves in the development of the lymphatic system. This phenotype should include functional studies using tracer dye injections, immunohistochemistry and descriptions at the molecular level derived from by means of molecular and biochemical techniques. We have used this analysis to characterize the lymphatic phenotype of *Chy-3* mice.

Real-time PCR proved to be an effective method to determine the genomic *Vegfc* copy number and genotype *Chy-3* mice. Evans blue dye injections revealed a dysfunction of the lymph vasculature specifically in the hind region of *Chy-3* mice. This is consistent with the visual observation that only the hindlimbs of *Chy-3* mice are lymphedematous. Interestingly, whole mount immunofluorescence of *Chy-3* ear skin shows that *Chy-3* mice have hypoplasia of dermal lymphatic vessels.

The abnormal function of the lymphatic vessels of the hindlimbs and lymphatic hypoplasia in *Chy-3* mice mirrors the published findings in *Vegfc*$^{+/-}$ mice. The lack of the *Vegfc* gene is likely the major or only cause of the *Chy-3* lymphatic phenotype. The *Chy-3* mouse can be useful to further study the role of *Vegfc* and its interaction with other genes in the development of the mammalian lymphatic system.

REFERENCES

1. Augustin HG(Ed.) (2005): *Methods in Endothelial Cell Biology.* Springer Lab Manuals, 383pps. ISBN#3-540-21397-X.
2. Cattanach B.M., Burtenshaw M.D., Rasberry C., Evans E.P. (1993): Large deletions and other gross forms of chromosome imbalance compatible with viability and fertility in the mouse. *Nature Genet.* 3:56-61.
3. Jeltsch M., Kaipainen A., Joukov V., Meng X., Lakso M., Rauvala H.,

Swartz M., Fukumura D., Jain R.K., Alitalo K. (1997): Hyperplasia of lymphatic vessels in VEGF-C transgenic mice. *Science* 276: 1423-1425.

4. Karkkainen M.J., Ferrell R.E., Lawrence E.C., Kimak M.A., Levinson K.L., McTigue M.A., Alitalo K., Finegold D.N. (2000): Missense mutations interfere with vascular endothelial growth factor receptor-3 signaling in primary lymphedema. *Nature Genet.* 25: 153-159.

5. Liu D.P., Schmidt C., Billings T., Davisson M.T. (2003): Quantitative PCR genotyping assay for the Ts65DN mouse model of Down syndrome. *Biotechniques* 35: 1170-1179.

6. Veikkola T., Jussila L., Makinen T., Karpanen T., Jeltsch M., Petrova T.V., Kubo H., Thurston G., McDonald D.M., Achen M.G., Stacker S.A., Alitalo K. (2001): Signalling via vascular endothelial growth factor receptor-3 is sufficient for lymphangiogenesis in transgenic mice. *EMBO.* 20: 1223-1231.

THE AVIAN CHORIOALLANTOIC MEMBRANE AS A TOOL TO MONITOR TUMOR LYMPHANGIOGENESIS AND INVASIVENESS

Maria Papoutsi[1], Monica Hecht[2], Lothar Schweigerer[1] and Jörg Wilting[1]

[1] Children's Hospital, Pediatrics I, Georg-August-University, Robert-Koch-Strasse 40, 37075 Göttingen, Germany

[2] Department of Oncology and Hematology, Charité, Humboldt University Berlin, Schumanstr. 20/21, 10117 Berlin, Germany

Abstract

The avian chorioallantoic membrane (CAM) is easily accessible for experimental studies on tumor host interactions. It is lined by an outer, ectodermal epithelium and contains all types of vessels including lymphatics. We have studied the hem- and lymphangiogenic potency of human A375 melanoma cells on the CAM. The cells produce Vascular Endothelial Growth Factor (VEGF)-A and –C and form huge vascularized tumours on the CAM. Transfection of the cells with cDNA encoding the soluble forms of VEGF receptor(R)-1 (sflt-1) and VEGFR-3 (sflt-4) inhibit hemangiogenesis and lymphangiogenesis, respectively. Inhibition of lymphangiogenesis does not prevent growth of the tumors. In contrast, sflt-1-transfected cells do not form solid tumors on the surface of the CAM. However, invasiveness of the cells is not affected by either of the transfections. They massively invade both blood and lymphatic vessels. Since the CAM is lined by a tight epithelium, and only tumor cells with high invasive potencies are able to cross this barrier, it is highly suited to study the mechanisms of tumor invasiveness. We have studied the significance of the Hepatocyte Growth Factor (HGF)/c-Met receptor interaction for its potential to induce invasion of tumor cells into the CAM. For this purpose we have inoculated human neuroblastoma cells, which constitutively express c-Met and STAT3, on the CAM. We show that HGF stimulates expression of proteolytic enzymes and invasiveness of the cells, which can be inhibited in vivo by specific inhibitors of the MAP kinase cascade and expression of dominant negative STAT3 in vivo and in vitro respectively. Our studies show that the CAM is a highly suitable organ to discriminate between different mechanisms of tumor progression.

Introduction

Tumor progression and metastasis is a complex

phenomenon. It involves diverse mechanisms such as proliferation, inhibition of apoptosis, hem- and lymphangiogenesis and invasivness. Tumor progression can hardly be studied *in vitro* because of specific tumor stroma interactions. In vivo models are required, which, however, are time consuming, expensive, and restricted by the law for the protection of animals. An *in vivo* (*in ovo*) model that circumvents these difficulties is the avian chorioallantoic memebrane (CAM) model (1).

The CAM is an extraembryonic organ with respiratory functions. It consists of an ectodermal chorionic epithelium, an endodermal allantoic epithelium and, in between, a vascularized mesodermal stroma. In the differentiated CAM, the conduit vessels are located within the stroma, whereas the capillaries are situated within the chorionic epithelium. Additionally, a dense plexus of lymphatics can be found along the blood vessels, which obviously drain excess fluid from the allantois. The CAM is easily accessible to the experimenter and, in most countries it is not regarded by law as an animal model. Proteins, viruses, tissues and tumor cells can be applied on the CAM.

Results

We have studied the effects of various members of the vascular endothelial growth factor (VEGF) family by applying the proteins on the CAM. Whereas VEGF-A induces a hemangiogenic response, VEGF-C and –D induce lymphangiogenesis (1). VEGF-A binds to two receptors, which are expressed on blood vascular endothelial cells (BECs): VEGFR-1 (flt-1) and VEGFR-2 (KDR, flk-1). VEGF-C and –D bind mainly to VEGFR-3 (flt-4), which is specifically found on lymphatic endothelial cells (LECs).

We have studied the hem- and lymphangiogenic potency of various tumor cells on the CAM. A375 human melanoma cells, which produce both VEGF-A and –C, form solid vascularized tumors seven days after the application of the cell suspension. With specific markers for LECs, such as VEGFR-3 and Prox1, we have been able to show that the melanoma cells induce development of intra- and peritumoral lymphatic vessels. Tumor lymphangiogenesis is greatly reduced after transfection of the cells with cDNA encoding the soluble form of VEGFR-3 (*sflt-4*), whereas hemangiogenesis is not affected (2). In contrast, tumor hemangiogenesis is largely reduced, when the cells are transfected with cDNA encoding the soluble form of VEGFR-1 (*sflt-1*). The in vivo behaviour of the cells is drastically altered. They do not form solid tumors, but are still able to invade the CAM, survive within the stroma and form tumor nodules (Fig. 1A-C). Numerous lymphocytes and macrophages can be seen within the

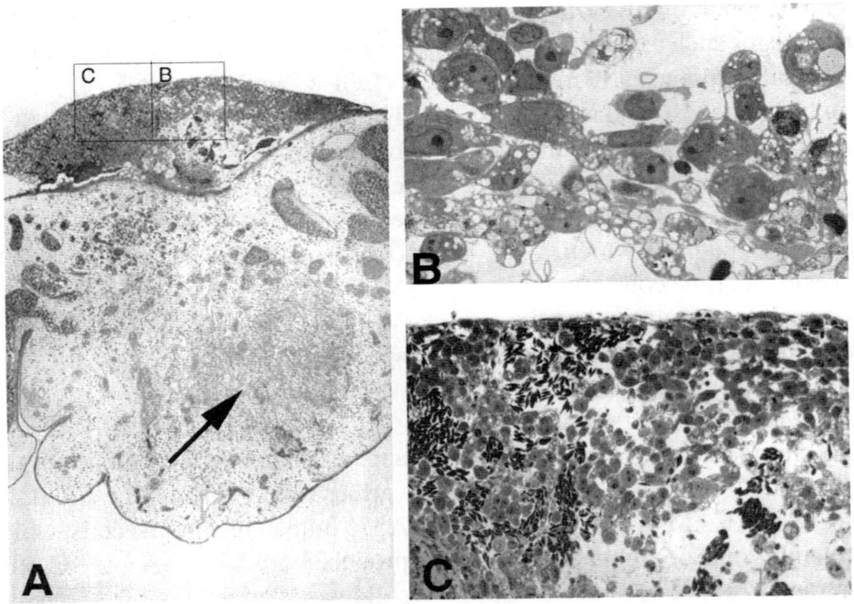

Fig. 1A-C. Semithin section showing sflt-1 transfected A375 melanoma cells on the CAM. Tumor cells have invaded the CAM and form nodules (arrows) within the stroma (A). Tumor cells on top of the CAM are mostly necrotic (B). Note that there is no formation of blood vessels but hemorrage (C).

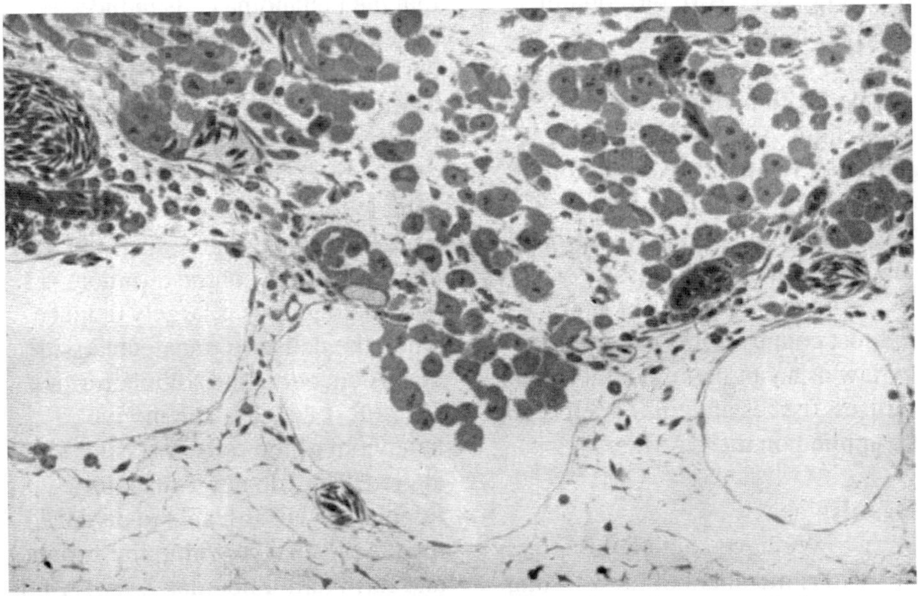

Fig. 2. Higher magnification of Fig. 1. Note invasion of tumor cells into a dilated lymphatic vessel.

stroma, which may account for a secondary hemangiogenic reaction. Tumor lymphangiogenesis does not seem to be affected, and the melanoma cells invade lymphatics at the tumor periphery (Fig. 2). This shows that tumor hemangiogenesis, lymphangiogenesis and invasiveness are separate processes, which are regulated by distinct but overlapping mechanisms. Whereas VEGF-C is a major regulator of lymphangiogenesis, VEGF-A induces hemangiogenesis. As described in the literature, Hepatocyte Growth Factor/Scatter Factor (HGF/SF) and its receptor c-Met are of utmost importance for invasive processes. Since the CAM is lined by an ectodermal epithelium, which has to be destroyed by the tumor cells in order to get access to the vascularized stroma, we sought to determine if the CAM may be a useful model to study tumor invasiveness.

The crucial roles of HGF and c-Met in the progression of malignancies of the adult are now well established, however, pediatric solid malignancies have not been studied yet. We have investigated the function of HGF/c-Met in human neuroblastomas *in vitro* and *in vivo*. Three out of nine neuroblastoma cell lines (NMB, SH-EP, SK-N-SH) express c-Met at RNA and protein levels. Application of HGF induces autophosphorylation of c-Met as early as 15 minutes after application. HGF does not induce proliferation of the neuroblastoma cells. In contrast, invasiveness of the cells is more than 100-fold increased as shown *in vitro* in a Matrigel invasion assay. The same behaviour of the cells can be observed *in vivo* in the CAM assay. Without HGF stimulation the neuroblastoma cells are hardly able to penetrate the CAM epithelium. Only in 2 out of 14 cases, we found formation of very small tumors. In contrast, after HGF stimulation multiple large and vascularized tumors are formed on the CAM (12 out of 14 cases). This effect can be blocked by inhibitors of the HGF/c-Met signalling pathway, such as inhibitors of the mitogen-activated protein kinase (MAPK) and phospholipase C-γ. This shows that the HGF/c-Met pathway is essential for neuroblastoma invasiveness (3).

Discussion

Tumor progression is a complex mechanism leading to increased malignancy of the cells in conjunction with increased proliferation, loss of apoptosis, induction of vascular supply, increased invasiveness and formation of metastases (4). Some aspects of tumor progression can be studied *in vitro*, however, the biological relevance can only be studied *in vivo*. Animal models are time consuming, expensive and formally high regulated. The avian chorioallantoic membrane

(CAM) represents a highly valuable model to study various aspects of tumor progression. The CAM is easily accessible to the experimenter and allows studies on tumor cell stroma interactions for a period of about 8 days. The CAM contains both blood and lymphatic vessels, and can therefore be used to study tumor induced hem- and lymphangiogenesis. We have demonstrated the essential roles of VEGF-A in hemangiogenesis and of VEGF-C and –D in lymphangiogenesis in the CAM assay.

The CAM can also be used to study invasiveness of tumor cells. The chorionic epithelium represents a barrier, which has to be destroyed before the tumor cells get access to the vessels of the CAM. Cells that are not invasive enough will not form solid vascularized tumors. Invasiveness of tumor cells can be increased or decreased by local application of specific drugs, which is a clear advantage to the mouse or rat model of tumor growth. We have shown that activation of the receptor c-Met by application of the ligand HGF/SF increases invasiveness of neuroblastoma cells through the activation of proteases such as MMP2 and uPA (Hecht et al., 2004). Neutralising antibodies against HGF and inhibitors of the c-Met signalling cascade reduce invasiveness and tumor formation (3).

In summary, the tumor-CAM model is a highly useful tool to study tumor hemangiogenesis, lymphangiogenesis and invasiveness and can be combined with studies on the effects of drugs that may inhibit either of these mechanisms.

References

1. Wilting, J, M Schneider, M Papoutsi, et al: An avian model in studies of embryonic lymphangiogenesis. Lymphology 33 (2000), 81-94.
2. Papoutsi, M, G Siemeister, K Weindel, et al: Active interaction of human A375 melanoma cells with the lymphatics in vivo. Histochem. Cell Biol. 114 (2000), 373-385.
3. Hecht, M, M Papoutsi, HD Tran, J Wilting, et al: Hepatocyte growth factor/c-Met signaling promotes the progression of experimental human neuroblastomas. Cancer Res. 64 (2004), 6109-6118.
4. Wilting, J, T Hawighorst, M Hecht, et al: Development of Lymphatic Vessels: Tumour Lymphangiogenesis and Lymphatic Invasion. Curr. Med. Chem. (2005), In press.

GLYCOPROTEINS PROFILE IN LYMPH OF NORMAL SUBJECTS AND PATIENTS WITH LYMPH STASIS

Interewicz B., Olszewski W.L., Dominiak A.

Department of Surgical Research & Transplantology, Medical Research Center, Polish Academy of Sciences, Warsaw, Poland

The importance of the lymphatic system in the performance of the cardiovascular and immune systems is often overlooked until it becomes compromised by processes which hamper or block the return of fluid to the systemic circulation and elimination of foreign antigens. This leads to development of lymphedema.

The lymph proteome is derived from filtrated plasma, metabolic products of connective tissue cells and population of recirculating lymphoid cells. The lymphatic endothelium also contributes to the lymph proteins and cytokines. They remain to be identified and characterized.

AIM

To determine the presence of glycoproteins and colloidal composition of lymph and plasma collected from healthy subjects and patients with obstructive lymphedema.

METHODS

Study groups: 1) Normal subjects (n=14) and 2) patients with

GLYCOPROTEINS IN PLASMA

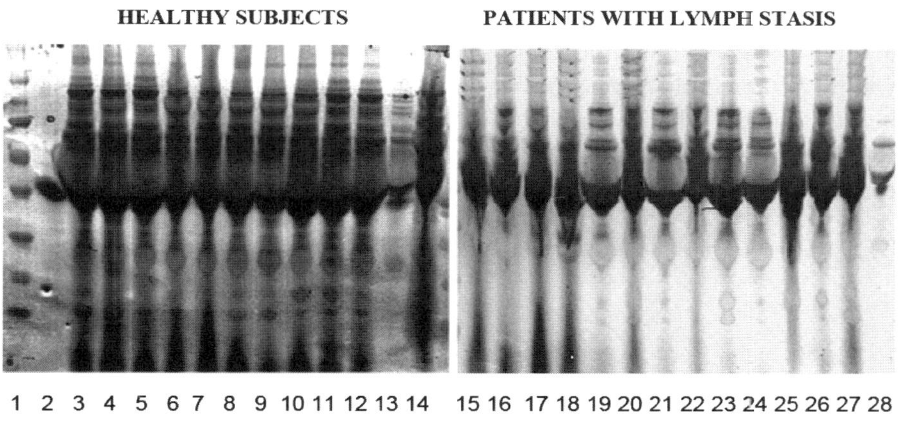

Lane 1- marker, lane 2- positive control (peroxidase), lanes 3 – 28 samples

DENDROGRAM SHOWING DIFFERENCES IN GLYCOPROTEINS IDENTIFIED IN PLASMA

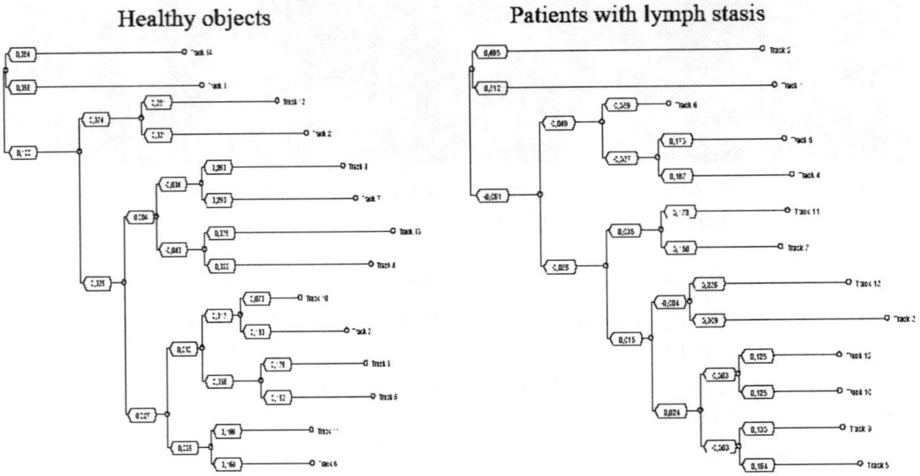

leg lymphedema. All subjects had their leg lymphatics cannulated and lymph samples were collected over a 24h period. Glycoproteins were examined using PAS and PAGE detection system, collagen and fibrinogen were detected by immunoblotting.

RESULTS

There was more glycoproteins of high molecular weight detected in lymph from healthy subjects than lymph from lymphedematous limbs. No differences in the glycoproteins profile of plasma samples were found. There was significantly more of different size collagen fragments in stagnant than normal lymph. Fibrinogen was not detected in normal lymph, while 3 bands of high molecular weight were detected in the stagnant lymph.

CONCLUSION

The glycoprotein, collagen and fibrinogen profile is more complex and differentiated in lymph of patients with lymph stasis than in normal subjects.

LOW-MOLECULAR WEIGHT PROTEINS IN NORMAL SUBJECTS AND PATIENTS WITH LYMPH STASIS

Interewicz B.[1], Olszewski W.L.[1], Leak L.V., [2,3] Petricoin E.F.[2], Ross S.[2], Liotta L.A.[3]

[1]Dept. of Surgical Research & Transplantology., Medical Research Center, Polish Academy of Sciences, Warsaw, Poland; [2]Clinical Proteomics Program of Therapeutic Proteins, CBER, Food and Drug Administration, Bethesda, USA; [3]Laboratory of Pathology, National Cancer Institute, National Institutes of Health, Bethesda, USA

Lymph contains a number of proteins that are similar to blood plasma as it is generally referred to as an ultrafiltrate of plasma. What are the components of human afferent lymph and how similar or different are they compared with plasma, remains largely undetermined.

In afferent lymph we expect presence not only of proteins and peptides derived from filtered plasma, but also metabolic products of keratinocytes and connective tissue cells, cytokines, chemokines, growth factors and antibacterial peptides originating from immune cells normally present in tissues.

The identification and validation of tissue fluid and lymph proteins under normal conditions and associated with a particular disease have so far been carried out only sporadically.

In the absence of protein databases for afferent lymph in comparison with those well established for plasma, there is a need for a rapid multiparametric and reproducible method for the identification and analysis of lymph protein components.

AIM

To define lymph and plasma peptide profile collected from healthy subjects, patients with obstructive lymphedema and patients with rheumatoid arthritis using the ProteinChip SELDI TOF MS system.

RESULTS

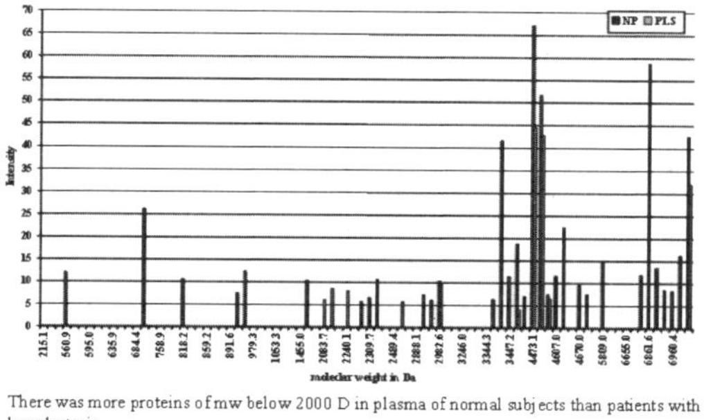

There was more proteins of mw below 2000 D in plasma of normal subjects than patients with lymph stasis.

The final map view of protein profile of normal plasma (NP) and plasma from patients with rheumatoid arthritis (PRA)

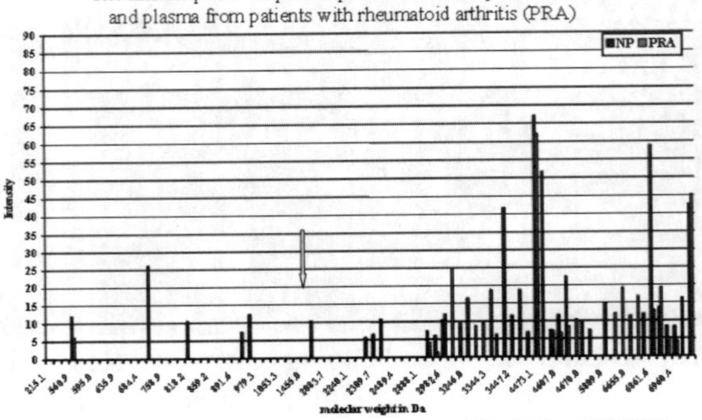

- Plasma of RA patients contained two clusters of proteins (between 3000 – 3500D and 6500-7000D) not present in normal plasma.
- There were no very low mw proteins (less than 2000 D) in plasma of RA patients.

The final map view of protein profile of normal lymph (NL) and lymph from patients with lymph stasis (LLS)

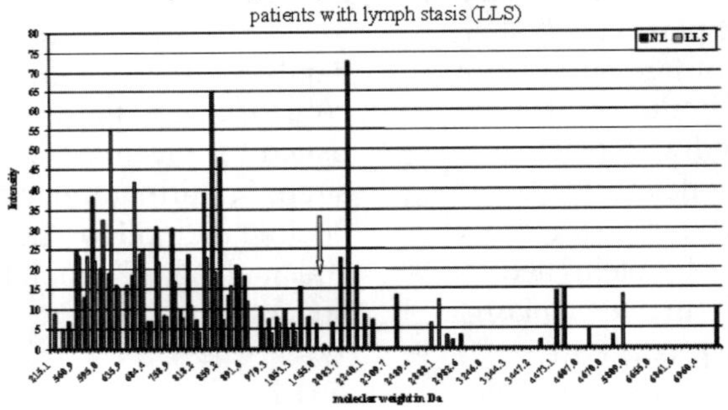

- The protein profile of normal lymph and lymph of patients with lymphedema was similar only in the range of proteins of mw below 2000D).
- Evident differences between normal lymph and lymph of patients with lymph stasis were found in protein profile ab 2000D.

The final map view of protein profile of normal lymph (NL) and lymph from patients with rheumatoid arthritis (LRA)

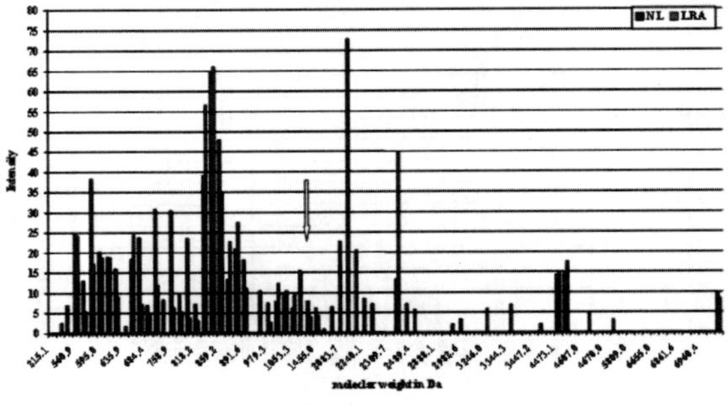

- The protein profile of lymph of RA patients was similar to that of normal lymph.
- Minor differences were observed in proteins between 2500 – 2700D and 3300 – 3400D.

The final map view of protein profile of normal plasma (NP) and normal lymph (NL)

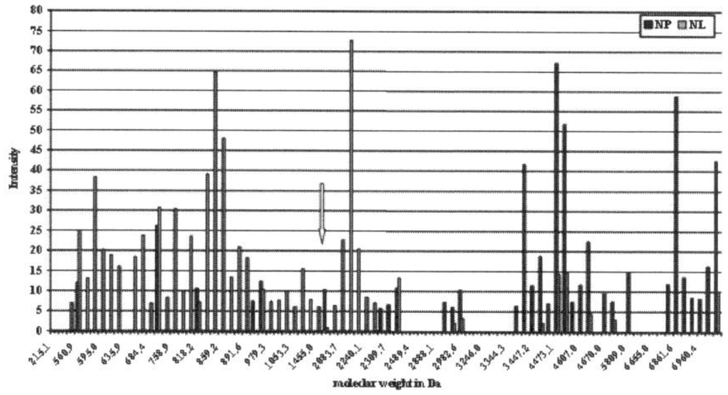

•Fourteen identical proteins, although of different relative intensity, were found in normal lymph and plasma.
•There were many very low mw proteins (below 2000 D) in normal lymph not detected in plasma.

The final map view of protein profile of plasma (PLS) and lymph (LLS) from patients with lymph stasis

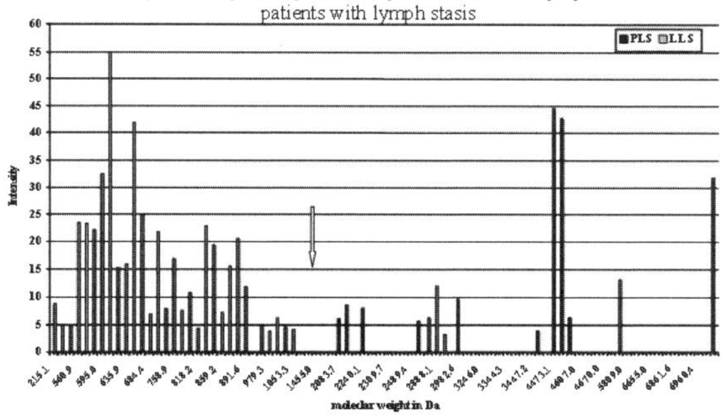

•The protein profile of plasma and lymph of patients with lymph stasis was different.
•There were very low mw proteins (below 2000 D) in lymph of patients with lymph stasis absent from plasma.

The final map view of protein profile of lymph from patients with lymph stasis (LLS) and lymph from patients with rheumatoid arthritis (LRA)

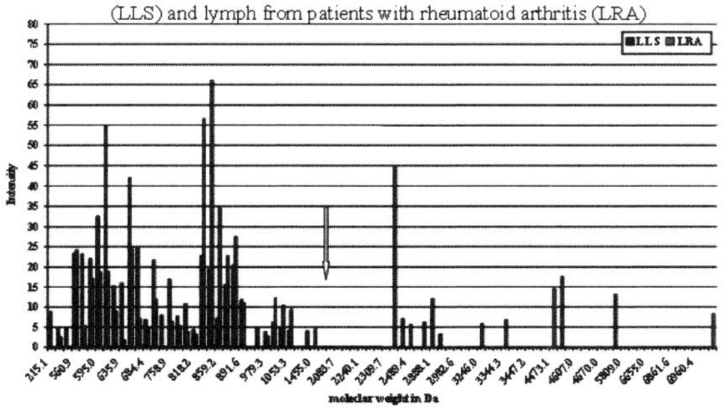

•The protein profile of lymph of patients with lymph stasis and lymph of patients with rheumatoid arthritis is similar in the range of very low mw. Proteins (less than 2000D)

•The protein profile ab 2000D is different.

CONCLUSIONS

Normal prenodal leg lymph contains low mw proteins absent from plasma and conversely plasma contains proteins not detectable in lymph.

Lymph from obstructed lymphatics and RA patients contains low mw proteins not present in plasma.

There are differences between low mw proteins between stagnant and RA lymph samples.

Low mw lymph proteins may be products of parenchymal cells and digested fragments of filtered plasma proteins.

Function of lymph low mw proteins remains to be determined.

Lack of low mw proteins in plasma not diffusing to the tissue fluid suggests their binding to albumin or other plasma proteins.

Detection of low molecular weight proteins in plasma absent from lymph challenges the concept of the transcapillary transport of proteins inversly related to the molecular weight.

PROTEASES IN HUMAN PERIPHERAL LYMPH IN NORMAL SUBJECTS AND INFLAMMATORY CONDITIONS

Interewicz B., Olszewski W.L., Dominiak A.

Dept. of Surgical Research & Transplantology, Medical Research Center, Polish Academy of Sciences, Warsaw, Poland

Long-lasting edema of the skin and subcutaneous tissue of limbs is caused by destruction of lymphatics and nodes by infection, trauma, irradiation or lack of tissue fluid drainage because of malfunction of initial lymphatics and inborn malformations of lymphatics.

Lymph contains proteins and peptides derived from plasma, products of connective tissue cells, components of extracellular matrix and proteins produced by lymph immune cells.

Controlled degradation of the extracellular matrix (ECM) is required for removal of its damaged components and to allow cell migration and angiogenesis.

Protease expression is one of the major events in the process of remodeling of the extracellular matrix (ECM) and restoring tissue integrity. A key step in degradation of ECM is the extracellular secretion of metalloproteinases (MMPs). The proteolytic MMPs profile of human normal, inflammatory and stagnant lymph has so far not been evaluated.

AIM

to determine proteolytic properties of peripheral lymph and plasma collected from:

1 healthy subjects
2 patients with lymph stasis
3 patients with rheumatoid arthritis

MATERIAL AND METHODS

Twelve subjects in each group, had lymph samples collected from leg lymphatics.

Zymography. Proteolytic profiles were examined using gelatin copolymerized in polyacrylamide gels. Cell free samples of lymph and plasma were subjected to PAGE-SDS under nonreducing conditions. After electrophoresis, gels were renaturated by overnight incubation at 37 °C in developing buffer. Then, gels were stained with colloidal Coomassie brilliant blue.

TIMP-1 and TIMP-2 were determined by Western blotting with use of specific antibodies.

PROTEASES IDENTIFIED IN PLASMA AND LYMPH BY ZYMOGRAPHY IN GELATIN POLYACRYLAMIDE GELS

MMP9 Complex
Pro MMP9
Active MMP9
Pro MMP2
Active MMP2

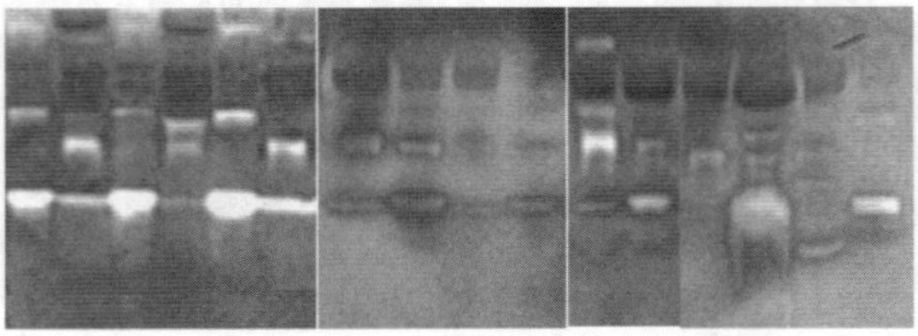

P L P L P L P L P L P L P L P L
1 2 3 4 5 6 7 8 9 10 11 12 13 14 15 16

P-plasma, L-lymph
Lanes 1-6 healthy subjects,
Lanes 7-10 patients with rheumatoid arthritis
Lanes 11- 16 patients with obstructive lymphedema

PROTEASES IDENTIFIED IN PLASMA AND LYMPH BY ZYMOGRAPHY IN CASEINE POLYACRYLAMIDE GELS

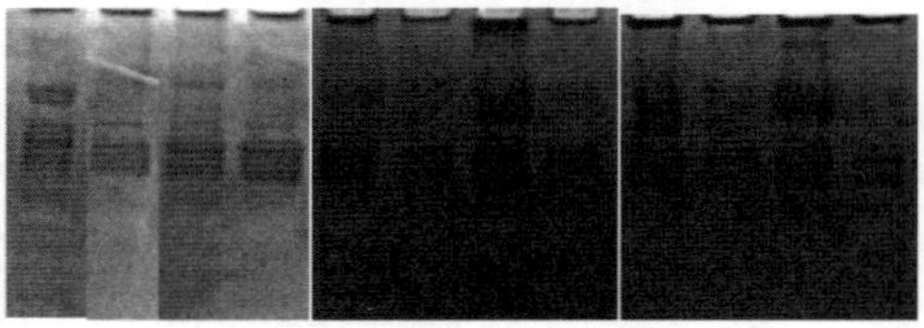

P L P L P L P L P L P L
1 2 3 4 5 6 7 8 9 10 11 12

P-plasma, L-lymph
Lanes 1-4 healthy subjects,
Lanes 5-8 patients with rheumatoid arthritis
Lanes 9- 12 patients with obstructive lymphedema

RESULTS

The gelatin zymography of normal lymph samples showed 6 bands. In lymph from lymphedematous limbs the number of bands varied in different patients. Up to11 bands could be detected. In lymph from patients with rheumatoid arthritis the proteolytic profile was similar but the band representing activated MMP-2 was missing.

There were differences in the proteolytic profile of plasma samples in patients with lymphedema.

The casein zymograms showed pattern of hydrolysis without significant differences between samples.

TIMP-1 was present in all analysed plasma and normal lymph samples, but it was not detected in the inflammatory lymph.

TIMP-2 was present in normal plasma but could not be found in normal and inflammatory lymph and plasma.

CONCLUSION

Different proteolytic enzymes were found in lymphedematous lymph compared to other samples.

MERCURY DETECTION IN RAT LYMPH NODES

Cunha EM, Cherdwongcharoensuk D, Costa-e-Silva A and Águas AP

Department of Anatomy, ICBAS (Abel Salazar Institute for Biomedical Sciences), and UMIB (Unit for Multidisciplinary Investigation in Biomedicine), University of Porto

Summary

Accidental exposure of mercury (Hg) can cause harmful effects in humans, namely the induction of autoimmune disease. This investigation was aimed at the distribution of Hg inside lymph nodes, a key organ of the immune system. For that, we have performed *in situ* detection of Hg particles in mouse popliteal lymph nodes using scanning electron microscopy coupled with elemental analysis (SEM-XRM). We found that Hg particles reach the lymph node via afferent vessel and are ingested by macrophages located firstly in the reticular network of the outer layer of the cortex. A few particles of Hg were seen in macrophages of the medulla. This study provides the first high-resolution evidence of the localization of Hg inside the lymph node.

Introduction

Mercury (Hg) is one of the most toxic metal agents present in the environment (1). It is a naturally occurring element existing in multiple forms and various oxidation states (2). In addition to the neurotoxicity of Hg, this metal induces changes in the functioning of the immune system leading to autoimmune disease that resembles lupus (3). In a previous study, we have investigated how Hg was distributed in mouse kidney, liver and spleen after intraperitoneal injection of $HgCl_2$ (4). Our goals now was to study the distribution of Hg inside the lymph nodes since cellular changes in this organ, as well as in the spleen, are associated with the Hg-induced autoimmune disease of rodents (5). By the use of scanning electron microscopy coupled with elemental analysis, we have aimed at the *in situ* detection of Hg particles in the two major domains of the lymph node, i.e. the cortex and the medulla. The arrangement of cells in the lymph node permits the contact between foreign substances, such as Hg, and macrophages and also T and B lymphocytes. This interaction is likely to modify the immune physiology of the lymph node. We have used here Wistar rats to detect Hg particles in their popliteal lymph nodes after subcutaneous or intraperitoneal injection of $HgCl_2$.

Material and Methods

Animals. Twenty-eight female Wistar rats, weighing about 350 g, were kept under standard housing conditions, and had unrestricted access to food and water. They were treated in accordance with the European Union law on animal protection (directive 86/609/EC).

Stimulation of Popliteal Lymph Nodes. Animals were injected subcutaneously at the footpads with 100 µL of complete Freund´s adjuvant in right footpads and of incomplete Freund´s adjuvant in the left footpads (each mL contain 1 mg of *Mycobacterium tuberculosis*). After 7 days of the first treatment, the immunized mice were reinjected with the same amount of adjuvant.

Hg injection. 24 hrs after the adjuvant treatment, 4 mice per each group were injected with various concentrations of $HgCl_2$ (from a stock solution of 25 mg of $HgCl_2$ in 500 µL of PBS, several dilutions were made: 5, 7.5, 10, 20, 50 and 100) both in subcutaneous area below the popliteal fossa and in the peritoneal cavity.

Scanning Electron Microscopy coupled with X-ray Elemental Microanalysis (SEM-XRM). Popliteal lymph nodes were fixed in an aldehyde mixture, dehydrated in ethanol and critical point-dried in a Balzer´s apparatus using carbon dioxide as the transitional fluid. The preparations were mounted on metal stubs and coated by carbon under vacuum, and examined in a JEOL JSM-6301F scanning electron microscope (SEM) that was coupled to a Noran Voyager x-ray elemental microanalyser (XRM) with EDS (Energy Dispersive Spectrometry) detection system. SEM-XRM allows the *in situ* identification of Hg upon the detection of the characteristic elemental spectra of the metal (6). SEM micrographs of the samples were derived from secondary and backscattered electron imaging modes, the latter being used to detect Hg *in situ* by x-ray microanalysis (4).

Results

Detection of Hg by SEM-XRM in the rat popliteal lymph nodes was achieved only in the rats that had received the lethal dose of $HgCl_2$ (25 mg in 500 µL of PBS). This dose killed the animals within 2-4 min. In the Hg-positive samples, the few Hg particles that were detected in the lymph node were always found inside cells with the surface morphology of macrophages. The localization of the Hg-positive macrophages was the following: a diffuse disposition of Hg particles in the cortical area of the lymph node and a residual number of Hg dots in the medulla. The metal localization suggested a gradient of dissemination of Hg-positive macrophages through the outer and inner cortex, medulla and, finally, through efferent lymphatic vessels. Thus, Hg appeared to be translocated by macrophages from afferent lymphatic vessels through reticular networks in the cortex and medulla in the direction of efferent lymphatics.

Discussion

In our previous study, we found that Hg injected in the peritoneal cavity of rodents was later seen accumulated as minute dots inside cells of liver, kidney and spleen (4). We report now that Hg can also be detected inside the rat lymph node, provided that a high dose of Hg is injected subcutaneously. The Hg particles were located mostly in the cortical areas of the lymph node and they were inside macrophages. Lymph nodes are divided into two domains: cortex and medulla. Both areas have reticular network containing macrophages and reticular cells. The lymph reaches the lymph node through afferent vessels that enter the cortex and it is transported through the medulla and efferent lymphatic vessels (7). Our observations with Hg suggest that the metal particles of Hg also reach the lymph node via afferent vessels and were mostly captured by macrophages surrounding the reticular network of the cortex. A few of Hg dots were also capture in the medulla of the lymph node indicating that the Hg-positive macrophages may migrate from the outer layers of the node into deeper regions, before leaving this lymphoid organ.

Acknowledgments

The authors are grateful to Professor Carlos M. Sá, director of CEMUP and to Dr. Daniela Silva for

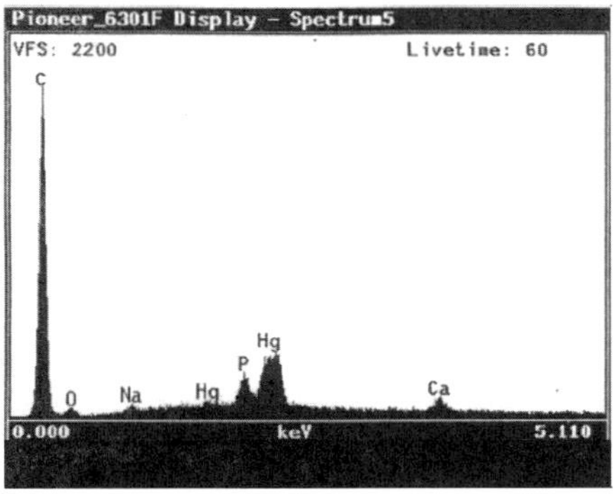

Fig. 1. X-ray elemental microanalysis spectrum of particles in mouse popliteal lymph node inclusion observed by SEM and containing Hg as revealed by the two peaks marked as Hg.

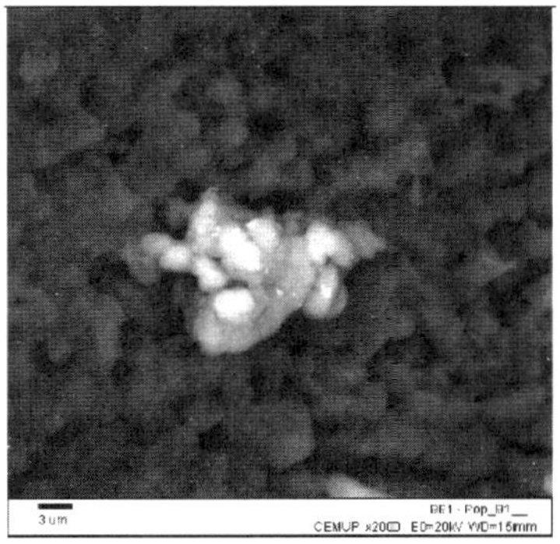

Fig. 2. SEM micrograph (backscattered electron imaging mode) of a macrophage from a lymph node. The Hg particles are visualized as white spots. Black bar, 3 μm.

expert help with SEM-RXM. This work was funded by grants from FCT /POCTI/BSE/36180/2000 and UMIB (Unit for multidisciplinary Investigation in Biomedicine), Portugal.

References

1. Clarkson, T. W., Magos, L, Myers, GJ: The toxicology of mercury: current exposures and clinical manifestations. N. Engl. J. Med. 349 (2003), 1731-1737.
2. Kales, S. N., Goldman, RH: Mercury exposure: current concepts, controversies, and a clinic´s experience. J. Occup. Environ. Med. 44 (2002), 143-154.
3. Silbergeld, E. K., Silva, IA, Nyland, JF: Mercury and autoimmunity: implications for occupational and environmental health. Tox. Appl. Pharmacol. 207 (2005), 282-292.
4. Cunha, E.M., Águas, AP: Relative loading of mouse viscera by lethal mercury: a study by scanning electron microscopy coupled with X-ray microanalysis. Toxicol. and Industrial Health 19 (2003), 55-61.
5. Haggqvist, B, Hultman, P: Effects of deviating the Th2-response in murine mercury-induced autoimmunity towards a Th1-response. Clin. Exp. Immunol. 134 (2003), 202-209.
6. Cunha, E.M., Silva, DP, Águas, AP: High-resolution identification of mercury in particles in mouse kidney after acute lethal exposure. BioMetals 16 (2003), 583-590.
7. Eses, G: Ultrasound of superficial lymph nodes. Eur. J. Radiol. 7 (2006), *in press*.
8. Cunha, E.M., Oliveira, MJ, Ferreira, PG, Águas, AP: Mercury intake by inflammatory phagocytes: *in vivo* cytology of mouse macrophages and neutrophils by X-ray elemental microanalysis coupled with scanning electron microscopy. Human & Exp.Tox. 23 (2004), 447-453.

SPLEEN CHANGES AND DECREASE IN BLOOD CELLS IN CALICIVIRUS INFECTION OF RABBITS

P.G. Ferreira, A. Costa-e-Silva, M.J.R. Oliveira, E. Monteiro, A. Ribeiro, A.P. Aguas

Department of Anatomy, ICBAS (Abel Salazar Institute for Biomedical Sciences) and UMIB (Unit for Multidisciplinary for Biomedical Research), University of Porto, Largo Professor Abel Salazar, 2, Porto 4099-003, Portugal, European Union.

ABSTRACT

Calicivirus infection causes the so-called rabbit haemorrhagic disease (RHD) that kills more than 90% of adult animals whereas young animals are naturally resistant to the disease. We have investigated changes in the morphology of spleen and liver in young (resistant) and adult (susceptible) rabbits. The infection of adult rabbits resulted in marked histological changes in liver and spleen; this is in contrast with the absence of significant lesions in spleen of infected young rabbits. A severe leukopenia characterizes the late stage of disease in adult rabbits. We postulate that these differences between young and adult rabbits may contribute to the different responses to the calicivirus infection (susceptibility versus resistance) observed in young and adult rabbits.

Calicivirus infection is lethal for adult rabbits, whereas young rabbits (less than 8-week-old) are resistant to the same infectious agent (1). The virus replicates in the liver and causes a fulminant hepatitis in adult rabbits leading, within 24-72 hours of viral infection, to rabbit haemorrhagic disease (RHD) (2,3). This is in contrast with the subclinical disease caused by calicivirus infection in young rabbits that is characterized by a mild and transient hepatitis (4,5). We have investigated here changes in morphology of spleen and liver in young (resistant) and adult (susceptible) rabbits. We have also followed changes in the number of blood cells during the calicivirus infection.

MATERIAL AND METHODS

Rabbits

Twenty four New Zealand White rabbits (*Oryctolagus cunicu-*

lus) were used in this study. All of the rabbits were maintained under standard conditions of housing with unrestricted access to food and water; this was done according to the European Union Directive no. 86/609/CEE.

Calicivirus infection

Ten adult (10-week-old) and 10 young (4-week-old) rabbits were injected intramuscularly with PBS suspension of caliciviruses that had a 2^{12} titer in haemagglutination units. The group of young animals were sacrificed 48 hours after viral inoculation. The infected adult rabbits were closely followed until death that occurred between 36 and 48 hours of infection. Controls were made up of two young and two adult rabbits that were injected with PBS (vehicle used in the calicivirus inoculum); they were sacrificed 48 hours later. Spleen, liver and blood samples were collected and studied by light and electron microscopy. The rabbits were sacrificed after an intravenous injection of an anaesthetic mixture of xylazine (Rompun®, Bayer Co., Portugal, 3mg/kg) and ketamine (Imalgéne 1000®, Merial, Portugal, 10 mg/kg).

Light and Transmission Electron Microscopy

For light microscopy, liver and spleen samples were fixed by immersion in 10% buffered formalin and processed as described before (4,5). For electron microscopy, samples were fixed by immersion in an aldehyde mixture made up of 4% formaldehyde, 1.25% glutaraldehyde, and 10 mM $CaCl_2$ in 0.05 M cacodylate buffer, pH 7.2, and processed as described before (2,3,6).

RESULTS

All 10 of the infected adult rabbits died of RHD within 36-48 hours of the calicivirus inoculation. In contrast, none of the 10 infected young rabbits died after the same viral infection. In adult rabbits, there was fulminant hepatitis and massive infiltration of the spleen by inflammatory cells, namely by heterophils. Lymphocytic necrosis occurred in the white pulp whereas diffuse cellular depletion affected the red pulp (Fig. 1). Congestion in red pulp was also presented. In the liver of adult rabbits, infiltrates were made up mostly of heterophils and they were located near hepatocytes showing severe cellular damage. In contrast, no significant lesions were detected in the spleen of RHD-resistant young rabbits, and liver leukocyte infiltrates were dominated by lymphocytes that depicted membrane contacts with the cell surface of undamaged hepatocytes. A marked decrease in circulating leukocytes was detected in infected adult rabbits, whereas this phenomenon was transient in the infected young rabbits. In adult rabbits both heterophils and lymphocytes participate in the leukopenia, whereas only heterophils are decreased in infected young rabbits.

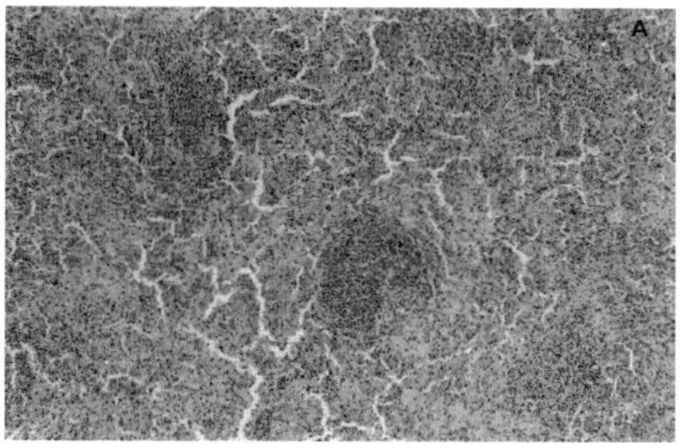

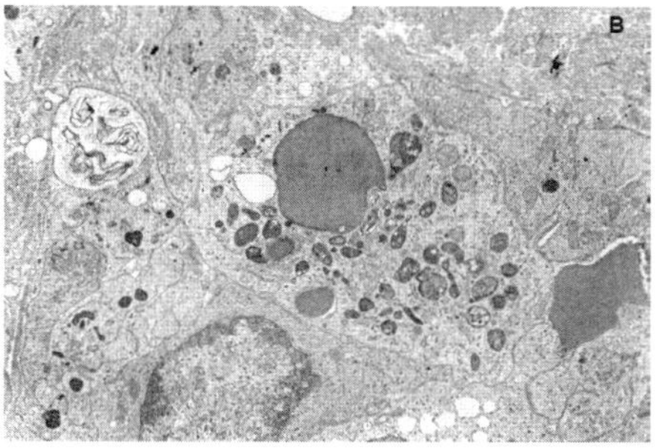

Fig. 1. Light (A) and electron (B) micrographs of spleen of adult rabbit dying from infection with calicivirus (36 hours after viral inoculation). (A). Splenic nodules were diminished in size. Haematoxylin-eosin stain. 100x. (B). The macrophage at the centre of the figure show phagocytic vacuoles in cytoplasm. A lymphocyte (bottom) and a cell with cellular debris in cytoplasm (left) are seen in contact with the macrophage.

DISCUSSION

This study compares changes in spleen and liver morphology attending the infection by caliciviruses of adult and young rabbits. We documented that calicivirus infection causes marked histological changes in spleen and liver of adult rabbits (susceptible to RHD), namely lymphocytic necrosis and death of a large of hepatocytes. This is in contrast with the absence of significant lesions in the liver and spleen of infected young rabbits. Electron microscopy also showed that the cellular inflammatory response of the liver to calicivirus infection is different in rabbits that are susceptible (adult) or resistant (young) to RHD. Leukocyte infiltration of the adult liver by heterophils is probably directed at the removal of dead hepatocytes (7), whereas the liver lymphocytic infiltration of young rabbits suggests the expression of viral antigens on the surface of liver cells (8,9). We also illustrated that a severe leukopenia characterizes calicivirus infection of adult rabbits, whereas the decrease in circulating white blood cells is a transient event in young rabbits. Necrosis of lymphocytes that are present in spleen of the infected adult rabbits could contribute to the decrease in lymphocyte counts. The sharp decline of the heterophils in RHD may be derived from sequestration of leukocytes out of circulation (e.g., in the infected liver where large numbers of inflammatory cells are observed).

In conclusion, this study establishes important differences in morphology of spleen and liver in young (resistant) and adult (susceptible) rabbits. It offers also a vision of alterations of cellular parameters of the blood of young and adult rabbits that were experimentally infected with calicivirus. We postulate that the herein reported differences between young and adult rabbits, namely regarding spleen morphology and haematological changes, may contribute to different responses to the calicivirus infection (susceptibility versus resistance).

ACKNOWLEDGMENTS

We thank Mrs. Manuela Silva for technical assistance. This work was funded by grants from FCT (POCTI/FEDER), Portugal.

REFERENCES

1. Parra F, M Prieto: Purification and characterization of a calicivirus as the causative agent of a lethal hemorrhagic disease in rabbits. J. Virol. 64 (1990), 4013-4015.
2. Ferreira PG, A Costa-e-Silva, MJR Oliveira, et al: Liver enzymes and ultrastructure in rabbit haemorrhagic disease (RHD). Vet. Res. Commun. 30 (2006), 393-401.
3. Ferreira PG, A Costa-e-Silva, MJR Oliveira et al: Severe leukopenia and liver biochemistry changes in adult rabbits after calicivirus infection. Res. Vet. Sci. 80 (2006), 218-225.
4. Ferreira PG, A Costa-e-Silva, E Monteiro, et al: Transient decrease in blood heterophils and sustained liver damage caused by calicivirus infection of young rabbits that are naturally resistant to rabbit haemorrhagic disease. Res. Vet. Sci. 76 (2004), 83-94.
5. Ferreira PG, A Costa-e-Silva, Águas AP: Liver disease in young rabbits infected by calicivirus through nasal and oral routes. Res. Vet. Sci. (2006) (In press).
6. Ferreira PG, A Costa-e-Silva, MJR Oliveira et al: Leukocyte-hepatocyte interaction in calicivirus infection: differences between rabbits that are resistant or susceptible to rabbit haemorrhagic disease (RHD). Vet. Immunol. Immunopath. 103 (2005), 217-221.
7. Marcato PS, C Benazzi, G Vecchi, et al: Clinical and pathological features of viral haemorrhagic disease of rabbits and the European brown hare syndrome. Rev. Sci. Tech. Off. Int. Epiz. 10 (1991), 371-392.
8. Prieto JM, F Fernandez, V Alvarez, et al: Immunohistochemical localisation of rabbit haemorrhagic disease virus VP-60 antigen in early infection of young and adult rabbits. Res. Vet. Sci. 68 (2000), 181-187.
9. Shien JH, HK Shieh, LH Lee: Experimental infections of rabbits with rabbit haemorrhagic disease virus monitored by polymerase chain reaction. Res. Vet. Sci. 68 (2000), 255-259.

CHANGES IN PLEURAL MILKY SPOTS DUE TO NOISE POLLUTION

Maria João R. Oliveira, António S. Pereira, Paula G. Ferreira, Alexandrina Ribeiro, Nuno R. Grande, Artur P. Águas

Department of Anatomy, ICBAS, Abel Salazar Institute for Biomedical Sciences, UMIB, University of Porto

ABSTRACT

Exposure to low frequency/ high intensity noise (greater than or equal to 90 dB, less than or equal to 500 Hz) is known to induce structural and functional changes in the pleural mesothelium and in the local immune system. We have studied here if the pleural milky spots (MS) response to infectious agents that reach the pleural space is modified by noise stress. The MS of rats that were infected with Mycobacterium avium and not exposed to noise were compared by light microscopy with MS of rats that were both submitted to M. avium infection and noise aggression. Our data show that exposure to low frequency/high intensity noise inhibits the normal response of MS in the pleural space that is associated with clearance of infectious agents. This findings is consistent with the higher frequency of pleural disorders in workers of industrial facilities (e.g. aeronautical and textile plants) where there is environmental noise aggression.

Milky spots (MS), also known as Kampmeier´s foci, are pleural structures that are confined to the parietal leaflet of the pleura and act as a barrier to the spreading of mediastinum infections, playing phagocytic and immune functions (1,2). Pereira *et al* (1994) have shown that these structures can mount different immune responses in accordance with the stimuli that reach the pleural space showing that they, therefore, work as fully competent lymphoepitheloid organs (3).

Chronic exposure to noise of large pressure amplitude (? 90dB) and low frequency (? 500Hz) (LPALF) for large periods of time (over 10 years), can damage different organs and systems of the human body. Taken together these disorders have led to the concept of Vibroacoustic Disease (VAD) (4-5). One of the systems that is damaged by this aggression is the respiratory system, and pleural effusions have been described in VAD patients (6). Previous studies of ours have shown that LPALF can induce changes in cell membrane projections such as cilia and microvillus of the respiratory epithelium and pleural mesothelium (7-10). Changes in the immune system were also previously described (11,12). In the herein experimental study we aimed at the investigation of the dynamics of MS, namely with regards to the response to infectious agents reaching the pleural space of rats also submitted to noise stress.

MATERIALS AND METHODS

Animals: 20 adult male Wistar rats that were purchased to a Spanish breeder (Charles River Laboratories España, SA, Spain). All animals had unrestricted access to food (commercial chow) and water, and were treated in accordance with the European Union laws on animal protection (directive 86/609/EC).

Experimental Protocols: The rats were divided in 4 groups of 5 animals: I) control and sham operated rats; II) exposed to intrapleural infection by *M. avium* only; III) exposed to 1696 cumulative hours of LPALF noise; IV) exposed to 2184 cumulative hours of LPALF noise. Following noise exposures, rats from groups 4 and 5 were injected in the pleural space with 0,2 ml of a saline solution containing $4x10^7$ viable *M. avium* bacilli (ATCC-25291strain, sereotype 2). The rats were sacrificed 21 days after infection and sections of the retrocardiac pleural leaflets were observed by a light microscopy using the Ziehl-Neelsen staining method to visualize the mycobacteria followed by background staining with toliudine blue. Martius Scarlet Blue staining was also performed.

Quantification of MS response to M. avium infection: The effect of the mycobacterial infection on the pleural MS was quantified by measuring the width of these structures instead of counting individual MS (3). The latter type of quantification was not possible because the mycobacterial infection leads to a marked increase in the MS size with fusion of individual MS. MS width are presented as means ± standard deviation; statistical comparison of values from different experimental groups was made using a Student´s test; p< 0,01 was accepted as statistically significant.

RESULTS

Our data showed that intrapleural infection by *M. avium* resulted in statistically significant increase in the MS width in all the experimental groups of rats (II, III and IV) in comparison with the rats of the control group (Graph 1).

The increase width was due to hypercellularity of the MS, mainly caused by an enhancement number of mononuclear cells, and the formation of large granulomas rich in mycobacteria (Figs. 1 and 2).

In addition, we found that rats exposed to 2184 hours of LPALF noise (group IV) presented a statistically significant decrease in MS width when compared either with groups II or III (exposed to intrapleural *M. avium* infection, but not to noise, and exposed to 1696 cumulative hours of LPALF noise followed by *M. avium* intrapleural infection) (Graph 1). Alterations of the hypertrophic MS, namely partial necrosis of these lympho-epithelial structures, were also found.

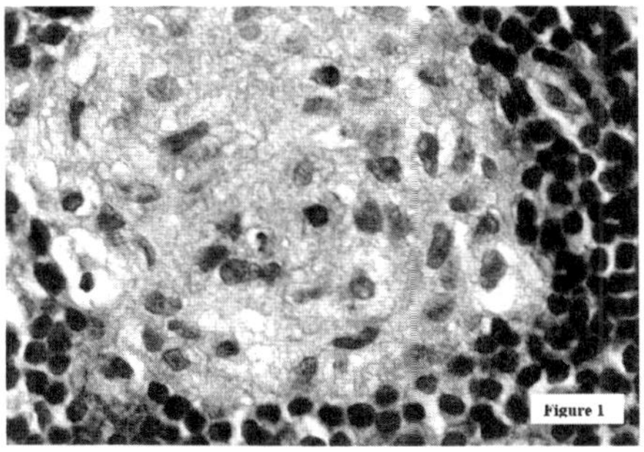

Fig. 1. Light microscopy micrograph of paraffin sections of pleural MS, from a rat submitted to 1696 hours of LPALF and to mycobacterial infection (group III). A large granuloma is seen in this MS (Martius Scarlet Blue). X 1000.

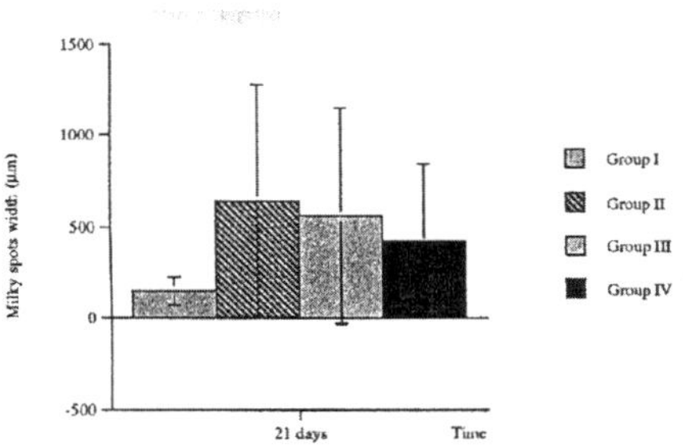

GRAPH 1. Changes in the MS width in response to intrapleural infection with $4x10^7$ viable bacilli of *M. avium*, in rats exposed to low frequency noise environment. Group I – control; Group II – *M. avium* infection and no noise exposure; Group III – 1696 hours of LPALF noise exposure followed by *M. avium* infection; Group IV – 2184 LPALF hours of noise exposure followed by *M. avium* infection. MS width is presented as means±sd.

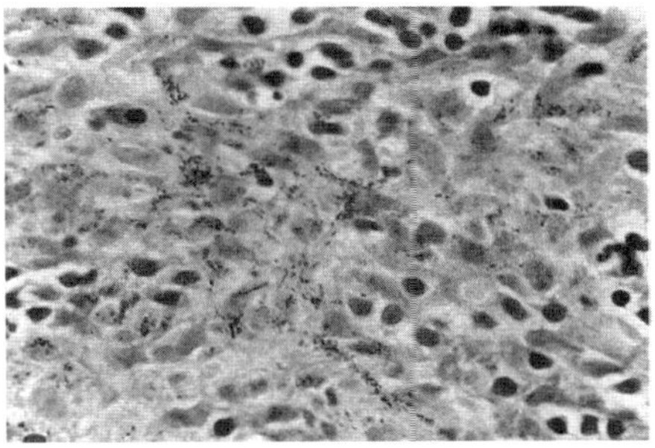

Fig. 2. Light microscopy micrograph of paraffin sections of pleural MS from a rat submitted to mycobacterial infection and kept in silent environment (group II). This enlarged MS shows that mycobacteria have been ingested by macrophages (Ziehl–Neelsen staining followed by toluidine blue). X 1000.

DISCUSSION

Noise pollution is an environmental hazard of modern life and is particularly severe in industrial facilities where large amounts of noise machinery are used. Occupational exposure to large pressure and low frequency (LPALF) noise is known to cause a multi-systemic disorder named Vibroacoustic Disease which includes respiratory and immune system disorders (4-6,11,12). MS are lymphoid organs located in the parietal leaflet of the pleura. These structures have an important role in the clearance of the pleural space from foreign particles or microbes due to their phagocytic abilities and capacity to mount different immune responses according to he stimuli that reach the pleural space (3). In order to investigate whether exposure to LPALF noise interfered with the normal immune response of rat MS, we have performed an intrapleural infection with *M. avium* after the rats were submitted to chronic noise aggression for 1696 and 2184 hours. Our data show impairment in the MS ability to remove the bacilli from the pleural space in the rats submitted to noise previous to infection, which was more severe in the animals that were exposed to longer hours of LPALF noise. These results may indicate a correlation between the length of exposure and the severity of the lesions.

These findings suggest that exposure LPALF noise alters MS dynamics namely by decreasing their response to infectious agents that enter the pleural space; this change may compromise the clearance of this ceolomic cavity. This investigation offer experimental data that is useful to understand the disorders of the pleural space found in patients with vibroacoustic disease.

ACKNOWLEDGMENTS

This experimental work was funded by grants from FCT (POCTI/FEDER/POCTI/CBO/ 40915/01).

REFERENCES

1. Pereira A. S., Grande NR: Particle clearance from the canine pleural space into thoracic lymph nodes: An experimental study. Lymphology 25 (1992), 120.
2. Cooray G. H.: Defense mechanisms in the mediastinum with special reference to the mechanics of pleural absorption. J Path Bact. 61 (1949), 551.
3. Pereira A. S., Águas AP, Oliveira MJR, *et al*:. Experimental modulation of the reactivity of pleural milky spots (Kampmeier´s foci) by Freund´s adjuvants, betamethasone and mycobacterial infection. J Anat. 185 (1994), 471.
4. Castelo Branco N. A. A.; Rodriguez E: The Vibroacoustic Disease – An emerging pathology. Aviat Space Environ Med. 70 (1999), A1.
5. Alves-Pereira M: Noise-induced extra-aural pathology: A review and commentary. Aviat Space Environ Med. 70 (1999), A7.
6. Castelo Branco NAA: A unique case of Vibroacoustic Disease: A tribute to an extraordinary patient. Aviat Space Environ Med. 70 (1999), A27.

7. Pereira AS, Grande NR, Monteiro E, *et al.*: Morphofunctional study of the rat pleural mesothelia cells exposed to low frequency noise. Aviat Space Environ Med. 70 (1999), A78.
8. Oliveira MJR, Pereira AS, Castelo Branco NAA, *et al.*: *In utero* and postnatal exposure of Wistar rats to low frequency/high intensity noise depletes the tracheal epithelium of ciliated cells. Lung 179 (2002), 225.
9. Oliveira MJR, Pereira AS, Ferreira PG, *et al.*: Reduction of rat pleural microvilli caused by noise pollution. Experimental Lung Research 29 (2003), 445.
10. Oliveira MJR, Pereira AS, Ferreira PG, *et al.*: Arrest in ciliated cell expansion on the bronchial lining of adult rats caused by chronic exposure to noise. Environmental Research 97 (2005), 282.
11. Águas AP, Esaguy N, Grande NR, *et al.*: Effect of low frequency noise exposure on BALB/C mice splenic lymphocytes. Aviat Space Environ Med. 70 (1999), A128.
12. Águas AP, Esaguy N, Grande NR, *et al.*: Acceleration of lupus erythematosus-like processes by low frequency noise in the hybrid NZB/W mouse model. Aviat Space Environ Med. 70 (1999), A131.

BONE FRACTURE AND HEALING EVOKE RESPONSE OF THE REGIONAL LYMPHATIC (IMMUNE) SYSTEM

Szczesny G., Zaleska M., Gorecki A., Olszewski W.L.

1 Department of Surgical Research & Transplantology, Medical Research Center, Polish Academy of Sciences, Warsaw, Poland; 2 Department of Orthopedics & Traumatology of the Locomotor System, Medical University, Warsaw, Poland

Mechanical injuries evoke response in the lymph nodes draining the site of trauma. Our previously reported clinical and experimental observations showed increased lymphatic outflow from traumatized limb and enlargement of regional lymph nodes.

Our experimental investigations showed increased autotransformation and responsiveness to PHA of lymphocytes from lymph nodes draining the traumatized tissues. Moreover, using fluorescence activated cell sorter (FACS) a proportional increase in all cell populations were observed. Both observations pointed to activation of regional lymph nodes, most probably caused by molecular mediators released from the traumatized / healing tissues.

The question arises how does the lymphatic system react to fracture. Is there any difference in the response of the regional lymphatic system of the extremity to normally healing and non healing fractures?

AIM

To identify the cell phenotypes and structural proteins in the fracture gap in the healing and non-healing fractures.

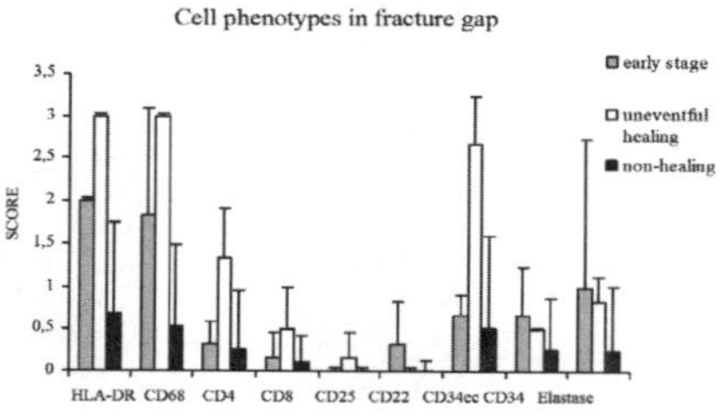

The question arises how does the lymphatic system react to fracture. Is there any difference in the response of the regional lymphatic system of the extremity to normally healing and non healing fractures?

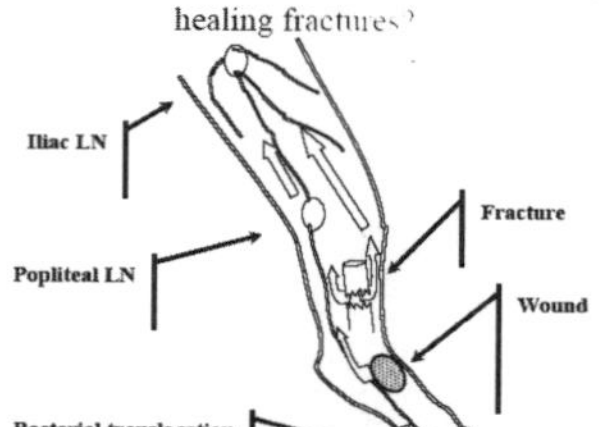

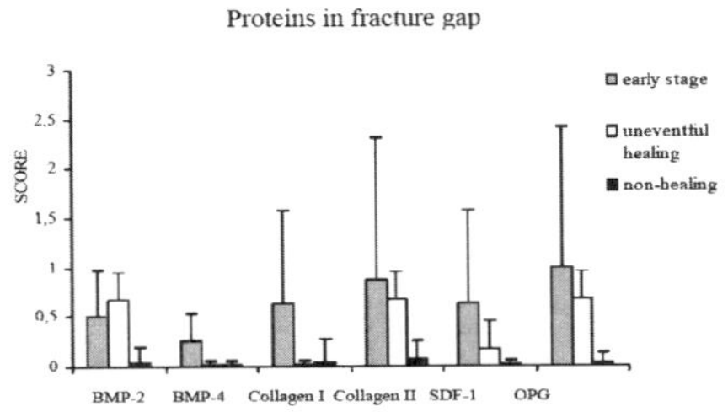

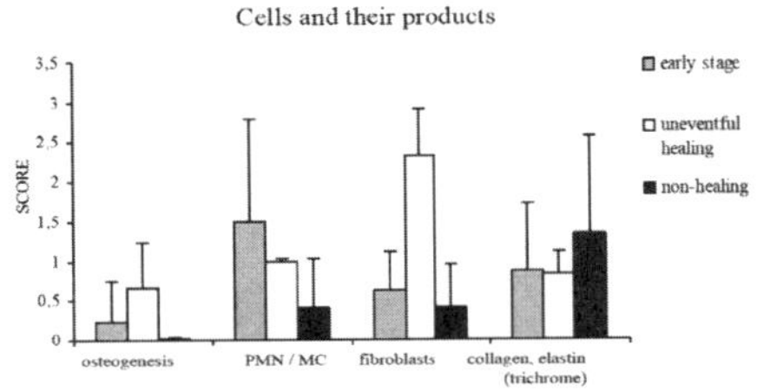

Aim of study

to visualize lymphatics and lymph nodes draining sites of closed fracture in the healing and non-healing bones of lower extremities.

Patients

Twenty five randomly selected patients with fractures of lower leg without skin trauma. Twelve patients were qualified to the early union (group 1) and thirteen to the non-union group (group 2). There was no suppuration at the facture site during the follow-up period.

Methods

1 Lymphoscintigrams were obtained from both extremities remaining in a horizontal position 30 and 120 minutes after subcutaneous injection of 99mTc-Nanocol (3 mCi) into the first web space, using a gamma camera. Data were expressed as indexes obtained from the equations:

2 **ILV or LN Index = STrLV or LN/SCLV or LN**

3 where SLV or LN were surface of lymph vessels or lymph nodes measured on the injured (Tr) and contralateral (C) extremity.

Results - union

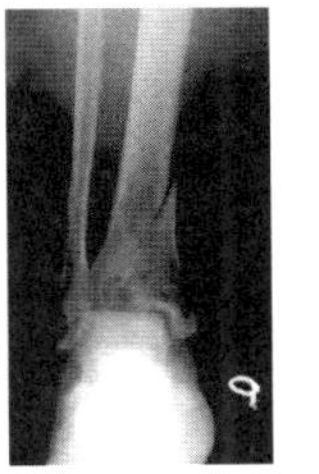

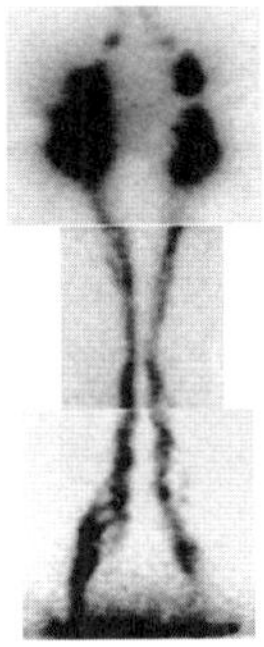

Results – non union

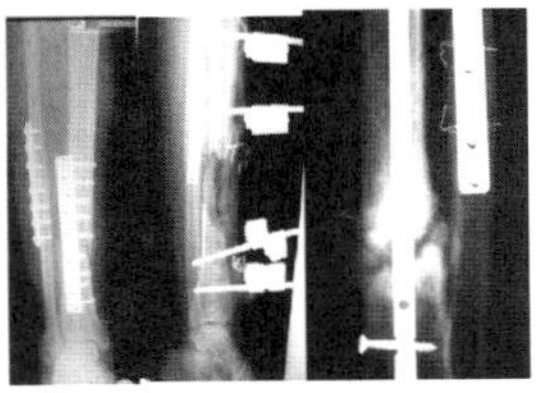

Fracture of right tibia

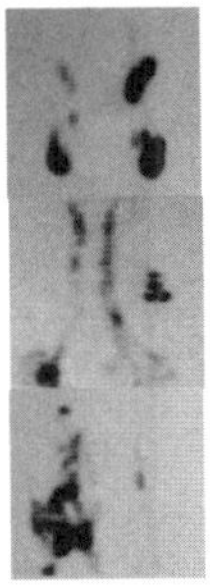

Numerical data of lymphoscintigrams of inguinal lymph nodes, thigh and calf lymphatics expressed as indices (surface traumatized extremity vs contralateral). Data are means +/- SD (*) <0.05

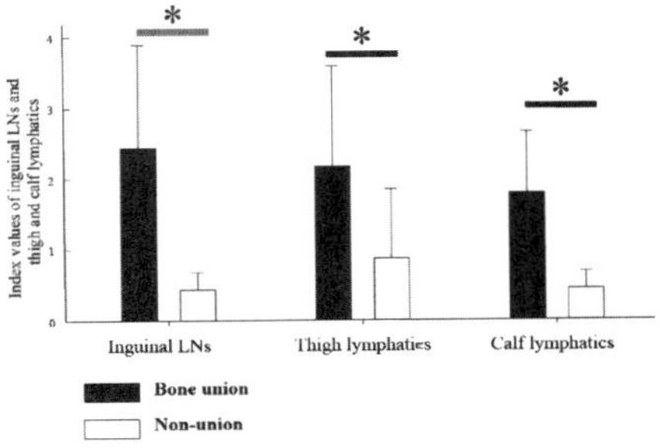

CONCLUSIONS

Closed bone fractures evoke immune response in local lymphatics and nodes but do not cause systemic symptoms of autoimmunity. In the fast healing fractures enlarged nodes and dilated lymphatics are observed. Lack of fracture healing results in decrease of regional lymph nodes mass (probably depopulation and fibrosis). The mechanism of these changes remains unclear. The question arises how does the efferent arc of immune response affect fracture healing.

Chapter 2
Epidemiology and Prevention of Lymphatic Disorders

UPPER LIMB LYMPHEDEMA FOLLOWING BREAST CANCER SURGERY: PREVALENCE AND ASSOCIATED FACTORS

Bergmann, A; PT, PhD[1]; Koifman, RJ; MD, PhD[2]; Koifman, S; MD, PhD[2]; Ribeiro, MJP[1], Mattos, IE; MD, PhD[2]

[1] National Cancer Institute / Cancer Hospital III; [2] National School of Public Health / FIOCRUZ

Abstract

Introduction: Lymphedema is one of the main complications following breast cancer surgery, and affects the quality of life of patients. This study aimed to determine the prevalence of lymphedema in women following breast cancer treatment, as well as associated risk factors. **Methods**: A cross-sectional study was carried out with 394 women undergoing breast cancer surgery. Personal data, tumor size, treatment and post surgical complications were collected. Risk estimates between lymphedema and selected independent variables were ascertained as odds ratios (OR) and their 95% confidence intervals were calculated. Unconditional logistic regression was performed to select the model that better explained the risk of lymphedema after breast cancer treatment. **Results**: The prevalence of lymphedema was 20.8%. The best adjusted model included the following variables: axillary radiotherapy (OR = 4.44; CI 95% 1.97 – 9.96), obesity (OR = 3.11; CI 95% 1.22 – 7.93), arm infection (OR = 5.01; CI 95% 1.80 – 13. 95), and reduced shoulder range of movement (ROM) (OR = 2.64; CI 95% 1.13 – 6.14). **Conclusion:** The prevalence of lymphedema was 20.8%. The variables which best explained the development of lymphedema were axillary radiotherapy, obesity, ROM and history of arm infection.

Keywords: Lymphedema, prevalence, breast cancer, complications.

Introduction

Breast cancer is a major public health problem, due to the magnitude of its incidence and mortality worldwide. The management strategy advocated for women with breast cancer depends, directly, on tumor stage (TNM); thus, as the tumor is diagnosed in more advanced stages, therapeutic resources become more limited and mutilating, with increased post-treatment morbidity. In Brazil, late diagnoses are still part of daily practice, and therefore a significant number of women have to live with physical and functional sequels as a result of more aggressive treatments. Among the complications resulting from breast cancer treatment, upper limb lymphedema is a major one. The onset of lymphedema following surgical treatment of breast cancer leads to major physical, social and psychological changes and its symptoms should not be disregarded on account of its non-lethal condition [1].

The prevalence of post breast cancer surgery upper limb lymphedema ranges between 9% and 40% in different studies, depending on the follow-up time, on the classification and criteria used for its definition, and on the time elapsed after surgery[2]. The risk factors associated with lymphedema described in the literature can be divided into three major categories: factors associated with the treatment; with the tumor; with practice and the patient[3]. A more in-depth understanding of the factors associated with lymphedema is required, so one is able to intervene preventively, changing life activities of women at risk as little as possible. The aim of this study was to determine the prevalence of lymphedema in a cohort of women undergoing medical follow-up after breast cancer treatment in a public referral hospital, as well the factors associated with its development.

Materials and Methods

A study on the prevalence of lymphedema in women undergoing medical follow-up for breast cancer surgical treatment in the outpatient service of a public referral hospital, was conducted from April to August 2000. Excluded from the study were women with: bilateral breast cancer; absence of axillary lymphadenectomy; active locoregional or distant disease; reported functional change in upper limbs prior to treatment for breast cancer; surgical treatment performed less than 6 months before the date of the interview; treatment in other hospitals; and those who were in no condition to answer the questions. Women who met the inclusion criteria were informed about research objectives, and upon acceptance, signed an informed consent. Data was attained through a semi-structured interview and physical examination, and complemented through a review of patient's records. All measurements were performed by a single professional (A.B.) following intra-observer standardization of procedures. Data collection was carried out through standardized devices and validated through the application of a pre-test in 20 women undergoing follow-up in a different institution, and also performed by the same researcher (A.B.). The lymphedema case definition adopted was based on the volume of the limb, estimated from five circumference measurements

(21 cm, 14 cm and 11.5 cm above the olecranon; 7.5 cm, 14 cm and 24 cm below the olecranon), treating every limb segment as a pair of circumferences (truncate cone). The segment volume was given by: $V = h * (C^2 + Cc + c^2) / (\pi * 12)$, where V is the limb segment volume, C and c are the circumferences between the points, and h is the distance between circumferences (C,c). The sum of the differences for every point equaled the estimated final volume[7], in which differences equal to or greater than 200 ml were considered as lymphedema. Variables studied were the ones associated with patient characteristics (age at diagnosis, ethnic background, marital status, educational background, predominant side, reported remunerated work at the date of interview, menopause prior to breast cancer, smoking at the date of surgery, body mass index, background of systemic hypertension, and presence of mycosis in the upper limb), treatment characteristics (time of postoperative follow-up, type of breast surgery performed, type of axillary surgery, reported total days with suction tube and surgical stitches, performance of radiotherapy, drainage chains irradiation, neo and/or adjuvant chemotherapy, hormone therapy, performance of breast reconstruction, side of the surgery and number of axillary lymph nodes removed), tumor characteristics (status of the axillary lymph nodes, tumor stage, tumor location, histological type, and tumor size), and postoperative complications (reported early edema, reported infection in the upper limb on the affected side or in the surgical scar associated with the use of antibiotics, reported necrosis, reported seroma with required aspiration/puncture, reported sensory symptoms at the intercostobrachial nerve area, presence of winged scapula, reduced shoulder joint amplitude and hematoma requiring surgical intervention). The characteristics of women meeting inclusion criteria were compared by using the x^2 test with a 5% ($p < 0.05$) level of significance. Means and medians were presented for continuous variables, and a frequency distribution was present for categorical variables. Logistic regression analysis was performed using the enter method to select a model to best represent the risk for lymphedema. Epi-Info 6.0 and SPSS 8.0 softwares were used for data analysis.

Six hundred and fifty one women came to the outpatient service for follow-up. Of the total, 189 (29%) were excluded because they failed to meet inclusion criteria and 68 (14.72%) refused to participate. Comparison between data obtained from medical records of the eligible women and of those who refused to participate did not show statistically significant differences, in relation to age, educational background, stage or number of lymph nodes removed. The type of surgery performed showed a borderline statistical level of significance between both groups, with a slight predominance of radical surgery among the ones who agreed to participate (x^2 = 3.72; p value = 0.05). Axillary status differed statistically between both groups, i.e., women participating in the study presented a greater number of impaired lymph nodes, as compared to the ones who refused (x^2 = 5.28; p value = 0.02).

Results

The prevalence of lymphedema ascertained in the study was 20.8%, based on the diagnostic criteria established. Table 1 shows the distribution of continuous variables statistics in the study. Considering women altogether, the mean volume difference between the affected limb and the counterlateral one, estimated by the circumference, was 112.7 ml (median = 68.28; percentile 25 = 20.52; percentile 75 = 172.46).

Most women were Caucasians (60%) with incomplete elementary school (63%). In regard to their marital status, 43.4% shared a home with a companion, having household chores as their main occupation (80%). Menopause was already present at the time of breast cancer diagnosis in more than half the women (59%), and on the date of the interview, there was an additional of approximately 25% due to the breast cancer treatment.

Surgeries performed were mostly radical ones (73%). According to patient records, axillary lymphadenectomy (three axillary levels) was the most frequently found (60%). Postoperative radiotherapy treatment was performed in 56.0 % of women, 19.7% of them also had the axillary irradiated. Chemotherapy was performed in 61.2% and hormone therapy with Tamoxifen was given to 44% of women. Injury to the intercostobrachial nerve, seroma and pain were reported in more than half the women examined. Winged scapula was found in 6.3% and reduced shoulder range of movement in 15% (table 2).

Table 1 – Mean, median, standard deviation and amplitude of variance of continuous variables

Variable	Mean	SD	Median	Variance amplitude
Age at diagnosis (years)	55.3	11.1	54	28 - 94
Follow-up (months)	59.5	48.9	46	7 - 287
Closed suction drainage (days)	9.3	4.9	8	0 - 30
Number of lymph nodes removed	17.2	6.9	16	2 - 48
Number of metastatic lymph nodes	1.9	4.2	0	0 - 38
Body Mass Index (BMI)	27.4	4.5	27.3	16 - 44
Sum difference in limb volume (ml)	112.6	68.3	68.3	- 362 / 1873

Table 2 – Prevalence of patient characteristics

Variable	N	%
Surgery performed		
Halsted Mastectomy	18	06.2
Modified radical Patey mastectomy	203	70.0
Modified radical Madden mastectomy	69	23.8
Conservative	101	25.6
Axillary Lymphadenectomy		
Partial (up to level II)	237	60.2
Total (up to level III)	81	20.6
Adjuvant Treatment		
Chemotherapy	241	61.2
Radiotherapy	221	56.1
Radiotherapy (with lymph drainage chains)	39	17.6
Hormone therapy	172	43.7
Stage		
0	5	01.3
I	59	15.0
II	209	53.1
III	108	27.4
Postoperative complications		
Arm infection	36	09.1
Seroma	214	54.3
Necrosis	14	03.6
Sensory symptoms at intercostobrachial nerve	218	55.3
Winged scapula	25	06.3
Reduced shoulder range of movement (ROM)	60	15.0

Variables with a statistically significant association with lymphedema in the bivariate analysis are shown in Table 3. The other variables showed no statistical significance in this study.

Table 3 – Non-adjusted prevalence ratios and respective 95% confidence intervals

Independent variable	**Lymphedema**			
	Yes	**No**	**RP***	**CI****
Axillary radiotherapy				
Yes	20	19	**2.81**	**1.79 – 4.41**
No	29	130		
BMI				
Overweight	70	204	**2.53**	**1.43 – 4.50**
Adequate / Thinness	12	107		
Arm infection				
Yes	16	20	**2.41**	**1.58 – 3.69**
No	66	292		
Stage				
> II B	51	129	**2.01**	**1.33 – 3.05**
up to II A	28	171		
Metastatic lymph nodes				
Yes	48	121	**1.84**	**1.24 – 2.72**
No	34	186		
Radiotherapy				
Yes	57	164	**1.76**	**1.15 – 2.70**
No	25	146		
Shoulder range of movement				
Limited	19	40	**1.76**	**1.14 – 2.71**
Normal	61	272		
Total of days with tube				
8 days and +	58	179	**1.60**	**1.04 – 2.46**
up to 7 days	24	133		
Early edema (report)				
Yes	32	84	**1.51**	**1.03 – 2.23**
No	50	224		
Early edema (symptoms)				
Yes	43	125	**1.48**	**1.01 – 2.18**
No	39	187		

* Prevalence ratio

** 95% confidence interval

Logistic regression was performed in order to find the model that best explained the risk for a woman to present with lymphedema after breast cancer treatment. The model which showed the best adjustment (explaining 80% of variance) was the one that included the following variables: radiotherapy in drainage chains, overweight or obesity, history of arm infection, and reduced shoulder range of movement (ROM) homolateral to surgery (table 4).

Discussion

The prevalence of lymphedema in this study was similar to results reported by other authors, considering the differences in methods used for the diagnosis of lymphedema, follow-up interval, type of treatment performed and chosen cut-off point for edema distributions [4-7].

The women selected to take part in this study, but who refused to participate, presented a significantly higher frequency of conservative

Table 4 – Adjusted odds ratio and corresponding 95% confidence intervals for axillary radiotherapy, BMI, Arm infection and ROM.

Independent variable	OR	CI
Axillary radiotherapy Yes No	**4.44**	**1.97 – 9.96**
BMI Overweight Adequate / Thinness	**3.11**	**1.22 – 7.93**
Arm infection Yes No	**5.01**	**1.80 – 13.95**
Shoulder range of movement Limited Normal	**2.64**	**1.13 – 6.14**

Estimated by unconditional logistic regression adjusted by selected variables.

surgeries as well as lesser lymph node impairment than participants, which could have caused overestimation of the prevalence observed. However, we do not find the fact significant, since there was no difference in regard to the number of lymph nodes removed or the axillary lymphadenectomy level.

Age was not associated with lymphedema, and this result was similar to that observed by some other authors [5,7-12]. Other studies found an increased risk for the elderly [13,14] and a further one for a younger age [4].

Obesity was the only variable related to the patients' characteristics that showed association with lymphedema. This is in agreement with results of other studies[5,6,10,12,13,15,16]. According to Kocak and Overgaard [3], the risk factors involved in the physiopathology of upper limb lymphedema associated with obesity remain unknown. However, obesity represents a risk factor for infection and delayed wound healing, and it may indirectly play a role in the development of lymphedema.

Time of follow-up was not associated with the development of lymphedema in the bivariate analysis, regardless of the cut-off point (2, 3, 4 or 5 years). Such results are in agreement with the ones reported by Kissin et al [17]. After lymphatic obstruction, compensating mechanisms are put into action in order to avoid the onset of lymphedema[18]. Such mechanisms aim to reestablish lymphatic circulation and maintain the affected upper limb without edema. However, this balance can be altered by other factors such as: "depletion" of the compensating mechanism; fibrosclerosis of the lymphatic vessels as of the fourth decade of life; local trauma; surgical lesion of collectors; inflammation; excessive muscle stress; exposure to high temperatures; and atmospheric pressure changes. Thus, it should be expected that the longer the time elapsed since lymphatic obstruction, the greater would be the risk for a lymphatic system unbalance, leading to the onset of lymphedema. Some studies have shown a significant trend towards an increased incidence of lymphedema along time, corroborating the theory described above [13,18,19].

Women undergoing radical treatment presented an increased risk for lymphedema, although without statistical significance. Other studies did not report a significant association of this variable with lymphedema either [8,13-16]. A possible explanation for the increased risk found in the current study, could be that the later the diagnosis the more radical the performed surgeries usually are.

Axillary radiotherapy played a major role in the development of lymphedema. Similar results were found by others authors [6,7,11,14,20-22]. We recommended that women with an indication for axillary radiotherapy be included in rehabilitation programs, aiming at the prevention of lymphedema.

Women with metastatic axillary lymph nodes were at a significantly higher risk for the development of lymphedema, but this observation was not sustained subsequently in the logistic regression performed. Similar results were found in other studies [4,5,14,20].

Women diagnosed at late tumor stages (> II B) presented a statistically greater risk for the development of lymphedema, as compared to those diagnosed at early stages, but when confounding and interaction were controlled, that variable lost its statistical significance. Heard-Smith et al [14], Ozaslan and Kuru [6] and Hinrichs et al [7] found no association between this variable and lymphedema.

Early edema was not associated with lymphedema in our results. Arm edema occurring shortly after surgery is usually transient, and tends to disappear after the development of compensating mechanisms [3,23].

Upper limb infection was associated with lymphedema in our study, a result also found by Petrek et al [13]. This variable should be investigated in depth, in order to establish the relationship between lymphedema and infection. The results of such studies could influence the current view concerning preventive guidance and adaptive management for women undergoing treatment for breast cancer [23,24].

Hematoma was a major risk factor for lymphedema in this study, but due to the limited sample size the observation was not statistically significant. This variable was not analysed in other studies.

Reduced shoulder range of movement was associated with lymphedema. Nevertheless, we cannot consider it to be a risk factor, given it was not possible to establish a true trend, and it may be acting either as a cause or as a consequence. Women with joint restriction should be encouraged to join a rehabilitation program, aiming to fully recover joint amplitude of the affected limb.

As information is achieved simultaneously in cross-sectional studies, it is often impossible to establish whether the condition preceded or resulted from the disease. A further limitation of this design derives from the fact that prevalent cases were analyzed and so the data may reflect disease survival determinants. As a result, cross-sectional studies may suggest possible risk factors, rather than establish the etiology of the disease [25]. Prospective studies are required if the major risk factors in the etiology of lymphedema are to be established.

Conclusion

The observed prevalence of lymphedema was 20.8%, which is in agreement with the results achieved in other reports. Sensory symptoms as intercostobrachial nerve, seroma and pain were present in more than half of the women examined. The variables which best explained the development of lymphedema were axillary radiotherapy, obesity, reduced shoulder range of movement and history of arm infection.

References

1. Velanovich V, Szymanski W. Quality of life of breast cancer patients with lymphedema. American Jounal of Surgery 1999; 177: 184-8.
2. Bergmann A, Mattos IE, Koifman RJ. Diagnóstico do linfedema: análise dos métodos empregados na avaliação do membro superior após linfadenectomia axilar para tratamento do câncer de mama. Rev Bras Cancerol 2004; 50(4): 311-20.
3. Kocak Z, Overgaard J. Risk factors of arm lymphedema in breast cancer patients. Acta Oncol 2000; 39: 389-92.
4. Warmuth M, Bowen G, Prosnitz L et al. Complications of axillary lymph node dissection for carcinoma of the breast: a report based on a patient survey. Cancer 1998; 83: 1362-8.
5. Edwards TL. Prevalence and aetiology of lymphoedema after breast cancer treatment in southern Tasmania. Aust N Z J Surg 2000; 70(6):412-8.
6. Ozaslan C, Kuru B. Lymphedema after treatment of breast cancer. Am J Surg 2004; 187(1):69-72.
7. Hinrichs CS, Watroba NL, Rezaishiraz H, Giese W, Hurd T, Fassl KA, Edge SB. Lymphedema secondary to postmastectomy radiation: incidence and risk factors. Ann Surg Oncol 2004; 11(6) : 573-80.
8. Kuehn T, Klauss W, Darsow M et al. Long-term morbidity following axillary dissection in breast cancer patients – clinical assessment, significance foi life quality and the impact of demographic, oncologic and therapeutic factors. Breast Cancer Res Treat 2000; 64: 275-86.
9. Yap KPL, McCready DR, Narod S et al. Factors influencing arm and axillary symptons after treatment for node negative breast carcinoma. Cancer 2003; 97: 1369-75.
10. Meric F, Buchholz TA, Mirza NQ et al. Long-term complications associated with breast-conservation surgery and radiotherapy. Ann Surg Oncol 2002; 9(6): 543-9.
11. Deo SV, Ray S, Rath GK et al. Prevalence and risk factors for development of lymphedema following breast cancer treatment. Indian J Cancer 2004; 41(1):8-12.
12. Clark B, Sitzia J, Harlow W. Incidence and risk of arm oedema following treatment for breast cancer: a three-year follow-up study. QJ Med 2005; 98: 343-8.
13. Petrek JA, Senie RT, Peters M, et al. Lymphedema in a cohort of breast carcinoma survivors 20 years after diagnosis. Cancer 2001; 92(6): 1368-77.
14. Heard-Smith A, Russo A, Muraca MG, et al. Prognostic factors for lymphedema after primary treatment of breast carcinoma. Cancer 2001; 92(7): 783-7.
15. Freitas Junior R, Ribeiro LFJ, Tala L, et al. Linfedema em pacientes submetidas a mastectomia radical modificada. RBGO 2001; 23(4): 205-8.
16. Veen PVD, Voogdt ND, Lievens P, et al. Lymphedema development following breast cancer surgery

with full axillary resection. Lymphology 2004; 37: 206-8.
17. Kissin M, Querci G, Easton D, et al. Risk of lymphedema following the treatment of breast cancer. Br J Surg. 1986; 73: 580-4.
18. Kiel K, Rademacker A. Early stage breast cancer: arm edema after wide excision and breast irradiation. Radiology, 1996; 279 – 83.
19. Casley-Smith, JR. Measuring and representing peripheral oedema and its alterations. Lymphology 1994; 27: 56-70.
20. Johansen J, Overgaard J, Blichert-Toft M, et al. Treatment morbidity associated with the management of the axilla in breast-conserving therapy. Acta oncol 2000; 30(3): 349-54.
21. Powell SN, Taghian AG, Kachnic LA, et al. Risk of lymphedema after regional nodal irradiation with breast conservation therapy. Int J Radiation Oncology Biol Phys 2003; 55(5): 1209-15.
22. Kwan W, Jackson J, Weir LM, et al. A Chronic arm morbidity after curative breast cancer treatment: prevalence and impact on quality of life. J Clin Oncol 2002; 20(20): 4242-8.
23. Rockson S, Miller LT, Senie R et al. Workgroup III – Diagnosis and management of lymphedema. Cancer 1998; 83 Suppl: 2882-5.
24. Casley-Smith JR. Lymphedema initiated by aircraft flights. Aviation, Space and Environmental Medicine 1996; 67 (1): 52-6.
25. Szklo M, Nieto J. Quality assurance and control. In: Epidemiology - Beyond the basics. Editora An Aspen Publication, 2000.

LYMPHOLOGY IN EMERGENCY ROOM

Maccio', A. F. Boccardo, C. Eretta, L. Marinelli, C. Campisi

Dept. of Surgery, Lymphology and Microsurgery Center, University Hospital S. Martino, Genoa, Italy

Lymphology is often underestimated among medical fields of interest; underlying physio-pathologic mechanisms are frequently unknown by general practitioners and medical operators from various specialities. This is particularly true when considering emergency rooms in Italian hospitals.

Since a lymphologist is not available even in the most advanced hospitals, the same pathological process such as and erysipeloid acute lymphangitis could be seen by a physician specialized in internal medicine, general surgery, vascular surgery or infectious diseases. The patient with lymphatic pathology usually follows a non-standardized, and often inappropriate, diagnostic and therapeutic process.

In emergency rooms, inflammatory-infectious pathology of lymphatic-lymph nodal structures, such as lymphangitis and lymphadenitis is the lymphatic pathology which is more frequently diagnosed.

Many other clinical manifestations involving the lymphatic system are almost never taken into consideration because of the low incidence. Among them we report lymphocele, chylous ascitis and peritonitis, chylopericardium, chylothorax and, considering traumatic injuries, thoracic duct lesions.

Lymphangitis is usually defined as a inflammatory process involving derma and hypoderma, with acute or chronic course, involving mostly lymphatic-lymph nodal structures and often recognizing bacterial aetiology. Since involved in immune processes, these lymphatic structures are involved in many infectious disorders; anyway, we are going to consider the pathological processes which involve the lymphatic system primarily and which pose a serious prognostic treat quoad valetudinem and quoad vitam.

Lymphatic infections are frequently caused by group A beta-haemolytic streptococcus or other saprophytic bacteria, but sometimes bacteria which are less sensitive and more harmful, such as staphylococcus aureus or pyogenes, may have a prominent role in the pathogenesis (ref).

From a clinical point of view, lymphangitis appears as an intense inflammatory process where all five typical semeiological signs can be found (rubor, calor, dolor, tumor, laesa functio); it can show erysipeloid features with sharp margins and the typical "step sign". Abscesses or involvement of muscular fascia (necrotising fasciitis) is less frequent.

From a nosological point of view we can distinguish:

1 "perilesional" lymphangitis, of limited extension and where a "way in" can be seen (e.g. trophic lesions)
2 so-called "truncular" lymphangitis, where the path lymphatic collectors involved in the pathological process can be seen
2 "reticular" or "spread" lymphangitis, where there is a wide involvement of tissues (often the whole limb)

All these pathological pictures can be associated to a satellite lymphadenitic involvement.

The clinical picture is variable: body temperature is almost always raised (up to 41°C and more), the process evolves quickly, shaking shivers and altered state of consciousness appears. Sometimes septic shock may appear.

In Emergency rooms, lymphangitis incidence is underestimated and, in our knowledge, no reliable data are available in international scientific literature. This study involves more than 1500 patients admitted to emergency rooms and evaluated by lymphologists.

After admission in emergency rooms, patient's anamnesis is collected, with particular attention to risk factors ad precipitating events, and a complete clinical evaluation is done. If necessary, the Doppler velocimetry and echography of lymph nodes which could be interested by secondary lesions or abscesses is performed. Blood biochemical and serological tests are also performed, in order to estimate the degree of systemic involvement (5-6).

During acute phase, full dosage antibiotic therapy is mandatory. Amoxicilline associated with Clavulanic acid and macrolids are the first choice drugs, followed by cephalosporines as a second choice. Use of slow release penicillin should be used only for prophylaxis (8-18). Non steroidal antiinflammatory drugs or, better, escine based drugs, along with adequate gastroprotection, can be useful in order to control the symptoms.

Avoiding the use of a rigid elasto-compression (multistrate bondages or "unna boot") with topic antibiotic and zinc-oxide application is considered malpractice (9-10).

The limb must be held unloaded during rest and a moderate motor activity can be suggested, in order to improve lymphatic drainage by the muscle pump. In patients with any comorbidity, a period of observation in hospital could be suggested. Those who present initial signs suggesting septicaemia should be admitted to emergency department where resuscitation facilities are present (picture 4). Even those patients who initially present milder symptoms should be carefully monitored when peculiar socio-economic factors could impair the follow-up at home (aged, immunocompromised and drug-addicted patients).

Septic shock is the most worrisome complication of lymphangitic and lymphadenitic processes; this condition can be mortal in 20% of cases (4). Lymphangitis, even if limited in extension, can damage lymphatic collectors, which usually are in high number in most individuals. In patients affected by a pre-existent insufficient lymphatic network, even sub clinical, collectors involvement can promote lymphedema, causing increasing lymphangitic relapses (11).

After acute treatment, patients should be followed by a lymphologist to monitor the recovery. In about 77% of patients who undergo a lymphangitic relapse, an underlying chronic lymphatic insufficiency can be demonstrated (12).

It must be underlined that more than a quarter of normal subjects has a congenitally deficient lymphatic system: adequate diagnostic procedures can reduce chronic lymphatic conditions and the social costs related to pathological conditions that can derive (13-14).

Emergent lymphatic pathology includes many less frequent and under diagnosed conditions such as lymphocele, chylothorax, chylopericardium and chyloperitoneum (or chylous ascitis) (15-16). Chyloperitoneum can evolve in chyloperitonitis, which accounts for 1 of 20000 patients in University Center (17). This condition shows up with a pseudo-peritonitic picture resembling acute appendicitis because of pressure exerted by the liquid in right parietocclic space; if properly diagnosed can simplify the surgical approach through the drainage of chyle (19). Traumatic injury of thoracic duct is extremely rare and mostly following weapon lesions or vertebral fractures; the treatment needs specific expertise (20-21).

Data collected by our personal experience in emergency rooms come from 2437 patients admitted from April 2004 to July 2005 have shown that 34 of them (1,39%) were affected by lymphatic disorders and, among these patients, 80% presented inflammatory or infectious conditions (such as acute erysipeloid lymphangitis), while the remaining 20% presented chronic conditions such as lymphedema and primary limphoadenopathies. If extended to the over 40 million admissions in national emergency rooms every year, the prevalence we report can lead to estimate a huge amount of lymphatic pathology which is unlikely to be recognised.

Bibliography

1. Dove va la Linfologia Italiana. S. Michelini, Linfologia Italiana 1/2004, Edit. pg 3
2. Prehospital Care. Black Well T.: Emerg. Med. Clin, Northam, 1993, 11:1-11..
3. Il triage. M. Costa, Mc Graw Hill, 1997.

4. The Epidemiology of Sepsis in the United States from 1979 through 2000. Greg S. Martin, New England Journal of Medicine, Vol. 348: 1546-1554
5. Erysipelas: recognition and management. Bonnetblanc JM, Bedane C, Am J Clin Dermatol. 2003;4(3):157-63.
6. Dizonario di Linfologia. Maccio'A., Campisi C, Ed. Minerva Medica 2003
7. Severe streptococcus pyogenes cutaneous infections. Olivier C., Arch. Pediatr. 2001 Sep;8 Suppl 4:757s-761s
8. La linfologia nella pratica quotidiana del MMG. Visitin A., Workshop: la Linfologia nella cultura medica attuale" – 7° Congresso Nazionale IFC 2003, Udine
9. The treatment of lymphedema. Foeldi E., Cancer. 1998 Dec 15;83(12 Suppl American):2833-4. Review.
10. Prevention of dermatolymphangioadenitis by combined physiotherapy of the swollen arm after treatment for breast cancer. Foeldi M. Lymphology. 1996 Jun;29(2):48-9.
11. Chronic inflammatory reaction in lymphedema. Hussain S.A., Phlebolymphology n° 28, 24-29
12. Lynphoscitigraphic evaluation in patients after erysipelas. de Godoy JM. et Al., Lymphology. 2000 Dec;33(4):177-180
13. Guidelines of the Societa Italiana di Linfangiologia: excerpted sections. Campisi C., Michelini S., BoccardoF., Lymphology. 2004 Dec;37(4):182-4.
14. Lymphedema after treatment of breast cancer. Ozaslan C, Kuru B. Am J Surg. 2004 Jan;187(1):69-72.
15. Chylous ascites: treated with total parenteral nutrition and somatostatin. Huang Q, Jiang ZW, Jiang J, Li N, Li JS., World J Gastroenterol. 2004 Sep 1;10(17):2588-91.
16. Laparoscopic repair of chylous ascites. Geary B, Wade B, Wollmann W, El-Galley R. J Urol. 2004 Mar;171(3):1231-2.
17. Peritonitis. Cadernas A., Harward Medical School Ed., 2002
18. Prophylaxis of recurrent lymphangitis complicanting Lymphedema. Babb RR., JAMA 1966 Mar 7;195(10) 871-3
19. Chyledema. Casaccia M, Campisi C., J Mal Vasc. 1988;13(2):145-53. French.
20. Lesioni Violente e Soccorsi d'Urgenza. Midolla C., Cremonese Ed. 1934 (historical)
21. Management of thoracic duct complex lesions (chylothorax): experience in 16 patients. Cariati E. et Al. , Lymphology. 1996 Jun;29(2):83-6.

PREVENTION OF SECONDARY ARM LYMPHEDEMA FROM A PROSPECTIVE RANDOMISED CONTROLLED STUDY TO THE PROPOSAL OF A PREVENTIVE PROTOCOL

Boccardo FM[1], MD, PhD, Michelini S[6], MD, Eretta C[1], MD, Pertile D[1], MD, Campisi Corrado[1], MS, Ansaldi F[2], MD, Icardi G[2], MD, Bellini C[5], MD, Accogli S[4], PT, Macciò A[1], MD, Taddei G[3], MD, Villa G[3], MD, Campisi Corradino[1], MD

[1]Department of Surgery – Unit of Lymphatic Surgery and Microsurgery
[2]Department of Statistics and Epidemiology
[3]Unit of Nuclear Medicine
[4]Rehabilitation Unit
S. Martino Hospital – University of Genoa, Italy
[5]Unit of Neonatal Pathology – G.Gaslini Institute, Genoa, Italy
[6]Center of Neuro-Vascular Rehabilitation – S.Giovanni Battista Hospital – Rome

Secondary arm lymphedema is a common and disabling complication of breast cancer treatment. A degree of arm swelling in the early postoperative period may only be a transient reaction to the surgical and radiotherapy treatments and tend to settle spontaneously within a matter of weeks[1-3]. Lymphedema may arise at any time, months or years after breast cancer surgery (till over 20 years after the initial treatment)[4-6]. About 75 per cent of cases, however, occur in the first year after surgery[7-10]. Quoted prevalence rates for secondary arm lymphedema vary from 5 to 60% in different studies[11-12], perhaps as a consequence of differences between the number of cases examined, different levels of awareness of the problem, measurements methods, lack of a universal definition of criteria used for the diagnosis of lymphedema, duration of follow-up, surgical procedures. The major risk factors for later development of arm lymphedema comprise "rough" surgical technique, the extent of axillary dissection, axillary radiotherapy, and complications in wound healing including those caused by bacterial infection[13]. Using atraumatic surgical technique, tissues are minimally injured and resprouting of lymphatics is facilitated[14] allowing for new lymphatic-lymphatic or lympho-venous connections. Such lymphangiogenesis and lymphvasculogenesis improve the lymphatic transport capacity[15].

The potential later development of lymph stasis in the upper extremity is probably unavoidable after axillary nodal dissection including sentinel node(s) removal. It is only a matter of time (sometimes years) before the first episode of dermatolymphangioadenitis (DLA) occurs, and lymphedema becomes clinically manifest[13].

The question remains open, however, which patient will develop overt lymphedema and in whom lymphedema will remain "latent". This prospective randomised controlled study was designed to objectively determine the effects of a specific protocol of prophylactic measurements on the development of secondary lymphedema and to assess the role of early lymphoscintigraphy in evaluating the extent of lymph stasis and in predicting the likelihood of later development of arm lymphedema.

PATIENTS AND METHODS

Patients scheduled to undergo breast-conserving surgery or modified radical mastectomy for breast cancer were randomly allocated to either the PG or CG after informed consent was obtained. The mean age of the women in this study was 54.07 years (SD = 10.54) and 48 % underwent breast-conserving surgery. As concerns radiotherapy, there was little difference between the two groups in the sites that were irradiated with the breast being the most common site, then the chest wall, supraclavicular fossa and internal mammary chain in decreasing frequency.

Fifty-five of the 73 women scheduled for breast cancer surgery during the study period met the inclusion criteria preoperatively. Four patients were excluded postoperatively when the planned axillary dissection was not performed. The remaining 18 women were excluded due to: refusal to perform lymphoscintigraphy preoperatively, and difficulty to accurately follow the protocol guidelines.

Each woman was assessed preoperatively and then postoperatively at 1 (1 mo.) month, three (3 mo.), six (6 mo.), twelve (12 mo.) and twenty-four (24 mo.) months.

The volume (VOL) of each woman's arms were assessed using water displacement and measured to the nearest 5 ml. The difference between the VOL measurements of both arms (operated arm OA – unoperated arm UOA) was determined. Both arms were measured at each review period and compared to preoperative data. The use of the difference between the two arms ensures that changes measured in the operated arm (that may have indicated early lymphedema) are not due to variability in arm volume over time. The criteria used to identify early secondary lymphedema included a difference of over 200 ml from preoperative VOL measurements (OA – UOA VOL)[16-17].

The preventive protocol for the PG women (25) included preoperative upper limb lymphoscintigraphy (LS)[18-19], principles for lymphedema risk minimisation[20] and early management of this condition when it was identified[21].

LS reveals different lymphatic patterns, including no useful lymph drainage with marked tracer dispersion (dermal back flow) throughout the arm (severe lymphatic impairment – LI), partially intact lymphatic collectors but with tracer dispersion in the forearm (mild to moderate LI), intact trunks without dermal back flow (no LI).

In women (18) with negative LS (NEG LS) the preventive protocol included the use of blue dye (Blue Patent V) injected at the volar surface of the arm at the time of breast cancer surgery in order to point out and try to preserve lymphatic vessels coming from the arm stained in blue. Patients (7) with positive LS (POS LS) underwent a microsurgical operation of lymphatic-venous multiple anastomoses[22] at the volar surface of the proximal third of the arm performed at the same time of axillary nodal dissection (Fig.1).

The NEG LS group was followed-up clinically (VOL) and by lymphoscintigraphy (at 6 mo. post-op).

When post-op LS pointed out disruption or blockage of arm lymphatic drainage before the onset of limb swelling, women underwent early use of elastic sleeves, supplemented by manual lymphatic drain-

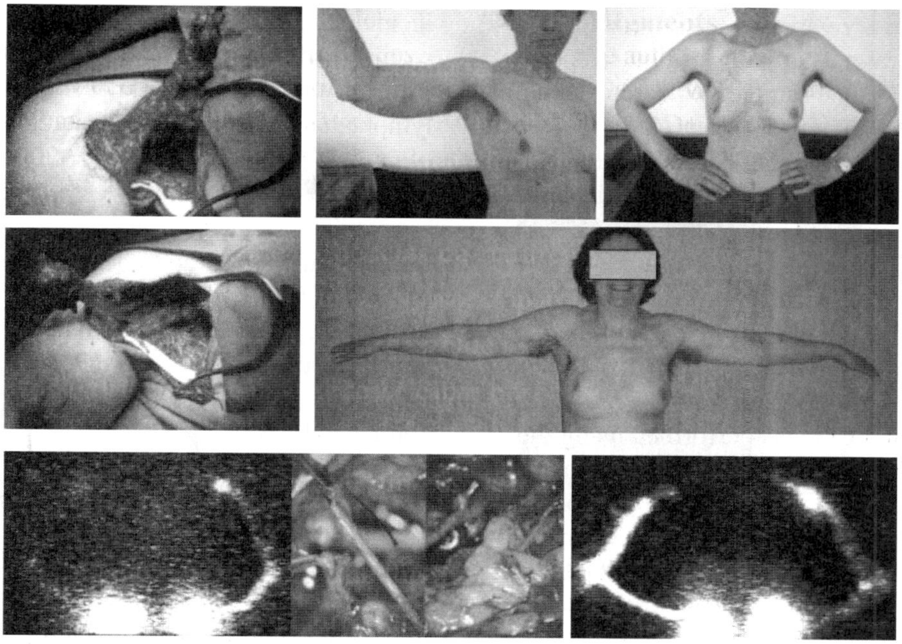

Fig. 1. Patient with positive lymphoscintigraphy undergoing microsurgical operation of lymphatic-venous multiple anastomoses at the volar surface of the proximal third of the arm, at the same time of axillary nodal dissection.

age, prophylactic external compression, and remedial exercises[23].

In case of appearance or worsening of lymphedema notwithstanding the physical methods, the patients underwent early microsurgical operation[24].

Statistical analysis

The comparison between scale variables age, BMI, lymphonodes removed, metastatic lymphnodes (MLN), surgical procedure, axillary dissection level, site of radiotherapy, wound infection, operated arm (OA) volume at baseline in PG and CG was performed using t-test as data were normally distributed (one-sample Kolmogorov-Smirnov p-value NS for every variables). As variable "MLN" was not normally distributed both in PG (one-sample Kolmogorov-Smirnov p-value=0.004) and CG (p-value=0.003), Mann Whitney-test was used. Nominal baseline variables were compared using Chi square or Fischer's Exact Test.

The comparison between percentage increase in comparison with baseline volume after 1, 3, 6, 12 and 24 months from operation in PG and CG was performed using the Mann Whitney test (between groups) and Wilcoxon test (between timing), as data are not symmetrically distributed and normal distribution could not be assumed as demonstrated using one-sample Kolmogorov-Smirnov test (see Results section). The percentage increase was represented by box plots showing the median, interquartile range, outliers and extreme cases of variables. Number of patients with increase >10% at different timing in PG and CG were compared using 2-sided Fischer's Exact Test.

RESULTS

Assessments at 2 years postoperatively were completed for 89% (49) of the 55 women who were randomly assigned to either PG (25) or CG (24).

Of the 49 women with unilateral breast cancer surgery who were measured at 24 mo., 10 (21%) were identified with secondary lymphedema using the VOL (OA-UOA). The PG women had an incidence of 8% (2) and the CG women had an incidence of 33% (8). Clinically significant secondary lymphedema was confirmed in 100% of cases by an increase of over 200 ml in the VOL at 24 mo.

The frequency of lymphedema appeared to be higher in women who had breast-conservation surgery than in those who had a mastectomy.

Data Analysis

The demographic and surgical data and OA baseline volume are reported in Table 1. No significant difference was observed as regards age, BMI, lymphonodes removed, MLN, surgical procedure, axillary dissection level, site of radiotherapy, wound infection, operated arm (OA) volume.

Table 1. The study population.

	New Protocol	Control	p-value
Subjects (n.)	25	24	
Age Mean±Standard Deviation (years)	53.4±7.2	54.6±7.9	NS
BMI Mean±Standard Deviation (Kg/m²)	27.3±5.4	29.9±6.8	NS
Lymphonodes Removed Mean±Standard Deviation (n.)	15.2±3.8	15.1±3.8	NS
MLN Mean±Standard Deviation (n.)	1.5±1.8	1.4±1.7	NS
Surgical Procedure (n.)			
CLE & AD	12	13	
MRM & AD	13	11	NS
Axillary dissection level			
I	4	5	
II	17	13	
III	4	5	NS
Radiotherapy (n.)			
Breast	15	14	
Chest wall	4	3	
Internal mammary chain	3	2	
Supraclavicular fossa	3	3	NS
Wound infection (n.)	3	3	NS
OA Baseline Volume (cc)			
Mean±Standard Deviation	2144±618	2163±623	NS
95% Confidence Interval	1889-2400	1901-2427	
Median	2140	2143	
Min-Max	1235-3100	1235-3100	

MLN=metastatic lymphonodes
OA=operated arm

The baseline volumes in PG and CG were overlapping both in terms of central trend index (mean and median) and absolute dispersion (standard deviation and range). The percentage increase in comparison with baseline volume after 1, 3, 6, 12 and 24 months in PG and CG is reported in Table 2. The data distribution is not normal for PG at 3 months (one-sample Kolmorov-Smirnov test p-value=0.001) and 6

Table 2. Percentage increase in comparison with baseline volume.

	Time after operation (months)				
	1	3	6	12	24
PG women					
Mean±Standard Deviation	3.8±1.7	0.9±1.6	2.4±4	1.1±0.6	1.3±0.7
95% Confidence Interval	3.1-4.5	0.3-1.6	0.7-4	0.9-1.4	1-1.6
Median	3.5	0.5	1.2	1.2	1.1
N. (%)>10	0	0	2 (8)	0	0
Wilcoxon p-value (in comparison with the previous timing)		<0.001	<0.001	0.036	0.022
CG women					
Mean±Standard Deviation	3.7±1.7	2.8±6.3	6.2±8.6	7.8±9.8	8.3±10.1
95% Confidence Interval	3-4.4	0,2-5.5	2.6-9.9	3.7-11.9	4-12.5
Median	3.4	0.5	1.4	1.7	1.9
N. (%)>10	0	2 (8.3)	6 (25)	8 (33.3)	8 (33.3)
Wilcoxon p-value (in comparison with the previous timing)		0.028	<0.001	NS	<0.001

months (p-value=0.001) and for CG at 3 months (p-value<0.001), 6 (p-value=0.003), 12 (p-value=0.008) and 24 (p-value=0.011) months.

PG and CG showed similar percentage increase at1 month (Mann Whitney test p-value=0.873) and 3 month (p-value=0.734). The increase of volume was higher in the Control group in comparison with PG group at 12 month (p-value=0.038) and 24 month (p-value=0.012), while at 6 month the difference was not statistically significant (p-value=0.17). The number of patients with a volume increase>10% is showed in Table 2 and the proportion was higher in the CG at 12 month (Fischer's Exact Test p-value=0.004) and 24 month (p-value=0.004) – Fig.2.

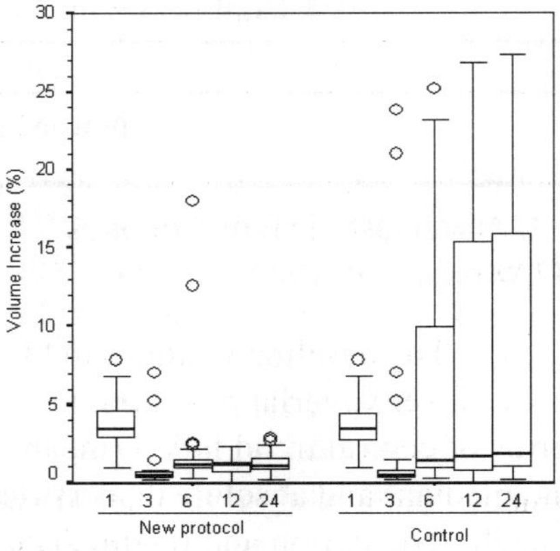

Fig. 2.

DISCUSSION

The incidence of clinically evident secondary lymphedema at 2 years after unilateral breast cancer surgery was 21%. All women were at risk of developing secondary lymphedema due to the surgical excision of the axillary lymph nodes. The clinical changes in the operated arm were confirmed by an increase of at least 200 ml from the pre-operative volumetric measurements. At 2 years, 33% of the CG women had been identified with secondary lymphedema compared to only 8 % of the TG women.

Most of the CG women detected with an increase of 200 ml from their pre-operative volumetry had persistent changes in arm volume from 6 to 12 months postoperatively. For two of the TG women, secondary lymphedema was first detected at 24 months but there tended to be a steady progression in the difference between the OA and UOA. In comparison, the pattern of change in volume measurements was inconsistent for the surviving women in the TG or CG, and in the majority of cases, did not exceed the clinical criteria. There are a few CG women who have increases in their volume but at the time of their 2 years review did not have clinically significant lymphedema.

Using the volumetric criteria and clinical signs, this study has demonstrated that the incidence of early secondary lymphedema at 24 months is similar to that detected previously in women who were assessed at later stages postoperatively when the only postoperative difference between the arms was considered. In the majority of women, changes consistent with lymphoedema were detected from 6 mo. postoperatively suggesting the early onset of significant secondary lymphedema may be detected with clinical assessment and objective measurement within the first year postoperatively. The early detection may result in more effective management and the resolution of acute lymphedema before it develops into a more chronic condition, identifying as a high priority the early detection of and possible benefits of early intervention for secondary lymphoedema[21].

Secondary arm lymphedema has been identified in 21% of the women who were assessed at 2 years after unilateral breast cancer surgery using a comparison a comparison to the preoperative measurements for each woman. The criteria, an increase of >200 ml from the preoperative volumetric conditions, was determined to be a sensitive measurement to detect early clinically significant secondary lymphedema.

The qualitative results of this study suggest that the strategies incorporated into the preventive protocol for the prevention and early intervention of secondary lymphedema do influence the occurrence and severity of secondary lymphedema in the TG women compared to those in the CG. At 24 months after breast cancer surgery, the CG women have almost three times the incidence of secondary lymphedema compared to the TG and in two-thirds of the CG women it was detected from 6 months postoperatively. The extension of this study to monitor the progress of the surviving women for another 3 years postoperatively will continue to provide further information on these early effects on the incidence and progression of secondary lymphedema after breast cancer surgery due to the use of this diagnostic and therapeutic preventive protocol.

REFERENCES

1. Pain SJ, Purushotham AD. Lymphoedema following surgery for breast cancer. British Journal of Surgery 2000; 87: 1128 1141.
2. Clodius L. More on axillary lymphadenectomy. Lymphology 2003; 36; 1-6.
3. Roses DF, Brooks AD, Harris MN, Shapiro RL, Mitnick J. Complications of level I and II axillary dissection in the treatment of carcinoma of the breast. Annals of Surgery 1999; 230(2): 194-201.
4. Pressman P. Surgical treatment and lymphedema. Cancer 1998; 83: 2782-2787.
5. Kissin MW, Querci della Rivere G, Easton D, Westbury G. Risk of lymphoedema following the treatment of breast cancer. Br J Surg 1986; 73: 580-4.
6. Schunemann H, Willich N. Lymphoedema of the arm after primary treatment of breast cancer. Anticancer Res 1998; 18: 2235-6.
7. Hardy JR. Lymphedema – Prevention rather than Cure. Annals of Oncology 1991; 2: 532-533.
8. Burstein HJ, Winer EP. Primary Care for Survivors of Breast Cancer. N Engl J Med 2000; 343: 1086-1094.
9. Hoe AL, Iven D, Boyle GT, Taylor I. Incidence of arm swelling following axillary clearance for breast cancer. Br J Surg 1992; 79: 261-262.
10. Duff M, Hill AD, McGreal G, Walsh S, McDermott EW, O'Higgins NJ. Prospective evaluation of the morbidity of axillary clearance for breast cancer. Br J Surg 2001 Jan; 88(1): 114-7.
11. Mortimer PS, Bates DO, Brassington HD, Stanton AWB, Strachan DP, Levick JR. The prevalence of arm oedema following treatment for breast cancer. Q J Med 1996; 89: 377-80.
12. Lin PP, Allison DC, Wainstock J. Impact of axillary lymph node dissection on the therapy of breast cancer patients. J Clin Oncol 1993; 11: 1536-1544.
13. Olszewski WL. Axillary dissection for breast cancer. Lymphology. 2002 Mar; 35(1):41-2.
14. Clodius L. Minimizing Secondary Arm Lymphedema from Axillary Dissection. Lymphology. 2001 Sept; 34(3):106-10.
15. Foldi M. On the pathophysiology of arm lymphedema after treatment for breast cancer. Lymphology. 1995 Sep; 28(3):151-8.
16. Box RC, Reul-hirche HM, Bullock-Saxton JE. The intra- and inter-tester reliability of three measurement methods for the early detection of lymphoedema after axillary dissection. Eur J Lymph 1999; 27: 74-79.

17. Starritt EC, Joseph D, McKinnon JG, Lo SK, de Wilt JHW, Thompson JF. Lymphedema after complete axillary node dissection for melanoma: assessment using a new objective definition. Annals of Surgery 2004; 240(5): 866-874.
18. Mariani G, Campisi C, Taddei G, Boccardo F. The current role of lymphoscintigraphy in the diagnostic evaluation of patients with peripheral lymphedema. Lymphology 1998; 31 (Suppl): 316-9.
19. Bourgeois P, Leduc O, Leduc A. Imaging techniques in the management and prevention of posttherapeutic upper limb edemas. *Cancer* 1998 Dec 15; 83 (12 Suppl American): 2805-13.
20. Clodius L. Minimizing secondary arm lymphedema from axillary dissection. Lymphology 2001; 34(3): 106-110.
21. Consensus document of the International Society of Lymphology. The diagnosis and treatment of peripheral lymphedema. Lymphology. 2003 Jun;36(2):84-91.
22. Campisi C, Boccardo F. Microsurgical techniques for lymphedema treatment: derivative lymphatic-venous microsurgery. World J Surg. 2004 Jun;28(6):609-13.
23. Földi M. The therapy of lymphedema. Eur J Lymph 1994; 14: 43-49.
24. Campisi C, Boccardo F. Lymphedema and microsurgery. Microsurgery. 2002;22(2):74-80.

INTERNATIONAL INTERNET PATIENT SURVEY: FOUR-YEAR OUTCOMES

Saskia R.J. Thiadens, RN; Jane M. Armer, RN, PhD; Mugur V. Geana, MD

National Lymphedema Network; Sinclair School of Nursing University of Missouri at Columbia; Health Communication Research Center University of Missouri at Columbia

The National Lymphedema Network (NLN) is an internationally recognized non-profit organization founded in 1988 by Saskia R.J. Thiadens, R.N., to provide education and guidance to lymphedema patients, health care professionals, and the general public by disseminating information on the risk reduction and management of primary and secondary lymphedema. For the current research, online and paper-based surveys administered by the NLN between March 2001 and May 2005 were used to collect data from persons with lymphedema. The research instrument was designed by the NLN Medical Advisory Committee. A self-report convenience sample of 4389 participants responded to the survey

Respondents were from forty different countries, but predominately from the United States (n=4161), followed by Canada (n=79), England (n=29) and Australia (n=25). The vast majority of the respondents were females (88%, n=3880) and of Caucasian origin (78%, n=3428). Secondary lymphedema was reported by 72% of the total number of respondents (n=2959), while 28% (n=1147) reported primary lymphedema.

The mean age of respondents with secondary lymphedema was 56 years, while the mean age for those with primary lymphedema was 42 years. Thirty-five percent (n=401) of the respondents with primary lymphedema reported age of onset between 11 and 20 years of age, with a range of reported onset from less than one year of age to 80 years of age (Fig. 1).

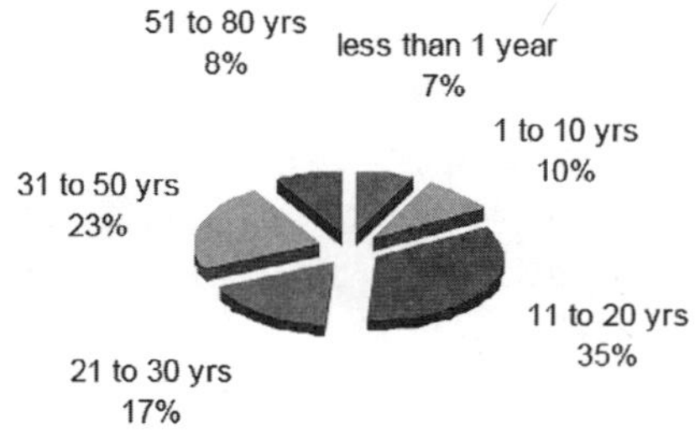

Fig. 1. Reported age of onset of primary lymphedema (n=1063).

Twenty-two percent (n=248) of those with primary lymphedema (n=1147) reported a living family member with lymphedema. Of these 248 respondents,

84% had a single living relative affected with primary lymphedema.

Of the total number of participants, 61% (n=2480) reported they were diagnosed by a physician, while 18% (n=732) reported they self-diagnosed (Fig. 2).

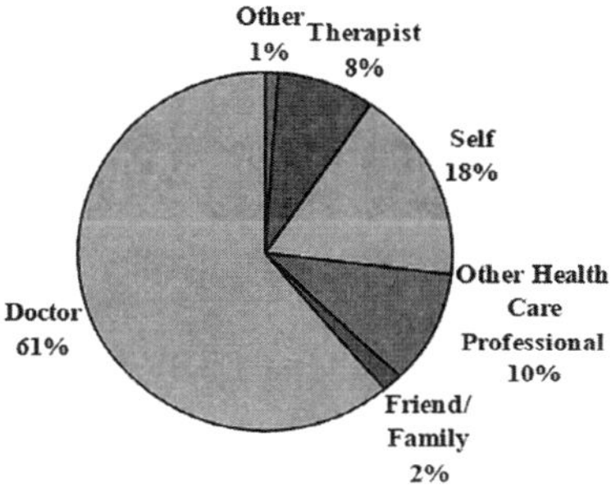

Fig. 2: Patient report of by whom they were diagnosed (n=4065).

Cancer treatment is the most common cause of secondary lymphedema. For the respondents that had been treated for cancer and subsequently developed lymphedema, 78% (n=2094) had breast cancer related surgery (Fig. 3). The high percentage of respondents with breast-cancer related lymphedema is reflective of breast cancer being the leading cause of secondary lymphedema in the general population in developed countries (ACS, 2006).

Surgery (20%) and trauma (19%) were the leading reported causes of non-cancer related lymphedema (Fig. 4).

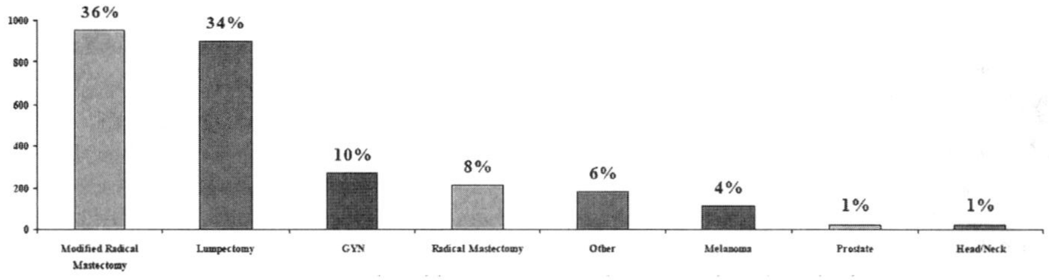

Fig. 3. Cancer-related history reported in secondary lymphedema (n=2684).

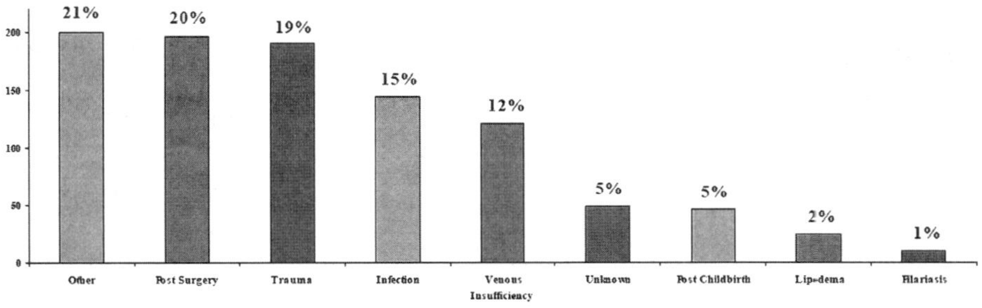

Fig. 4. Reported causes of non-cancer-related secondary lymphedema (n=978).

Twenty-two percent of respondents who underwent cancer surgery (n=603 of 2708) reported they were educated about lymphedema and risk reduction methods at the time of their surgery (Fig. 5).

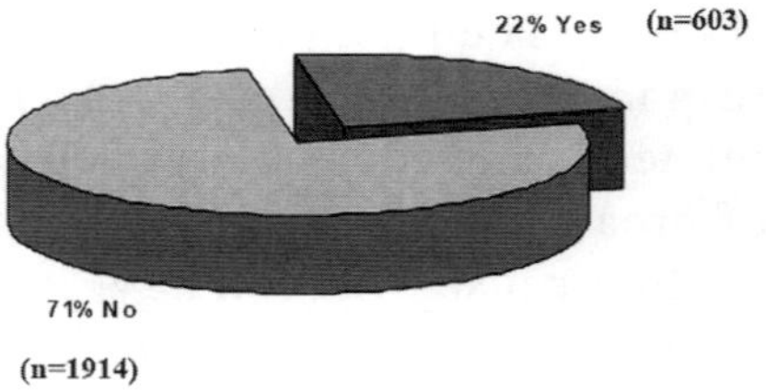

Fig. 5. Respondents reporting they were educated about lymphedema at time of cancer surgery.

Forty-four percent (n=1611) of respondents with lymphedema reported episodes of infection: 40% of those with secondary lymphedema and 54% of those with primary lymphedema. Nineteen percent (n=291) of those with a history of lymphangitis or cellulitis reported they were currently taking prophylactic antibiotics. Thirty percent (n=487) of the respondents that developed infections reported a single episode of infection, while 42% (n=682) reported 2-5 episodes, and 12% (n=200) reported more than 12 episodes of infection (Fig. 6).

Patient education was selected as the top issue by respondents when it came to the most pressing problems related to lymphedema (Fig. 7).

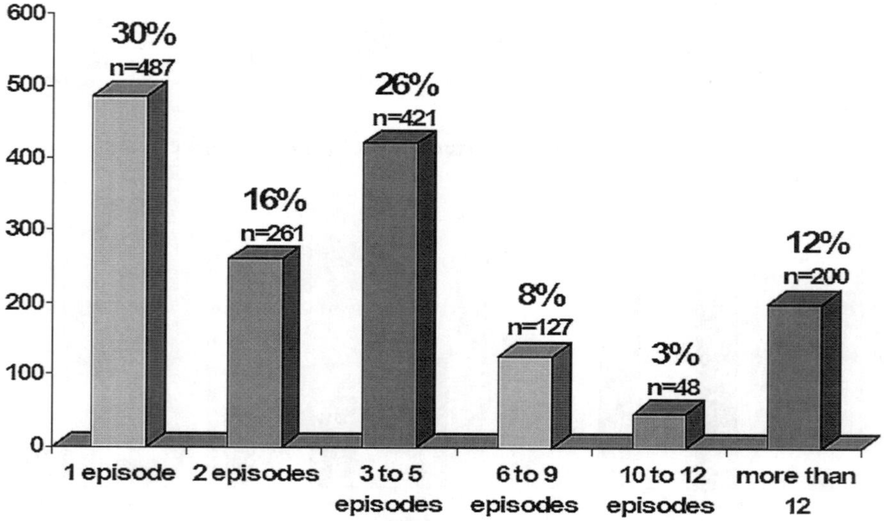

Fig. 6. Reported number of episodes of infection by those reporting previous cases (n=1611).

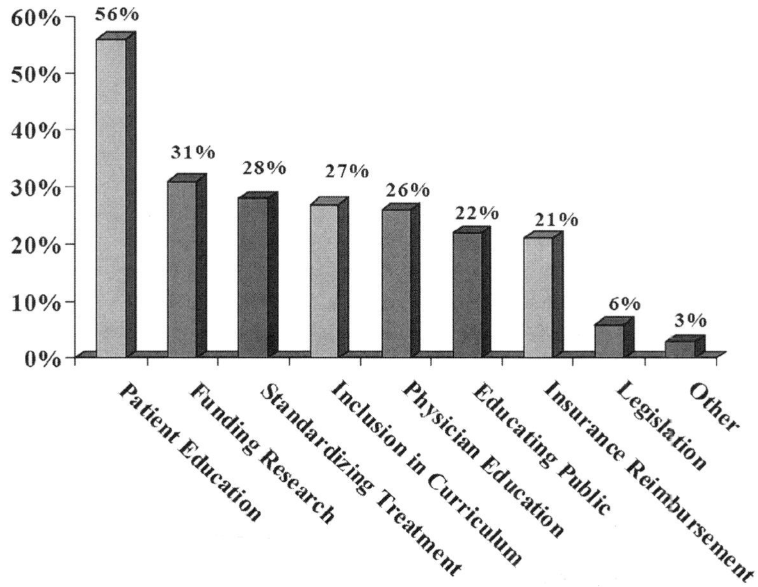

Fig. 7. Issues selected as top issues by respondents with lymphedema when asked, "What do you see as the top three (3) most pressing issues in LE?"

The impressive response to the NLN survey demonstrates the willingness and interest of persons with lymphedema to participate in research. One of the most interesting findings is the self-perception of patients living with lymphedema regarding the need for patient education, a very important issue that is poorly addressed: 71% of participants reported they were not educated in risk reduction guidelines post-cancer surgery, while only 22% reported they received education.

Further research is needed to explore the intricate relationship between patient education and therapeutic outcomes. Research is also needed to support the development of training materials and assessment instruments for lymphedema patients that are rigorously developed and tested and could prove useful for the early diagnosis and treatment follow-up for lymphedema.

References

1. American Cancer Society [ACS] (2006). Cancer facts and figures: 2006. Atlanta: American Cancer Society. Retrieved February 16, 2006 at http://www cancer.org/docroot/MED/content/MED_1_1_Most-Requested_Graphs_and_Figures_2006.asp
2. National Lymphedema Network (2005). Survey retrieved at www.lymphnet.org.

Chapter 3
Oncolymphology and Immunology

CHANGE OF PARADIGM FOR TREATMENT OF PRIMARY MELANOMA AND BREAST CANCER IN THE SENTINEL LYMPH NODE ERA: NEW DIRECTIONS FOR ONCOLYMPHOLOGY

Stanley P. L. Leong, MD, FACS - Professor of Surgery

University of California, San Francisco; Member, UCSF Comprehensive Cancer Center; Department of Surgery; UCSF Medical Center at Mount Zion

Key Words: Melanoma - Breast Cancer - Metastasis - Sentinel Nodes - Oncolymphology

ABSTRACT

Lymph node status is the most reliable prognostic indicator for patients with melanoma and breast cancer. Because it is the first node draining the primary cancer, the sentinel lymph node (SLN) is most likely to harbor metastatic cancer cells. The Breslow thickness of the primary melanoma and the size of primary breast cancer are highly correlated with SLN metastasis. If the SLN is negative, its negative predictive value for the remaining nodal basin exceeds 95%; thus, survival rates for melanoma and breast cancer increase when the SLN is negative. The rate of SLN identification is more than 95%, and the false-negative rate is about 5%. The therapeutic value of additional lymph node dissection after a positive SLN for melanoma or breast cancer is still controversial. In most cases, melanoma and breast cancer follow an orderly progression of metastasis to the SLN; however, a small subgroup may develop systemic dissemination without SLN involvement. Since treatments for metastatic cancer are still limited, early detection and resection are imperative. Better understanding of the molecular and genetic mechanisms of metastasis will be critical to select high-risk patients for adjuvant therapy. In the SLN era, new directions are coming forth in oncolymphology.

CANCER PROGRESSION AND METASTASIS IN THE PRE-SLN ERA

Various clinical and histological features have been utilized to predict the prognosis of primary melanoma [1] and breast cancer [2]. The Clark model is about 89% accurate in predicting survival in stage I melanoma based on tumor progression [3]. Melanoma typically progresses from in situ growth to a radial growth phase and then expands into a vertical growth phase associated with increased risk of metastasis. Breslow tumor thickness as measured from the stratum granulosum of the epidermis to the deepest point of the tumor is considered the best predictor of clinical outcome and is an integral part of the pathology report [4]. When melanoma is diagnosed early with Breslow thickness less than 1 mm, the cure rate is over 95%. The survival may drop to less than 50% when the thickness is over 4mm [5]. Regional nodal status correlates significantly with survival. The survival rate drops to single digits when metastasis is found beyond the regional lymph nodes, especially in visceral sites [5]. Likewise, breast cancer probably arises from in situ growth as ductal carcinoma in situ (DCIS). As the invasive carcinoma grows in size, the incidence of nodal involvement is increased [6]. The recent mortality rate for breast cancer has decreased [7], while the incidence of breast cancer increased 0.5% per year between 1987 and 1998 [8]. Over the past several decades, the size of breast cancer has significantly decreased [9]. The percentage of women 40 years of age or older who underwent mammography within the past 2 years increased from 29% in 1987 to 67% in 1998, the incidence of smaller tumors (less than 2.0 cm) more than doubled, and the incidence of tumors greater than 3.0 cm decreased by 27%.[10, 11].

In general, this is believed to be due to complete resection of early breast cancer detected by screening mammography. Indeed, when early breast cancer is treated appropriately, excellent survivorship may be achieved [12, 13]. In a retrospective analysis of a large population of breast cancer patients, Nemoto et al. [14]. showed that nodal status was the most important predictor of outcome, as it is in melanoma.

Various models of breast cancer metastasis have been proposed since the days of Halsted [15]. According to Halsted's model, tumor spreads first to the regional nodes. A positive lymph node is an indicator of tumor spread and the instigator of distant metastasis. Therefore, treatment involves aggressive locoregional control such as a radical mastectomy with extensive lymph node dissection [16]. On the other hand, Fisher et al. [17]. suggests that a systemic model is more appropriate because no orderly pattern of metastasis is apparent for breast cancer. Axillary dissection does not alter the incidence of systemic recurrence or patient survival. Thus, systemic treatment is equally important at the time of treatment for local disease. Over the years, it has become obvious that patterns of metastasis do not conform strictly to either model. In the spectrum model developed by Hellman [18, 19], tumor spreads via lymphatic vessels in early-stage disease and via blood vessels in late-stage disease. Based on the Swedish two-county trial of screening mammography, Tabar et al. [20, 21]. concluded that mammographic screening resulted in earlier diagnosis of breast cancer, which corresponded to smaller tumors, fewer tumor-involved lymph nodes, and less-aggressive histology. These features were significantly correlated with survival. They challenged the proposal that breast cancer was a systemic disease from its inception; they asserted that the proposal was either mistaken or not relevant to the treatment of node negative tumors that were less than 15 mm. Thus, cancer may spread based on the incubator hypothesis with the regional nodes as the gateway to metastasis and the marker hypothesis with simultaneous spread through the lymphatic and vascular system. For this reason, the emphasis is locoregional control in the early stage of disease. Effective axillary treatment should still be considered essential for early breast cancer [22]. In both melanoma [5, 23] and breast cancer [14, 24] nodal status is the most important predictor of clinical outcome. These studies of the pre-SLN era provided strong evidence that, in general, tumor progression in a primary site resulted in metastasis first to regional nodes and then to distant sites. Thus, the premise of treatment for melanoma and breast cancer rested on the eradication of the primary tumor and the nodal disease. Oftentimes, a regional lymph node dissection was performed to ensure that all lymph nodes were harvested for staging the cancer. Furthermore, if these lymph nodes harbored microscopic disease, their removal could potentially prevent systemic metastasis.

VALIDATION OF THE SLN CONCEPT FOR MELANOMA AND BREAST CANCER

The term SLN was first coined by Gould et al. [25] in 1960 as the guardian lymph node for the parotid nodal basin. Further studied by Cabanas [26] with use of the penile carcinoma model for SLN based on radiological identification. Using the blue dye technique, both the feline model [27] and clinical trial on selective sentinel lymphadenectomy (SSL) for melanoma [28] established the concept of an orderly and nonrandom progression of melanoma to the SLNs [23]. The 1992 report by Morton [28] was followed by an impressive succession of SSL studies [29] in melanoma and subsequently in breast cancer [30]. These publications have shown that, in general, both melanoma and breast cancer progress in an orderly fashion from the primary site to the SLN and beyond. The SLN concept has been further applied to other solid cancers [31]. The validation of the SLN concept is a turning point in the management of human solid cancers, particularly melanoma and breast cancer. SSL selects one or a few SLNs for an extensive histopathologic examination that would not be practical for the many nodes yielded by a standard lymph node dissection. If the SLN is negative, the negative predictive value of the remaining nodal basin for melanoma and breast cancer exceeds 95% [23, 30, 32-34]. Thus, most patients (about 80% with melanoma and 60% to 70% with breast cancer) can be spared the more extensive and morbid procedure of standard lymph node dissection. Thus, SSL is being applied widely as a screening procedure. The need for additional lymph node dissection after a positive SLN for melanoma or breast cancer is still controversial.

CLINICAL SIGNIFICANCE OF SLN MICROMETASTASIS

Outcome studies of melanoma patients undergoing SSL have shown that micrometastasis in SLNs is associated with a poorer prognosis. Multiple studies have shown that patients with positive SLNs have a poorer prognosis than patients with negative SLNs [29] Starz et al. [35, 36] have further defined and classified micrometastasis in melanoma SLNs. In a recent report by Morton et al. [37] of 1599 melanoma patients undergoing SSL, the overall survival rates at 5, 10, and 15 years were 70%, 65%, and 65% respectively. In comparing 322 patients with immunohistochemistry (IHC)-positive SLNs and 1277 patients with IHC-negative SLNs, the overall survival rates at 5, 10, and 15 years were 89%, 83%, and 81%, respectively ($P \leq 0.0001$). For breast cancer, micrometastasis was defined as a focus of tumor less than or equal to 2 mm in the draining lymph node in the pre-SLN era [38]. In general, micrometastasis to regional nodes had a poorer prognosis [39-42]. Some studies have shown a worse outcome for patients with an IHC-positive micrometastasis [2, 43-46] . However, these studies were performed on routine axillary lymph node dissections rather than SLNs. Since the clinical outcome associated with IHC-positive SLNs is not known, Ibarra [47] cautioned against the use of IHC as a guide for treatment decisions. A recent study showed that micrometastasis in breast cancer SLNs projected a poorer clinical outcome [48]. Using immunocytochemical staining with monoclonal anticytokeratin (CK) antibodies, Braun et al. [49] analyzed micrometastasis in bone marrow aspirates from 150 node-negative patients with stage I or II breast cancer. CK-positive cells were found in the bone marrow aspirates of 44 patients (29%) and in the lymph nodes of only 13 (9%). Only two patients had simultaneous microdissemination to bone marrow and lymph nodes. Decreased 4-year distant disease free and overall survival were each associated with positive cells in the bone marrow aspirates ($P = .032$ and $P = .014$, respectively) but not with lymph node micrometastasis. It should be noted that SLNs were not harvested and compared with the bone marrow status. Since the incidence of metastasis is reportedly higher in SLNs than non-SLNs obtained by routine axillary dissection (42% versus 29%) [50] further studies should be done to compare the clinical significance of micrometastasis in SLNs versus bone marrow. A prospective study under the American College of Surgeons Oncology Group (ACOSOG) Z0010 protocol (http://www.acosog.org) will address the clinical relevance of micrometastasis to SLN and bone marrow in early breast cancer.

CLINICAL SIGNIFICANCE OF MOLECULAR FINDINGS

Molecular markers based on reverse transcriptase polymerase chain reaction (RT-PCR) assay [51, 52] are now available to further assess SLNs that are negative by hematoxylin and eosin and/or IHC. Among patients whose SLNs are negative by histological and molecular assessments, survival is nearly 100%, indicating that melanoma with no metastasis to the SLN(s) can potentially be cured. Patients whose SLNs are histologically negative but RT-PCR positive have a significantly higher recurrence rate than patients whose SLNs are negative by both assays. In the study by Morton et al., [37] SLNs from 215 patients were studied by multimarker molecular assays. Of 162 patients with IHC negative SLNs, 49 (30%) had SLNs that expressed at least 1 of the 4 RT-PCR markers. These patients had significantly higher risk of disease recurrence and death than did patients with negative IHC and RT-PCR results ($P \leq 0.0001$). This difference suggests that IHC fails to detect 30% of SLN micrometastases. Thus, RT-PCR not only is more sensitive than IHC for detection of micrometastases in SLNs but also may be clinically significant for recurrence. It is possible that early dissemination of microscopic cells via the circulatory system may occur. Prospective clinical follow-up of patients will further define the validity of molecular staging. For breast cancer patients with positive SLNs fare much worse than patients with negative SLNs [53]. The role of IHC and RT-PCR in breast cancer has yet to be defined.

PARADIGM OF METASTASIS IN THE SENTINEL NODE ERA

Breslow thickness of a primary melanoma is linearly correlated with the SLN tumor status [54]. Likewise, there is a linear relationship between size of a primary breast cancer and tumor status of the SLN [55-57]. Because of the accuracy of SSL as a staging method, the 6th edition of the American Joint Committee on Cancer's staging manual incorporates SLN status for both melanoma and breast cancer [6]. Melanoma progression can be further defined in terms of primary melanoma proliferation, metastasis to the SLNs or distant sites, progression from SLNs to non-SLNs, and progression from SLNs or non- SLNs to systemic sites (Fig.

1). Early metastasis occurs mostly in the regional SLNs, and SLN metastasis is a poor prognostic factor with respect to disease-free and overall survival. Likewise, for breast cancer, metastatic cells are generated as a result of proliferation, and early metastasis may occur in the SLN (Fig. 1). Further, clinical follow-up is needed for recurrence and survival outcome. In general, the paradigm of metastasis for melanoma and breast cancer is a sequential progression from the primary tumor to SLNs, non-SLNs, and distant sites. Occasionally, tumor cells spread via systemic circulation to distant sites from the primary site, SLN(s) or non-SLN(s) (Fig.1). At what point in this progression can the cancer be arrested? If only the SLNs are involved, can the removal of these nodes be curative?

FUTURE PERSPECTIVES

Multifaceted aspects of micrometastatsis including proliferation and differentiation of various clones from the primary tumor, the acquisition of adhesion

molecules, the process of angiogenesis and host interaction with the microscopic tumor may shed new lights on the biology and mechanism of early metastasis. Molecular and genetic tools may be

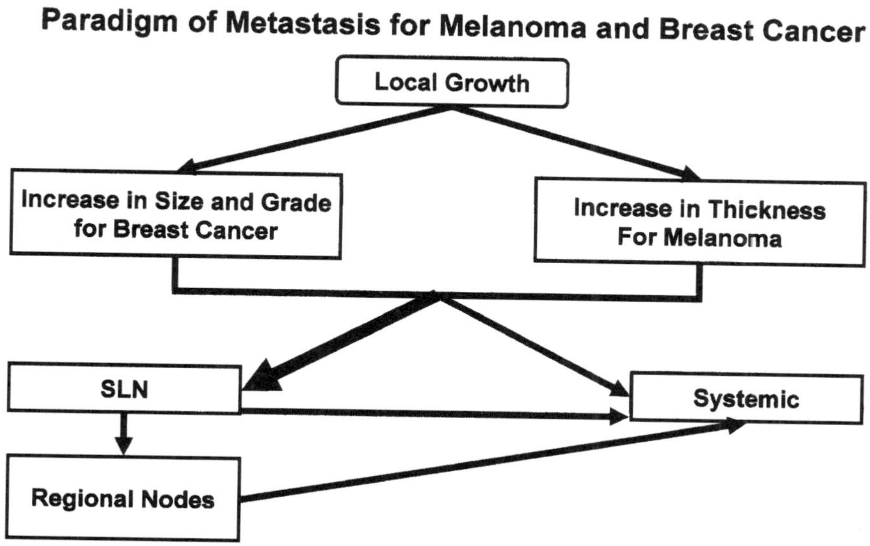

Fig. 1. The paradigm of metastasis for melanoma or breast cancer is similar with local growth at its inception. Subsequent proliferation results in more aggressive clones that may metastasize to SLNs and subsequently to non-SLNs. Metastasis to distant sites may ensue. Occasionally, tumor cells from the primary site, SLNs, or non-SLNs may spread via vascular channels to distant sites. (Source: Leong [58]. Reprinted with permission.)

used to dissect the mechanisms of lymphatic and hematogenous routes of metastasis. Different molecular markers may be associated with different patterns of cancer metastasis so that molecular markers may be used to subgroup cancer spreading through the lymphatic system versus the vascular system. As the SLN appears to be the gateway to systemic metastasis new directions in oncolymphology should be directed to the anatomic physiologic and molecular mechanisms of metastasis through the lymphatic system in addition to the hematogenous route. Understanding such mechanisms may help us to develop therapeutic strategies to prevent the process of micrometastasis.

CONCLUSION

In conclusion, cancer metastatic potential increases with its stage; the process is progressive. Most cases of melanoma and breast cancer follow an orderly progression of metastasis to the SLN. A small subgroup of patients may develop systemic dissemination without SLN involvement. Early diagnosis of melanoma through education and surveillance should be encouraged. Similarly, screening mammography should be continued to detect early breast lesions. Since treatments for metastatic cancer are still limited, it is imperative for oncologists to detect and resect an early cancer as soon as possible.

REFERENCES

1. Zettersten, E., et al., Prognostic factors in primary cutaneous melanoma. Surg Clin North Am, 2003. **83**(1): pp. 61-75.
2. Cote, R.J., et al., Role of immunohistochemical detection of lymph-node metastases in management of breast cancer. International Breast Cancer Study Group. Lancet, 1999. **354**(9182): pp. 896-900.
3. Clark, W.H., Jr., et al., Model predicting survival in stage I melanoma based on tumor progression. J Natl Cancer Inst, 1989. **81**(24): pp. 1893-904.
4. Liu, V. and M.C. Mihm, Pathology of malignant melanoma. Surg Clin North Am, 2003. **83**(1): pp. 31-60, v.
5. Balch, C.M., et al., Final version of the American Joint Committee on Cancer staging system for cutaneous melanoma. J Clin Oncol, 2001. **19**(16): pp. 3635-48.
6. AJCC, Cancer Staging Atlas. 2006, New York: Springer.
7. Niederhuber, J.E., Seeking calmer waters in a sea of controversy. Oncologist, 2002. **7**(3): pp. 172-3.
8. Von Eschenbach, A.C., NCI remains committed to current mammography guidelines. Oncologist, 2002. **7**(3): pp. 170-1.
9. Cady, B., et al., The new era in breast cancer. Invasion, size, and nodal involvement dramatically decreasing as a result of mammographic screening. Arch Surg, 1996. **131**(3): pp. 301-8.
10. Andersen, L.D., et al., Assessing a decade of progress in cancer control. Oncologist, 2002. **7**(3): pp. 200-4.
11. Begg, C.B., The mammography controversy. Oncologist, 2002. **7**(3): pp. 174-6.

12. Wood, W.C., et al., Can we select which patients with small breast cancers should receive adjuvant chemotherapy? Ann Surg, 2002. **235**(6): pp. 859-62.
13. Arnesson, L.G., S. Smeds, and G. Fagerberg, Recurrence-free survival in patients with small breast cancer. An analysis of cancers 10 mm or less detected clinically and by screening. Eur J Surg, 1994. **160**(5): pp. 271-6.
14. Nemoto, T., et al., Management and survival of female breast cancer: results of a national survey by the American College of Surgeons. Cancer, 1980. **45**(12): pp. 2917-24.
15. Chung, M.A. and B. Cady, New lessons from the sentinel node. Surg Oncol Clin N Am, 2001. **10**(2): pp. 461-73, xi-xii.
16. Halsted, W., The results of operations for the cure of cancer of the breast performed at The John Hopkins Hospital from June, 1889 to January, 1894. In: Operations for Cure of Cancer of the Breast. The Johns Hopkins Press, 1894. **Vol. 4.**: pp. 497-553.
17. Fisher, B., et al., Ten-year results of a randomized clinical trial comparing radical mastectomy and total mastectomy with or without radiation. N Engl J Med, 1985. **312**(11): pp. 674-81.
18. Hellman, S. and R.R. Weichselbaum, Oligometastases. J Clin Oncol, 1995. **13**(1): pp. 8-10.
19. Hellman, S., Karnofsky Memorial Lecture. Natural history of small breast cancers. J Clin Oncol, 1994. **12**(10): pp. 2229-34.
20. Tabar, L., et al., Reduction in mortality from breast cancer after mass screening with mammography. Randomised trial from the Breast Cancer Screening Working Group of the Swedish National Board of Health and Welfare. Lancet, 1985. **1**(8433): pp. 829-32.
21. Tabar, L., et al., The Swedish Two-County Trial twenty years later. Updated mortality results and new insights from long-term follow-up. Radiol Clin North Am, 2000. **38**(4): pp. 625-51.
22. Harris, J.R. and R.T. Osteen, Patients with early breast cancer benefit from effective axillary treatment. Breast Cancer Res Treat, 1985. **5**(1): pp. 17-21.
23. Reintgen, D., et al., The orderly progression of melanoma nodal metastases. Ann Surg, 1994. **220**(6): pp. 759-67.
24. Adjuvant therapy for breast cancer. NIH Consens Statement, 2000. **17**(4): pp. 1-35.
25. Gould, E.A., et al., Observations on a "sentinel node" in cancer of the parotid. Cancer, 1960. **13**: pp. 77-8.
26. Cabanas, R.M., An approach for the treatment of penile carcinoma. Cancer, 1977. **39**(2): pp. 456-66.
27. Wong, J.H., L.A. Cagle, and D.L. Morton, Lymphatic drainage of skin to a sentinel lymph node in a feline model. Ann Surg, 1991. **214**(5): pp. 637-41.
28. Morton, D.L., et al., Technical details of intraoperative lymphatic mapping for early stage melanoma. Arch Surg, 1992. **127**(4): pp. 392-9.
29. Leong, S.P., et al., Clinical significance of occult metastatic melanoma in sentinel lymph nodes and other high-risk factors based on long-term follow-up. World J Surg, 2005. **29**(6): pp. 683-91.
30. Cody, H.S., 3rd, Sentinel lymph node mapping in breast cancer. Oncology (Williston Park), 1999. **13**(1): pp. 25-34; discussion 35-6, 39, 43.

31. Leong, S., Y. Kitagawa, and M. Kitajima, Selective sentinel lymphadenectomy for human solid cancer. 2005, New York: Springer.
32. Thompson, J.F., et al., Sentinel lymph node status as an indicator of the presence of metastatic melanoma in regional lymph nodes. Melanoma Res, 1995. **5**(4): pp. 255-60.
33. Morton, D.L., et al., Validation of the accuracy of intraoperative lymphatic mapping and sentinel lymphadenectomy for early-stage melanoma: a multicenter trial. Multicenter Selective Lymphadenectomy Trial Group. Ann Surg, 1999. **230**(4): pp. 453-63; discussion 463-5.
34. Albertini, J.J., et al., Lymphatic mapping and sentinel node biopsy in the patient with breast cancer. Jama, 1996. **276**(22): pp. 1818-22.
35. Starz, H., et al., A micromorphometry-based concept for routine classification of sentinel lymph node metastases and its clinical relevance for patients with melanoma. Cancer, 2001. **91**(11): pp. 2110-21.
36. Starz, H., A. De Donno, and B.R. Balda, The Augsburg experience: histological aspects and patient outcomes. Ann Surg Oncol, 2001. **8**(9 Suppl): pp. 48S-51S.
37. Morton, D.L., et al., Lymphatic mapping and sentinel lymphadenectomy for early-stage melanoma: therapeutic utility and implications of nodal microanatomy and molecular staging for improving the accuracy of detection of nodal micrometastases. Ann Surg, 2003. **238**(4): pp. 538-49; discussion 549-50.
38. Huvos, A.G., R.V. Hutter, and J.W. Berg, Significance of axillary macrometastases and micrometastases in mammary cancer. Ann Surg, 1971. **173**(1): pp. 44-6.
39. Rosen, P.P., et al., Axillary micro- and macrometastases in breast cancer: prognostic significance of tumor size. Ann Surg, 1981. **194**(5): pp. 585-91.
40. Rosen, P.P., et al., Prognosis in stage II (T1N1M0) breast cancer. Ann Surg, 1981. **194**(5): pp. 576-84.
41. Clayton, F. and C.L. Hopkins, Pathologic correlates of prognosis in lymph node-positive breast carcinomas. Cancer, 1993. **71**(5): pp. 1780-90.
42. Fisher, E.R., et al., Pathologic findings from the National Surgical Adjuvant Breast Project (NSABP) Protocol B-17. Intraductal carcinoma (ductal carcinoma in situ). The National Surgical Adjuvant Breast and Bowel Project Collaborating Investigators. Cancer, 1995. **75**(6): pp. 1310-9.
43. Byrne, J., et al., A preliminary report on the usefulness of monoclonal antibodies to CA 15-3 and MCA in the detection of micrometastases in axillary lymph nodes draining primary breast carcinoma. Eur J Cancer, 1992. **28**(2-3): pp. 658-60.
44. Chen, Z.L., et al., Occult metastases in the axillary lymph nodes of patients with breast cancer node negative by clinical and histologic examination and conventional histology. Dis Markers, 1991. **9**(5): pp. 239-48.
45. Sedmak, D.D., et al., Prognostic significance of cytokeratin-positive breast cancer metastases. Mod Pathol, 1989. **2**(5): pp. 516-20.
46. Trojani, M., et al., Micrometastases to axillary lymph nodes from carcinoma of breast: detection by

immunohistochemistry and prognostic significance. Br J Cancer, 1987. **55**(3): pp. 303-6.
47. Ibarra, J.A., The pathologist in breast cancer: contemporary issues in the interdisciplinary approach. Surg Oncol Clin N Am, 2000. **9**(2): pp. 295-317.
48. Colleoni, M., et al., Size of breast cancer metastases in axillary lymph nodes: clinical relevance of minimal lymph node involvement. J Clin Oncol, 2005. **23**(7): pp. 1379-89.
49. Braun, S., et al., Comparative analysis of micrometastasis to the bone marrow and lymph nodes of node-negative breast cancer patients receiving no adjuvant therapy. J Clin Oncol, 2001. **19**(5): pp. 1468-75.
50. Giuliano, A.E., et al., Improved axillary staging of breast cancer with sentinel lymphadenectomy. Ann Surg, 1995. **222**(3): pp. 394-9; discussion 399-401.
51. Wang, X., et al., Detection of submicroscopic lymph node metastases with polymerase chain reaction in patients with malignant melanoma. Ann Surg, 1994. **220**(6): pp. 768-74.
52. Bostick, P.J., et al., Prognostic significance of occult metastases detected by sentinel lymphadenectomy and reverse transcriptase-polymerase chain reaction in early-stage melanoma patients. J Clin Oncol, 1999. **17**(10): pp. 3238-44.
53. Naik, A.M., et al., The risk of axillary relapse after sentinel lymph node biopsy for breast cancer is comparable with that of axillary lymph node dissection: a follow-up study of 4008 procedures. Ann Surg, 2004. **240**(3): p. 462-8; discussion 468-71.
54. Leong, S.P., Selective sentinel lymphadenectomy for malignant melanoma. Surg Clin North Am, 2003. **83**(1): pp. 157-85, vii.
55. Cox, C.E., C.J. Salud, and M.A. Harrinton, The role of selective sentinel lymph node dissection in breast cancer. Surg Clin North Am, 2000. **80**(6): pp. 1759-77.
56. Chen, M., et al., Role of primary breast cancer characteristics in predicting positive sentinel lymph node biopsy results: a multivariate analysis. Arch Surg, 2002. **137**(5): pp. 606-9; discussion 609-10.
57. Giuliano, A.E., et al., Sentinel lymphadenectomy in breast cancer. J Clin Oncol, 1997. **15**(6): pp. 2345-50.
58. Leong, S.P., Paradigm of metastasis for melanoma and breast cancer based on the sentinel lymph node experience. Ann Surg Oncol, 2004. **11**(3 Suppl): pp. 192S-7S.

CANCER AND THE LYMPHATIC SYSTEM

Kimberly Jones, MD,* Marlys H Witte, MD, Charles L Witte, MD

Department of Medicine (Oncology), University of Utah, Salt Lake City, UT* and Department of Surgery, University of Arizona, Tucson, AZ USA

Cancer has been known to involve the lymph nodes since as early as the 1700s and although this was nearly 75 years after Gaspar Asellius first described lymphatic vessels in 1627, it was still very much earlier than the importance of the related immune system's function of defense and surveillance became apparent in the 1940s. In the 19th century, when Virchow's cell theory became popular it was thought that the removal of all areas of tumor involvement had the highest chance for cure, and this concept led to the Halstedian operations or radical lymphadenectomies beginning in the late 1800's. With the use of vital blue dye lymphatic imaging in 1937, lymphography by cannulation in the 1950's, and application of the sentinel node approach initially in the 1960s, progressively less radical procedures were planned and by 1989 the sentinel lymph node was in widespread use. Furthermore, basic research during the last 25 years has led to isolation of lymphatic endothelial cells, replication of lymphangiogenesis in vitro, and more recently, with advances in molecular biology, elucidation of the process of lymphvasculogenesis/ lymphangiogenesis in growth and development, and interactions of the lymphatic system with other systems in health and disease.

Past research largely focused on one or another component of the lymphatic system alone rather than on the integrated system of lymphatic vessels, liquid lymph, lymphocytes, and lymph nodes, the interactions of both vasculatures and circulations (blood and lymph), and connections to the immune network. The concept of an extended circulation of extracellular fluid has emerged where the unidirectional lymphatic vascular system traverses the lymph nodes and returns to the bloodstream the fluid, macromolecules, and migrant cells that have leaked from the blood vessels or been added in the interstitium. The lymphatic system and lymph circulation acts as a mirror of tissue events and is the first barrier against the entry and spread of disease. This system can also be manipulated by microorganisms and abnormal cells to augment their own survival and spread.

When the blood-lymph circulatory loop becomes damaged or obstructed, a constellation of sequelae develops with edema, fibrosis, immunodysregulation, nutritional depletion, and/or disturbed lymphangiogenesis and hemangiogenesis. Specific clinical manifestations of tumor involvement within the lymphatic system ranges from primary vascular tumors, widely metastatic disease, significant morbidity of post-treatment secondary lymphedema, or even generation of new malignancies such as Stewart Treves syndrome – the highly aggressive angiosarcoma that develops in the setting of longstanding lymphedema. Cancer can also disrupt the balance between lymph formation (governed by Starling's Law), and lymph absorption by altering microvascular pressures, through direct involvement of the blood or lymph vasculature, or invasion of the stroma or surrounding tissues. Clinically, this could even represent the first sign of cancer spread or recurrence, i.e., malignant pleural or peritoneal effusion or limb lymphedema.

Key to examining mechanisms involved in the spread of cancer and impact of cancer treatment is a consideration of the interactions between the closely related vascular systems and the immune system that operates within them. The immune systems reaction to tumor cells is partially mediated through cytokine induced processes and theoretically it should recognize tumor cells as abnormal and provide a barrier to dissemination. In the clinical setting, this system is often faulty perhaps due to either tumor cell ability to avoid detection or through tumor cell mediated biochemical processes that disrupt the immune system's structure or function or a combination of both. For example, the TIE 2 receptor (tyrosine kinase receptor with immune and epidermal growth factor domains), the VEGF (vascular endothelial growth factor) family, and angiopoietin peptide family (Ang 1 and Ang 2), are involved not only in vasculogenesis but also in mammalian immunity and are especially influenced by the cytokine interleukin-1.

Involvement of adjacent lymph nodes remains one of the most important predictive prognostic features in cancer staging, and can be evaluated by relatively non-invasive lymphatic imaging techniques such as indirect lymphography, direct lymphography, and lymphangioscintigraphy, and positron-emission computed tomography. This staging is crucial in deciding surgical or combined modality treatment planning, direct endolymphatic infusion of cytotoxic agents, or intralymphatic immunotherapy.

Over the past 15 years, several lymphatic specific markers have been identified and fueled recent growth in research efforts. These include cell surface receptors, extracellular matrix proteins, and transcription factors. Some of the growth factors that regulate or influence lymphangiogenesis, particularly VEGFs ($C_1$1, R, and even A), as well as angiopoietins (1 and 2), appear to have distinct roles in the blood vasculature under different regulatory controls. For example, it has been shown that different gene expression programs are activated in lymphatic endothelial cells than in blood endothelial cells in response to the same receptor kinase signaling, which clinically would allow for different functions in response to the same stimulus. This concept is important as these pathways appear to be relevant in both tumor growth and metastasis as well as lymphangiodysplasia syndromes.

Members of the VEGF family are overexpressed in a wide variety of tumors with some studies showing a positive correlation to lymphatic spread and tumor vasculogenesis. Angiopoietins 1 and 2 play a context dependent agonist and antagonist role in vascular remodeling probably through the recruitment and sustenance of periendothelial cells and thus could be involved in tumor cell invasion. As mentioned before, the receptors for these growth factors are of the tyrosine kinase family, several other members of which have been implicated in cancer specific growth and appear to have overlapping downstream signaling pathways. As an example, a recently developed therapeutic agent, BAY 43-9006, designed to target the RAF/MED/ERK signaling pathway at the level of the RAF kinase, has shown a more pronounced antiangiogenic effect clinically and was found to exhibit cross reactivity and blocking of the signaling pathways of both the VEGFR 2 and PDGFR receptors. Recognizing these overlapping pathways could lead to more specific or complete targeting.

Other receptors and growth factors with lymphatic specificity are already in use as lymphatic markers within or around tumors. These include LYVE-1, the primary lymphatic endothelial receptor for hyaluronan, a mucopolysaccharide abundant in lymph;

PROX1, a transcription factor expressed in early embryogenesis during lymphatic budding from the cardinal vein; the sialomucoprotein podoplanin; and the D6 proinflammatory beta chemokine receptor.

In addition to these lymphatic markers, the use of reverse genetics in subpopulations of families afflicted with hereditary lymphangiodysplasia syndromes such as familial Milroy syndrome, lymphedema-distichiasis, and hypotrichosis-lymphedema-telangiectasia has led to the identification of other genes related to lymphatic growth, namely, VEGFR 3, FOXC2, and SOX18 respectively. Furthermore, chromosomal aneuploidy syndromes and rearrangements, as well as marker loci associated with specific subpopulations of patients with Aagenaes, Noonan, and Turners syndrome, implicate additional chromosomal regions (and genes contained within these regions) spanning almost the entire human genome in normal and pathologic lymphangiogenesis and lymphvasculogenesis pertinent to cancer.

How cancer cells gain entry into the lymphatics is still unclear. If tumors are categorized as liquid tumors versus solid or hematological malignancies versus organ tumors, different mechanisms of metastasis might be expected. However, this is not always the case. In order for successful metastasis to occur tumor cells must first experience a loss of cohesiveness, then enter into the lymphatic system or blood vascular system, survive in the circulation and successfully implant into another organ.

However, a variety of both of these tumors commonly metastasize to the central nervous system, an organ thought to lack true lymphatics. Thus the question persists as to whether metastasis is dependent on the formation and invasion of new lymphatics (tumor lymphangiogenesis) or whether tumors surround and co-opt the nearby normal lymphatics for this process. The distinct patterns of tumor vascularization thus far have generated some controversy, and this is partly due to methods of staining, different tumor types, and marker heterogenicity. For example, lymphatic vessels easily seen by H&E staining or by the expression of one marker are not all positive for another marker, and while head and neck cancers, melanoma, and pancreatic cancers commonly demonstrate proliferating lymphatics within the tumor, colorectal, breast, prostate and cervical tumors often demonstrate proliferating lymphatics only peritumorally or within the stroma. In addition, some of the tumor associated endothelial cells seem to express both venous and lymphatic markers.

Despite the solid evidence demonstrated by the study of the sentinel node, other dye experiments that have tracked tumor localized injections did not demonstrate physical continuity of intratumoral vessels with the draining lymphatic network. Nonetheless, it appears that tumor lymphangiogenesis is present in at least some tumors, is probably underestimated due to variable assays measurements, and remains misunderstood.

Use of currently available clinical tools does not always predict tumor behavior. For example, radionuclide lymphangioscintigrams can show severe disruption of the lymphatic system, seen by dermal backflow, high grade obstruction, and increased uptake in surrounding nodes in patients without any clinically evident metastasis. This raises the question about the indolent course of localized direct invasion, the natural history of untreated cancer, and lymphogenous spread.

Thus, in summary, the lymphatic system is involved in all phases of cancer from its development, progression, and spread to evaluation, prognosis, treatment, post-treatment complications, prevention, containment, and opportunities for cure. A recent approach to address this multiplicity of questions has led to an international symposium in San Francisco in April 2005 (The 1st International Conference on Cancer and the Lymphovascular System: A Rational Basis for Therapy, Organizer, University of California in San Francisco Professor of Surgery, Stanley Leong, MD), where concepts, ideas, and research were exchanged in a collaborative environment. This meeting, the Proceedings of which was published as a special issue of Cancer Metastasis and Reviews, June 2006 (1), was a major milestone. A 2nd Conference is planned for May 3-5, 2007. A variety of questions were raised and ways to address them explored. Some of the major areas discussed included the mechanisms and differences of lymphogenous from hematogenous spread and how the immune system either facilitates or contains this spread. Another was whether the lymphatics involved with or associated with tumors are pre-existing or new lymphatics. If they are newly formed, then are they using embryological differentiation patterns or patterns more typically seen in wound healing and paralleling hemangiogenesis? If both situations occur, what are the circumstances that determine this? The use of gene microarray to assess marker up regulation or down regulation and to correlate the phenotypic differences between normal lymphatics and those involved with or near tumors was discussed. And lastly, the physiological changes, for example flow, contractility, pressure gradient effect, destruction, invasion, at each level of the vasculature, from the capillaries to the larger collecting vessels and also within different organs in the presence of tumor involvement were examined and their importance recognized. This type of multidisciplinary approach will undoubtably lead to even more questions offering the opportunity to continue to advance our understanding and ultimately provide effective treatment of cancer that has invaded the lymphatic system and spread to regional lymph nodes and systemically.

REFERENCE

1. Witte MH, K Jones, J Wilting, et al: Structure function relationships in the lymphatic system and implications for cancer biology. Cancer Metastasis Rev 25 (2006), 159-184.

REVERSAL OF IMMUNOHISTOPATHOLOGICAL CHANGES IN LYMPHEDEMATOUS SKIN TRANSPLANTED TO SCID MICE

Moscicka M, Olszewski W. L., Zolich D.

Department of Surgical Research & Transplantology, Medical Research Center, Polish Academy of Sciences, Warsaw, Poland

INTRODUCTION

Lymphedematous skin, subcutaneous tissue and muscular fascia undergo major structural changes in course of time. Hyperkeratosis of epidermis, fibrosis of dermis, infections and inflammation are the commonly observed alterations. Stasis of tissue fluid and lymph and recurrent inflammatory episodes aggravate the destructive process.

Are the degenerative changes reversible and may they partially subside after restoration of lymphatic drainage?

AIM OF STUDY

To follow the changes in human lymphedematous skin transplanted into scid mice using immunohistochemical methods for evaluation of cells and ground matrix.

MATERIAL AND METHODS

SKIN SPECIMENS. Five by five mm large skin fragments of leg skin from patients with lymphedema of lower limbs, stage III and IV were harvested during debulking procedures. They were placed in 4C saline and transplanted within 4-6h after harvesting.

SKIN TRANSPLANTATION. Skin fragments were grafted onto the dorsum of scid mice and kept there for 3 to 4 weeks. Then, they were removed and snap-frozen for immunohistochemical staining. To evaluate the proliferating capacity of graft cells, some recipients received BrdU before graft harvesting.

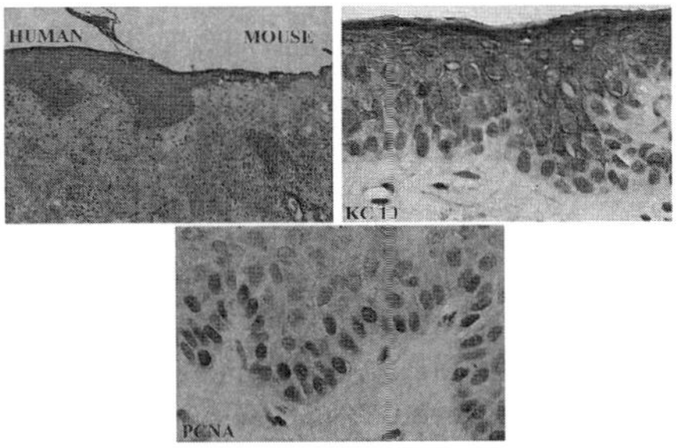

Lymphedematous skin after tx to scid mouse

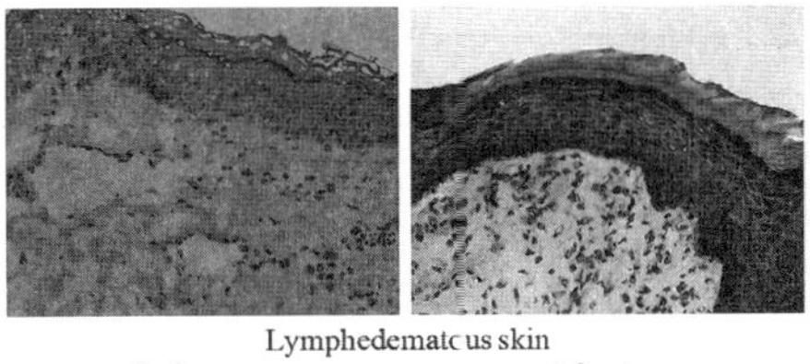

Lymphedematc us skin
Before After tx

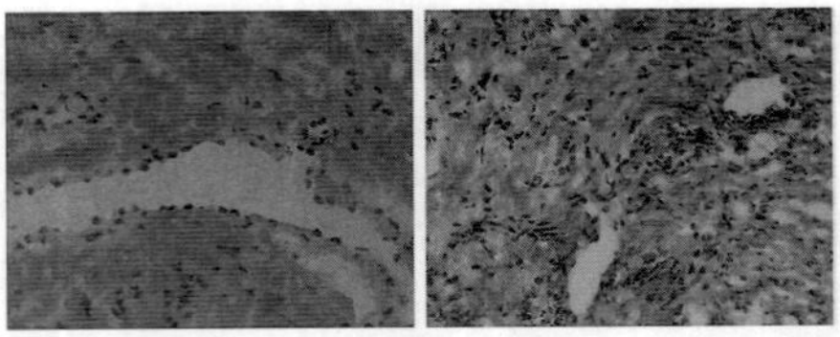

Lymphedematous skin
Before After tx

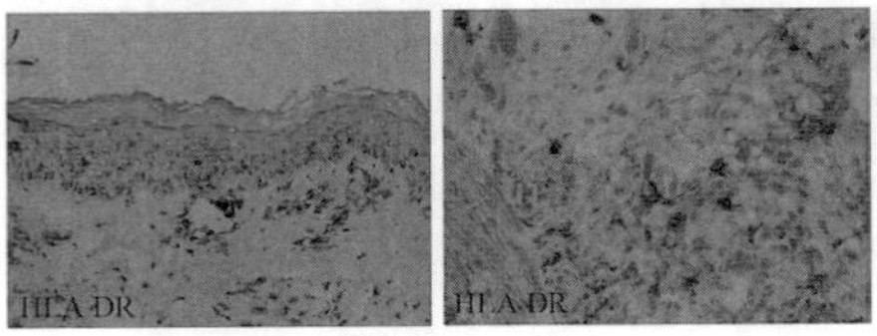

Lymphedematous skin
Before After tx

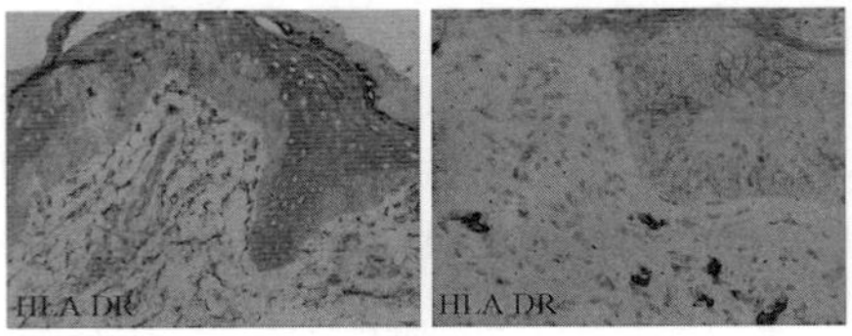

Lymphedematous skin
Before After tx

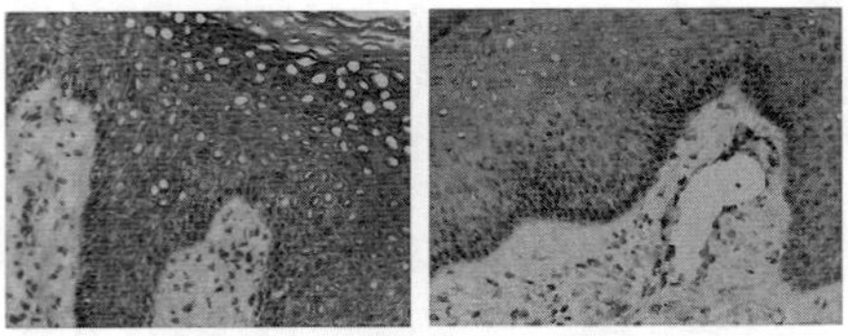

Lymphedematousskin after tx

RESULTS

Vigorous proliferation of keratinocytes was observed. They expressed PCNA, p63, CD29, keratin production.

CD1a Langerhans'cells were not present in epidermis. They presumably migrated out to recipient lymphoid organs.

The structure of dermis remained unchanged with a few blood vessels and fibroblasts. Dilated lymphatics collapsed.

CONCLUSIONS

Intensive proliferation of keratinocytes, persistence of dilated lymphatics and lack of changes in dermal structure indicate that no remodeling of lymphedematous skin took place within 4 to 12 weeks after transplantation to a normal environment.

Table 1. Bacterial isolates from lymphedematous skin before and after transplantation to scid mice (10 patients, 14-100 days transplants)

Isolates	before	after	other isolates
Staph.aureus	4	2	B.cereus, E.coli, Micrococcus spp
Staph.epidermidis	5	3	B.cereus
Staph.hominis	2	0	E.coli, Eubacterium lentum, Peptostrepotococcus
B.cereus	2	1	
E.coli	2	0	Staph.aureus 2
Enterococcus			
feacalis	2	3	B.cereus
feacium	2	1	Aeromonas spp.

THE UNIVERSITY OF ARIZONA EXPERIENCE IN STAGING AND MEASURING EFFICACY OF TREATMENT IN NON-HODGKIN LYMPHOMA USING POSITRON EMISSION TOMOGRAPHY

WH Williams

Department of Radiology (Nuclear Medicine), University of Arizona, 1501 N. Campbell Ave. Tucson, AZ, USA

Introduction

Non-Hodgkin Lymphomas (NHL) are malignancies of the lymphatic system and, are the sixth most common cancers in the US with an expected yearly incidence of 50,000 and; greater than 20,000 will die in 2005. For decades, Computed Tomography (CT) has been considered the standard procedure for evaluating Non-Hodgkin Lymphoma (NHL). Its high spatial resolution provides anatomic details that make CT an excellent tool in diagnostic and therapeutic procedures. However, there is no direct assessment of the functional or metabolic status of tumors.

2-(fluorine-18)-2-deoxy-D-glucose (^{18}F-FDG) is the radiotracer most often used in Positron Emission Tomography (PET). FDG follows the glucose pathway with metabolism blocked at the FDG-6-P step see Fig. 1.

FDG-PET imaging is performed and commonly used in staging of NHL. Chemotherapy can be curative in both Hodgkin disease and in non-Hodgkin Lymphoma. Residual masses at the end of chemotherapy may represent persistent fibrosis but residual or recurrent tumor can not be excluded. Ga-67 scintigraphy has been used but recent trials have demonstrated that FDG-PET is superior to gallium single photon emission tomography.

Intensive chemotherapy may cure high grade NHL. The other possibility is relapse. Since MRI and CT can not reliably differentiate between scar and recurrence, FDG-PET was tried and found to be predictive of outcome and overall survival[1].

Procedure

10 to 20 mCi of F-18 FDG was administered intravenously following a standard protocol. The patient fasted for greater than 6 hours and blood glucose was less than 150 mg/dl prior to FDG administered. Following injection of

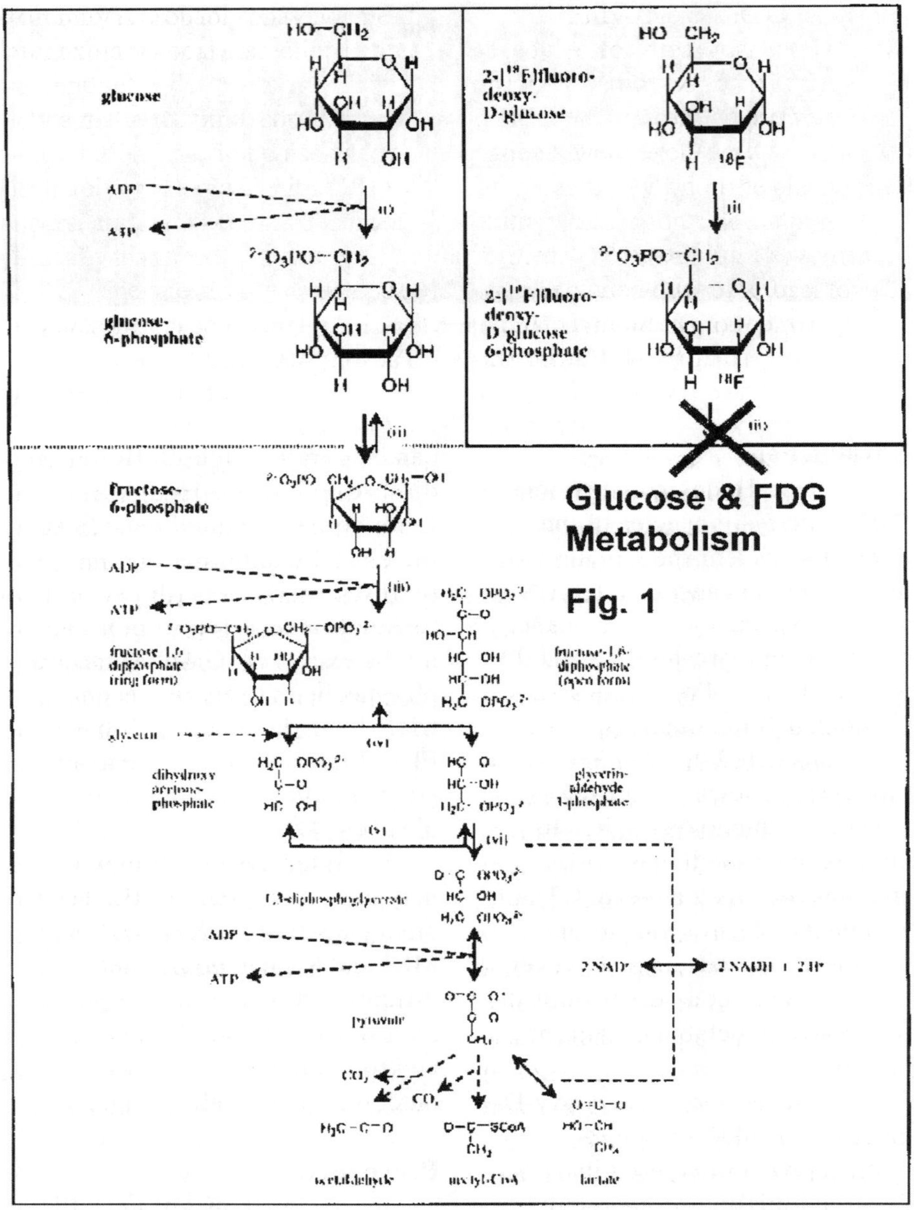

FDG and an uptake period of 60 minutes in a quiet darkened room, the patient was imaged on a Siemens/CTI ECAT EXACT PET scanner Fig. 2.

We report here our experience with 35 patients, ages 4 to 89 years, with a diagnosis of NHL. 14 of the 35 patients had multiple PET scans. 2-fluoro deoxyglucose (FDG)

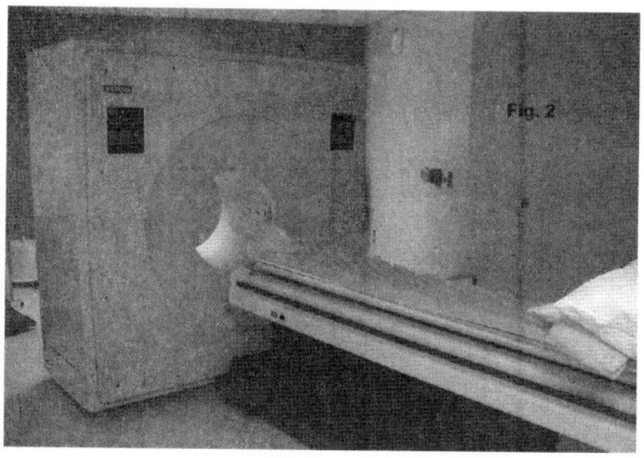

was administered IV following a standard protocol. Images were obtained from the orbit level to the mid-thighs. Image sets were reconstructed with attenuation correction based on a transmission scan and displayed in multiple tomographic and 3-dimensional orientations. Tumor lesions were described by size, location and Standard Uptake Values (SUV). SUV's greater than 2.5 were considered consistent with tumor.

Discussion

Two patients showed progression of disease (Fig. 3) and one marked progression. Our results showed dramatic resolution of FDG uptake (Fig. 4) in four patients after chemotherapy and

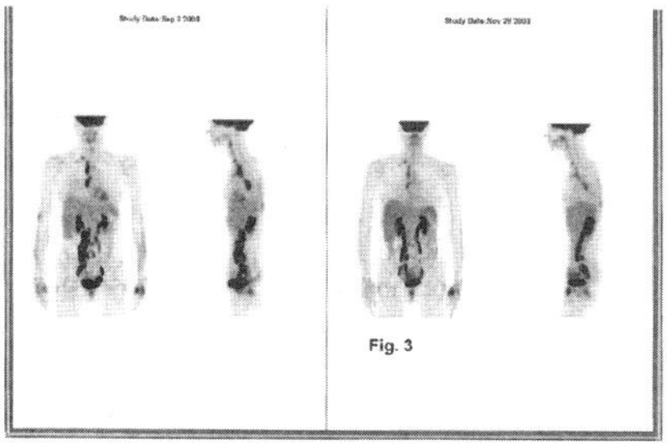

48 year old feamle with non-Hodgkin Lymphoma
Status post radiation and chemotherapy,
now with enlarging mediastinal, retropertioneal
and pelvic lymph nodes.

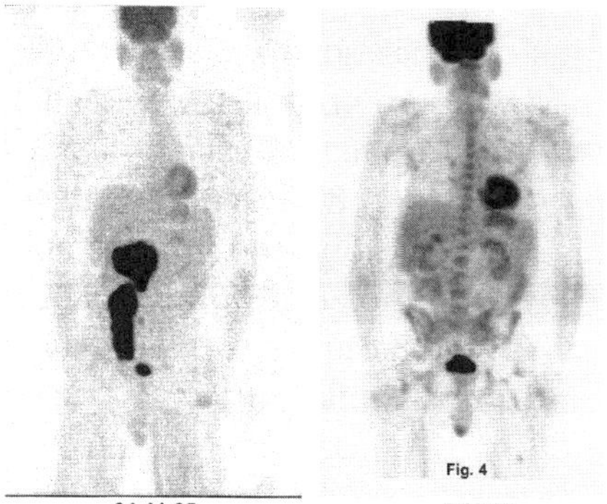

04-11-05 6-16-05
59 year old male with history of Non-Hodgkin Lymphoma, diagnosed 2-17-05.

radiation. The sizes and SUV's of active tumor seen in the patients in Fig. 4 are evaluated from sagittal, coronal and axial tomographic sections (Figs. 5 to 8).

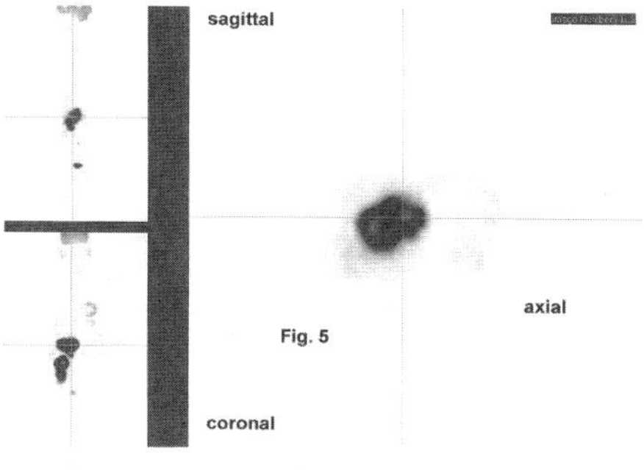

4-11-05

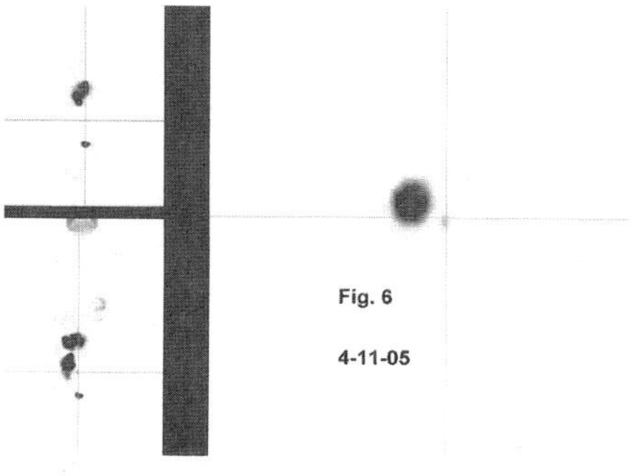

Two small nodes in the abdomen probabfy mesenteric and periaortic.

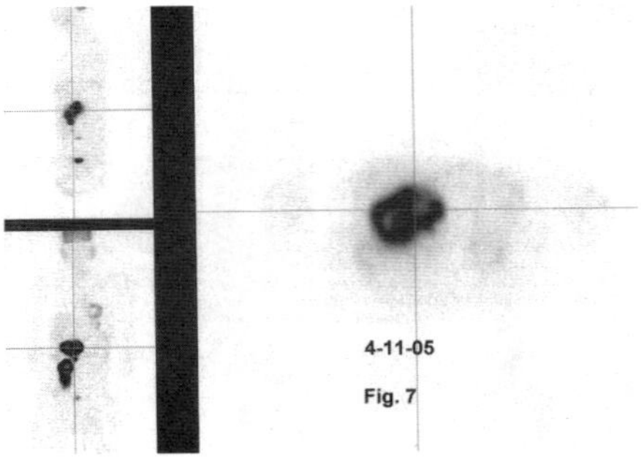

Fig. 7

Two large irregular foci of increased FDG uptake measuring approximately 15 cm each.

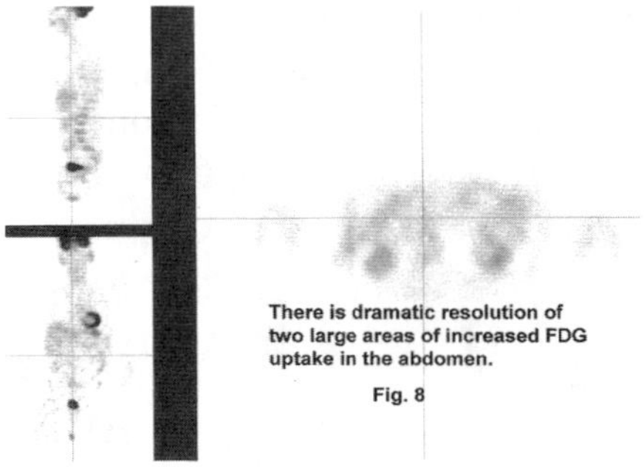

There is dramatic resolution of two large areas of increased FDG uptake in the abdomen.

Fig. 8

6-16-05

Seven of the patients with a diagnosis of non-Hodgkin Lymphoma who were scanned after chemotherapy and radiation treatment were normal. Three patients showed recurrence of disease greater than 6 years after the initial diagnosis and treatment.

Our patients are now imaged using PET/CT (typical schematic layout (Fig. 9) on a Siemens Biograph 6 PET/CT scanner (Fig. 10). Images are obtained from the orbits to the mid thighs and; can be obtained from the vertex to the feet. A concurrent CT scan was used for attenuation correction and localization purposes (by fusion imaging, Fig. 11) but not for diagnostic CT interpretation.

Conclusions

PET scanning is an excellent tool for the staging

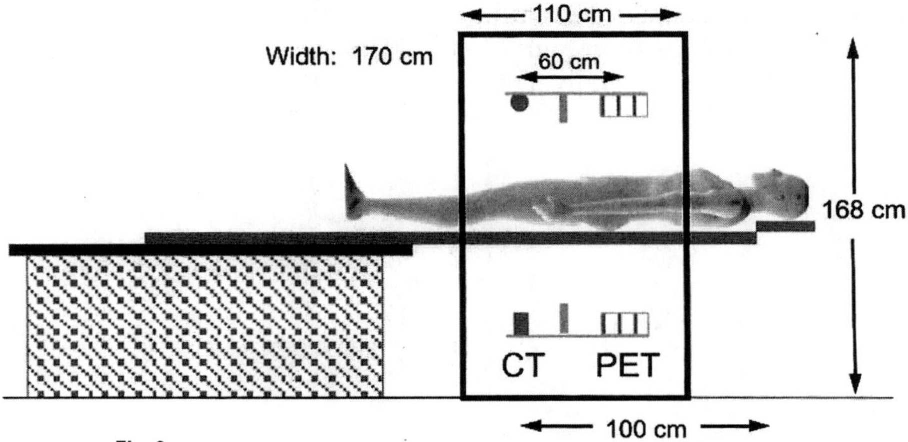

Fig. 9

PET-CT

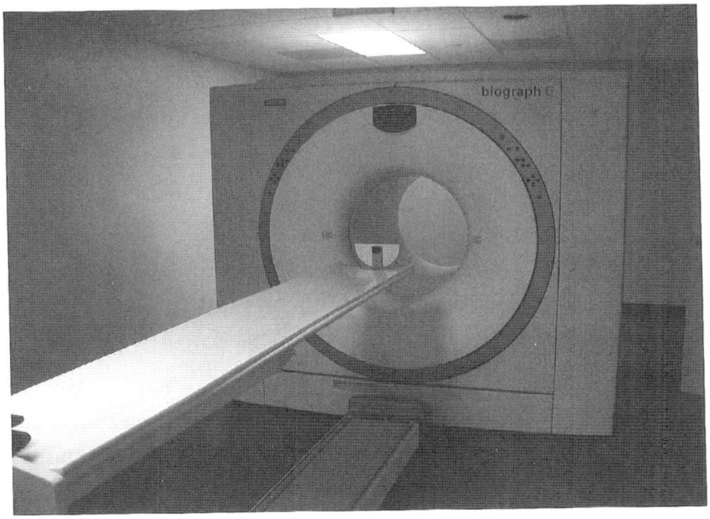

Fig. 10

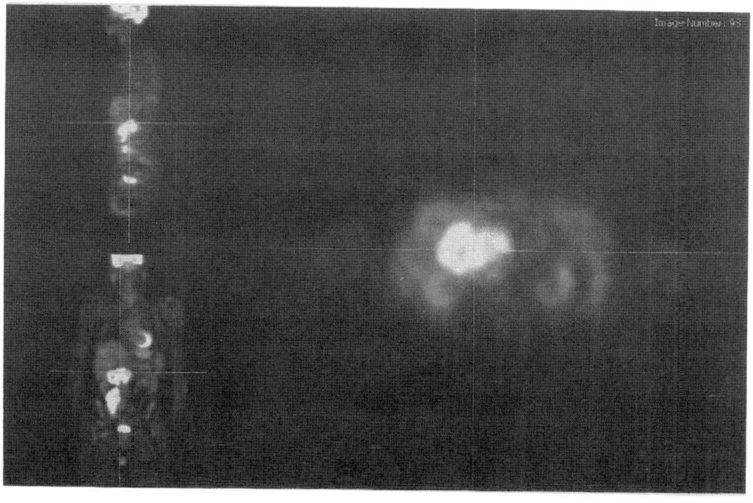

Fusion Images Fig. 11

and follow up of non-Hodgkin Lymphoma. Our instrumentation has been replaced with a PET-CT unit. Any current ambiguity in tumor location is solved by PET-CT Fusion imaging.

Reference

1. G Jerusalem, F Najjar, P Paulus etal. Early assessment of response to chemotherapy by FDG-PET is highly predictive of outcome in patients with high-grade Non-Hodgkin's Lymphoma. *J. Nucl Med 1998; 39: 147P.*

THE INNATE IMMUNE REACTION IN HUMAN SKIN TO INFECTION INVOLVES KERATINOCYTES, DENDRITIC CELLS, TISSUE FLUID AND LYMPHATIC SYSTEM

Olszewski W.L, Cakala M, Stanislawska J, Zaleska M, Galkowska H

Department of Surgical Research & Transplantology, Medical Research Center, Polish Academy of Sciences, Warsaw, Poland

The immune response of skin to infection involves keratinocytes (KC), Langerhans cells (LC) a subset of dendritic cells, then tissue fluid and lymph proteins, lymphatic endothelial (LEC) and lymph node cells. The mechanical barrier created by epidermis is only one factor protecting against penetration of microorganisms. This is the functional network of epidermal and skin resident and blood–derived migrating cells, their receptors and protein products that creates skin defence system. Aim. To identify defensins, HLA DR and toll-like receptors in KC, cytokines, chemokines, complement and lysozyme in tissue fluid and lymph, toll-like receptors in LEC and LC, and antigen presentation in LC-lymphocyte clusters in skin of human lower limbs. Methods. Studies were performed in 15 healthy volunteers undergoing tests for antibiotic penetration to tissue fluid. Ethical committee was obtained in each case. Skin biopsy was performed in lower leg above medial malleolus. The same site served cannulation of lymphatics for collection of lymph draining foot skin. Lymph samples were stored at –70. Toll-like receptors. Immunohistological staining was performed with anti TLR2 and 4 mabs (Santa Cruz). Defensins. Human ß-defensin-2 mab (Santa Cruz) was used. Cytokines and chemokines. ELISA assay (R&D) was used for determination of IL1, IL6, TNFα, TGFß, IL8, IL10, MCP1 concentration. Complement protein concentration was measured by immunodiffucion (Boehring). Lysozyme level was estimated using kits (Boehring). Activation markers. Monoclonal antibodies for CD1α, HLA DR and ICAM1 were used (Dako) for cell immunohistochemical staining. LEC were identified using LYVE1 mAb. Results. Keratinocytes from skin of lower leg expressed TLR 4, and weakly HLA DR and ICAAM1 in the basal and suprabasal layer. Around 40 CD1α LC per linear mm were detected in epidermis. No LC were seen in papillary or reticular dermis. ß-defensin-2 was present in epidermis..Lymph contained all investigated cytokines, chemokines and complement at level different from that of serum. The IL1 concentration was 40%, of IL6 920%, TNFα 190%, IL8 990, IL10 1200%, MCP1 387% of that of serum. The C1q level was 5% and of CD3 22%,respectively. Lysozyme concentration was 50% of that of serum. Five to eight percent of

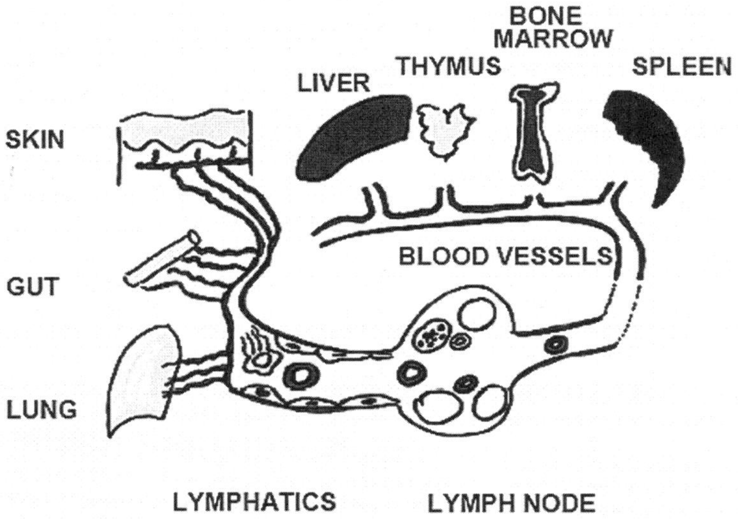

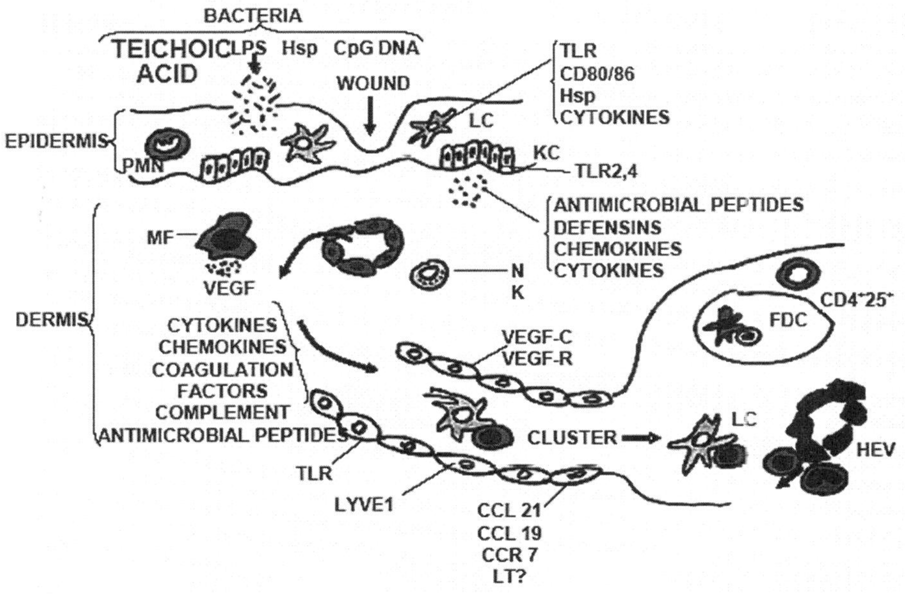

lymph LC formed clusters with CD4 and CD8 lymphocytes. Conclusions. Under physiological conditions skin from the medial aspect of human lower leg, a common site of ulcer formation, expresses antimicrobial receptors and contains proteins participating in immune processes. A high number of LC-lymphocyte clusters in lymph draining skin reflects a continuous immune alert in skin.

Innate immunity is an evolutionarily ancient part of the host defence mechanism. The innate immune processes both rapidly recognize foreigness of penetrating cells and substances as well as oddity of own cell debris and delivere them to the organized lymphoid tissue for elimination of reutilization. The same molecular modules are found in plants and animals. The immune cell receptors are fixed in genome and rearrangement is not necessary. Cells belong to non-clonal population, they possess conserved molecular pattern, act immediately and recognize between self and non-self. The innate and adaptive processes merge in lymph nodes where they up- or downregulate each other.

Innate immunity processes proceed in lymphoid tissue of lymph nodes. There are no tissues with environmental contact that would not be drained to the lymph node. Lymph nodes react to bacterial and allostimulation by increase in cell mass. Frequency of node populations does not change as if nodes were physiologically pre-prepared for a nonspecific stimulation. Presumably lymph node cells carry immune trait that is constantly active.

Innate immunity in skin and its lymphoid tissue intermingles with adaptive processes. Memory cells arise ready to eliminate foreign and self antigens. They become furious about foreign intruders but kind to own antigens. Why such difference in behavior?

THE RESPONSE OF REGIONAL LYMPH NODES TO SKIN BACTERIAL AND ALLOGENEIC ANTIGENS

Cakala M., Olszewski W.L.

Department of Surgical Research and Transplantology, Medical Research Center, Polish Academy of Sciences, Warsaw, Poland

INTRODUCTION

Food and leg skin are physiologically targeted by resident and environmental bacterial flora. Leg ischemia and venous stasis facilitate bacterial penetration and colonization with subsequent proliferation and host inflammatory response. Bacterial products damage draining lymphatics leading to their obstruction. The question arises how does lack of local lymphatic drainage affect the skin inflammation.

AIM OF THE STUDY

To characterize infiltrating cell populations in skin and regional lymph nodes after local human bacteria infection in animals with ligated afferent lymphatics.

MATERIALS AND METHODS

Group I bacteria were injected i.d. into the paw daily for 7 days.

Group II lymphatics leading to the popliteal lymph node were ligated prior to bacterial injections, as in group I.

Group III lymphatics were ligated without bacterial injections.

On day 8 specimens of paw skin and popliteal lymph node were harvested.

MATERIALS AND METHODS

Staphylococcus epidermidis was isolated from the lower part of leg skin of healthy volunteers and injected sc into Wistar rat paw.

For phenotyping the W3/13, W3/25, OX8, MHC II, OX7, OX43, OX33, OX45, OX12, CD31, CD54, ED1, OX62 and HIS48 monoclonal antibodies were used.

Subcutaneous bacteria injection.

Popliteal lymph node cell phenotypes identified by flow cytometry after injection of *Staphylococcus epidermidis* (n=3)

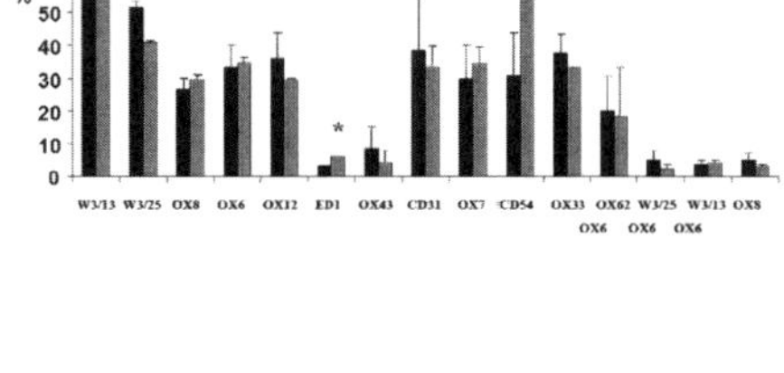

RESULTS

Paw skin. In group I, multiple (++) MHC II+, ED1+ and CD54+ cells were found in the subepidermal region. In group II, desquamation of epidermis, subepidermal and perivascular infiltrates reached +++. Lymphatics occluded by acellular substance were seen. In group III, no infiltrates were detected. Dilated lymphatics had open lumen without thrombi.

Lymph nodes. An increase in number of lymph node weight and cell concentration was observed in groups I and II. Most intensive changes in the paracortex and medulla with a high number of large cells in the medulla were seen in group I. The W3/25+, MHC II+, ED1+, HIS48+, OX7+, OX62+ and CD54+ cells accumulated in the follicles, paracortex and medulla. In group II, the density of cells was increased but without change in

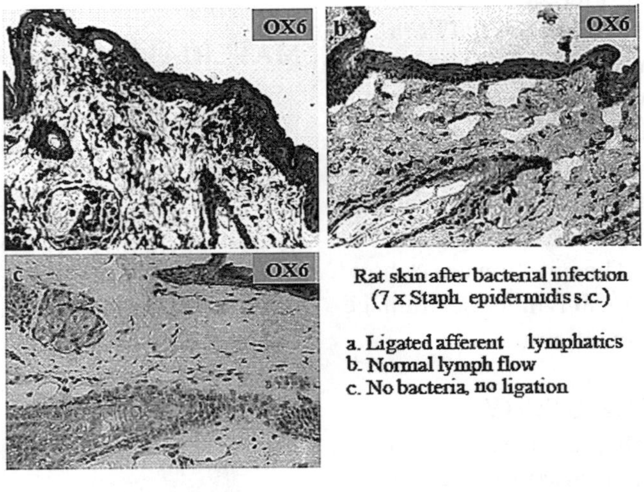

Rat skin after bacterial infection
(7 x Staph. epidermidis s.c.)

a. Ligated afferent lymphatics
b. Normal lymph flow
c. No bacteria, no ligation

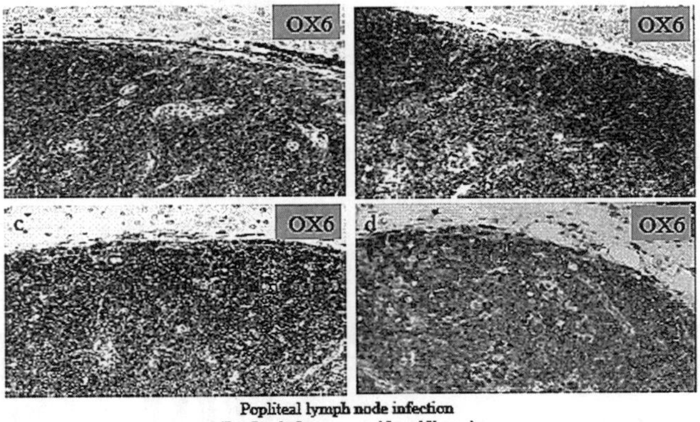

Popliteal lymph node infection
(7 x Staphylococcus epidermidis s.c.)
a. normal node, b. 7 d after infection, c. as b. + ligation of afferent lymphatics,
d. ligation of afferent lymphatics. Magn x 200

proportions of various subsets except of evident decrease of OX62+ cells (migrating dendritic). In group III, no changes were observed but lack of OX62+ cells.

CONCLUSIONS

Interruption of lymphatics draining skin regions infected with bacteria spares lymph nodes but evidently enhances local inflammatory reaction even leading to skin necrosis. These findings justify intensive antibiotic therapy in dermatitis in lymphedematous tissues (post-mastectomy, post-inguinal dissection).

Chapter 4
Lymphoscintigraphy and Diagnosis of Lymphatic Disorders

LYMPHOSCINTIGRAFY EVALUATION OF ASSIMPTOMATIC LYMPHATIC INSUFFICIENSY

Silvia Bacellar, Marcos Arêas Marques, Paulo Roberto Mattos da Silveira, Léa Miriam Barbosa da Fonseca, Arno von Ristow, Rivany Pires e Rosana Lucena.

Introduction

Lymphatic edema is an invalidating disease with high morbidity whereas prevention remains the best approach. Lymphatic edema related to cancer, mostly on the breast, and those related to filariosis are being studied by researches in all continents. Even assymptomatic patients may be diagnosed with lymphatic insufficiency after lymphoscintigraphy. Some studies described the relation between intense physical activities and collateral lymphatic circulation. The aims of this study were to identify by lymphoscintigraphy the incidence of lymphatic insufficiency in healthy patients and to correlate sedentarism and physical exercises in the development of lymphedema.

Method

Twenty five healthy volunteers were studied and submitted to anamneses, physical evaluation and lower limb lymphoscintigraphy.

Results

Only two out of 25 patients showed the normal lymphoscintigraphy pattern. These patients were the only athletes in the group. There was a high incidence of lymphatic insufficiency in sedentary assymptomatic patients.

Conclusion

We conclude that physical exercises could play an important role in the prevention of lymphatic edemas. We suggest that more studies should evaluate these sedentary patients, after a physical activity program during three, six and twelve months in order to analyze the lymphatic function. Furthermore, we recommend a review of the normal pattern for lymphoscintigraphy due to the high incidence of abnormal scans observed.

INTEREST OF THE LYMPHOSCINTIGRAPHY IN ROUTINE PRACTICE: THE SURGICAL POINT OF VIEW

F. Boccardo, G. Taddei*, G. Villa*, C. Bellini, C. Eretta, D. Pertile, A. Macciò, S. Michelini***, C. Campisi**

Department of Surgery – Section of Lymphatic Surgery and Microsurgery
S. Martino Hospital, University of Genoa, Italy
*Section of Nuclear Medicine – University of Genoa, Italy
**Center of Neonatal Pathology – G.Gaslini Institute, Genoa, Italy
***Center of Neuro-Vascular Rehabilitation – S.Giovanni Battista Hospital – Rome

Lymphoscintigraphy represents the common diagnostic examination which is usually performed by lymphedema patients addressed to an operation of lymphatic microsurgery, together with the study of venous circulation by means of duplex scan.

It is indispensable to study the conditions of vein circulation in order to decide which microsurgical technique is to use in the single case, derivative lymphatic-venous shunt or reconstructive lymphatic-venous-lymphatic plasty.

As concerns lymphoscintigraphy[1-6], the value of this investigation is very high in those cases of early stage peripheral lymphedemas, because it allows to study both superficial and deep lymphatic circulation in a very precise and not only functional but also morphological way, giving important data to the surgeon to establish the correct therapeutic strategy.

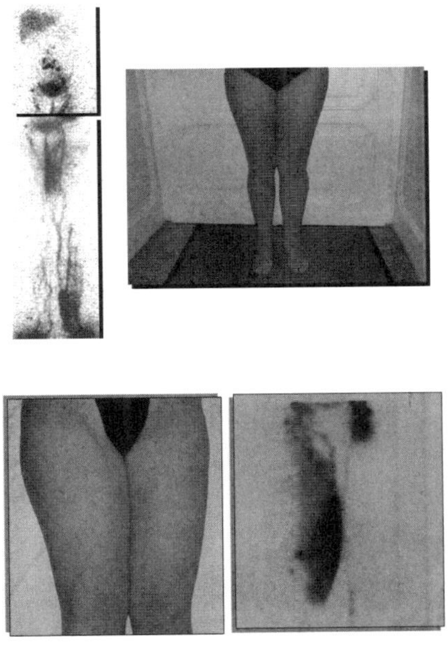

Figs.1,2. Lymphoscintigraphies in peripheral early stage lymphedemas showing the lymph stasis (dermal back flow) and the main lymphatic pathways coming up to the groin, site of the microsurgical anastomoses.

But, in the most advanced cases of lymphedema,

lymphoscintigraphy[7-12] proved not to be so reliable, as the tracer remains at the site of injection without any sign of progression. This outcome might lead to a misunderstanding of the etiology and physiopathological mechanism of the pathology, which can be wrongly interpreted as congenitally based on a condition of lymphatic and lymphnodal aplasia (so called Nonne-Milroy disease). On the contrary, it is only a problem of extremely difficult absorption of the tracer by the initial lymphatics, due above all to high interstitial pressure and tissular fibrosis.

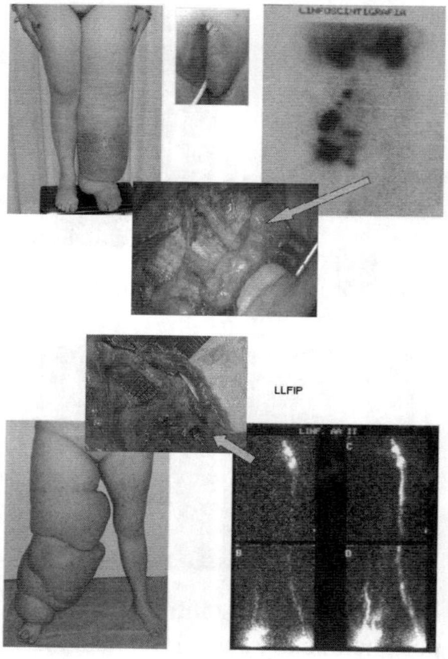

Figs.3,4. Lymphoscintigraphies in two cases of late stage peripheral lymphedemas show an apparent absence of lymphatic-lymphnodal structures that were in fact found at the time of surgery (dumb lymphoscintigraphies).

There are, however, sometimes even early stages in which the tracer does not progress from the site of injection, but in these cases we might think of a sort of inhibitory nervous signal from the proximal lymph nodes as it is for the kidney in case of ureteral stone obstruction: we called the phenomenon lymphatic-lymphnodal functional inhibiting phenomenon (LLFIP).

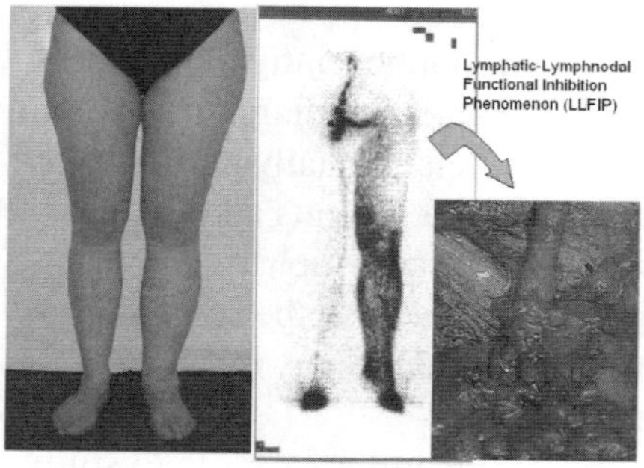

Fig. 5. Lymphoscintigraphy in a case of peripheral early stage lymphedema showing the LLFIP phenomenon.

The assessment of these cases was wrong by lymphoscintigraphy because when we operated on these patients we could find both lymphatic and lymph nodal structures, not pointed out by lymphoscintigraphy. The problem was of a lymph nodal fibrosclerosis but with good afferent lymphatic collectors that were anastomosed to a near vein.

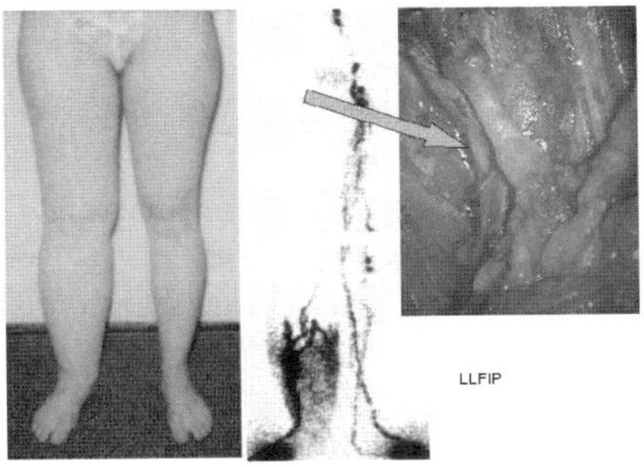

Fig. 6. Another case of lymphoscintigraphy in a later stage lymphedema showing the same LLFIP phenomenon.

Owing to these clinical observations, we suggest that in case of a complete absence of tracer progression along the limb, it is useful to inject the radiocolloid proximally at the root of the limb, a little distally to the groin or the axilla. This technical trick helps in visualizing the lymphatic structures present there and allow to properly interpret the pathology.

Finally, lymphoscintigraphy allows to assess the long term patency of microanastomoses, even over 10-15 years after microsurgical operation.

Efficacy of derivative lymphatico-venous anastomoses is confirmed by the following lymphoscintigraphic patterns: 1) reduced dermal back-flow; 2) rapid clearance with the blood stream of the tracer at the site of microanastomoses, and 3) earlier tracer uptake by the liver indicative of more rapid entry into the bloodstream.

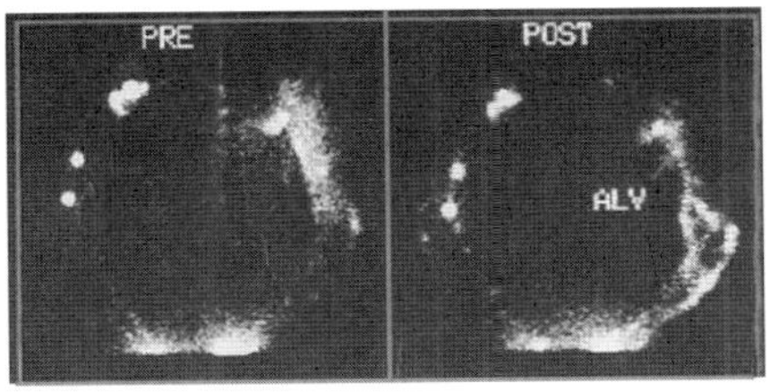

A B

Fig. 7. Usefulness of lymphoscintigraphy in the long term assessment of the patency of ve lymphatic-venous derivatmicroanastomoses. before (A) and after (B) microsurgery.

As concerns reconstructive technique, lymphoscintigraphy permits to visualize lymph flow through the venous grafts thus mirroring clinical improvement. The lymphoscintigraphic patterns correlated to the efficacy of the reconstructiv technique of interpositioned vein graft are: 1) reduced dermal back flow, 2) appearance of preferential ways of lymph drainage and 3) visualization of the intralymphatic interposition autologous venous grafts.

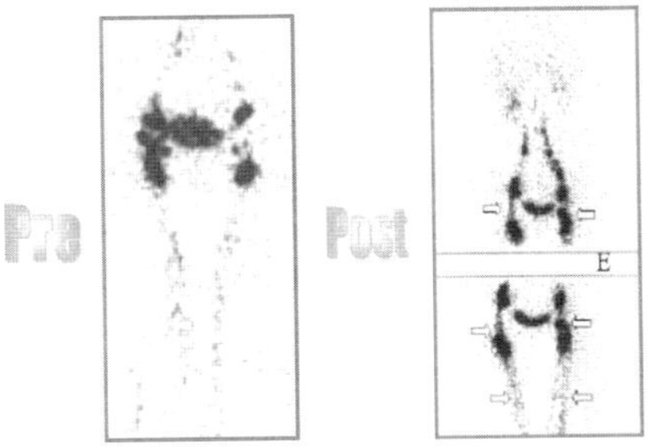

Fig. 8. Lymphoscintigraphy to evaluate the patency of reconstructive lymphatic-venous-lymphatic anastomoses with the visualization of vein grafts at long term distance from operation.

It is, finally, useful to underline how there might exist some cases of "dumb lymphoscintigraphy" notwithstanding the presence of proper lymphatic-lymphnodal structures.

REFERENCES

1. Bellini C, Arioni C, Mazzella M, Campisi C, Taddei G, Boccardo F, Serra G. Lymphoscintigraphic evaluation of congenital lymphedema of the newborn. Clin Nucl Med. 2002 May;27(5):383-4.
2. Biassoni P., C.Campisi, G.Villa, F.Boccardo: "Isotopic lymphography in the diagnosis and follow-up of lymphedemas treated by microsurgery". Lymphology 29 (Suppl): 101-105, 1996.
3. Bourgeois P., Wolter F.: "Lymphoscintigraphy demonstration of a protein loosing enteropathy". EJLRP 1990, 18, 44-46.
4. Campisi C., Boccardo F., Tacchella M.: "The present role of isotope lymphangioscintigraphy and conventional lymphography in delineating the status of lymphatic and chylous collectors". Lymphology 1994, 27 (Suppl), 282-285.
5. Michelini S, Campisi C, Failla A, Boccardo F. Proposal for stadiation of phlebolymphoedema. Europ J Lymphol Relat Probl 1995; 6(20): I-14.
6. Pecking AP, Gougeon-Bertrand FJ, Floiras JL, Garbay JR, Banzet P, Roussé J. Lymphoscintigraphy. Overview of its use in the lymphatic system. Lymphology 1998; 31 (Suppl): 343-346.
7. Witte C., McNeill G., Witte M. et Al.: "Whole-body lymphangioscintigraphy: making the invisible easily visible". Progress in Lymphology XII, Elsevier Science Publishers B.V., 1989, 123.
8. Campisi C, Davini D, Bellini C, Taddei G, Villa G, Fulcheri E, Zilli A, Da Rin E, Eretta C, Boccardo F. Lymphatic microsurgery for the treatment of lymphedema. Microsurgery. 2006;26(1):65-9.
9. Tommasi L, Mignone A, Caralis G, Morbelli S, Curti G, Santaniello B, Boccardo F, Campisi C, Peschiera F, Dinati L, Taddei G. Lymphoscintigraphy in the evaluation of lymphedema in the lower limbs after abdominal surgery. Lymphology 2004; 37 (S): 587-8.
10. Campisi C, Davini D, Bellini C, Taddei G, Villa G, Fulcheri E, Zilli A, Da Rin E, Eretta C, Boccardo F. Lymphatic microsurgery for the treatment of lymphedema. Microsurgery. 2006;26(1):65-9.
11. Bellini C, Boccardo F, Taddei G, Mazzella M, Arioni C, Villa G, Hennekam RC, Serra G, Campisi C. Diagnostic protocol for lymphoscintigraphy in newborns. Lymphology. 2005 Mar;38(1):9-15.
12. Campisi C, Boccardo F. Microsurgical techniques for lymphedema treatment: derivative lymphatic-venous microsurgery. World J Surg. 2004 Jun;28(6):609-13.

ISOTOPIC LYMPHOGRAPHY HELPS TO DETECT EDEMA OF VARIOUS ETIOLOGY AND TO ESTABLISH APPROPRIATE THERAPY

Olszewski W. L.

Department of Surgery and Transplantation, Medical Research Center, Polish Academy of Sciences, Warsaw, Poland

Lymphoscintigraphy has become a routine diagnostic procedure in our hands in each case of edema of limbs of non-systemic etiology. In combination with Doppler investigation of the venous system it allows to establish diagnosis with a high level of accuracy. Lymphoscintigraphy allows to: 1. show lack of absorption of tracer, 2. if absorbed to show speed of tracer flow, 3. visualize lymph nodes in anatomical and NON-anatomical "new" sites, 4. visualize lymphatic collaterals, 5. provide pictures of inflammatory foci in superficial and deep tissues due to extravasation and phagocytosis of tracer with aggregated albumin, 6. show flow of tracer after mechanical massage proving its efficiency, 7.abstain from massage in cases of vast clinically not diagnosed inflammatory changes, 8. show areas of more intensive edema requiring more massage, 9. compare the pre- and posttreatment pictures, 10. evaluate the patency of microsurgical shunt by measuring the radioactivity over liver. Taken together, lymphoscintigraphy gives insight into the topographical distribution of edema, its intensity, location of inflamed tissues, efficacy of mechanical drainage. This allows to modulate the therapeutic protocol and supplement massage with drugs and in some cases provide indications for microsurgical decompressing procedures.

The generally accepted notion that lymphedema is caused mainly by lack patency of lymphatics undergoes currently a fundamental revision. Lymph stasis (leading to lymphedema) is caused by all factors damaging lymphatic wall and valves, which subsequently affect tissue fluid/lymph transport irrespective of whether the lumen is patent or not.

CONDITIONS AFFECTING LOWER LIMB LYMPHATICS AND NODES

1. Nonspecific dermatits
2. Trauma: mechanical, surgical
3. Venous ulcer
4. Diabetic foot
5. Lymph node extirpation
6. Iatrogenic: venous and arterial surgery, vein harvesting
7. Arthritis
8. Thrombophlebitis

CLASSIFICATION OF LYMPHEDEMA

1. Postinflammatory (dermatitis, lymphangitis, lymphadenitis of various etiologies)
2. Postsurgical (after groin and axillary dissectionalso including radiotherapy; after arterial reconstructions and saphenous vein harvesting for coronary bypasses)
3. Posttraumatic (closed and open limb injuries with immobilization)
4. Mixed lymphatico-venous type in chronic various
5. Idiopathic (primary)
6. Parasitic (filarial)

EVALUATION OF LYMPHOSCINTIGRAMMES

necessary for establishing rational therapy

1. physiotherapy
2. elastic support
3. antibiotics
4. surgery (lymphovenous, scar removal)

CLASSIFICATION OF CHANGES ON LYMPHOSCINTIGRAMS

Tracer flow speed Calf – dilated lymphatics, extravasation and dermal back flow, absorption of tracer macrophages (inflammation), interrupted lymphatic pathways (collaterals), "new" lymph nodes"

Thigh - as above Inguinal lymph nodes – total area, collateral lymphatics, always compare with contralateral side

SUPERFICIAL AND DEEP LYMPHOSCINTIGRAPHY

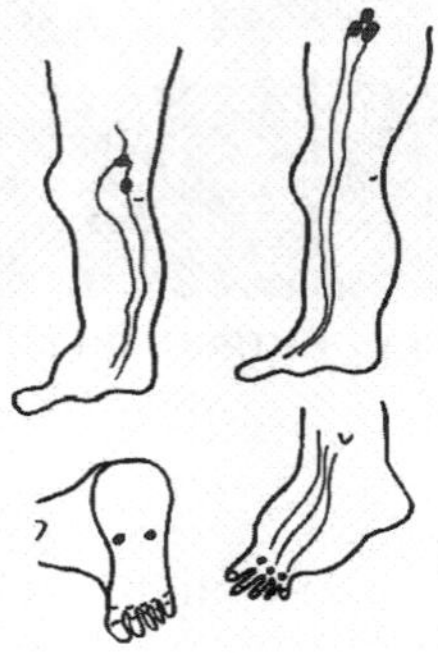

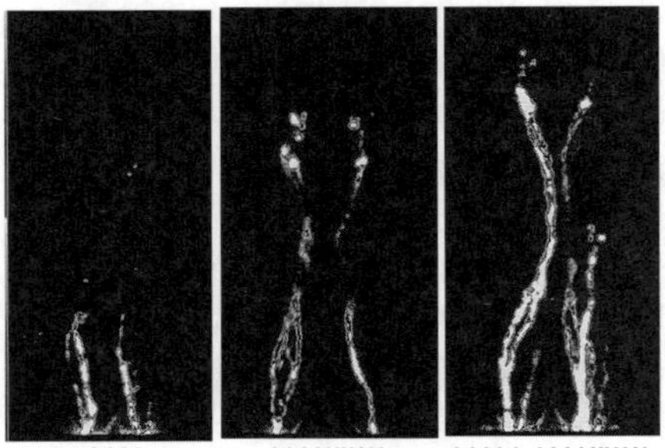

Deep Superficial Deep& superficial

INDICATIONS FOR LYMPHOSCINTIGRAPHY OF LIMBS

Post-
- dermatitis
- lymphangitis
- traumatic
- surgical
- phlebitis

Dermatoliposclerosis
Ulcers
Unknown origin (excluding systemic etiology)

INTERPRETATION OF LYMPHOSCINTIGRAMS

1 Tracer absorption rate from injection site

2 Consecutive pictures either static or after standard walking distance (at 30 min intervals up to 2.5 h)
3 Gross anatomical evaluation of pathways and nodes outline (deep and superficial limb systems)
4 Densitometry of calf and thigh lymphatics and sites of tracer accumulation (surface area)
5 Densitometry of inguinal lymph nodes pictures (surface area)
6 Comparison of data of swollen and contralateral limb

INTERPRETATION OF LYMPHOSCINTIGRAMS (2)

1 Deep and superficial systems should be visualized.
2 Prognosis and surgical indications for lympho-venous shunts and debulking surgery depend on obstruction of one or both systems

REFERENCES

Lymphoscintigraphy allows to:

1. show lack of absorption of tracer,
2. if absorbed, to show speed of tracer flow,
3. visualize lymph nodes in anatomical and non-anatomical "new" sites,
4. visualize lymphatic collaterals,
5. provide pictures of inflammatory foci in superficial and deep tissues created by extravasated and phagocytosed tracer (aggregated albumin)
6. show flow of tracer after mechanical massage, proving its efficiency,
7. abstain from massage in cases of diffuse, clinically not diagnosed, inflammatory changes,
8. show areas of intensive edema requiring more massage,
9. compare the pre- and posttreatment pictures,
10. evaluate the patency of microsurgical shunt by measuring the radioactivity over liver.
11. visualize inflammatory foci years after trauma or inflammation
12. creates new problems as TO TREAT? AND IF SO HOW? the detected changes

RHODAMINE-BASED OPTICAL IMAGING OF THE MURINE LYMPHATIC SYSTEM

Gideon Richards[1], Micheal Bernas[1], Robert Hunter[1], Brant Kaylor[2], Arthur Gmitro[2], and Marlys H. Witte[1]

[1]Department of Surgery and [2]Optical Sciences Center, University of Arizona, Tucson, Arizona, USA.

Introduction

The gold standard for high resolution lymphatic system imaging in mice is visual lymphangiography with Evans Blue dye (EBD) to highlight the superficial lymphatics, deep trunks and lymph nodes. This method is invasive and generally involves the sacrifice of the animals which limits its practical use for serial observations. In this study, fluorescence lymphangiography was evaluated for its ability to reliably and dynamically image lymph vessels and nodes in mice.

Method

Adult C57/Bl/6 mice were anesthetized with ketamine/xylene. Injection test sites were selected based on known regional lymphatic drainage basins. In each site, a tetrarhodamine-labeled 10,000 MW dextran was injected intradermally. Injection test sites were selected based on known regional lymphatic drainage basins. Imaging was performed with a bioluminescence box equipped with a specialized high resolution CCD camera optimized for low light level imaging of biological materials. The imaging technique was evaluated for its utility to document the anatomy and correlate to the EBD-observed lymphatic system findings.

Results

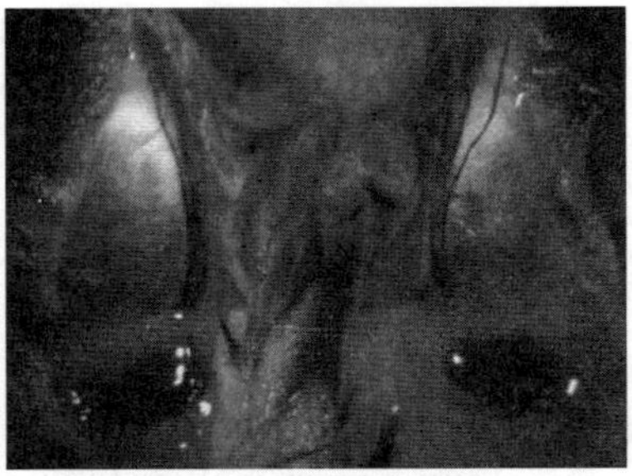

Fig. 1. Ventral aspect of the neck after removal of skin to reveal EBD highlighted lymph nodes and trunks.

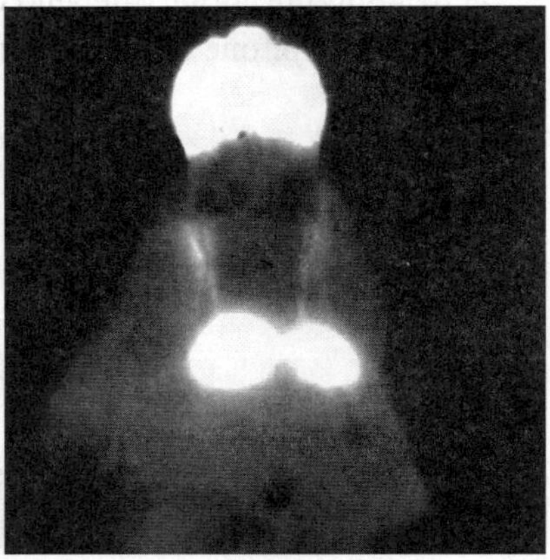

Fig. 2. Ventral aspect of the head and neck of a C57/BL/6 mouse. Image taken using Rhodamine-based fluorescent imaging. Lymph nodes are visible as are large lymphatic trunks.

Injections into the snout in all experimental animals clearly and reliably imaged the lymph channels and nodes. Other lymphatic drainage test sites failed to be imaged reliably. Fig. 2 shows a representative image. This image has enough resolving power to distinguish the two drainage channels on each side. However, this level of resolution was not a consistent finding (data not shown). The anatomy of the cervical lymphatic structures shown by EBD can be seen in Fig. 1.

Conclusion

Rhodamine-based optical imaging promptly, reliably, and dynamically demonstrates the normal anatomy of the superficial cervical lymphatic drainage basin. The minimally invasive nature of this imaging technique allows repeated, serial imaging in a single animal without disrupting the anatomy of the lymphatic trunks and nodes.

A variety of technical modifications may be useful in enhancing image resolution. Refinements of the technique should be useful in delineating the variations and alterations of lymphatic phenotypes.

LYMPHOSCINTIGRAPHY IN WOMEN AFTER BREAST CANCER TREATMENT. CAN IT HELP US BETTER UNDERSTAND PATHOPHYSIOLOGY OF POSTSURGICAL LYMPHEDEMA?

Andrzej Szuba[1], Ryszard Jasinski[2], Diana Jedrzejuk[3], Marek Wozniewski[2], Ryszard Andrzejak[1]

1 Department of Internal Medicine, Occupational Diseases and Hypertension, Wroclaw School of Medicine; 2 Department of Physiotherapy, School of Physical Education.
3 Department of Endocrinology, Wroclaw School of Medicine. Wroclaw, Poland

ABSTRACT

Introduction:
Postmastectomy arm lymphedema is a common problem affecting more than 30% of women after breast cancer treatment and it is still unclear why over 50% of women never develop lymphedema. The aim of this preliminary study was to evaluated lymphatic transport with lymphoscintigraphy in women after breast cancer surgery without lymphedema, and with mild (Ist stage) and severe (IInd stage) of lymphedema. ***Methods:*** 19 women after breast cancer therapy and axillary lymphnode dissection were recruited into the study. 5 women had no arm edema (stage 0, group I), 6 women had mild intermittent edema (stage 1, group 2) and 7 women had severe arm lymphedema (stage 2, group 3). One woman had a history a bilateral mastectomy and lymphnode dissection with no edema of one arm and stage 1 lymphedema of the second arm. Upper extremity lymphoscintigraphy with ^{99m}Tc Nanocoll was done in all patients and qualitative and quantitative analysis was performed. ***Results:*** Lymphatic transport to the axillary lymphnodes was significantly lower in patients with severe lymphedema (stage 2) comparing to patients with stage 1 or no edema. However there was no difference in tracer disappearance rate from the injection site regardless the edema stage (0+1 vs 2) and the patients arm (operated vs not operated). Qualitative analysis revealed accumulation of radiotracer in axillary lymphnodes of operated side in majority of patients in groups 1 and 2 and no patient in group 3. *Conclusion*: Preservation of functional axillary lymphnodes and drainage pathway correlates with

lack of or mild postmastectomy lymphedema. Overall lymphatic transport of the tracer from the injection site is not affected in all groups what suggest presence of efficient collateral circulation or/and peripheral lymphovenous communications.

KEYWORDS: lymphatic transport, postmastectomy lymphedema, axillary lymphnode dissection

INTRODUCTION

Postmastectomy arm lymphedema is a common problem affecting more than 30% of women after breast cancer treatment and despite identification of several risk factors it is still unclear why over 50% of women never develop lymphedema. Known risk factors for postmastectomy lymphedema include radiation therapy, stage of primary disease, obesity and hypertension. However arm lymphedema develops also in women without proven risk factors and, on the other hand presence of all risk factors does not necessary mean that lymphedema will develop. Several other factors may also play important role in pathophysiology of postmastectomy lymphedema including individual lymphatic and venous anatomy, infections, skills and technique of operating surgeon [1,2]. We decided to evaluate lymphatic transport by lymphoscintigraphy also in women after breast cancer surgery without lymphedema.

The aim of this preliminary study was to evaluated lymphatic transport with lymphoscintigraphy in women after breast cancer surgery without lymphedema, and with mild (Ist stage) and severe (IInd stage) of lymphedema.

METHODS

19 women after breast cancer therapy and axillary lymphnode dissection were recruited into the study. All women were examined by one physician and the arm circumferences were measured. Arm lymphedema (Stage 2) was diagnosed if the difference in arm circumference on any level exceeded 2 cm or there was detectable pitting in any area of the arm including hand. Stage 1 lymphedema was diagnosed if the arm circumference difference did not exceeded 2 cm but the patient reported intermittent arm swelling. Within the study group 5 women had no arm edema (stage 0, group I), 6 women had mild intermittent edema (stage 1, group 2) and 7 women had severe arm lymphedema (stage 2, group 3). One woman had a history a bilateral mastectomy and lymphnode dissection with no edema of one arm and stage 1 lymphedema of the second arm.

Upper extremity lymphoscintigraphy with ^{99m}Tc Nanocoll was done in all patients and qualitative and quantitative analysis was performed as desribed earlier [3]. Briefly: bilateral subcutaneous injection of 0.25 mCi of 99mTc-Nanocoll was performed in two interdigital spaces (total dose per patient 1mCi). Images were obtained immediately afterinjection and 2 hours post injection. Quantification of lymphatic transport were The counts in each ROI were measured immediately after injection (ROI^{0}) and 2h later (ROI^{2h})

Following parametres were calculated:

- AR^{2h} : Axillary ratio: operated side /not operated side 2h post injection, as a measure of impairment of lymphatic transport on the operated side
- TD^{2h}: Tracer disappearance rate from the injection site

The study was approved by the Bioethics Committee of the Wroclaw University of Medicine

RESULTS

The demographics of the studied group is presented in Table 1. Lymphatic transport to the axillary lymphnodes presented as axillary ratio after 2h was significantly impaired in women with severe lymphedema (stage 2) as compared to women with stage 1 or no edema (0,15 vs 0,4; p<0,05). However there was no difference in tracer disappearance rate from the injection site regardless the edema stage (0+1 vs 2) and the patient's arm (Table 2).

Table 1. DEMOGRAPHICS

	Group 1 (no edema)	Group 2 (stage 1)	Group 3 (stage 2)
Number of patients	5	6	7
Age (years) [range]	55.2 [47-66]	59.7 [52-72]	64.6 [52-76]
Time from surgery (years) [range]	9.6 [1-16]	7.5 [2-14]	5.1 [3-12]
Radiation therapy	1	3	7*
Chemotherapy	1	2	6*

Table 2. TRACER DISAPPEARANCE RATE (TD^{2h})
Differences are not significant.

	Group 1 (no edema)	Group 2 (stage 1)	Group 3 (stage 2)
Operated side (%)	24,2	28,8	33,3
Healthy side (%)	25,9	30,9	29,7

Qualitative analysis revealed accumulation of radiotracer in axillary lymphnodes of operated side in majority of patients in groups 1 and 2 and no patient in group 3.

DISCUSSION

Functional axillary lymphnodes and drainage pathways were found in women without or with mild, intermittent postmastectomy lymphedema. This findings suggests that presence of functional lymphatic vessels and preservation of lymphatic transport might be critical to avoid arm lymphedema after breast cancer surgery. Further studies are necessary to clarify if the lymphatics are preserved because of anatomical differences within the axillary fossa or due to regrowth of new lymphatic vessels. Further studies are necessary to clarify this issue. Overall epifascial lymphatic transport of the tracer from the injection site is not affected in all groups what is in agreement with earlier reports [4] and may suggest presence of efficient collateral circulation or/and peripheral lymphovenous communications.

Significant limitations of our preliminary study include small number of subjects and demographic differences between studied groups (age, radiation therapy). Larger, prospective study is currently prepared to confirm our preliminary findings.

REFERENCES

1. Segerstrom K, Bjerle P, Graffman S, Nystrom A. Factors that influence the incidence of brachial oedema after treatment of breast cancer. *Scand J Plast Reconstr Surg Hand Surg* 1992; 26(2): 223-7.
2. Szuba A, Rockson SG. Lymphedema: classification, diagnosis and therapy. Vasc Med. 1998;3:145-56.
3. Szuba A, Strauss W, Sirsikar PS, Rockson S: Quantitative radionuclide lymphoscintigraphy predicts outcome of manual lymphatic therapy in breast cancer-related lymphedema of the upper extremity. Nucl Med Commun. 2002 Dec;23(12):1171-5.
4. Stanton AWB, Svensson WE, Mellor RH, Peters AM, Levick JR, Mortimer PS. Differences in lymph drainage between swollen and nonswollen regions in arms with breast-cancer-related lymphoedema. Clin Sci. 2001;101:131–140.

RELATIONSHIPS BETWEEN LIMB SIZE AND COMPOSITION USING OBJECTIVE MEASURES. THEIR ROLE IN PROVIDING BETTER TREATMENT OUTCOMES

A L Moseley[1] & N B Piller[1]

[1]Department of Surgery & Lymphoedema Assessment Clinic, Flinders University & Medical Centre, Adelaide, Australia

Lymphoedema is a complex disorder which progresses from a condition of excess fluid in the tissues to one where there is also fibrotic induration[1-2] and at times adipose proliferation[3-4]. These different stages of lymphoedema often require a number of different measurement techniques and based upon analysis, different and individualised treatment regimes. Both the measuring equipment used and the instigated treatment regime will vary from country to country according to clinician preference and available resources. Discussed here will be validated measuring techniques that can be used to assess the state of the limb and guide its treatment.

One of the easiest, cheapest and traditional ways of measuring a lymphoedematous limb is by tape measure which involves taking circumference measurements at 4cm intervals along the axis of the limb. This not only gives an indication of limb size but can also be converted into limb volume. There are however some inherent problems with this method, with the accuracy of tape measurement being reliant upon operator experience, accurate tape spacing, measurements being taken at right angles and the tension placed upon the tape. The equations used to convert the circumference measurements into volume also often assume that the limb is in the shape of a cone or cylinder, where as lymphoedematous limbs can vary greatly in size and shape[5]. Therefore, as the field of lymphoedema has grown, so too have the techniques to measure it.

One technique that is emerging as a useful measuring tool is multi-frequency bio-impedance, as it can accurately quantify both body composition and fluid content having the ability to distinguish between the gain or loss of fluid from fat and muscle[6]. This reproducible technique[6-8] has previously been used to measure changes in general body composition and ICF/ ECF fluid in a number of conditions including; obesity, pregnancy and kidney dialysis. In particular it has successfully been used in both the detection[9] and management of lymphoedema[10-13]. This makes bio-impedance a reasonable option for following sequential changes in extracellular volume, and for this reason it has been successfully used in lymphoedema management.

A study by Moseley et al (2002) has also shown that the change in leg fluid volume measured by multi-frequency bio-impedance correlates with leg volume as measured via perometery ($r = 0.611$, $p = 0.000$; figure 1a.)[14]. The same research team (2004, unpublished) has also demonstrated a correlation in arm volume change as measured by both bioimpedance and perometry ($r = 0.839$, $p = 0.000$; figure 1b.)[15]. A study by Cornish et al (1996) has also found that multi-frequency bioimpedance was more sensitive than circumferential measurement, both in early lymphoedema diagnosis and in monitoring limb change[16].

In addition, some bio-impedance equipment has the ability to differentiate between fat and muscle, helping the clinician to better determine whether a patient is over weight or obese and the progression of the lymphoedema. The quantification of fat mass is particularly important in lymphoedema management, as increased subcutaneous fat exerts an additional load on the lymphatic system, with obesity also being shown to be a risk factor for the development of lymphoedema[17] and cellulitis[18].

Tonometry measures tissue resistance to pressure, giving an indication of the compliance of the dermis and extent of fibrotic induration[19] in the lymphatic territories which include the calf, anterior and posterior thigh, forearm, upper arm, anterior and posterior thorax. This not only gives an indication of areas of fibrotic induration (and therefore areas that require treatment) but also areas of inadequate lymphatic drainage, as induration will generally occur in areas were there is fluid and protein stasis[2].

Tonometry has been successfully used to monitor tissue changes in response to treatment in a number of clinical trials. Chen et al (1988) followed patients who had undergone lymphatico-venous anastomoses over 18 months and found that tonometry demonstrated tissue softening and correlated well with subjective feelings[20]. Tissue softening as measured by tonometry has also been demonstrated in response to laser therapy[21-22], mechanical and manual lymphatic drainage massage[15], oral Benzopyrones alone[23-24] and in combination with microwave therapy[25]. Importantly this device can also be used to detect deterioration in the tissues when there is no treatment regime implemented or when the regime has ceased.

Our clinic has conducted a pilot study investigating the inter-reliability of the mechanical tonometer which has shown that measurements taken by two trained clinicians do correlate (Moseley & Piller, unpublished)[26]. The tonometer used consisted of a central plunger (1 cm diameter) weighted to a mechanical load of 275.28 gms/cm^2, operating through a footplate that rests on the surrounding skin and which applied a load of 12.2 gms/cm^2. Thus, the plunger applies a differential pressure of 263gms/cm^2, and the degree of penetration of the plunger (arbitrary units) was measured by a micrometer on a linear scale.

Patients presenting at the Lymphoedema Assessment Clinic (Flinders Medical Centre, Adelaide, Australia) had tonometry measurements taken on the lymphatic territories of the lymphoedematous limb by two clinicians following a set protocol (see table 1a.). Results showed that the clinicians' measurements taken in the major lymphatic territories, including the anterior thigh, posterior thigh, calf, forearm and upper arm were strongly and significantly correlated (table 1b.). This demonstrates that the tonometer can be confidently used by different clinicians to reliably measure tissue consistency in different lymphatic territories.

Table 1a. Tonometry measurement protocol*

Territory	**Measurement**
Anterior Thigh	10cms up from the mid-line of the patella
Posterior Thigh	10cms up from the popliteal crease
Calf	10cms down from the popliteal crease
Forearm	10cms down from the cubital fossa
Upper Arm	10cms up from the cubital fossa

* All measurements were taken in the middle of the territory. The second clinician who took the repeat measurement did not take it exactly on the same point as the tonometer can push fluid out of the local area. Hence, using the exact same measurement point would have yielded an inaccurate reading. All readings were recorded by a third, independent clinician.

Table 1b. Inter-relater correlations for tonometry measurements of different lymphatic territories.

Territory	**Correlation**	**p =**
Anterior Thigh	0.902	0.000
Posterior Thigh	0.888	0.000
Calf	0.942	0.000
Forearm	0.966	0.007
Upper Arm	0.982	0.003

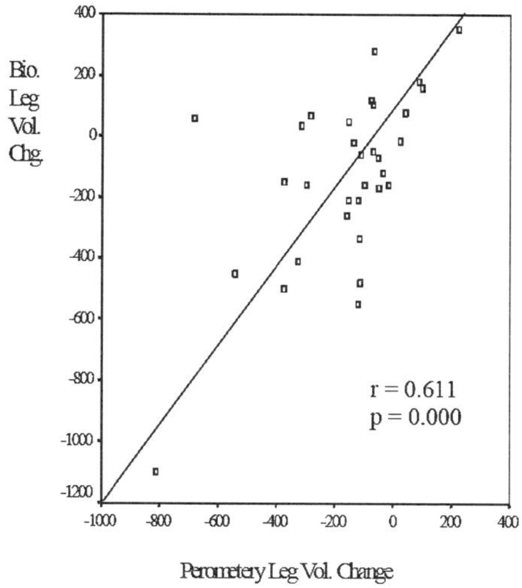

Figure 1a. Correlation between change in arm volume as measured by bioimpedance & perometry.

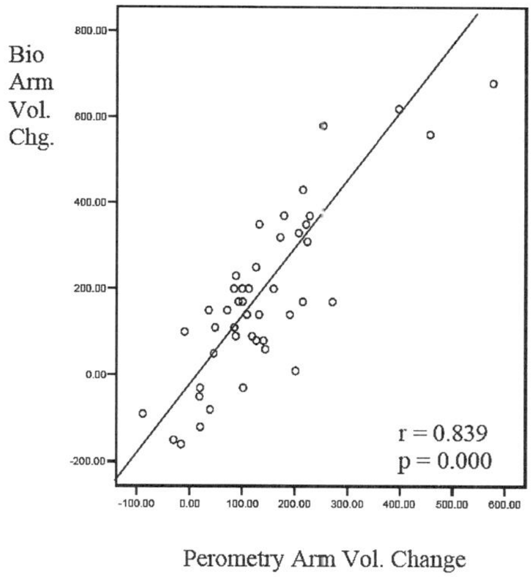

Figure 1b. Correlation between change in leg volume as measured by bioimpedance & perometry.

Objectively determining limb volume, composition and tissue compliance is important in lymphoedema as it establishes limb progression, treatment regimes and the response to the instigated regime. Ascertaining and monitoring body composition is also important as obesity certainly contributes to the morbidity of lymphoedema and is an additional component which needs to be treated and controlled. This is supported by studies which have shown that dietary modification and weight loss can actually benefit lymphoedematous limbs[27-28].

Of course these objective measures should not be considered alone, but in concert with quality of life (QOL) indicators and subjective symptom ratings, both of which can be determined by the use of rating scales such as the Likert or Visual Analogue Scales. These subjective indicators, when compared with the objective measurements will indicate whether objective improvements correlate with subjective ones or whether the instigated therapy needs to be modified as it has had no subjective benefits as reported by the patient. Consideration of both the objective and subjective domains will help in establishing treatment regimes that are more likely to be beneficial and complied to by the patient, as patient compliance is more likely to occur with regimes that result in both limb and subjective improvements.

In both the clinical and research setting it is vital that measuring equipment is used that is both reliable and validated so that both the patient and the lymphademated limb can be accurately assessed, treated and monitored. Measurement techniques such a multi-frequency bioimpedance can be used to monitor limb fluid and volume in additional to already established techniques such as perometery, with both forms of measurement being shown to correlate. Multi-frequency bioimpedance can also be used to monitor body composition, including fat mass which is becoming increasingly more important to control in lymphoedematous conditions. Tonometry has been shown to monitor tissue consistency in a number of clinical trials and to have clinician inter-reliability. These objective measurement techniques can be confidently used to accurately measure and quantify the lymphoedematous limb and in combination with subjective indicators, monitor both progression and response to instigated therapies.

References

1. Piller N & Clodius L. Lymphoedema of the rabbit ear following partial and complete lymphatic blockade; its effects on fibrotic development, enzyme types and their activity levels. Brit J Exper Pathol. 1978, 59(3):319-26
2. Knight KR, Collopy PA, McCann JJ, Vanderkolk CA, Coe SA, Barton RM, Chen HC & O'Brien B. Protein metabolism and fibrosis in experimental canine obstructive lymphedema. J Lab Clin Med Nov 1987 10(5): 558-566.
3. Casley-Smith JR. Clodius L & Piller NB. Tissue changes in chronic experimental lymphoedema in dogs. Lymphology. Sep 1980, 13(3):130-41
4. Brorson H. Liposuction in arm lymphedema treatment. Scand J Surg, 2003,92(4):287-95
5. Stanton A W B, Badger C & Sitzia J, Non-invasive assessment of the lymphedematous limb. Lymphology 2000 33: 122-35
6. Mikes D, Cha B, Dym C et al. Bioelectrical impedance analysis revisited. *Lymphology* 1999; **32** (4): 157-65
7. Kichula C, Sunyong S, Cheongmin S et al. Evaluation of segmental bioelectrical impedance analysis (SBIA) for measuring muscle distribution. *J Ichper* 1997; 11-14
8. Segal K, Gutin B, Presta E et al. Estimation of human body composition by electrical impedance methods: a comparative study. *Amer Physiol Soc* 1985; **85**: 1565, 1571
9. Hawes C, Borbasi S, Chapman Y, Piller NB, O'Brien N & DeCrespigny C. Our interest is swelling – a collaborative venture to establish the world's first free public screening for lymphoedema. *Collegian*, 2002; **9**(1): 23-6.
10. Moseley A, Piller N, Carati C & Esterman A. The Sun Ancon Chi Machine Aerobic Exerciser: a new patient focused, home based therapy for people with chronic secondary leg lymphoedema. *Lymphology,* June 2004, **37**: 53-61
11. Box RC. Reul-Hirche HM. Bullock-Saxton JE. Furnival CM. Physiotherapy after breast cancer surgery: results of a randomised controlled study to minimise lymphoedema. *Breast Cancer Res & Treat.* Sep 2002; **75**(1):51-64,
12. Ward L, Bunce I, Cornish B et al Multi-frequency bioelectrical impedance augments the diagnosis and management of lymphoedema

in post-mastectomy patients. *Euro J Clin Invest* 1992; **22**: 751-54

13. Watanbe R, Miura A, Inoue K et al Evaluation of leg edema using a multifrequency impedance meter in patients with lymphatic obstruction. Lymphology 1989; 22: 85-92
14. Moseley A, Piller N & Caratic C Piller N & Carati C. Combined opto-electronic perometry and bioimpedance to measure objectively the effectiveness of a new treatment intervention for chronic secondary leg lymphoedema. Lymphology; 2002, 35: 136-143
15. Piller N, Moseley A, Esplin M & Douglass J. 2004, A randomised trial of the effectiveness of manual lymphatic drainage and machine based massage on post mastectomy arm lymphoedema. Unpublished data.
16. Cornish B, Chapman M, Hirst C et al Early diagnosis of lymphedema using multifrequency bioimpedance. Lymphology 2001; 34(1): 2-11
17. Johansson K, Ohlsson K, Ingvar C, Albertsson M & Ekdahl C. Factors associated with the development of arm lymphedema following breast cancer treatment: a match pair case-control study.Lymphology. Jun 2002 35(2):59-71
18. Dupuy A, Benchikhi H, Roujeau JC, Bernard P, Vaillant L, Chosidow O, Sassolas B, Guillaume JC, Grob JJ & Bastuji-Garin S. Risk factors for erysipelas of the leg (cellulitis): case-control study. BMJ, Jun 1999, 318(7198):1591-4
19. Clodius L, Deak I, Piller N. A new instrument for the evaluation of tissue tonometry in lymphedema. Lymphology. 1976;9:1–5.
20. Chen HC, O'Brien BM, Pribaz JJ & Roberts AH. The use of tonometry in the assessment of upper extremity lymphoedema. British Journal of Plastic Surgery. Jul 1988, 41(4):399-402.
21. Carati CJ, Anderson SN, Gannon BJ & Piller NB Treatment of postmastectomy lymphedema with low-level laser therapy. Cancer Sep 2003 98(6): 1114-1122
22. Piller, NB & Thelander A Low level laser therapy: A cost effective treatment to reduce post mastectomy lymphoedema. Lymphology 29 (suupl 1): 297-300
23. Piller NB. Morgan RG. Casley-Smith JR. A double-blind, cross-over trial of O-(beta-hydroxyethyl) -rutosides (benzo-pyrones) in the treatment of lymphoedema of the arms and legs. British Journal of Plastic Surgery. 41(1):20-7, 1988 Jan.
24. Piller NB & Clodius L. The use of a tissue tonometer as a diagnostic aid in extremity lymphoedema: a determination of its conservative treatment with benzo-pyrones. Lymphology. 9(4):127-32, Dec 1976.
25. Chang TS. Gan JL. Fu KD. Huang WY. The use of 5,6 benzo-[alpha]-pyrone (coumarin) and heating by microwaves in the treatment of chronic lymphedema of the legs. Lymphology. 29(3):106-11, 1996 Sep.
26. Moseley A & Piller N. A pilot study of the inter-reliability of the mechanical tonometer. Unpublished.
27. Soria P. Cuesta A. Romero H. Martinez FJ. Sastre A. Dietary treatment of lymphedema by restriction of long-chain triglycerides. Angiology. 45(8):703-7, 1994 Aug.
28. Freilich G, Parbhoo S, Bennett H & Keenan C Obesity, weight loss and lymphoedema. Progress in Lymphology, 2004, 37(suppl): 277-83

Chapter 5
Clinics in Lymphology

DYSPLASIA OF THE TORACIC DUCT, CYSTERNA CHILI AND CHYLIFEROUS VESSELS WITH CHYLOUS PERITONITES

Campisi Corradino[1], MD, Eretta Costantino[1], MD, Pertile Davide[1], MD, Campisi Corrado[1], MS, Bellini Carlo[4], MD, Macciò Alberto[1], MD, Fulcheri Ezio[2], MD, Accogli Susanna[3], PT, Boccardo Francesco[1], MD, PhD

[1]Department of Surgery – Unit of Lymphatic Surgery and Microsurgery
[2]Institute of Pathological Anatomy
[3]Rehabilitation Unit
S. Martino Hospital – University of Genoa, Italy
[4]Unit of Neonatal Pathology – G.Gaslini Institute, Genoa, Italy

INTRODUCTION

From a nosographic point of view, the definition of 'chylous peritonitis' is substantially the same as 'chyloperitoneum', namely a disease caused by the leak of intestinal lymph - clinically called 'chylous'. It has a peculiarly milky colour, due to a dense and rich concentration of chylomicrons after long-chain fat and triglyceride absorption from intestinal lymph vessels or collectors. These vessels which, for their specific function, are called 'chyliferous' vessels, are located under the diaphragm and in the retro and intra-peritoneal compartment.

According to the by now conventional description of this disease made by Gruwetz[4] around thirty years ago, chyloperitoneum is classified into: 1) an acute form, also called 'chylous peritonitis', which has generally its onset after a heavy and specially fat meal, with acute pain and abdominal defence reaction, and 2) a 'sub-acute' or chronic form, with a more subtle, hence more insidious, clinical onset, due to a much slower and progressive chylous leak.

The first systematic investigations on both animals and human cadavers were originally conducted by Gaspare Aselli[5] and Jean Pecquet[6] back in the 17th century: They set up the basis for the excellent iconographic description of the lymphatic circulation system made in the following century by Paolo Mascagni[7]. However, the first clinical case of chyloperitoneum following an abdominal trauma was allegedly described by J. De Diemerbroeck[8] in 1685, followed by another case reported by R. Morton[9] four years later, which was caused by tubercular lymphoadenitis obstructing the thoracic duct and associated with chylothorax.

A recent detailed review of the by now numerous cases reported in the literature since then was published in 2000 by O. Aalami and coll.[10] in "Surgery". Further, we should also mention the outstanding investigations and experiences made by M. Serveuille[11], J.B. Kinmoth[12] and G. Gruwez[13] for their nosographic value. Personally, however, I believe that the actual incidence of this disease has been widely underestimated, since in hospital dismissal forms, diagnoses of 'chyloperitoneum, chylous ascitis or chylous peritonitis' are not normally reported as primary diseases, but as associated pathologies or complications.

In any case, even considering the above mentioned reservations, the incidence rate of chyloperitoneum is still today reckoned to be of 1 case every 50,000 hospitalised patients.

ETIOPATHOGENESIS AND PHYSIOPATHOLOGY OF CHYLOPERITONEUM

Chyloperitoneum may be 'primary' or 'secondary', depending on whether its root cause can be detected. Even in its more specifically clinical expression of 'chylous peritonitis', especially in children or young adults, its etiology is basically correlated with congenital dysplasic alterations and more or less extended malformations of chyliferous vessels, of the chylous cyst, and/or of the thoracic duct, as well as of loco-regional lymph nodes in this district or in affected districts. These forms are commonly considered to have a so called 'primary' etiogenesis and account for approximately 70% of all cases. Conversely, 'secondary' forms due to mechanical causes or obstructions of various nature, including trauma, have a much less important statistical value.

However, it should be pointed out that, as presented later on in this presentation, from a physiopathological point of view, malformation-related dysplasic alterations act as actual obstacles to antigravity lymph drainage, just like mechanical obstruction forms proper.

Among the forms of 'secondary' chylous leak, we should mention those found in tropical and subtropical regions that are endemically affected by *Filaria Bancrofti* parasite, namely, more specifically, India, Africa, and North-West Latin America. Due to sanitary-nutritional reasons, also related to poor socio-economic conditions of the native populations, these diseases record a very high incidence and are generally followed by post-tubercular forms, that are also promoted by the same poor socio-economic living conditions mentioned above for filariasis.

Conversely, in countries that, from a socio-economic point of view, are more developed, secondary chyloperitoneum is generally found as sub-acute or chronic chylous leak (chylous ascites) occurring most commonly as a consequence of:

- primary invasive or infiltrating malignant tumours, or

malignant lymphomas with abdominal and/or thoracic-madiastinal localisation;
- lymph node metastases;
- traumas;
- surgery of the thoracic-abdominal aorta (accidental lesion of iuxta-cisternal lymph vessels, of the chylous cyst or of the thoracic duct) or involving extensive retroperitoneal lymph node resections.

Then, there is a whole range of likely causes of secondary chyloperitoneum, from acute or chronic pericarditis, to acute or chronic pancreatitis, from retroperitoneal fibrosis to sarcoidosis, etc. All of them challenge the diagnostic acumen and therapeutic skills of clinicians, who have the hard task of handling these complex and difficult cases.

Conversely, with regard to 'primary' chyloperitoneum, what M. Servelle[11] first stated in 1981 is still valid, namely " ... il n'existe pas de chylopéritoine spontané sans malformation congénitale des chyliférese".

A malformation affecting the thoracic duct, Pecquet cyst, and/or chyliferous vessels underlines the previously mentioned physiopathological concept, but actually means that there is a significant obstacle to lymph drainage and, in particular, to intestinal drainage. Therefore, chyliferous vessels along the walls of the small intestine and of the mesentery become significantly dilated and abnormally stretched due to chylous stasis. The disease also features lymphatic megacollectors with more or less extensive chylous lymphangiectasia, often associated with lymphangiomiomatosis (Fig. 1)[15].

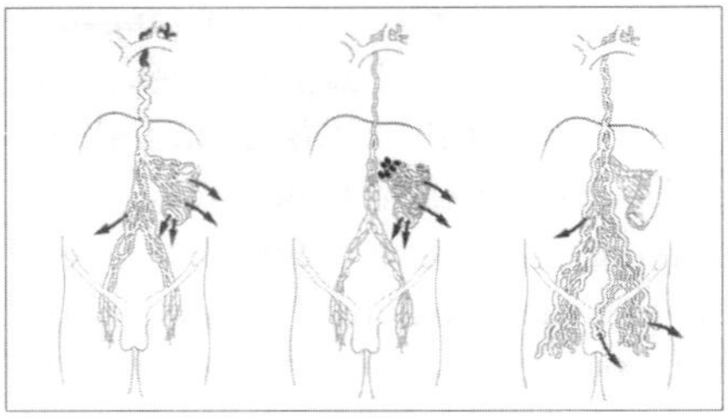

Fig. 1. Some patterns of chylous leak inside the abdominal cavity, following the break of chyliferous megalymphatics in one or two steps[15].

Now, looking at their position, they are not only located right below the visceral peritoneal layer with a mesh-like arrangement, but also throughout the small intestine and more specifically at the level of intestinal villi. Hence, dysplasic chyliferous mega-lymphatics may break due to a localised swelling (the so called 'mesentery chylous cyst'), or anywhere along the wall of an extremely ectasic collector, sometimes through a two-step process, namely, once the peritoneum is opened up by chylous with subsequent development of a 'chyloma', chylous begins to flow into the abdominal cavity. Also, in other cases, the chyliferous vessel at the centre of the villus breaks into the intestinal lumen, thus causing the loss of proteins, lipids, lipoproteins, and even calcium and glucose, which lead to metabolic disorders that are typical of so called 'Protein Losing Enteropathy' (PLE) (Fig. 2).

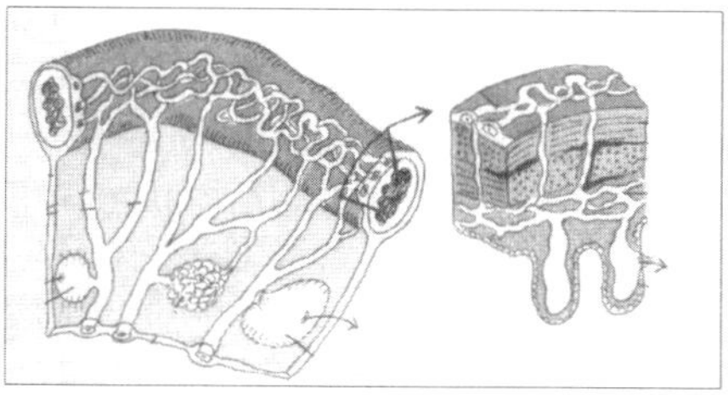

Fig. 2. The arrow points to the rupture of the central lymph vessel of the intestinal lumen villus; 'Protein Losing Enteropathy' (PLE)

Owing to the direct link between the septic intestinal environment and the inner part of chyliferous vessels, there may be recurrent attacks of acute lymphangitis and acute mesenteric lympho-angioadenitis which, in some cases, may even lead to septic shock or, at best, to a chronic process, while triggering a vicious circle with further worsening of the intestinal lymphatic drainage.

Chyloperitoneum and protein losing enteropathy may often be combined. Also, we should not forget that, apart from intestinal lymphatics, also lumbar lymphatics - collecting the lymph from the lower limbs, external genitalia, intra-abdominal organs, kidneys, adrenal gland, and the abdominal wall - flow into the chylous cyst. Further, considering the thoracic-mediastinal catchment basin of the thoracic duct and that lymphatic dysplasia can affect even one or more extra-abdominal districts, due to strange malformation combinations, chyloperitoneum can also be associated with a whole range of different pathologic pictures listed below (Fig. 3)[1]:

- mono or bilateral *chylothorax*
- *chylous cyst, mediastinal chyloma or chylomediastinum*
- *chylopericardium*
- *chyluria*
- *chylo-colpometrorrhea*
- *chylodema* of external genitalia and/or of one or both lower limbs, with *chylo-lymphostatic verrucosis* and subsequent chylo-lymphorrhea;
- *chylous joint effusion*

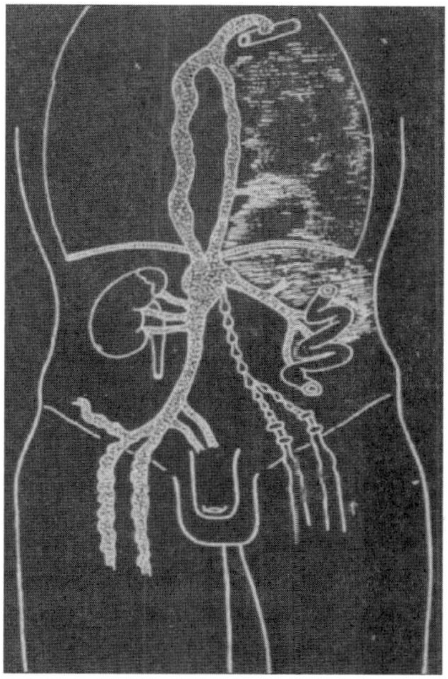

Fig. 3. Several bizarre anatomic clinical and topographic associations of dysplasia of chyliferous vessels, thoracic duct and chylous cyst, including chyloperitoneum.

The wide ranging extension of the above malformations and the complexity of their association with dysplasia of chylo-lymphatic vessels, thoracic duct, and chylous cyst explain why, in the newborn, sometimes these conditions affecting multiple-districts are incompatible with life. Further, upon clinical onset of the most severe cases, effective treatment may be difficult to achieve later in life, thus leading to more or less complex prognostic implications involving *'quoad valetudinem'* as well as *'quoad vitam'* issues.

CLINICS, LABORATORY AND INSTRUMENTAL DIAGNOSTICS

In case of an isolated picture of chyloperitoneum, it should be pointed out that, owing to the 'primary' nature of the disease, specially in children and young adults, the presence of more or less extended cutaneous hemangiomas in the chest or the limbs - normally flat, of a 'milk and coffee' or 'Port wine' colour - may be a sign of the disease. No familiarity has yet been confirmed for these malformations.

Obviously enough, information about the *patient's medical history* and a *clinical examination* are fundamental for diagnosis and must be conducted in the most accurate possible way.

According to some Authors, the definition of 'acute chylous peritonitis' is not accurate, since pain is caused by the quick swelling related to chylous leak into the intra-peritoneum, rather than to direct chylous action irritating the peritoneum. However, in our own experience and in the experience of many other authoritative Authors [11,12,13], intra-operative findings as well as peritoneal biopsies have shown the presence of a more or less significant acute inflammation process. This would confirm the typical clinical picture of 'acute abdomen' which, in 50% of cases, could initially mislead to wrong diagnoses of 'perforated gastro-duodenal ulcer', 'acute appendicitis', or acute 'cholecystitis'.

These acute forms are unlikely to be complicated by septic shock.

For a proper differential diagnosis, *paracentesis* is fundamental: this procedure allows to verify the nature of effusion and confirm clinical and imaging (US and CT) results. It is generally employed to confirm clinical assumptions, while lab tests are useful to show the presence of leukocytosis and related lymphopenia.

Subacute and chronic forms are more subtle, where chylous leak is slow and progressive, with practically no pain, which the patient feels as an annoyance or burden due to abdominal distension. Distension which, in turn, raises the diaphragm, with subsequent significant breathing capacity reduction and related subjective and objective symptoms. Vomiting is frequent in children.

In case of slow chylous leak, adult patients show a higher adjustment capacity, until some sort of spontaneous, probably unstable balance is reached, even for longer periods (weeks, months, even years), depending on the severity and cause of chyloperitoneum.

In the majority of cases, malnutrition is present, with more or less significant hypoproteinemia - specially affecting the albumin fraction - and weight loss. Respiratory problems and steatorrhea are also often present, in PLE associated forms.

The chylous nature of the effusion can be confirmed not only from its peculiar milky colour, but also by chemical analysis, which will show a high fat concentration (cholesterol, lipoproteins, chylomicrons).

Specially in acute onset forms, bacteriological analysis, also coupled with an antibiogram, is useful, in order to implement a targeted antibiotic therapy, if necessary.

SURGICAL TIMING

In our opinion, all the above described pictures, even in the case of acute onset, should not undergo surgery too quickly, until at least a proper diagnosis has been made as to the nature and site of the likely

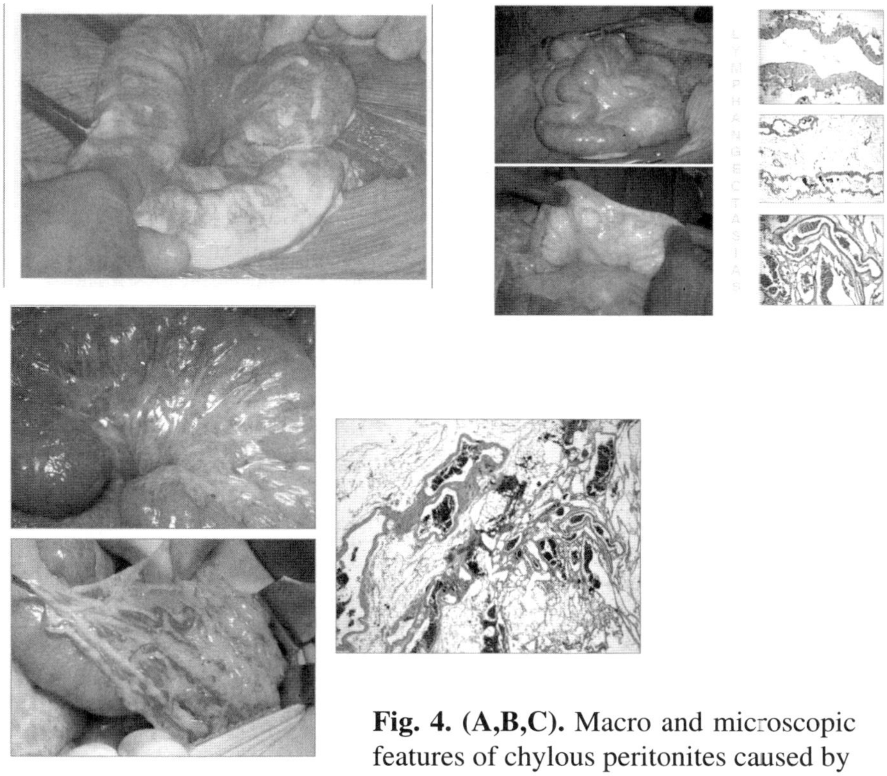

Fig. 4. (A,B,C). Macro and microscopic features of chylous peritonites caused by chylo-lymphangio-adenodysplasia.

leak. During this period, the patient must be properly metabolically compensated, through an appropriate diet, with protein integration and limited lipid input confined only to medium chain triglycerides (MCT). As a matter of fact, in these cases MCTs, rather than being absorbed through intestinal chyliferous lymphatic roots, follow the portal root pathway.

For a quick reinstatement of a proper metabolic balance, total parenteral feeding (TPF) is recommended early on, in order to significantly limit the chylous leak volume.

Further, in this phase of 'initial approach' to this complex problem, specially in acute and subacute onset cases, a *videolaparoscopy* can be useful, also in order to help in the proper positioning of one or more peritoneal drains, having the correct size. These drains will be used to drain the effusion in one or more steps, depending on its volume, while being careful not to cause 'ex vacuo' haemorrhages and keeping in mind that chylous is a dense fluid, hence this procedure is to be preferred over the US or CT guided positioning of smaller drains, which are more likely to get clogged with time.

Once in place, these drains can be used 'on demand', also for washings with a Trémolliéres sterile solution (concentrated lactic acid) combined with an antibiotic (250-500 mg of sodium rifamicine). The sclerotizing effect of this drug has proved beneficial, specially in the treatment of post-surgical chyloperitoneum (mostly occurring after lymph node resections performed close to the mesentery root). Also, in our experience, in these cases of surgical origin where the onset of chylorrhagia occurs in the early days after surgery and can be observed through the same drains placed upon surgery completion, in the great majority of cases, washing with Trémolliéres associated with a rigorous total parenteral feeding has proved to be successful in solving this condition in two, maximum three weeks. Actually, the great majority of chylorrhagia cases were due to extended lymphadenectomy in kidney cancer surgery. In this way, timely treatment of chylorrhagia as a post-operative complication will help prevent the onset of secondary chyloperitoneum. This is a likely complication in these types of oncological surgery, specially when abdominal drains are removed too early, also because, as mentioned above, in the first week after surgery, they are useful 'sensors' for the recognition and prompt treatment of chylorrhagia.

Conversely, primary chyloperitoneum caused by dysplasia or malformations is a much more complex condition. An accurate diagnostic assessment is required for its proper treatment, depending on associated clinical pictures, namely:

- *$^{51}CrCl_3$ test*, to gain evidence of any major abdominal protein leak (> 2% of fecal radioisotope disposal within 5 days following intravenous - 30 μ Ci - administration of this substance. Specially in children, care must be paid not to mix feces with urine, since 30% of this isotope is disposed in the urine).

- *Small intestine barium enema*, to demonstrate any remarkable thickening due to lymphedema, which is generally greater in the submucosa of the intestinal wall, and subsequent protrusion of intestinal folds and villi;
- *Small intestine endoscopy,* in particular with biopsy of the duodenum-jejunum segment, which will show significantly stretched chyliferous vessels at the centre of villi (Fig. 5)[15];

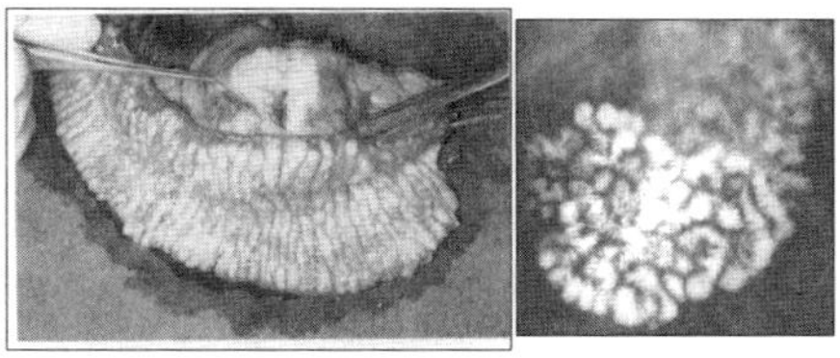

Fig. 5. Typical anatomic-clinical and radiological pictures of Protein Losing Enteropathy (PLE)[16].

- *Lymphoscintigraphy*, with evidence not only of tracer leak into the peritoneal cavity, but also of a more or less severe dysplasia involving also other compartments, like external genitalia and the lower limbs (Fig. 6). This method is an excellent tool to assess microsurgery outcome (as we will better illustrate here below);

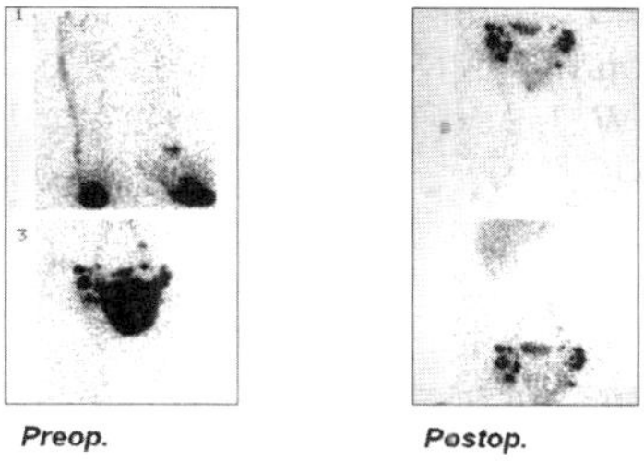

Fig. 6. Lymphoscintigraphic pictures, before and after microsurgery, of gravitation chylous reflux, also involving external genitalia and the lower limbs (please note the significant reflux reduction after microsurgery).

- Standard *lymphangiography* (with liposoluble ultrafluid contrast medium injected with microsurgical technique after isolation and incannulation of the lymphatics of the extensor digitorum muscle. If coupled with a CT scan, it allows a more accurate assessment of disease extension, as well of the site of the obstacle and of chylous leak source;

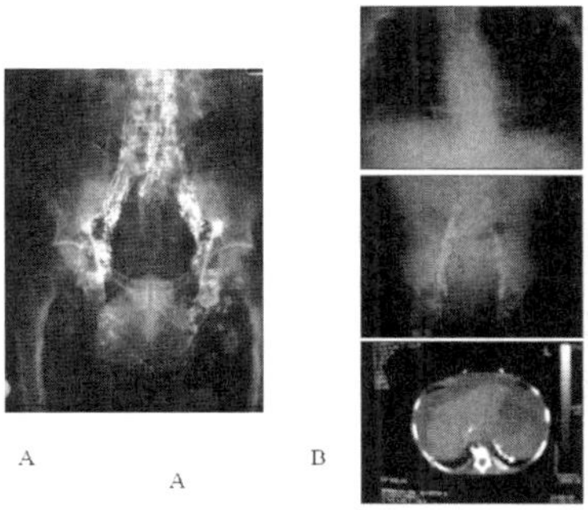

Fig. 7. (A and B). Lymphangiography is still a fundamental investigation method in the diagnosis of dysplasia of chyliferous vessel, the 'cisterna chyli' and the thoracic duct, especially when associated with CT scan (B).

- *Magnetic resonance* (Fig. 8) which, by digital subtraction method of the fatty tissue, will allow the get a more in-depth demonstration of dysplasia-related impairment of the lymph vessels (lymphangio-MR).

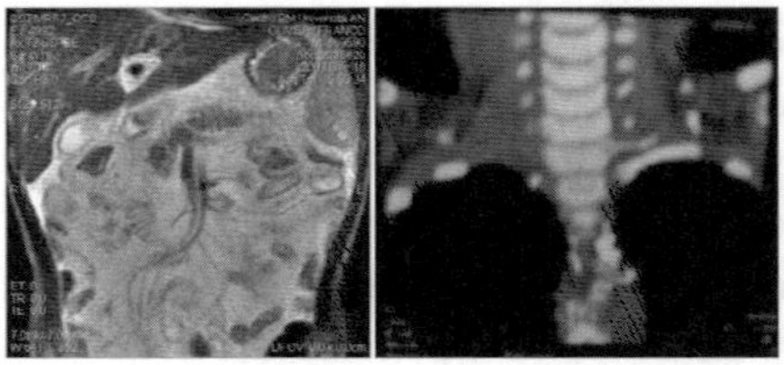

A B

Fig. 8. (A and B). Magnetic resonance is often a useful complement in the diagnosis of this disease.

In order to demonstrate a concurrent Protein Losing Enteropathy (PLE), *albumin labelled (^{99m} Tc) scintigraphy* may be quite useful for a more complete diagnosis. PLE can be observed inside the intestinal lumen in scans taken 1-24 hours after intravenous administration of 740 mBq.

Finally, in case of more complex pictures associated with more or less widespread hemo-angiodysplasia, also *selective digital angiography* of the compartments affected by vascular visceral and/or peripheral malformation, and *angio-CT* are advantageous complements to the above mentioned instrumental diagnostic process.

At this point, surgical timing will be defined, to be designed also on the outcome of the various conservative treatments already implemented, namely: hyper-protein and hypo-lipidic diet (e.g. exclusively based on medium-chain fats and triglycerides) and TPN; proper antibiotic protection, which is necessary to prevent and treat the not so rare septic complications of this disease; and even seriated paracentesis, which mainly aims at gradual chylous effusion drainage and subsequent reduction in intra-abdominal pressure.

In this as well as in subsequent treatment phases, the - intravenous, intramuscular, and subcutaneous, respectively - administration of somatostatin or ocreotide can be quite useful. Both substances have proved successful in reducing chylous effusion - in some cases also in a remarkable way - and even as anti-proliferation agents of vascular and, more specifically, lymphatic cells and endothelia (N. Browse, G. Burnard and P. Mortimer, 2003[15]).

Therefore, surgery will be designed, on a case by case basis, depending on the primary or secondary nature of chylous effusion, clinical severity, and the number of chylous leaks. Hence, through different associations, the following types of surgery procedures can be performed to treat this disease:

- Chyloperitoneous *drainage*;
- *Identification* of the site or sites of chylorrhagy;
- *Removal* of chylous cysts and/or chylomas;
- *Resection* of lymphangiectasic - lymphangiodysplasic tissue,

which could also be combined with other 'ad hoc' solutions;

- *"Spaced-out" antigravity ligatures* of incompetent and ectasic chyliferous lymphatic vessels, in order to treat gravitation chylous reflux - following the teachings of Servelle and Tosatti - and if necessary also
- *CO_2 -Laser.* When applied at low power, it has a welding effect already proven on lymphatics, as well as on many other tissues and blood vessels up to one millimetre diameter;
- *Derivative* (*lymphatic-venous anastomosis*) or *reconstructive* (*lymphatic-venous-lymphatic plasty*) *microsurgery*: When applicable, its efficacy has been extensively proven by our personal experience and by other authors as well. With these techniques, functional solutions can be fashioned allowing for anti-gravitation discharge into lumbar, iliac-pelvic, and inguinal lymph nodes - depending on each single case - and, when suitable, ectasic collectors can be harvested.
- In the most difficult cases and those affected by constant recurrences, a *peritoneal-jugular shunt* (Denver, Le Veen), which, however, has some major limitations in children.

In extreme cases, entero-mesentery lymphangiectasia may be so severe that a full resection of the intestinal segment mostly affected by dysplasia may be required.

Videolaparoscopy as a support to *laparotomy* - when the former cannot be performed as an exclusive procedure - and often associated with Co_2 Laser assisted microsurgery - is the most successful therapeutical approach so far, as also demonstrated by our own experience (Table I, II, and III).

For a better recognition of chyliferous vessels, the administration of a fatty meal (60 g of butter in a cup of milk) can be useful, when taken by the patient 4-5 hours before surgery, according to the teachings of Servelle.

In Figures 9-12, taken from our own surgical case series, surgical procedures are presented that have proved most successful and effective in the treatment of chylous peritonitis.

Table I. Our clinical experience.

Men	14
Women	2

Adults	10
Children	6

Table II. Clinical registry of surgical cases in adults (10) and children (6).

ADULTS

Chylous peritonitis (CP)	4
CP+ chylous reflux+ lymphangiectasia+ lymphochyloedema of the lower limbs and external genitalia	2
CP+chylothorax	1
CP+ chylous reflux+ iliac-pelvic lymphangiectasia+lymphangiomatosis	1
CP+ chylous reflux+ inguinal lymphangiectasia+lymphangiomatosis	1
CP+spontaneous rupture of the thoracic duct+chylothorax+lymphochyloedema of the breast and of the left arm	1

CHILDREN

CP + chyluria	1
CP+ PLE + retroperitoneal lymphangiectasia + chylous cyst and thoracic duct dysplasia	1
CP+lymphedema of the left arm+PLE	1
CP+ peritoneal-vaginal duct patency and chylocele	1
CP+ chylous reflux+ lymphochyledema of the lower limbs and external genitalia	1
CP+chylopericardium	1

Table III. Summary of therapies and obtained results.

Regression of chyloperitoneum (5 year follow-up) in 15 out of 16 patients.
Laparotomic approach associated with resection and on demand Co_2Laser
Significant reduction of chylothorax after disappearance of chyloperitoneum
Recurrent chyloperitoneum treated with peritoneal-jugular shunt.

In conclusion, I think I have to point out, quite humbly, that, considering the etiopathogenesis as well as the nature and complexity of chyloperitoneum, the treatment of these difficult pictures and its outcome significantly depend on the skills and hands of physicians/surgeons and on the technology of available equipment. For this reason, it is highly recommended that these patients be referred to the few centres that have a specific surgical experience in the treatment of this disease.

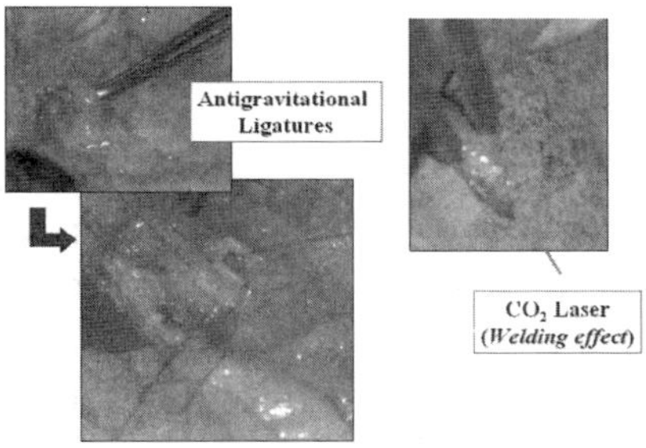

Fig. 9. Laser-assisted anti-gravitation ligatures of dilated and incompetent collectors.

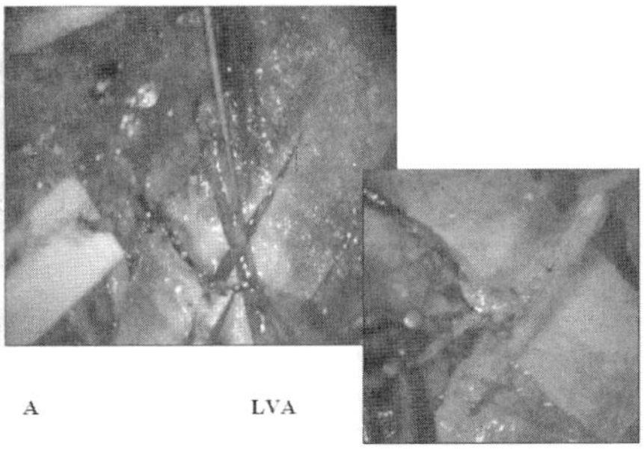

Fig. 10A. Derivative (lymphatic-venous anastomosis LVA) microsurgery.

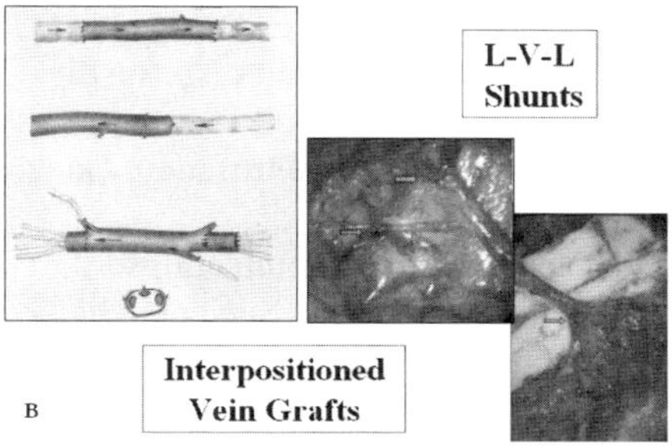

Fig. 10B. Reconstructive (lymphatic-venous-lymphatic plasty - LVLA) microsurgery.

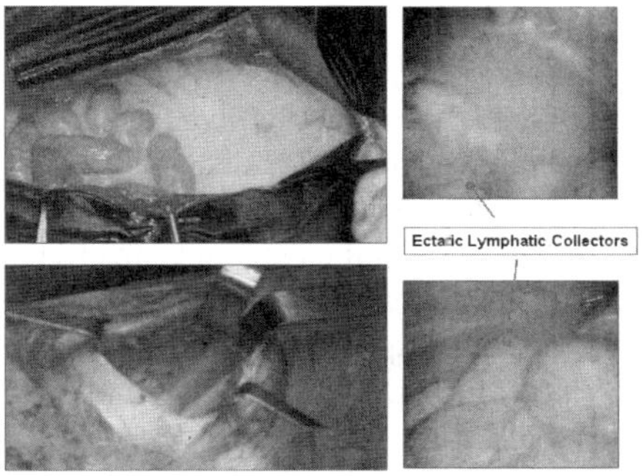

Fig. 11. Videolaparoscopy and laparotomy pictures of acute chyloperitoneum.

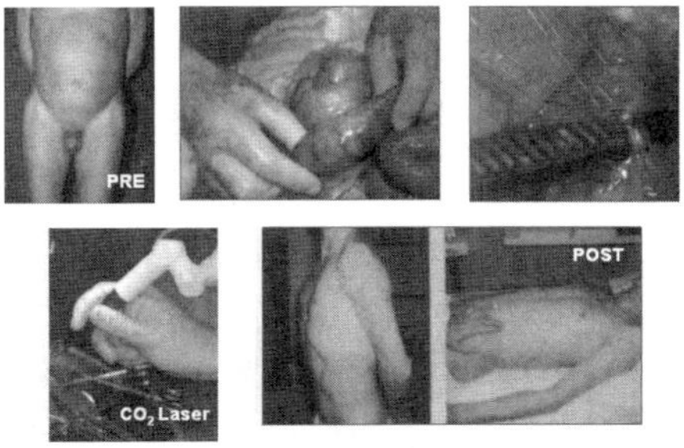

Fig. 12. Chyloperitoneum treated with peritoneum-jugular shunt.

REFERENCES

1. Tosatti E, Cariati E, De Mauro D, Ricco G. Linfonodi, cisterna di Pecquet e dinamica antigravitazionale linfatica. Gazz. Sanit., 3:83, 1964.
2. Casaccia M. Peritoniti chilose. Atti VI Congresso della Società Italiana di Chirurgia d'Urgenza (SICU), Padova, 1977.
3. Casaccia M, Campisi C. Chyloedèmes. Journal des Maladies Vasculaires, 13:145-153, 1988.
4. Gruwez J., Dive C, Vyncke G, Baert A, Lacquet A, Vanden Brouck J, Tallegaert W. Les eddusions chyleuses. VI Int. Congress of Angiol., Barcellona, 1967.
5. Aselli G. De lactibus sive lacteis venis. Milano, G.B.Bidelli, 1627.
6. Pecquet J. Experimenta nova anatomica quibus incognitum chyli receptaculum, et ab eo per thoracem in ramos uque subclavis vasa lactea deferguntur. Paris, S&G Carmoisy, 1651.
7. Mascagni P. Vasorum lymphaticorum corporis humani historia et ichnographia. Siena, Pazzini Carli, 1787.
8. De Diemerbroeck I. Opera omnia anatomica et medica. Utrecht, Dreunen, 1685.
9. Morton R. Phythysiologica sen exertationes de phythysi. Lib. I. London, Smith, 1689.
10. Aalami OO, Allen DB, Organ CH Jr. Chylous ascites: a collective review. Surgery 2000; 128:761-78.
11. Servelle M, Noguès C. The chyliferous vessels. Expansion Scientifique Francaise, Paris, 1981.
12. Kinmonth JB. The lymphatics. Surgery, lymphography and diseases of the chyle and lymph systems. E.Arnold, London, 1982.
13. Gruwez J. Lymphoedema, basic mechanism, clinical problems, indications for therapy. Chylous reflux. ISL Congress, Tucson, Arizona, 1973.
14. Press OW, Press NO, Kaufmann SD. Evaluation and management of chylous ascites. Annals of Internal Medicine 1982; 96:358-64.
15. Browse N, Burnand KG, Mortimer PS. Diseases of the lymphatics. Arnold, London, 2003.
16. Campisi C, Boccardo F. Lymphedema and microsurgery. Microsurgery 2002;22:74-80.

TWO CASES OF SEVERE LYMPHORRHEA TREATED WITH CILOSTAZOL

M. Masuzawa, A. Maeda, M. Masuzawa, T. Miyata, K. Katsuoka

Department of Dermatology, Kitasato University School of Medicine, Japan

INTRODUCTION

Lymphorrhea is caused by damage to the lymphatic system due to trauma, neoplasm, infection and congenital malformation among others. Severe lymphorrhea is a serious disorder leading to hypoproteinemia. Improvement of lymphorrhea is almost despairing.

Cilostazol, sold as"Pletaal," is an antiplatelet drug made by Otsuka, Tokyo, Japan1). In the ICL of 2003, we had presented an efficacy study of cilostazol in 30 cases of lymphedema. This time, we present the 2 cases with severe lymphorrhea treated by the oral administration of cilostazol.

CASE 1: FILARIASIS

A 59-year-old man had lymphedema of the right leg for 20 years and severe lymphorrhea (2-3 liter per day) from the scrotum for 12 years, caused by obstruction of the thoracic duct with filariasis. In this case the efficacy of cilostazol for lymphorrhea was discovered, when cilostazol was administered for the treatment of his cold feet. After one month his lymph oozing from the scrotum began decreasing remarkably (Fig. 1). Hypourine and

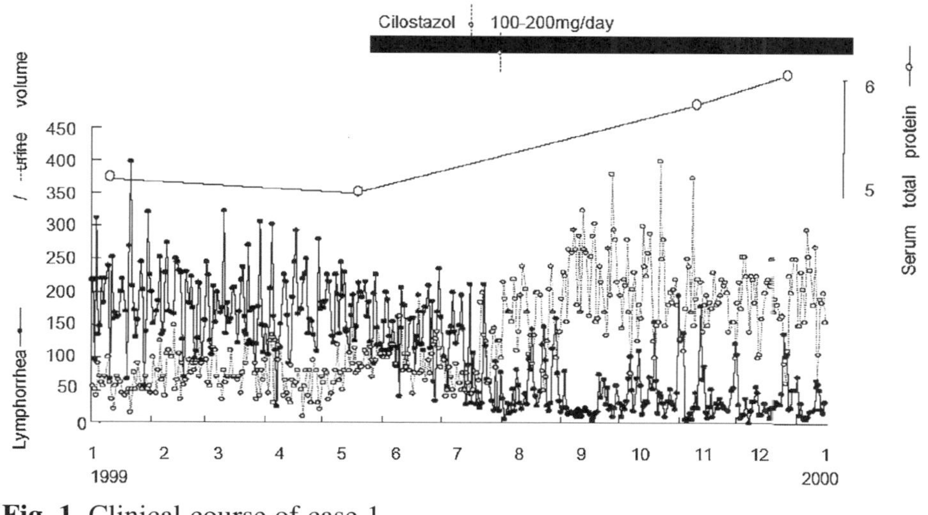

Fig. 1. Clinical course of case 1.

hypoproteinemia also recovered to normal levels and the milky-wet scrotum gradually dried up (Fig. 2).

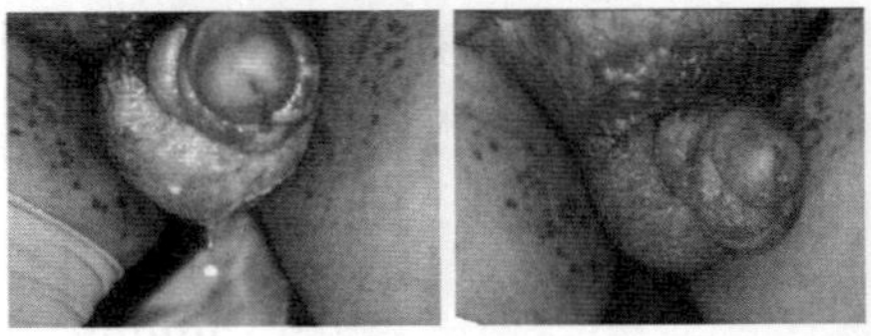

Fig. 2. In case 1, severe lymphorrhea from the scrotum was improved by the treatment of cilostazol. Left: the milky-wet scrotum before treatment, Right: the dry scrotum after one year's treatment.

CASE 2: CONGENITAL LYMPHATIC DEFORMITY

A 19-year-old female had severe lymphorrhea (1-2 liters per day) leaking from the right labium due to a congenital deformity of the intrapelvic lymphatics since she was 6 years old. Her family has been looking for an effective therapy not only in Japan but also in the United States. Even though local resection of the right major labium was performed, the lymphorrhea could not be stopped. The parents read our paper2) on the case described above and consulted us in April of 2004.

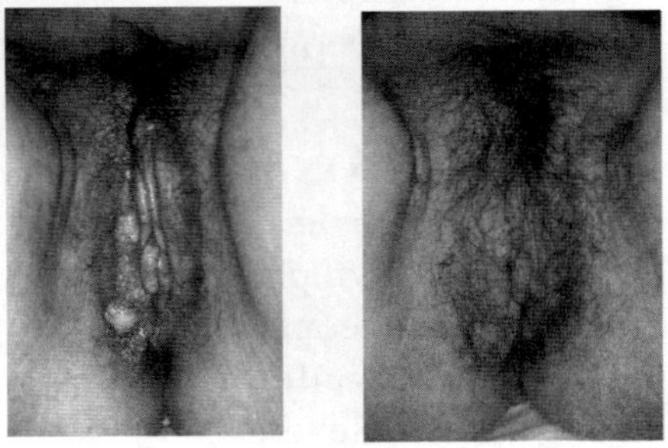

Fig. 4, 5. In case 2, secondary lymphangiomas on the major labium were reduced by the treatment of cilostazol. Left; at first visit, Right; after one and half years' treatment.

We administered cilostazol immediately. Her lymphorrhea was almost stopped in 2.5 months and serious hypoproteinemia was improved as well (Fig. 4). Secondary lymphangiomas on the major labium

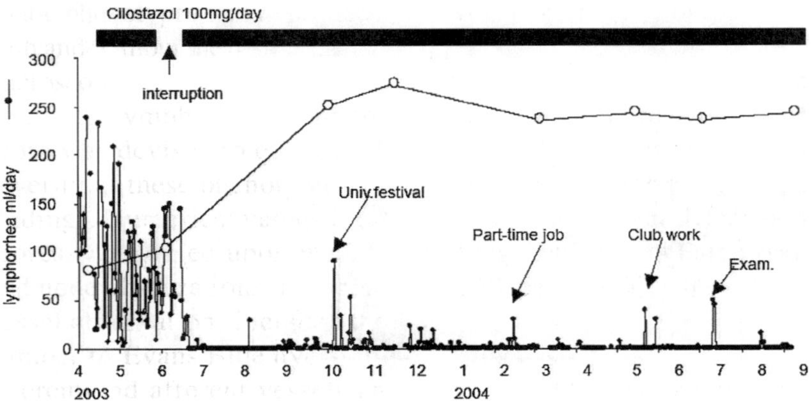

Fig. 3. Clinical course of case 2.

were reducing (Fig. 5). Some times, fatigue, exercise or menstruation produce a small amount of lymphorrhea (Fig. 4), but her good condition is being maintained with continuous administration of cilostazol.

CONCLUSIONS

Cilostazol acts as an antiplatelet but also dilates blood vessels and promotes blood flow3,4). We supposed that the pharmacological functions of cilostazol may promote absorption of lymph from tissue into the blood vessels, resulting in the decrease of lymphorrhea. This mechanism is supported in the evidences that hypoproteinemia and hypourine improved after administration of cilostazol. Our results suggest that cilostazol, administered orally, is effective in the treatment of lymphorrhea.

REFERENCES

1. Sorkin, EM, A Markham: Cilostazol. Drugs & Aging 14(1999), 63-71.
2. Masuzawa, M, H Hara, T Miyata, et al.: Severe lymphorrhea and lymphedema caused by filariasis: The efficacy of oral treatment with cilostazol. Jpn J. Dermatol. 111(2001),179-183. (in Japanese)
3. Kawamura, K, K Watanabe, Y Kimura: Effect of cilostazol, a new antithrombotic drug on cerebral circulation. Arzneim-Forsch/Drug Res 35 (1985), 1149-1154.
4. Kamiya, T, S Sakaguchi: Hemodynamic effects of theantithrombotic drug cilostazol in chronic arterial occulusion in the extremities. Arzneim-Forsch/Drug Res 35(1985), 1201-1203.

CD 44 IN LYMPHEDEMA-RELATED ACUTE DERMATITIS

M. Ohkuma

Department of Dermatology, Sakai Hospital, Kinki University, School of Medicine, Osaka, Japan

INTRODUCTION

CD 44 is a membrane penetrating protein,80-90 kDa (Fig.1) with location of gen in 11th chromosome, bound to counter receptor of HEV, bound to actin filament related skeleton and found in the blood cells, intestine, muscle, nerve and skin. It is a kind of adhesion molecule and 3 types are known; constitutively active, inducible and inactive form. Its structure is shown in Fig. 1. It is associated with lymphocyte homing, ligand of hyaluronate, fibronectin, laminin and collagen, agglutination of erythrocytes with T cell, Il-1 production by T cell activation, bone marrow proliferation, carcinoma's metastasis and inflammation (Fig. 2). The receptor of LYVE-1, i.e., CD 44 mainly observed in the lymphatics is associated with hyaluronic acid and in case of lymphedema

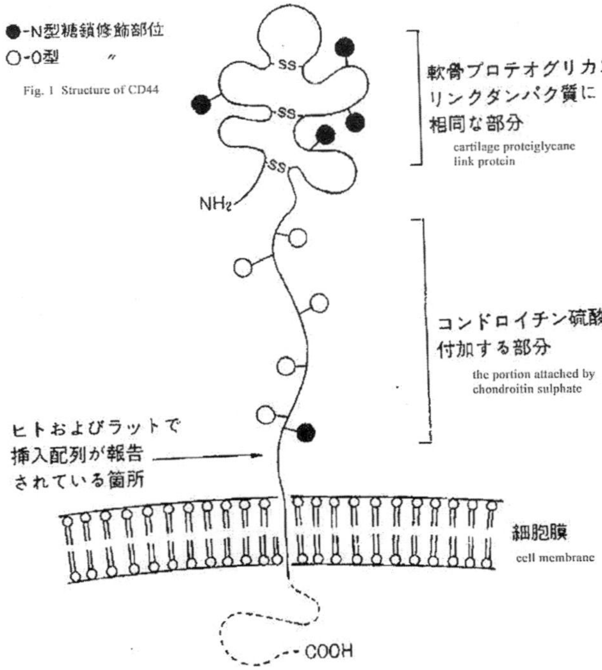

Fig. 1 Structure of CD44

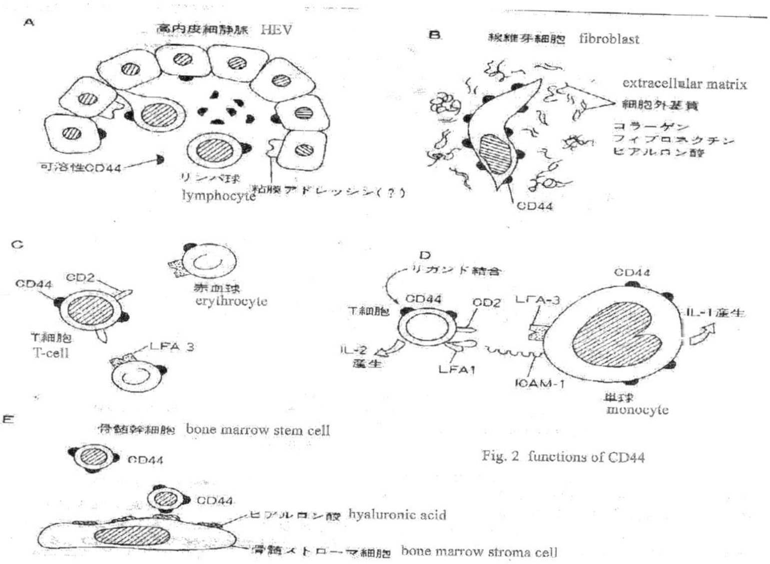

Fig. 2 functions of CD44

hyaluronic acid is increased (1,2). This molecule may play an important role in lymphedema and its acute inflammatory complication. That is why this investigation has been performed.

MATERIAL AND METHOD

Five ml of heparinized blood was taken from five cases of lymphedema during lymphedema-related acute dermatitis. For the control 5 cases of lymphedema and 2 normal volunteers were examined in the same way. The blood was evaluated for CD 44 by means of flow cytometry using labeled antibody.

RESULT

There is no statistical difference between the lymphedema-related acute dermatitis and the lymphedema without complication (Table 1) (Fig. 3).

Fig.3

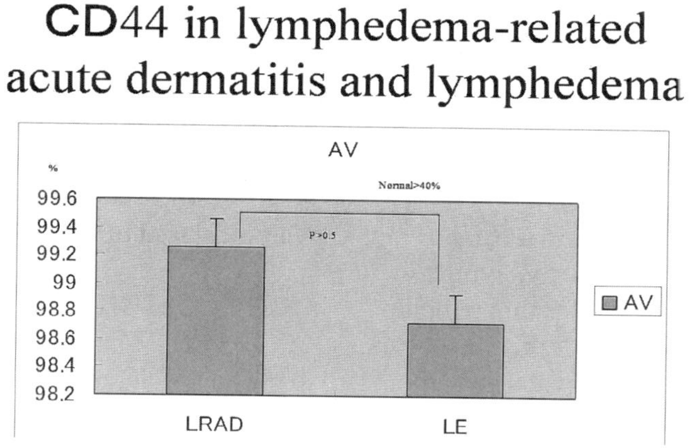

Table 1

Examined patients

No.	name	age	sex	location	duration 1°	disease	episode	result
Lymphedema with acute dermatitis								
1.*	TY	41	M	bil.lower	18Y		x 5	98.7%
2.	SI	57	F	bil.lower	2Y	nephritis?	-	98.7%
3.	EK	70	F	lt.lower	1Y	arthritis ope.	-	98.9%
4.	AM	62	F	lt.lower	1Y	hysterectomy,ca.	x3	98.9%
5.	TS	71	F	lt.lower	6Y	hysterectomy,ca.	x10	99.6%
Lymphedema without acute dermatitis								
6.	MK	71	M	rt.lower	2M	rectum ca.	-	97.6%
7.*	CW	49	F	lt.lower	26Y		+	99.7%
8.	MK	67	F	rt.lower	1Y	arthritis,ope.	+	99.4%
9.	RM	74	F	lt.lower	32Y	breast ca.	+	99.8%
10.	HY	86	F	rt.lower rt.femur	1Y	epiphyse-necrosis	+	99.4%
Normal volunteer								
11.	YO	56	F					98.4%
12.	MO	68	M					98.6%

* primary lymphedema, all others secondary lymphedema
F:female, M:male, bil:bilateral, lt:left, rt:right, Y:tear, M:month,
Ope.:operation, ca.:cancer

The normal volunteers are also within normal limit (>90%) although the number of investigated cases is small.

DISCUSSION

It is well known from a clinical point of view that lymphedema gets worse after this lymphedema-related acute dermatitis occurs. Its reason is not known. The author has suspected if CD 44 is intensified and hyaluronic acid is increased in the tissue, the lymphedema gets worse. However this process has not been concluded. This may attributed to other reasons such as changed tissue with increased bFGF (3).

CONCLUSION

CD 44 has not been proved to play a special role in case of lymphedema-related acute dermatitis.

REFERENCES

1. Liu NF, Zhang LR: Changes of tissue hyaluronan in peripheral lymphedema. Lymphology 31 (1998), 173.
2. Ohkuma M: Hyaluronic acid in lymphedema; its change after a new physiotherapy and its difference between primary and secondary lymphedema. Lymphology 37 (Suppl) (2004), 319.
3. Ohkuma M: VEGF, c-GMP & AMP, bFGF and EGF in lymphedema-related acute dermatitis. Lymphology 37(Suppl) (2004), 297.

AXILLARY WEB SYNDROME AFTER LYMPH NODE DISSECTION: RESULTS OF 1,004 BREAST CANCER PATIENTS

Bergmann, A; PT, PhD[1]; Mattos, IE; MD, PhD[2]; Pedrosa, E; PT[1]; Nogueira, EA; PT[1]; Koifman, RJ; MD, PhD[2].

[1] National Cancer Institute / Cancer Hospital III; [2] National School of Public Health / FIOCRUZ

Abstract

Introduction: Axillary web syndrome (AWS) occurs in patients submitted to surgical treatment for breast cancer due to injury of superficial lymphatic vessels during lymph node dissection. Its incidence and risk factors are unknown. The purpose of this study was to evaluate the incidence and risk factors of AWS in breast cancer patients.
Methods: Prospective cohort of 1,004 breast cancer patients submitted to axillary clearance at the National Cancer Institute (INCA), between August 2002 and November 2002. Women with prior conditions of the upper arm were excluded. The following variables were collected: age at operation, body mass index (BMI); marital status; years of schooling; neoadjuvant radiotherapy, chemotherapy or tamoxifen; number of lymph nodes removed; number of metastatic lymph nodes; type of axillary surgery; total days with closed suction drainage; TNM stage (pathology); type of surgery; early arm edema (volume > 200 ml). Univariate analysis was performed for describing population profile. Bivariate analysis and logistic regression were performed in order to identify risk factors involved in the development of AWS. This study was approved by the Ethics and Research Committees of INCA and FIOCRUZ.
Results: The follow-up period was 24 months. The sample comprised 1,004 women, with a mean age of 55 years, 48% were married, 53% had not completed elementary school and 70% were obese. Mastectomy was performed in 65%, the mean number of lymph nodes removed was 17. As for staging, 47% of the cases were considered in an advanced stage (higher than IIB). The incidence of AWS was 38.2%. The variables that showed significant statistical association with AWS (logistic regression) were: early arm edema (RR=2.27 IC 1.10-4.65) and number (continuous) of lymph nodes removed (RR=1.01 IC 1.00 – 1.03).

Conclusion: AWS is a common condition after axillary lymphadenectomy for breast cancer and was statistically associated with the number of lymph nodes removed and with early arm edema.

Keywords: Axillary web syndrome, breast cancer, complications, lymphadenectomy

Introduction

The most important factor for survival in breast cancer is the presence of lymph node metastasis. Axillary clearance (AC) or sentinel node biopsy (SNB), depending on the characteristics of the tumor, are recommended for its appropriate staging [1].

Axillary web syndrome (AWS) is a condition that occurs in the early postoperative period after AC and SNB, characterized by axillary pain irradiation down the ipsilateral arm, shoulder range-of-motion limitation and axillary web of tissue most obvius during the abduction of the arm [2].

This syndrome is rarely described in the literature. Hoffman and Rolff [3] observed three patients who developed painful bands across the axilla after breast surgery and AC, suggesting thrombosis, obstruction and inflammation of lymphatic channels as the probable pathogenesis. Similar observation after AC was described recently in four studies [4-6]. Morkovitz et al [2] in a retrospective study of 750 women, found a prevalence of 6% of AWS after AC. Leidenius et al [7] observed a prevalence of 72% after AC and 20% after SNB, in 85 patients submitted to breast cancer surgery. Pappo et al [8] described three cases after SNB.

The factors associated with AWS following breast cancer surgery are still not clear. After performing biopsies of axillary webs, Markowitz *et al* [2] suggested that the pathogenesis of AWS was related to a lymphovenous injury that might occur in the retraction of tissue and patient positioning during AC; stasis of lymphovenous channels induced by removal of axillary lymphatics draining to the arm; and a hypercoagulability in surrounding tissues due to tissue injury during operation and releasing of tissue factor.

The aim of this study was to evaluate the incidence and risk factors associated with AWS after axillary clearance in patients submitted to breast cancer surgery.

Materials and Methods

We conducted a prospective cohort study of 1,004 breast cancer patients submitted to axillary clearance at the Cancer Hospital III / National Cancer Institute (HCIII/ INCA) in Rio de Janeiro, between August 2002 and November 2002. Women with breast cancer submitted to conservative surgery or mastectomy, associated with axillary clearance (level I, II or III) were eligible for the study. Women with prior alterations of the upper arm, bilateral breast cancer, absence of axillary clearance, treated in other hospitals and who were in no condition to answer the questions were excluded. Eligible women gave informed consent and this study was approved by the Committees of Ethics and Research of the National Cancer Institute and of the Oswaldo Cruz Foundation. Women were evaluated in the preoperative, on the first day, and on months 1, 6, 12, 18 and 24 after axillary clearance. Variables related to the characteristics of patients, treatment, the tumor and postoperative complications were studied. The variables age, body mass index, and the number of removed and metastatic lymph nodes were tested in the regression model as continuous and categorical. AWS was defined as the presence of a visible web in the axilla and/or arm, associated or not with pain and shoulder range-of-motion limitation.

The characteristics of women meeting inclusion criteria were compared and the x^2 test with a 5% ($p < 0.05$) level of significance was performed in order to determine statistical significance. For continuous variables, we presented the mean and the median, and categorical variables were described through frequency distribution. A bivariate analysis was performed in order to explore the magnitude of the association between AWS and study variables. A model to best represent the risk for lymphedema was searched by unconditional logistic regression using the enter method, adopting as criterion for entrance $p \leq 0.10$ and for exit $p \geq 0.11$ of the tested variables. Epi-Info 2000 and SPSS 10.0 software were used for data analysis.

Results

We studied 1,004 women submitted to axillary clearance. The mean age of the population studied was 56 years (SD ± 13.08). In relation to Body Mass Index (BMI), 28.9% of the patients had adequate weight, 31.9% were overweight and 36.5% were obese. Mastectomy was performed in 65% of the patients, with predominance of the modified radical mastectomy of Madden. Most patients (79%) were submitted to axillary clearance until level III, with a mean of 17 (SD ± 6.77) lymph nodes removed, of which 47% were metastatic. Together, stages IIA and IIB answered for more than half of cases (55.8%). In relation to oncologic treatment, 70% of the women received adjuvant chemotherapy and 63% were submitted to radiotherapy and axillary lymph drainage was necessary in 43% of them.

The incidence of AWS was 38.2%. We observed that women with an increased volume of the arm (> 200 ml) in the first six months after AC (early edema), had 1.54 more risk (IC 95% 1.13 – 2.10) of AWS in comparison with those with a normal volume. Other variables analyzed associated with AWS did not show statistical significance (table 1).

The adjusted model that better predicted the risk for developing AWS after AC consisted of two variables: number of lymph nodes removed (continuous), showing a 1% increase in risk for each lymph node removed (RR 1.01 IC 95% 0.99 – 1.03) and the occurrence of early edema (RR=2.27;IC 95% 1.10 – 4.65).

Discussion

The study population, whose origin was a public reference hospital for breast cancer in Rio de Janeiro - Brazil (HCIII/INCA), consisted of a group of women that have routine physiotherapy care and are assessed with standardized instruments, allowing prevention and early identification of complications.

The incidence of AWS in our study (38.2%) was below the one observed by Leidenius et al [7], who found an incidence of 72% by evaluating 36 women submitted to AC. We did not find other studies on the incidence of AWS in the literature reviewed. In both studies, AWS was evaluated by inspection and palpation of the axilla and the arm. The differences observed in the incidence of AWS could probably be due to heterogeneity of the population studied and to different study procedures.

Leidenius et al [7] found that AWS after AC was not associated with shoulder range-of-motion limitation in the preoperative and with axillary metastases. In our study, women with shoulder range-of-motion limitation previous to AC were excluded and we did not find a statistically significant association with axillary metastases. Our results were different from those of Leidenius et al [7] in relation to BMI, as we did not find an association of this variable (categorical or continuous) and AWS and in their study, women with AWS presented lower BMIs (p=0.01) in relation to those of the ones without such complication. Possibly, the identification of AWS in obese women is difficult, due to poor visualization of lymphatic vessels, and this fact could justify the results observed by these authors.

Moskovitz et al [2] analyzed 750 women submitted to AC for breast cancer between 1980 and 1996, in a retrospective study, and found a 6% prevalence of AWS. Among the cases of AWS observed by these authors, 11% developed lymphedema in the early or late postoperative, 4.5% developed postoperative complications (seroma, necrosis and infection), 64% were submitted to conservative surgery and 49% presented axillary metastasis. The retrospective methodology and the definition of AWS used by the authors do not allow a comparison with the data from our study.

Patients submitted to SNB were not part of our study population. Leidenius et al [7] found an incidence of 10% in this group, which was lower than that observed in the group submitted to AC (74%) (p <0.000). Other authors published reports of cases of AWS after SNB [2,8].

The etiology of AWS after surgical treatment of breast cancer is still not clear. However, published studies agree that AWS occurs

Table 1. Relative risks between AWS and selected variables

Variable	AWS Yes	AWS No	RR**	IC*
Patient age				
≤ 55 years	200	321	1.09	0.86 – 1.18
> 55 years	184	299		
Body mass index (BMI)				
≥ 25	265	421	1.04	0.88 – 1.24
< 25	111	189		
Surgery				
Mastectomy	252	400	1.03	0.87 – 1.22
Conservative	132	220		
Immediate reconstruction				
Yes	18	40	0.80	0.54 – 1.19
No	366	580		
Number of lymph nodes dissected				
≥ 18 lymph nodes	179	315	0.90	0.77 – 1.05
< 18 lymph nodes	205	304		
Number of metastatic lymph nodes				
≥ 4	66	103	1.13	0.88 – 1.45
< 4	95	179		
Stage				
II B e III	175	273	1.04	0.89 – 1.22
< II B	206	343		
Early edema				
Yes	18	13	1.54	1.13 – 2.14
No	366	607		
Hematoma				
Yes	10	27	0.70	0.41 – 1.19
No	374	592		
Wound Infection				
Yes	46	81	0.94	0.74 – 1.20
No	336	538		
Seroma				
Yes	227	381	0.91	0.77 – 1.07
No	144	207		

*** 95% Confidence interval**
**** Relative risk**

because of axillary surgery, as cases after breast surgery only were not observed [2,7,8]. The smaller the axillary surgery, the lower seems to be the occurrence of AWS. In our study the number of lymph nodes removed increased in 1% the risk of AWS for each lymph node removed.

Morkovitz et al [2], observing fibrin clot in superficial veins and lymphatics of biopsied axillary webs in 4 patients, suggested that lymphovenous injury, stasis, and hypercoagulability after axillary surgery in breast cancer could contribute to the development of AWS. Due to surgical trauma, the thrombosis of lymphatic vases could be followed by local coagulation and fibrina deposition, which would induce cellular proliferation along the vase [9]. Our results showed a significant association with early edema and AWS (RR=2.27 IC 95% 1.10 – 4.65) after AC. A possible explanation for these findings could be the common pathophyisiology of those complications, beginning with axillary lymphatic obstruction.

Conclusion

The incidence of AWS AC for breast cancer was 38.6%. The best model to explain the risk of AWS after AC was made up of two variables: number of axillary lymph nodes removed (RR 1.01 IC 95% 0.99 – 1.03) and development of early edema (RR=2.27 IC 95% 1.10 – 4.65).

References

1. Cody B. Consensus on sentinel node biopsy. The Breast Journal 2002; 8(3): 123-5.
2. Morkovitz AH, Anderson BO, Yeung RS, Byrd DR, Lawton TJ, Moe RE. Axillary web syndrome after axillary dissection. The American Journal of Surgery 2001; 181: 434-9.
3. Hoffman J, Tolff M. Axillary band contractures after axillary lymph node dissection (abstract). Ugeskr Laeger 1992; 154 (18): 1280-1.
4. Kroon KE, Roumen RM. Two women with painful bands after axillary lymph node removal: lymphatic thrombosis end fibrosis (abstract). Ned Tijdschr Geneeskd 2004; 148 (26): 1312-3.
5. Reedijk M, Boerner S, Ghazarian D, McCready D. A case of axillary web syndrome with subcutaneous nodules following axillary surgery. Breast 2005; oct 27 (abstract).
6. Ferreira-Rezende L, Laier Franco R, Costa Gurgel MS. Axillary web syndroem: practical implications. Breast Journal 2005; 11 (6): 531.
7. Leidenius M, Leppanen E, Krogerus L, Smaitten KV. Motion restriction and axillary web syndrome after sentinel node biopsy and axillary clearance in breast cancer. The American Journal of Surgery 2003; 185: 127-130.
8. Pappo I, Wasserman I, Stahl-Kent V, Sandbank J, Halevy A. Mondor's disease if the axilla: a rare complication of sentinel node biopy. The Breast Journal 2004; 10(3): 253-5.
9. Marsch W, Haas N, Stuttgen G. Mondor´s phlebitis – a lymphovascular process. Dermatologica 1986; 172: 133-8.

LYMPHEDEMA
THINKING OUTSIDE OF THE BOX

Nancy J. Fortin, Boc CO, CLT Lana

Hyperbaric Oxygen/Problem Wound Clinic
St. Joseph Hospital

INTRODUCTION

Patient is a 41year old, married mill worker with 11+ years of recurrent ulcers at both lower extremities, worse in the medial and lateral malleolar regions of both ankles. He now presents with a wound at his distal,medial left thigh for 2+ years which has never closed. The patient has a previous history of postphlebotic syndrome and recent acute cellulites. Prior diagnosis include postitive history for DVT bilateral lower extremities 1993, veinstripping in 1997. Has received 45+ treatments with Hyper Baric Oxygen. BP 134/82, Appropriate INR, Greenfield filter in place. Multiple varicosities. Patient is on his feet when working in the mill for approximately six hours a day. Elevated white blood count. Feet are deep purple with webbing bilateral second and third toes. Presently on Keflex,Coumadin and aspirin.

METHOD

Patient treated with Hyperbaric Oxygen treatment 45+ times. Minimal results with normal TCOM's. Referred to Lymphedema Clinic for treatments. Patient has been attending the Lymphedema Clinic for approximately six weeks. He received Manual Lymphatic Drainage, pneumatic compression pumping, and compression bandaging three times a week. Wound care involves application of Accuzyme and Sorbsan following protection of the periwound area with a sealant and cover dressing under the compression bandages.

PLAN A

1 Hyperbaric evaluation (20-40 treatments with bed rest) started on 7/15/04.
2 Chest xray
3 Cardiogram
4 Keflex,coumadin,aspirin therapy
5 Application of accuzyme, sorbsan with final layer of a commercial sealant and softsorb w/o compression.

PLAN B

1 Referred to the lymphedema/ edema clinic February 8, 2005. Aproximately 1 year later.
2 T.I.D. treatments of MLD/CDP followed by compression pumping with pneumatic pump (Lymphapress) and compression bandaging.

RESULTS

Patient started with a wound on his distal medial left thigh of approximately 13cm (L) x 9cm (w) x .3cm (D) on July 15, 2005 at the Hyperbaric/Problem Wound Clinic. Patient was referred to the Lymphedema Clinic on February 5, 2005. As of March 23, 2005 his wound measured 9.5cm (L) x 4.5cm (W) x .1cm (D). Patient continues to improve daily. We are also working on his nutritional and psychological progress to make sure he continues to make gains.

CONCLUSION

Patients who have any type of wound be it vascular, diabetic, etc. can improve from continuous Manual Lymphatic Drainage, pneumatic compression pumping and compression bandaging. Proper skin care and nutrition should continue to be the long term focus as well as consideration for possible psycho/ social involvement.

INCIDENCE OF PSYCHOLOGICAL ASSISTANCE IN PATIENTS AFFECTED BY LYMPHEDEMA

Susana Gulias, Psych Lic and Salvador Nieto, MD, FICA.

Salvador Nieto Foundation ("For the Development of Lymphedematology")

PURPOSE

The objective of this study was the identification of psychological aspects of patients affected by lymphedema as a consequence of oncological treatment, or due to congenital or genetic factors. The purpose of the study, on one hand, was to identify and address psychological issues patients experienced so that these issues did not amplify their physical ailments nor interfere with their medical treatment, thus allowing patients to differentiate the ailments caused by physical distress due to their illness from the ailments caused by psychological distress associated with their illness. On the other hand, the purpose was to analyze the efficacy of psychological intervention on those patients affected by lymphedema, their receptiveness to the medical treatment, and their acceptance of the results the treatment utilized.

MATERIAL AND METHODS

We performed this study on 44 patients. A psychological evaluation test was administered to all patients at the beginning of their medical treatment for lymphedema, both to those who received psychological intervention (22 patients) and those who did not receive any psychological intervention (22 patients) in conjunction with their medical treatment, utilizing a HADS scale (Hospital Anxiety and Depression Scale) for analysis of depression and anxiety. At the end of the treatment period, another psychological evaluation was done utilizing the same methodology and HADS scale.

RESULTS

A significant reduction in the anxiety of patients was noted in those patients who received psychological intervention in concurrence with their lymphedema treatment; no changes in levels of anxiety were noted in those patients who did not receive any such intervention. In respect to depression, no significance was noted in levels of depression in either group of patients except for a few cases which were classified as not being related to their lymphedema. A very notable result was that all patients in this study expressed great emotional relief at being able to speak openly about their condition and exhibited a notable improvement in their attitude and acceptance of their treatment. In another respect, this improved the doctor-patient relationship resulting in significantly better results from the therapeutic treatment.

DISCUSSION

Providing psychological support to patients undergoing lymphedema treatment requires commitment of the medical professionals and health and insurance organizations involved. One should utilize an integrated approach (physical, psychological and social) to the patient seeking treatment, not just for humanitarian reasons, but also to optimize the results of the medical treatment received, keeping in mind that the psychological aspects of each patient as well as their personality, can greatly affect the etiology of the illness.

CONCLUSION

Patients affected with lymphedema as a consequence of oncological treatment or due to congenital or genetic factors, require psychological support whether it be for the condition of cancer itself, for anxiety and suffering that cancer can cause, or for the disfigurement of one's body and the related physical, workplace and social difficulties that accompany those with the condition of lymphedema. If the emotional aspects involved are considered, one then has an integral understanding of the patient and can anticipate, prevent, as well as successfully treat any complications that eventually appear during medical treatment. One must recognize that the inability to measure and standardize patients' emotions continues to considerably limit incorporating psychological intervention into therapeutic medical treatments.

RECOMMENDATION

As such, based on what has been concluded in this study, the recommendation is, in general, to incorporate psychological intervention into medical treatments, especially those directed to treatment of patients with lymphedema resulting from oncological treatment or due to congenital or genetic factors.

PROPHYLAXIS OF LYMPHEDEMA-RELATED ACUTE DERMATITIS BY EXTERNAL APPLICATION OF ANTIMICROBIOTIC (NADIFLOXACIN) LOTION

M. Ohkuma

Department of Dermatology, Sakai Hospital, Kinki University School of Medicine, Osaka, Japan

INTRODUCTION

The author has already reported a prophylactic effect of nadifloxacin cream for lymphedema-related acute dermatitis with an excellent result (1). However lotion is easier to apply and the applied skin condition is better because it is not sticky.

MATERIAL AND METHOD

Fifteen cases of lymphedema which have had at least once an attack of the complication in the past one month are tried give an daily application of the 1 nadifloxacin (Fig. 1) lotion to the whole area of the lymphedematous skin after bath for 3 to 48 months. Any occurrence of the complication has been checked. Twelve patients out of the 15 are complicated with tinea, which are treated at the same time.

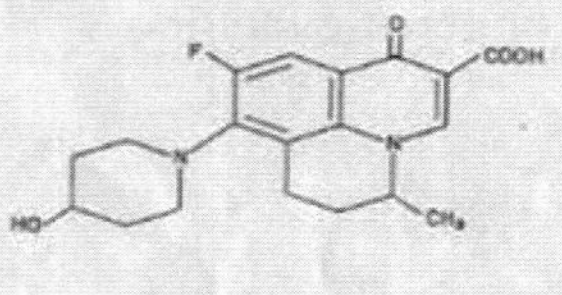

$C_{19}H_{21}FN_2O_4$
360.39 (MW)

(±)-9-fluoro-6,7-dihydro-8-(4-hydroxy-1-piperidyl)-5-methyl-1-oxo-1*H*,5*H*-benzo[*ij*]quinolizine-2-carboxylic acid

Fig. 1. Chemical structure of nadifloxacin.

RESULT

All cases have become free from the attack but a patient in which the complication came once by the time the complicated tinea became healed 2 weeks after onset of the prophylactic treatment (Table 1). No complication of new mycotic infection is observed even after the antimicrobiotic treatment for up to 48 months.

DISCUSSION

It has been concluded that nadifloxacine lotion is as effective as its cream. Many patients have mentioned that the skin condition is better with the lotion. The author has already reported its more frequent incidence in the tinea complicated lymphedema (2). The above prophylactic effect may be partly due to treated tinea. Pharmacological effects of antimicrobiotic are 1. Inhibit the formation of cell wall (absent in animal cell), 2. Disturb the function of plasma membrane, 3. Inhibit protein synthesis of

Table 1. Prophylactic effect of nadifloxacin lotion for lymphedema-related acute dermatitis tried in lymphedema

No.	name	age	sex	involved extremity	tinea	duration of Tx	Results
1.	SY	49	F	bil. lower It.foot	+	6.5 months	+ after 2W
	- after 3W						
2.	RH	54	F	It.lower It.foot	+	8 months	-
3.	TI	*41	M	bil.lower feet	+	14 months	-
4.	Ry	65	F	rt.upper	+	7 months	-
5.	KU	48	F	rt.lower rt. foot	+	3 months	-
6.	AA	*56	M	It.lower It. foot scrotum	+	36 months	-
7.	SM	73	M	bil.lower feet	+	4 months	-
8.	KY	73	F	It.lower feet	+	3 months	-
9.	KY	59	F	rt.lower feet	+	8 months	-
10.	TS	75	F	It.lower It.foot	+	14 months	-
11.	MW	67	F	rtlower	+	12 months	-
12.	SI	67	F	bil.lower feet	+	18 months	-
13.	SS	68	F	bil.lower feet	+	9 months	-
14.	TM	68	F	It.lower It.foot	+	48 months	-
15.	AN	68	F	It.upper	+	5 months	-

*primary lymphedema & all others secondary; F: female, M: male, bil.: bilateral, lt.: left, rt.: right.

ribosomes, 4. Inhibit folic acid synthesis, 5. Inhibit nucleic acid synthesis. The antimicrobiotics are characterized by 1. Inducing a resistant bacteria less frequently, 2. Reaching to the foci more easily, 3. The less incidence in adverse effect, 4. No post antibiotic effect (ex. yellow teeth by tetracycline). The surface skin shows such resident bacteria such as staphylococcus epidermidis or corynebacterium. If systemic antibiotics are given, it has the same prophylactic effect but it causes more serious adverse effects such as liver, renal or intestinal bacteria flora disturbances. Mycotic skin complication is seen after long period use of antibiotics which has not been observed in this trial. Even it does happen, the dermatologist can easily diagnose and manage it.

CONCLUSION

Nadifloxacin lotion is effective in prophylaxis for lymphedema-related acute dermatits.

REFERENCES

1. Ohkuma M: Prophylactic treatment of acute cellulitis in lymphedema by application of antimicrobiotic cream. Lymphology 29(Suppl.) (1996), 317.
2. Ohkuma M, Kubo S, Furuta I: Skin surface bacteria in uni- and bilateral lymphedema– the second report. Lymphology 31(Suppl.) (1998), 547.
3. Ohkuma M: Incidence of acute cellulitis in lymphedema, trial in treatment dispensing antibiotics and its relation to mycotic infection–the second study. Lymphology 29(Suppl.), (1996), 313.

WHY AND WHEN SHOULD ANTIBIOTICS BE USED IN PATIENTS WITH LYMPHEDEMA OF LIMBS

Olszewski W. L.

Department of Surgery and Transplantation, Medical Research Center, Polish Academy of Sciences, Warsaw, Poland and Norwegian Radium Hospital, Oslo

There is convincing evidence for low-dose long-term penicillin administered as a prophylactic modality to stop advancement of tissue changes in lymphedematous limbs and drastically lower the incidence rate of recurrent acute attacks of dermato-lymphangio-adenitis (DLA). Poor lymphatic drainage brings about retention of microbes that colonized deep layers of skin and subcutis. These microbes belong to our "physiological" flora populating skin surface. Any inflammation at any place in the body remote from the lymphedematous tissues may evoke inflammatory reaction, where similar microbes colonize deep tissue acting as the so called "recall antigens". In some cases microbes break capillary barrier and cause septicemia. Fatal cases have been recently reported. Inflammation in lymphedematous tissue causes piling up of immune cells, their products as cytokines and chemokines and tissue cellular debris. Our widely accepted protocol is based on the knowledge that bacterial colonies can be kept dormant at low concentrations of simple antibiotics. This happens in the nature as we carry a big load of bacteria and at the same time produce own antibiotics (tounge, gut etc). We administer a low dose of 1200.000 u of bicillin every 3 weeks im. In a recent study based on 100 patients followed for 12 months the rate of DLA attacks decreased from 100 percent to 6-15. There were no cases of septicemia. Bacteriology of tissue fluid, lymph and lymph nodes showed a significant decrease in number of isolates.There was no rise in resistance to antibiotics. We estimate that more than 10 million people follow our protocol.

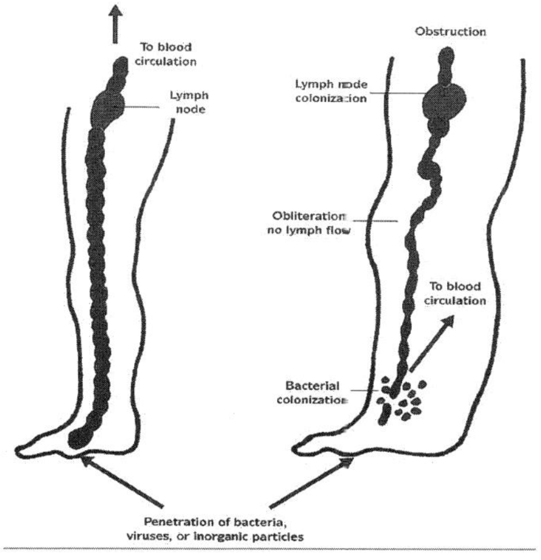

Prevalence of bacterial isolates on skin surface in subcutaneous tissue, lymph nodes, tissue fluid and lymph of the lymphedematous limb in patients with "filarial" lymphedema (treated and non-treated patients) (% of positive cultures, n – number of specimens)

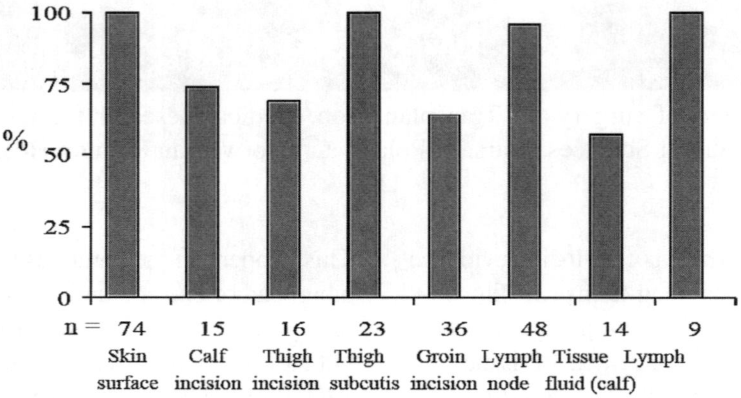

WHAT IS CAUSING INFLAMMATION?
a) bacterial cells,
b) DNA CpG,
c) lipoplysaccharide (LPS)
d) superantigen (e.g. Staphylococcus).

ANTIBIOTIC ADMINISTRATION PROTOCOL
Oral: one table of Potassium Penicillin G 800 000 units, every night, for one year.
Parenteral: Long-acting Penicillin (Benzathine), 1 200 000 unit, i.m., every 21 days, for one year.

Table 1. Prevalence of bacterial isolates from specimens obtained from swollen extremities of 38 European patients with secondary lymphedema (isolates identified in 10 patients (25%))

Strain	Toe-web swab	Calf skin swab	Surgical incision	Lymph	Lymph node
Micrococci	23* (7)**	30 (37)	0 (0)	14 (0)	66 ND
Staphylococci	67 (71)	51 (37)	75 (0)	71 (0)	33 ND
Streptococci	2 (0)	3 (0)	0 (0)	0 (0)	0 ND
Others (gramcocci, bacilli, coryneforms)	11 (21)	14 (24)	25 (0)	14 (0)	0 ND

* per cent of isolates of a given strain
** in parentheses values obtained from normal controls

Other antibiotics:
According to the investigator, under the condition they will be given for one year.
Local:
Neomycin, gentamycin, erythromycin, fungizon, ointment on foot (between toe-webs and around nails), daily.
THERAPY SHOULD LAST FOR MONTHS OR YEARS DEPENDING ON THE STAGE OF THE DISEASE

TOPICAL DRUGS

1. should penetrate epidermis
2. evoke reaction of keratinocytes, dendritic and endothelial cells
3. change chemical milieu for bacteria
4. bacteriostatic or bacteriocidal, antifungal
5. Facilitate penetration of other drugs

Toe-web and calf skin bacterial strains after 3 months topical administration of gentamycin, erythromycin, neomycin and clotrimazole in 11 patients with secondary lymphedema of lower limbs.

No changes in types of isolated bacterial strains were observed.

PROTOCAL FOR TOPICAL APPLICATION OF ANTIBIOTICS ON FOOT AND CALF SKIN IN PATIENTS WITH LYMPHEDEMA

Normal daily hygienic regimen
Gentamycin (0.03%)
Neomycin (0.05%) Ointment
Erythromycin (1.0%)
Clotrimazole (1.0%)
Thin layer on toe-web and sole skin, around nails, dorsum of foot and lower part of calf, application every 2nd or 3rd day

Table 2. Leg skin antibiogrammes 72h after topical application of antibiotics.

Antibiotic	n	Strains/skin swab before/ 72h after antibiotics		No growth %	Growth %	Resistant strains
Erythro+ Genta + Neomycin + Clotrimazole	17	2.5	0.17	76	24	Bacilli *
Gentamycin	7	2.6	0.85	43	57	Cocci *
Neomycin	7	2.5	0.7	57	43	Cocci Bacilli *
Erythromycin	7	1.6	1.1	28	72	Bacilli Cocci *
Clotrimazole	7	1.4	0.85	43	57	Cocci Bacilli

* Candida

THE EFFECT OF TOPICAL APPLICATION OF LOW-CONCENTRATION ANTIBIOTIC (GENTAMYCIN, NEOMYCIN, ERYTHROMYCIN, CLOTRIMAZOLE) OINTMENT ON FOOT AND CALF SKIN IN 11 PATIENTS FOR A 3-MONTHS PERIOD

Skin bacteria	Skin infiltrates	Clinical data
Cocci ↓ 50%	20% ↓ to +	DLA recurrency 20%
Candida ↑ 45%	25% ↓ to ++	Reported improvement 45%
	55% no change	

AIM OF STUDY

Retrospective evaluation of the effects of administration of Penidur on

a) recurrency rate of DLA,

b) changes in bacterial spectrum on skinsurface and in deep tissues and fluids,

c) sensitivity to penicillin and other antibiotics

PREVALENCE OF RECURRENCIES OF DLA IN A 12 M STUDY

	No of patients	% of patients with DLA attacks	
		Before	after
		treatment	
I. Penidur-treated	40	100	15.6
II. Non-treated	34	100	76.4

The ratio of 12 months penidur-treated (P+) to non-treated (P-), patients in material taken from various anatomical sites of the lymphedematous extremity

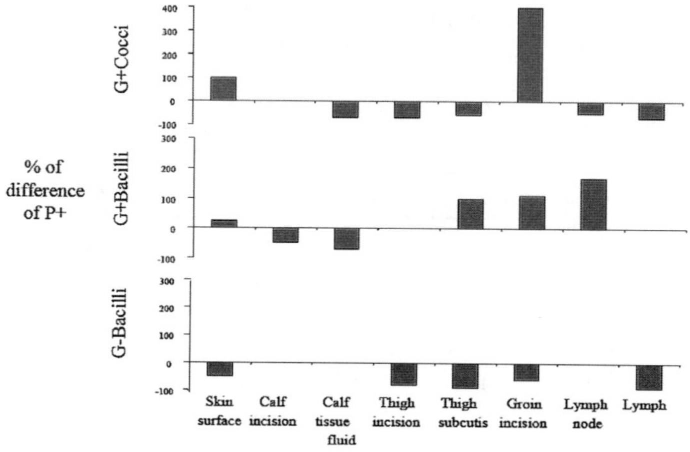

Table 3. Prevalence of sensitivity to antibiotics of bacterial species isolated from subcutaneous tissue, lymph nodes, tissue fluid and lymph in penidur treated and non-treated patients with "filarial" lymphedema (% of sensitive strains).

	G+ Cocci		G+ Bacilli		G- Bacilli	
	P+	P-	P+	P-	P+	P-
Penicillin	44	59	53	31	58	57
Tobramycin	80	81	68	59	56	36
Gentamycin	84	86	72	65	89	64
Tetracyclin	84	77	66	70	52	54
Erythromycin	76	73	86	82	nd	nd
Lincomycin	84	76	79	41	nd	nd
Rimfapicin	92	95	100	100	nd	nd
Vancomycin	92	91	96	94	nd	nd
Cotrimoxazole	72	78	94	94	83	92

* sensitivity +++, nd – not done

SUMMARY

The effects of Penidur administration in "filarial" lymphedema patients:

A significant decrease in recurrency rate of DLA

Change in the frequency distribution of Cocci and Bacilli on the skin surface

Decrease in prevalence of isolates in tissue fluid and lymph and lymph nodes

Lack of significant changes in sensitivity to antibiotics both of the surface and deep tissue bacterial flora

THE PLACEBO EFFECT: GOOD NEWS FOR THOSE WITH LYMPHOEDEMA?

A L Moseley[1] & N B Piller[1]

[1]Department of Surgery & Lymphoedema Assessment Clinic, Flinders University & Medical Centre, Adelaide, Australia

Lymphoedema is a condition caused by dysfunctional lymphatic drainage and which can effect a significant number of people, from those who are born with a dysplastic system to those who develop it secondary to surgery, injury or filiaratic infestation. The subsequent swelling is particularly distressing to the sufferer, as it can cause limb disfigurement and an array of symptoms which result in discomfort, such as pain, heaviness, tightness, bursting sensations and elevated skin temperatures. The chronicity of the condition can also be hard to endure for patients as their symptoms and the inconvenience never seemingly abates, with the condition itself needing constant attention to keep it from getting out of complete control. Although a number of beneficial therapies do exist for lymphoedema, a definitive cure still remains elusive and therefore as clinicians we need to consider how we may best maximize current therapies to the patient's best advantage.

This brings us to the controversial subject of the 'placebo effect'. A placebo can be defined as a sham medication or intervention (ie: machine switched off) which delivers no treatment to the patient. The placebo effect is when the patient shows an actual or perceived improvement to the instigated sham treatment. This effect is well known and documented, with the anticipation of receiving treatment being shown to produce biological responses such as the release of brain endorphins[1]. A recent systematic review has also shown that placebos had small benefits in studies with continuous subjective outcomes[2]. This positive response in subjective outcomes is particularly relevant to the area of lymphoedema, as various clinical trials which have involved a placebo group have shown this trend of subjectively responding to inactive treatment.

There are a limited number of studies in the area of lymphoedema that have involved a true 'placebo' group, as lymphoedema is generally considered to be a condition that worsens over time researchers and ethic committees often find it unethical to have a group that receives sham or no treatment. However, there are a few studies that have used placebo groups and where patients have responded to (placebo) treatment or reported improvements in subjective symptoms which were not accompanied by a significant reduction in objective measures such as limb size or volume (summarized in table 1). Most of the studies to date have involved randomized, double-blinded, placebo controlled trials of oral preparations (flavanoids) for lymphoedema. A trial investigating the effects of Coumarin (400mg) in post mastectomy lymphoedema by Loprinzi et al (1999)[3] showed that despite an arm volume increase in both groups, the positive responses to arm swelling, tightness, heaviness and in arm mobility were similar for Coumarin and placebo, with no differential effect with active treatment. Interestingly, after 12 months the women indicated that they slightly preferred the placebo period over the Coumarin period (25% v's 24%).

Similar results were seen in a study by Pecking et al (1997)[4] also involving women with post mastectomy lymphoedema, this time investigating the effects of Daflon (500mg). Both the placebo and active group reported statistically significant reductions in arm discomfort ($p = 0.002$, $p < 0.001$ respectively) and an improvement in constant heaviness, with the active group experiencing a 30.4% reduction and the placebo group a 22.9% reduction. Objectively the active group experienced an improvement in lymphatic migration speed ($p = 0.005$) and half life over time ($p = 0.034$) as detected by lymphoscintigraphy, however there was no significant improvement in these parameters in the placebo group. Another two trials involving arm lymphoedema have also shown increases in objective parameters but improvements in subjective symptoms. Cluzan et al (1996)[5] investigated CYCLO-FORT versus placebo and found after 3 months that percentage oedema increased by 2.5% in the placebo group whilst the treatment group had a reduction of 12.9%. Despite the increase in percentage oedema, the placebo group reported improvements in both arm heaviness and mobility.

A trial by Mortimer et al (1995) investigated O-(?-hydroxyethyl)-rutoside (3g) versus placebo in arm lymphoedema over a 6 month period[6]. Results from this study showed that the ratio of arm volume (the ratio of the swollen arm to the unaffected arm) had increased over the course of 6 months in the placebo group whilst the treatment group showed decreases at months 1, 2 , 3 and 6. By trial end, the increase in arm volume ratio in the placebo group was statistically significant ($p = 0.028$). From the data displayed in the accumulative symptom table, it would also appear that both groups reported an improvement in the accumulated subjective symptoms. A trial by Casley-Smith et al (1993)[7] demonstrated the greatest increases in limb volume in the placebo groups over a

6 month period. This study investigated the effect of 5,6-benzo-[á]-pyrone (200mgs) in comparison to placebo in patients with either arm (post mastectomy) or leg (various causes) lymphoedema and demonstrated an increase in arm volume of 490mls and in leg volume of 300mls. Both these increases were significant ($p < 0.03$) in comparison to the treatment groups who both had reductions in limb volume. Again, despite the increases in limb volume, both placebo groups (arm and leg) reported slight improvements in swelling, well being, tightness, heaviness and hardness, although the improvements were more pronounced in the treatment groups.

Two studies, one which investigated exercise and the other which investigated handheld laser also included placebo groups which demonstrated positive subjective improvements. Box et al (2004)[8] studied the effects of hydrotherapy compared to a control group who essentially did not receive any treatment. Although after 7 weeks the control group demonstrated an increase in arm volume of 50mls, they also reported improvements (along with the treatment group) in aching, limb appearance, heaviness, tightness and work/leisure activities. The handheld laser study by Carati et al (2003)[9] involved the placebo group receiving sham laser for 3 weeks followed by 1 and 3 month follow ups. At the 3 month follow up the placebo group had had an increase in arm volume of 32.1mls but also reported improvements in the overall mean perceptual score ($p < 0.05$) and in activities of daily living.

From the aforementioned studies it can be concluded that the placebo effect, in terms of positively responding to instigated 'sham' treatment certainly occurs in those with lymphoedema. This effect occurs with different treatment regimes and over different time periods (7 weeks to 6 months). However, instead of seeing this effect as a negative outcome, there is the possibility of embracing and using it to the advantage of both the therapist and patient. Studies have shown that certain factors can accentuate the placebo effect, these include the patients expectations, the therapist's belief in the treatment being offered and the patient-therapist relationship[10-12]. Being aware of these influences may help the therapist to initiate improvements in subjective symptoms even if this is not necessarily followed by changes in more objective parameters.

This synergistic relationship between the clinician and the therapy offered is aptly summed up by Plato who once said "the cure for the headache was a kind of leaf, which required to be accompanied by a charm, and if a person would repeat the charm at the same time that he used the cure, he would be made whole; but that without the charm the leaf would be of no avail"[13]. Essentially what this is showing us is the importance of not only providing therapy but also empowering the patient. The only way we can know what needs are truly important to the patient is by consulting them and making them partners in their own health management. Obviously all treatments need to be assessed in terms of cost, whether they have any benefit or are contraindicated. However, considering lymphoedema is a condition which requires diligent maintenance, any therapy which does not do harm and is felt to be beneficial by the patient is probably worth instigating. Even if it does not result in a direct reduction in limb size or volume, it may improve the patient's quality of life and frame of mind and encourage them to undertake other treatments which will.

References

1. Haour F. Mechanisms of placebo effect and of conditioning: neurobiological data in human and animals. M S-Medecine Sciences Mar. 2005 21(3):315-9
2. Hrobjartsson A & Gotzsche P C. Is the Placebo Powerless? An Analysis of Clinical Trials Comparing Placebo with No Treatment. The New England J of Med, May 2001, 344(21),1594-1602

Table 1. Summary of research trials which have included a control group; representing changes in objective results and subjective improvements

Control	Duration	Objective Results	Subjective Improvements	Reference
Not stated	7 weeks	Arm vol: ↑ 50mls (p = n.s.)	Aching, limb appearance, heaviness, tightness & work/leisure activities (p = n.s.)	Box et al (2004)
Sham laser applied 3 x wk for 3 wks	Follow up @ 3mths	Arm vol: ↑ 30mls (p = n.s.)	Mean perceptual score ($p < 0.05$) Activities of daily living (p = n.s.)	Carati et al (2003)
3 placebo capsules 3 x a day	3 months	Arm oedema: ↑ 2.55% (p = n.s.)	Tissue softness, heaviness, mobility (p = n.s.)	Chzan et al (1996)
Lactose tablets, 2 x tablets, 2 x day	6 months	Arm vol: ↑ 21mls (p = n.s.)	Swelling, pressure, tightness, heaviness, mobility (p = n.s.)	Loprinzi et al (1999)
Placebo tablets, 2 tablets, 1 x day	6 months	Arm vol: ↑ 10% (p = n.s.)	Discomfort ($p = 0.002$)	Pecking et al (1997)
Placebo tablet, 1 x day	6 months	Arm vol: ↑ 490mls Leg vol: ↑ 300mls ($p = 0.03$ compared to tx)	Slight improvement in: swelling, well being, tightness, heaviness, hardness	Casley-Smith et al (1993)
Placebo tablet, 1 x day	6 months	Arm ratio*: ↑ 0.15% ($p = 0.028$)	Improvement in accumulated symptoms	Mortimer et al (1995)

* The ration of the swollen arm to the unaffected arm

3. Loprinzi, C.L., Kugler, J.W., Sloan, J.A., Rooke, T.W., Quella, S.K., Novotny, P., Mowat, R.B., Michalak, J.C., Stella, P.J., Levitt, R., Tschetter, L.K. and Windschitl, H. Lack of effect of Coumarin in women with lymphedema after treatment for breast cancer. The New England Journal of Medicine (1999), Feb; 340(5): 346-350.
4. Pecking, A.P., Fevrier, B., Wargon, C. and Pillion, G. Efficacy of Daflon 500mg in the treatment of lymphedema (Secondary to conventional therapy of breast cancer). Angiology (1997), Jan; 48(1): 93-98.
5. Cluzan, R.V., Alliot, F., Ghabboun, S. & Pascot, M. Treatment of secondary lymphedema of the upper limb with Cyclo 3 Fort. Lymphology (1996), 29: 29-35
6. Mortimer, P.S., Badger, C., Clarke, I. and Pallet, J. A double-blind, randomized, parallel-group, placebo-controlled trial of O-(β-hydroxyethyl)-Rutosides in chronic arm oedema resulting from breast cancer treatment. Phlebology (1995), 10: 51-55.
7. Casley-Smith, J.R., Morgan, R.G. & Piller, N.B. Treatment of lymphedema of the arms and legs with 5,6-BENZO-[á]-PYRONE. New England Journal of Medicine (1993), 329 (16): 1158-1163
8. Box, R., Marnes, T. & Robertson, V. Aquatic physiotherapy and breast cancer related lymphoedema. 5th Australasian Lymphology Association Conference Proceedings (2004): 47-9
9. Carati, C.J., Anderson, S.N., Gannon, B.J. and Piller, N.B. Treatment of postmastectomy lymphedema with low-level laser therapy. Cancer (2003), 98(6): 1114-1122.
10. Benson, H. and Friedman, R. (1996). Harnessing the power of the placebo effect and renaming it "remembered wellness". Annual Review of Medicine, 47: 193-99.
11. Kaptchuk, T.J. (2002). The placebo effect in alternative medicine: Can the performance of healing ritual have clinical significance? Annals of Internal Medicine, 136(11):817-825.
12. Papakostas, Y.G. and Daras, M.D. (2001). Placebos, placebo effect, and the response to the healing situation: The evolution of a concept. Epilepsia, 42(12): 1614-1625.
13. Jowett B. Dialogues of Plato. Chicago: Univ Chicago Pr; 1952

UPPER EXTREMITY VENOUS SYSTEM VARIANTS AND PROTECTION FROM POSTMASTECTOMY LYMPHEDEMA

Ryszard Jasinski[1], Marek Wozniewski[1], Andrzej Szuba[2]

[1] Department of Physiotherapy, School of Physical Education; [2] Department of Internal Medicine, Wroclaw School of Medicine, Wroclaw, Poland

Abstract

Introduction: Superficial venous system of upper extremity serves as the main blood draining system from the arm. Anatomical variants of upper extremity venous system (M, Y and N type) may correlate with efficiency of upper extremity muscular pump and in consequence venous outflow.

Hypothesis: Anatomical variants of the antecubital superficial venous pattern correlate with the efficiency of upper extremity venous pump and , due to differences in venous pressure, with development of postmastectomy lymphedema. *Methods:* 70 healthy women and 36 women after mastectomy were studied. The antecubital venous pattern were visualized after brief placement of constriction band on the upper arm. Types M, N, and refer to specific antecubital venous patterns. Atypical patterns were called type Z and non-visible veins - type X. Venous pump effect was studied with photoplethysmography using Rheo Dopplex II device (Huntleigh Inc). Venous pump effect (VP) was calculated automatically from the venous emptying curve. *Results:* In the group of healthy women 140 upper extremities were studied. Venous pattern M was found in 63% , N in 24% and Y in 43% of extremities respectively. The efficacy of venous pump was highest in type Y (mean VP= 41,63 for the right arm and 38,27 for the left arm) and was significantly lower both for type M (mean VP= 23,29 for the right arm and 24,80 for the left arm) and type N (mean VP= 30,00 for the right arm and 26,00 for the left arm). In the group of women after mastectomy 14 (38%) had lymphedema. Analysis of venous patterns of arms on the operated side revealed presence of type M in 33%, type Y in 44%; type Z in 16% and type X in 8% of all women. In women with arm lymphedema type M was found in 35% , type Z also in 35% , type X in 21% and type Y in 7% (1 women). *Conclusion:* Efficacy of upper extremity venous pump differs between anatomical variants of antecubital venous system. Type Y is characterized by highest venous pump efficacy and may have a protective effect on development of postmastectomy lymphedema.

Key words: photoplethysmography, venous pump, upper extremity venous system

Introduction: Superficial venous system of upper extremity serves as the main blood draining system from the arm. The anatomy of arm superficial veins in humans is highly variable. Several major anatomical variants were described on the basis of patterns of superficial veins in the antecubital fossa. Most common described anatomical patterns include M, Y and N type. Their functional significance remain unclear however the types may vary in efficiency of upper extremity muscular pump and in consequence venous outflow [1].

We hypothesize that anatomical variants of the antecubital superficial venous pattern correlate with the efficiency of upper extremity venous pump and that antecubital superficial venous pattern may vary in women with postmastectomy lymphedema

Material and Methods: 70 healthy women and 36 women with history of mastectomy and axillary lymphnode dissection due to breast cancer were studied. The antecubital venous pattern were visualized after brief placement of constriction band on the upper arm.

Types M, N, and refer to specific antecubital venous patterns. Atypical patterns in women with postmastectomy were called type Z (collateral circulation pattern) and non-visible veins - type X.

Venous pump effect was studied with photoplethysmography using Rheo Dopplex II device (Huntleigh Inc). Venous pump effect (VP) and venous return time were calculated automatically from the venous emptying curve.

Results: 140 upper extremities in 70 healthy women (mean age 21,03 ± 1,65 years; range 19-25 years) were studied. Venous pattern M was found in 63% , N in 24% and Y in 43% of extremities respectively. The mean efficacy of venous pump in type Y was 39,95 (±9,8), significantly higher than in type M : 24,05 (±8,4) and type N: 28,0 (± 8,2); (p< 0,001).

The group with history of breast cancer surgery consisted of 36 women (mean age 56,4± 9,0 years). 14 women (38%) in this group had arm lymphedema. Analysis of venous patterns of arms on the operated side revealed presence of type M in 33%, type Y in 44%; type Z in 16% and type X in 8% of all women. In women with arm lymphedema type M was found in 35% , type Z also in 35% , type X in 21% and type Y in 7%. In the group without lymphedema type Y was found in 68% and type M in 32% of studied women and no type Z or X were identified. The difference in prevalence of type Y was statistically significant (p< 0,01)

Discussion: Upper extremity lymphedema is a frequent sequel of breast cancer surgery affecting about 30% of operated patients [2,3]. The pathophysiology of postmastectomy lymphedema is still not fully understood. The role venous pathology in development of arm lymphedema after mastectomy was postulated already by Halstead and later by several other authors [4,5,6], however never physiological variants of venous anatomy were linked to development of arm lymphedema . We have found that type Y of venous pattern is rare in women with lymphedema and much more frequent in women without this complication. We have also found that type Y, linked to higher physical activity [7], is characterized by more effective venous pump capability and possibly better venous outlow. It led us to the conclusion that type Y of antecubital venous pattern may characterized women less prone to arm lymphedema secondary to axillary lymphnode dissection.

References

1. Jasinski R, Wozniewski M , Pietrzyk D, Pawlowska K, Szuba A,: Evaluation of Venous Pump in Upper Extremities by Photoplethysmography. *International Journal of Angiology* 2005;14(1):22-25
2. Schunemann H, Willich N. [Lymphedema after breast carcinoma. A study of 5868 cases]. *Dtsch Med Wochenschr.* 1997;122:536-41.
3. Goltner E, Gass P, Haas JP, Schneider P. The importance of volumetry, lymphscintigraphy and computer tomography in the diagnosis of brachial edema after mastectomy. *Lymphology.* 1988;21:134-43.
4. Halsted WS. The swelling of the arm after operation for cancer of the breast, elephantiasis chirurgica, its causes and prevention. *Bull J Hopk Hosp* 1921;32:309-313.
5. Gruffaz J. [Venous component in lymphedema of the upper extremity after radio- surgical therapy of cancer of the breast]. *Phlebologie* 1986;39:517-25.
6. Svensson WE, Mortimer PS, Tohno E, Cosgrove DO. Colour Doppler demonstrates venous flow abnormalities in breast cancer patients with chronic arm swelling. *Eur J Cancer* 1994;30A:657-60.
7. Jasinski R, Wozniewski M.: Architecture types of the superficial forearm veins. *Phlebology* 1995, Suppl. 1: 1022-1024.

TUBEROUS SCLEROSIS ASSOCIATED WITH CONGENITAL LYMPHEDEMA

Andrade M, Carvalho Sobrinho AC, Martins ACP, Neves CB

Dept. Of Surgery, Univ. of Sao Paulo, Brazil

INTRODUCTION

Tuberous Sclerosis Complex (TSC) is a dominantly inherited disease of high penetrance, characterized pathologically by the presence of hamartomata in multiple organ systems. Well known clinical manifestations include epilepsy, learning difficulties, behavioral problems, and skin lesions. Many patients have renal lesions, usually angiomyolipomas and renal cysts [1]. Cardiac rhabdomyomas and brain tumors are present in some cases. Webb found skin abnormalities in 126 of 131 patients with tuberous sclerosis. Hypomelanotic maculae were found in 80 patients, 32 of these had more than 5 such maculae [2]. Congenital lymphedema is a rare association of tuberous sclerosis and only three cases were found in the literature. A number sign is used with this entry because tuberous sclerosis exhibits genetic heterogeneity. Mutation in the TSC1 gene is the cause of the form linked to chromosome 9q34, but mutations in TSC2 (16p13), TSC3 and TSC4 have also been found [3,4].

Lymphedema usually results from lymphatic agenesis, hypoplasia, or obstruction. If the disorder manifests at birth or before one year of age, it is referred to as congenital lymphedema (10% of cases).

The association between Tuberous sclerosis and Lymphedema congenital has been related previously (Cottafava et al. 1986; Hirsch et al. 1999; Voudris et al. 2003) [5,6,7]. This report refers to this association foun in two patients from our service in Brazil.

CASE REPORTS

A 4 year-old female patient with congenital lymphedema presented to our institution and her mother referred an episode of infection in the edematous lower extremity at one year of age that had subsided after treatment with antibiotics. No familial history of Lymphedema was disclosed. Her father was followed elsewhere for tuberous sclerosis and presented maculae, cerebral tumors and arrhythmia. Our patient had hypomelanotic maculae and a non-pitting edema of the left lower leg. Mental development was normal for her age. Echocardiogram showed cardiac rhabdomyomas and her brain CT and renal ultrasound were normal.

The other patient was also a female with 6 years of age and presented the same clinical signals: maculae and congenital right lower limb lymphedema, no mental retardation reported and no familial history either of tuberous sclerosis or lymphatic disorders. However, the CT scan showed brain tumors. Cardiac and renal examinations were normal. The maculae and lymphedema in the right lower extremity are showed in the figure 1.

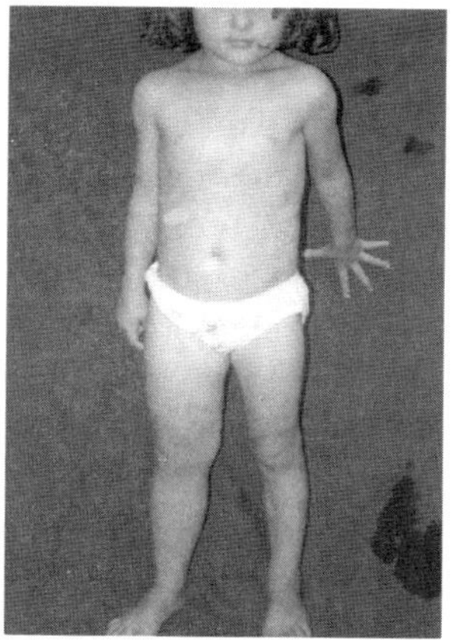

Fig. 1. The maculae and lymphedema in the right lower extremity.

CONCLUSION

We report two cases of congenital lymphedema in association with tuberous sclerosis. Although this association may be coincidental, clinicians should be aware of the potential link between these entities. Further cases will help to more clearly define the relationship between congenital lymphedema and tuberous sclerosis.

REFERENCES

1. Cook JA, Oliver K, Mueller RF, Sampson J. A cross sectional study of renal involvement in tuberous sclerosis. J Med Genet 1996 33: 480-484.
2. Webb DW, Clarke A, Fryer A, Osborne JP. The cutaneous features of tuberous sclerosis: a population study. Brit J Dermatol. 1996 135: 1-5.
3. Sampson JR, Janssen LAJ, Sandkuijl LA, et al. Linkage investigation of three putative tuberous sclerosis determining loci on chromosomes 9q, 11q and 12q. J Med Genet 1992 29: 861-866.
4. Short MP, Haines JL, Bove C, et al. Linkage and heterogeneity in tuberous sclerosis: linkage to chromosome 16 and resolution of old problems. 1992 Am J Hum Genet 51: A201.
5. Hirsch RJ, Silverberg NB, Laude T, Weinberg JM. Tuberous sclerosis associated with congenital lymphedema. *Pediatr Dermatol.* 1999 Sep-Oct; 16(5):407-8.
6. Cottafava F, Cosso D, Brida di Prio S, Grossi-Bianchi ML, Fedi M, Fontana F, Racugno A, Tosca P.A case of Bourneville's tuberous sclerosis with elephantiasis (caused by lymphedema) of the left leg. *Minerva Pediatr.* 1986 Jan 31;38(1-2):49-52.
7. Voudris KA, Skardoutsou A, Vagiakou EA. Tuberous sclerosis and congenital lymphedema. Pediatr Dermatol. 2003 Jul-Aug; 20(4):371-3.

CHYLOUS ASCITES SECONDARY TO AORTIC ANEURYSM REPAIR

Andrade M, Carvalho Sobrinho AC, Martins ACP, Neves CB

Dept. Of Surgery, Univ. of São Paulo, Brazil

Introduction

Chylous ascites is an uncommon complication of aortic surgery, being responsible for less than 1% of all complications related to surgical aortic approach[1]. It is as rare in aortic aneurysm repair as in aortic reconstructions for occlusive disease. Nevertheless, aortic surgery is the main cause of chylous ascites after retroperitoneal manipulation. English language literature is rich in case reports, but it is hard to find a single author with large experience[6, 11, 13]. The biggest series have reported not more than 18 patients.

Marked nutritional depletion, associated to the important drop in lymphocyte counts and also the mechanical factor present in large ascites, facilitates infectious complications, which respond for most of the morbidity and mortality cases[1,4].

Treatment of this condition involves total parenteral nutrition (TPN); high protein medium chain triglyceride diet and repeated paracentesis, isolated or associated to each other[4]. Poor response to conservative management makes direct intervention mandatory to repair chylous leakage or peritoneal-venous shunt insertion[5].

Case Report

A 64 years old woman presented to our Hospital complaining of abdominal pain due to a justarenal aortic aneurism and undergone surgical repair, with an aortoaortic dacron graft, through a left extraperitoneal approach.

She developed two severe infections during the postoperative period, bronchopneumonia and central catheter related infection. In association she had a transitory BUN rise.

Two months after her discharge, she returned complaining of abdominal pain and distention. She had no fever. The CT scan showed a large heterogeneous fluid collection restricted to the right hemi abdomen, from rib to iliac crest, with a liquid-air level characteristic of chylous collection (Fig. 1). A paracentesis was performed with drainage of 5 liters of a sterile bright white liquid and a tubular 15 F drain was inserted and remained in place for 4 weeks. The patient was kept under total parenteral nutrition until the drainage volume reached less than 100 ml a day. Then, a medium chain triglyceride diet was introduced.

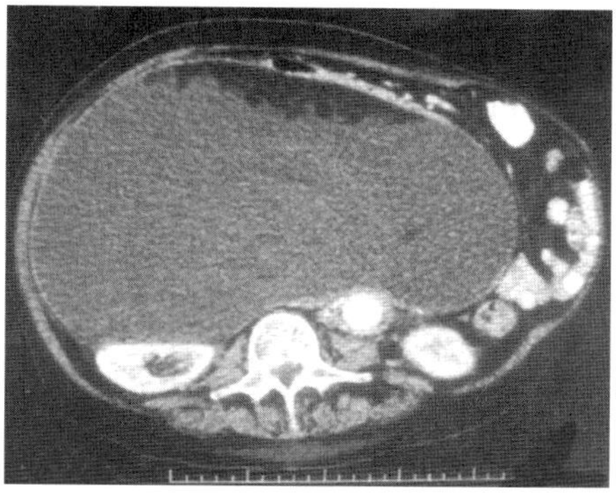

Fig. 1. Voluminous chylous ascites two months after aortic reconstruction. Heterogeneous aspect of the fluid and a liquid-air level.

During the following two weeks, drainage volume decrease and control CT showed a residual cavity (Fig. 2). Drain tube was removed and the patient was discharged without any infectious complications.

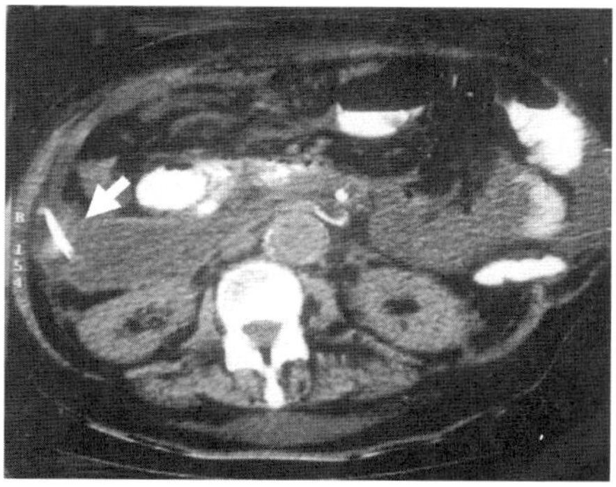

Fig. 2. Two weeks after paracentesis and conservative treatment. Residual cavity and drain tube (arrow).

Another control TC 6 months after discharge showed no cavity at all (Fig. 3). During the 4 years follow-up there was no resume of the chylous ascites, although the patient developed a thoracic aorta aneurysm, and an open repair is to be programmed.

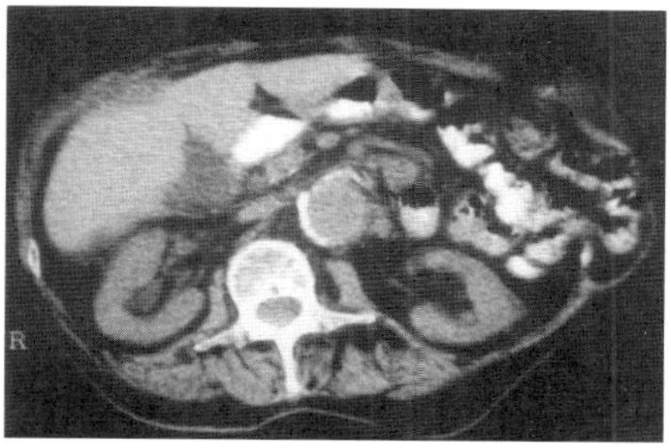

Fig. 3. Late CT showing no residual ascites.

Discussion

Literature is rich in case reports of chylous ascites after manipulation of the retroperitoneal space. Urologic cancer surgery and kidney transplantation with extensive manipulation of retroperitoneum are some examples of situations that may be complicated with chylous ascites[3, 6, 8, 10, 11, 13]. Nevertheless, abdominal aortic surgery is the leading cause of secondary chylous ascites after retroperitoneal manipulation, being responsible for 81% of lymphatic surgical complications, and up to 1 % of all complications. Besides that, it is a rare complication.

The important nutritional deficit (due to protein and fat loss combined with micronutrients deficit), in association to the drop of lymphocyte counts and diaphragm compression (mechanical factor) lead to a higher risk of infectious complications, one of the most important causes of death[1, 5, 12]. The initial management of this condition involves conservative measures: medium chain triglyceride, high protein, low salt diet, associated to diuretics, total parenteral nutrition and use of somatostatin[2, 7, 8].

The immunological insufficiency in this situation is characterized as a lymphocytopenia secondary to leakage of lymphocyte-rich lymph. Due to a continuous protein loss, these patients present hypogammaglobulinemia which, associated with lymphocyte depletion, predispose this population of patients to a higher risk of bacterial infections[1]. A mechanical factor (diaphragm restriction) is also responsible for a greater risk of infectious complications.

After ingestion of a fatty meal, the lymph flow through thoracic duct may increase from 1 ml/kg/h up to 200 ml/kg/h. That is the reason why fat ingestion restriction and parenteral nutrition play such an important role in the management of this condition. Long-chain triglycerides are incorporated to chylomicrons to be absorbed into the lymphatic system. Medium and short-chain triglycerides may be absorbed across the enterocyte layer and diffuse directly to the portal venous system, so they must be part of the fat supplement during the treatment of these patients. An obstruction to the normal outflow of lymph may lead to a loss of chyle to the peritoneal cavity or intestinal lumen. This protein-losing enteropathy manifests with hypoproteinemia, edema, steatorrhea, asthenia, tetany and chylous ascites[1].

Despite the fact that the exact mechanism of action of somatostatin is not fully understood, it has been used in the treatment of chylous ascites and chylothorax with some good results[2, 7, 8]. It must be used in association with other conservative measures in order to promote a decrease in lymph flow, in an attempt to cease the lymph leakage.

When the conservative measures are not successful, surgical approach with suture of the lymphatic fistula is indicated. Some authors have treated this complication with minimally invasive approach, through laparoscopic suture of the lymphatic leakage and fibrin glue[11]. When it is not possible or not efficient, an alternative is to implant a peritoneal-venous shunt[1, 5, 12]. Even when surgical correction is considered it is important to keep the medium chain triglyceride diet and the others clinical measures in order to ensure a low lymphatic drainage, what is related to a better surgical outcome.

Conclusion

Chylous ascites secondary to aortic operations is a rare condition and its management may be challenging to the attending surgeon. Among the great variety of causes of chylous ascites, surgical intervention in retroperitoneal space is of particular importance. Additionally, as oncological barriers become wider, surgical procedures tend to become more complex, being hard to define a limit. A rise in frequency of this complication can be expected. Surgeon's awareness of this condition is important to diagnose and treat it as soon as possible. Conservative measures precede any surgical intervention, reserved to the refractory cases, or patients with poor evolution.

References

1. Aalami, OO; Allen, DB; Organ, CH. Chylous ascites: A collective review. Surg, 2000; 128: 761-778.
2. Berzigotti, A; Magalotti, D; Cocci, C; Angeloni, L; Pironi, L; Zoli, M. Octreotide in the outpatient therapy of cirrhotic chylous ascites: A case report. Dig. Liver Dis., 2006; 38: 138-142.
3. Boran, N; Cil, AP; Tulunay, G; Ozgul, N; Kose, MF. Chylous ascites following para-aortic lymphadenectomy: a case report. Gynecol. Oncol., 2004; 93: 711-714.
4. Browse, NL; Wilson, NM; Russo, F; Al-Hassan,H; Allen,DR. Aetiology and treatment of chylous ascites. Br. J. Surg., 1992; 79: 1145-1150.
5. Campisi, C; Bellini, C; Eretta, C; Zilli, A; Rin, E; Davini, D; Bonioli, E; Boccardo, F. Diagnosis and management of primary chylous ascites. J. Vasc. Surg., 2006; 43: 1244-1248.
6. Caumartin, Y; Dujardin, T. Postoperative chylous ascites in urology. Prog. Urol., 2005; 15: 1046-1055.
7. Collard, JM; Laterre, PF; Boemer, F; Reynaert, M; Ponlot, R. Conservative Treatment of Postsurgical Lymphatic Leaks With Somatostatin-14. Chest, 2000; 117: 902-905.
8. Giovannini, I; Giuliante, F; Chiarla, C; Ardito, F; Vellone, M; Nuzzo, G. Non-surgical management of a lymphatic fistula, after laparoscopic colorectal surgery, with total parenteral nutrition, octreotide, and somatostatin. Nutrition, 2005; 21: 1065-1067.
9. Gloviczki, P. Primary chylous ascites. J. Vasc. Surg., 2006; 43: 1297-1298.
10. Jensen, EH; Weiss, CA. Management of chylous ascites after laparoscopic cholecystectomy using minimally invasive techniques: a case report and literature review. Am. Surg., 2006; 72: 60-63.
11. Link, RE; Amin, N; Kavoussi, LR. Chylous ascites following retroperitoneal lymphadenectomy for testes cancer. Nat. Clin. Pact. Urol., 2006; 3: 226-232.
12. Noel, AA; Gloviczki, P; Bender, CE; Whitley, D; Stanson, AW; Deschamps, C. Treatment of symptomatic primary chylous disorders. J. Vasc. Surg., 2001; 34: 785-791.
13. Takeuchi, S; Kinoshita, H; Terasawa, K; Minami, S. Chylous ascites following operation for para-aortic lymph node dissection in a patient with cervical cancer. Int. J. Gynecol. Cancer, 2006; 16 Suppl 1: 418-422.

Chapter 6
Surgical Lymphology

LYMPHATIC MICROSURGERY: INDICATIONS, TECHNIQUES AND RESULTS

Campisi Corradino[1], MD, Eretta Costantino[1], MD, Pertile Davide[1], MD, Campisi Corrado[1], MS, Bellini Carlo[4], MD, Macciò Alberto[1], MD, Michelini Sandro[5], MD, Fulcheri Ezio[2], MD, Accogli Susanna[3], PT, Boccardo Francesco[1], MD, PhD

[1]Department of Surgery – Unit of Lymphatic Surgery and Microsurgery
[2]Institute of Pathological Anatomy
[3]Rehabilitation Unit
S.Martino Hospital – University of Genoa, Italy
[4]Unit of Neonatal Pathology – G.Gaslini Institute, Genoa, Italy
[5]Center of Neuro-Vascular Rehabilitation – S.Giovanni Battista Hospital – Rome

Introduction

Lymphedema is characterized by an impaired or blocked lymphatic circulation of the affected limb, with progressive evolution of the disease and onset of recurrent acute lymphangites, which are responsible for a further rapid increase in edema volume and thickness[1,3,5].

Commonly, lymphedema is treated and controlled firstly by conservative medical-physical therapies. This therapy has to be intensive, carried out for several months and repeated twice or three times a year. Patients need to wear bandages and elastic garments. Edema undergoes a certain entity of reduction and reaches a decrease of lymphedema beyond which it is extremely difficult to go only by physical treatment.

Surgical techniques used in the past[4-8] for the treatment of lymphedema aimed at reducing the limb volume with a debulking resection approach and were merely symptomatic solutions.

On the contrary, Microsurgery represents a functional therapeutic solutions aimed at treating the real cause of lymphedema by draining the lymphatic flow or reconstructing lymphatic pathways with a direct approach to the lymphatic structures[9-17].

Materials and Methods

First direct approaches to lymphatic-lymph node structures were represented by multiple antigravitational ligatures of incompetent lymphatic and chyliferous vessels according to Servelle and Tosatti[18], for the treatment of lymphochyloedema due to gravitation reflux and Kinmonth[19] operation (entero-mesenteric bridge operation), which consisted in the anastomosis between iliac-inguinal lymph nodes and a segment of the ileum with its mesenteric peduncle after mucosa removal.

Today, microsurgical operations include derivative and reconstructive techniques[20].

Derivative techniques[21] aim at restoring the lymphatic flow at the site of obstruction through a lympho-venous drainage which uses lymph nodes or lymphatics directly.

The most commonly used techniques are multiple lymphatic-venous, end-to-side or end-to-end anastomoses. Depending on the anatomic situation determined at the time of surgery, they are performed directly with the use of major veins or their collateral veins at the medium or upper third of the volar surface of the arms and at the inguino–crural area for the lower limbs[22] (Figs.1-3).

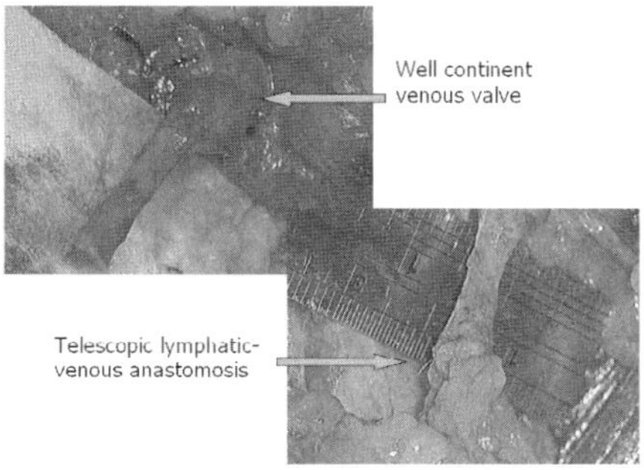

Fig. 1. Lymphatic-venous derivative anastomosis by telescopic technique. Of note, a perfectly continent venous valve which avoids blood to come in contact with the lymphatics.

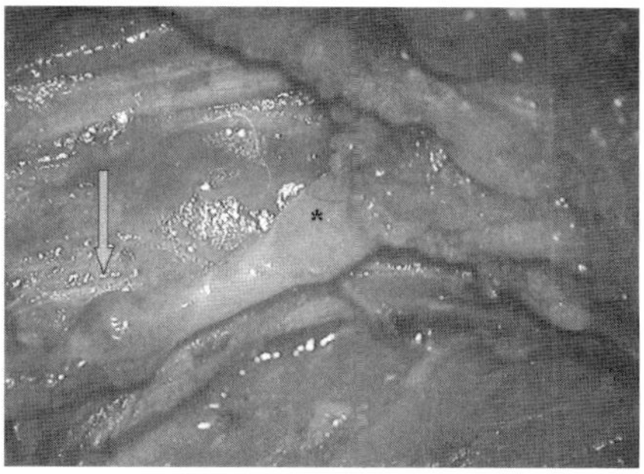

Fig. 2. Telescopic lymphatic-venous anastomosis using a perfectly continent venous branch (arrow indicates the valve). Note the passage of the blue dye inside the vein (*).

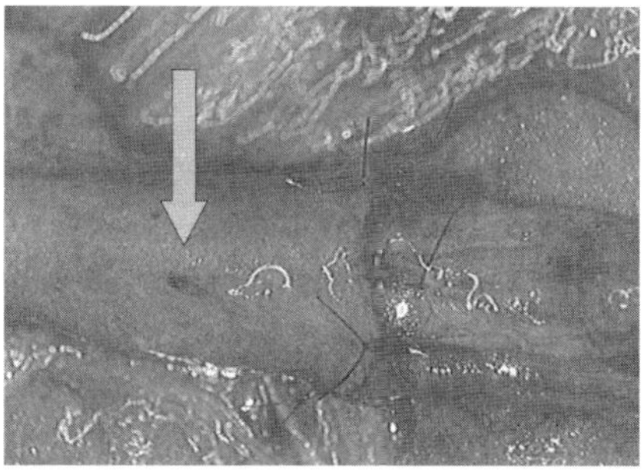

Fig. 3. High magnification lymphatic-venous anastomosis. Note that the U-shaped stitch used to pull lymphatic collectors inside the vein is finally removed (arrow), thus avoiding to close lymphatics by a transfixed stitch. The vein is still filled with lymph coloured in blue.

Conversely, with reconstructive microsurgery techniques, the lymphatic flow can be resumed by by-passing the site of the block by the interposition of autologous lymphatic or venous segments connecting the collectors upstream and downstream the obstacle (LVLA).

As concerns the interposition of autologous venous grafts between lymphatic collectors above and below the obstacle[23], venous grafts are taken from the same affected site or from the volar surface of the arm, with a length ranging from 7 to 25 cm and a caliber of 1.5-5 mm. At the lower limb, vein grafts are implanted just above and below the inguinal region, using a telescopic anastomosing method (Figs. 4-5).

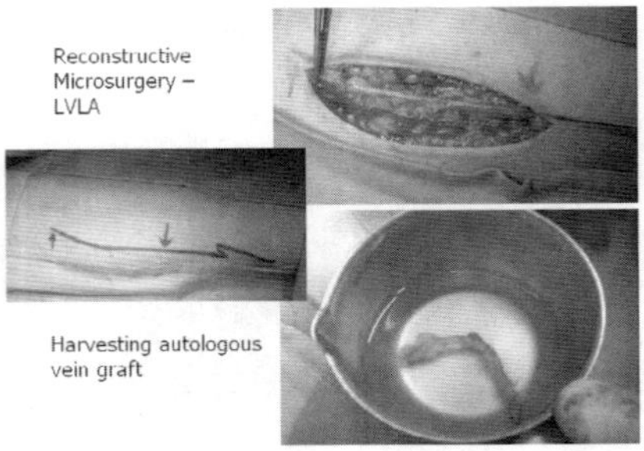

Fig. 4. Reconstructive technique of interpositioned vein graft: the venous segment is harvested from the volar surface of the forearm (cefalic vein).

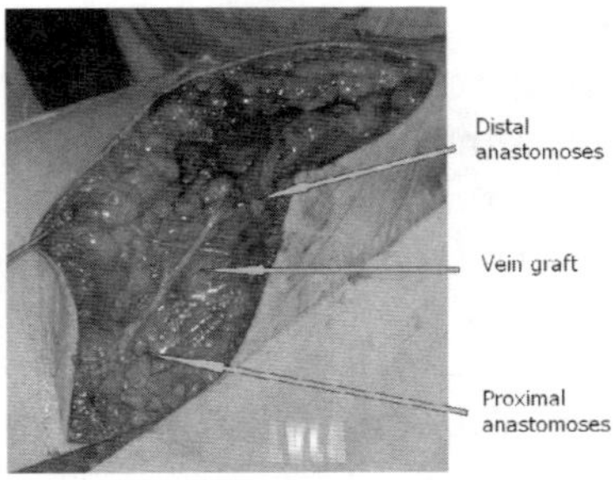

Fig. 5. Lymphatic-venous-lymphatic reconstructive anastomoses at the end. Note that the vein graft is already filled with lymph. Distal and proximal lymphatic-venous anastomoses are performed by telescopic technique.

Indications for the various lymphatic microsurgery techniques are based on the presence of a proper lymphatic venous pressure gradient in the affected limb[24]. Derivative techniques are not indicated in cases where lymphostatic disease is associated with venous flow impairment (varices, venous hypertension, valvular incontinence). In these cases, reconstructive microsurgical techniques are used, unless the venous disease can also be corrected, during the same surgery for lymphedema treatment or as a preliminary phase to it.

Following the above indications, patients must be studied by means above all of lymphoscintigraphy[25] and Doppler venous flowmetry and manometry. Lymphangiography is used in case of chylous disorders. Based on a proper patient selection, microsurgical techniques for the treatment of lymphostasis thus allow to obtain successful results with 50% to 75%, and even up to nearly 100% reduction in edema volume and thickness - depending on disease staging[25] - from the original pre-operative conditions: the earlier is the treatment, the better is the edema reduction.

In the clinical (volumetric assessment) and instrumental (lymphoscintigraphy) follow-up of patients treated with lymphatic microsurgery for lymphedema of the limbs, these results have proved to be stable and long-lasting up to 15 years from surgery.

Our clinical experience by the Center of Lymphatic Surgery and Microsurgery of the University of Genoa includes over 1500 cases of peripheral lymphedema of the limbs and external genitalia treated with Microsurgery from 1973 until today, of whom 968 have been followed up at least from 5 to 15 years after surgery. Females prevail (1.5:1) Age ranges from 2 to 68 years (26 years on average). Patients affected by lymphedema of the upper limb are 291, of whom 57 primary and 234 secondary lymphedemas. Lower limb lymphedemas are 677, of whom 358 primary and 319 secondary lymphedemas.

In all primary lymphedemas, lymphadenodysplasia was present with or without lymphangiodysplasia[27]. The presence of typical lymphatic-lymph node impairment was confirmed by histopathological examination[28] of the lymph nodes resected during microsurgery, which also justified the obstructive behavior of these forms of lymphedema and, hence, the successful result obtained with either derivative or reconstructive microsurgery.

Secondary lymphedemas were mainly due to oncologic surgery, associated with regional lymphadenectomy and, in many cases, with radiotherapy.

With regard to disease staging, surgery was performed in patients with Stage I lymphedema in 55 cases (3%), Stage II in 381 cases (41%), Stage III in 443 (49%) and Stage IV-V in 89 (7%) cases.

The time from onset of lymphedema and microsurgery treatment varied: in primary lymphedemas, this interval ranged from 5 to 15 years, with an average of 7 years, whereas in secondary lymphedemas it ranged from 1 to 10 years, with an average of 4 years.

In almost all patients with both primary and secondary lymphedema, complications were reported featuring acute or recurrent, more or less severe, lymphangitic episodes[29], which were being treated pre-operatively with broad spectrum antibiotics. A significant reduction in these infection episodes was reported after microsurgery, owing to lymph flow stasis reduction and a better lymphatic flow in the lymphedematous limb.

Before undergoing microsurgery, all patients had to follow intensive medical-physical therapy courses for at least 6-9 months (2-3 cycles of physiotherapy). This allowed to obtain a certain decrease of edema, which was only partial and not so significant. Afterwards, microsurgery was used and supplied a quick and marked reduction of lymphedema volume and consistence. Furthermore, after that, physiotherapy was applied again and permitted to stabilize and even improve the outcome.

Derivative microsurgery has been used in the most cases. However, in the presence of venous flow impairment with venous hypertension and valvular incontinence, the reconstructive technique of lymphatic-venous-lymphatic anastomosis was performed.

Results

Volumetry and lymphoscintigraphy were used to evaluate clinical outcome.

Very good results (with over 75% edema volume reduction from pre-operative conditions) were reported in 723 patients (75%), good (over 50% edema reduction) in 218 cases (22%), and fairly good (up to 25% edema reduction) in 27 patients (3%).

The follow-up of patients treated by microsurgery included periodic controls at 1,3,6,12 months and then once a year for at least 5 years. About 15% (145 cases) of patients had a follow-up of more than 15 years. Lymphatic scintigraphy, which was performed at various intervals from surgery (1,3,5,15 years), in 116 patients (85 who had undergone derivative, and 31 reconstructive microsurgery, respectively) permitted to confirm that all derivative or reconstructive microsurgery anastomoses were patent[30] (Figs. 6-9).

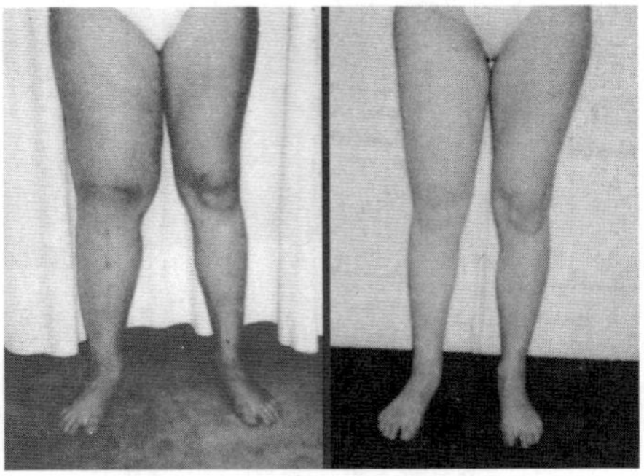

A B

Fig. 6. Secondary right lower limb lymphedema (A) treated by microsurgical lymphatic-venous anastomoses at the right inguino-crural region: outcome at over 5 years from operation (B).

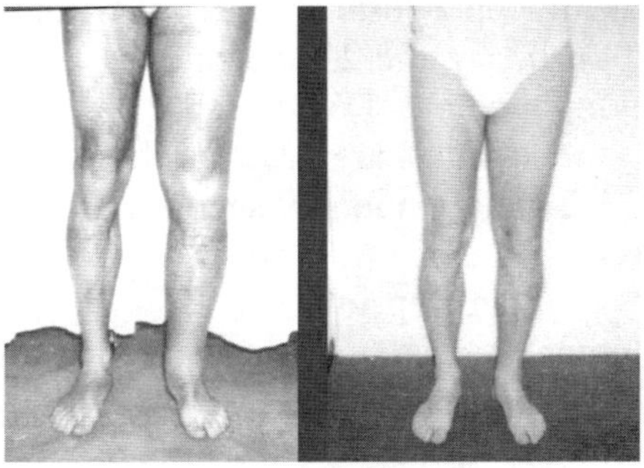

A B

Fig. 7. Primary left lower limb lymphedema (A) treated by microsurgical anastomoses and followed-up at over 7 years (B).

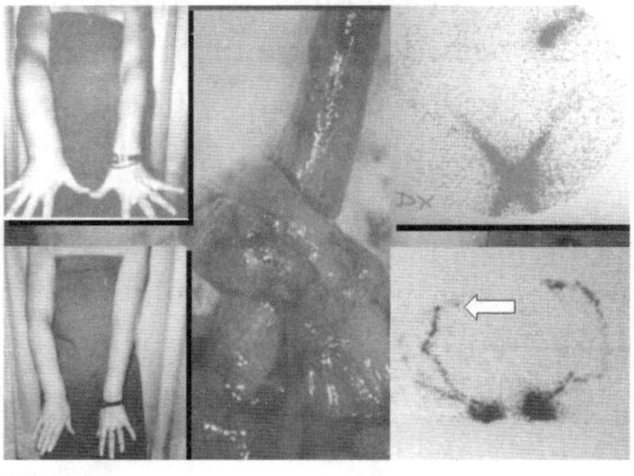

Fig. 8.

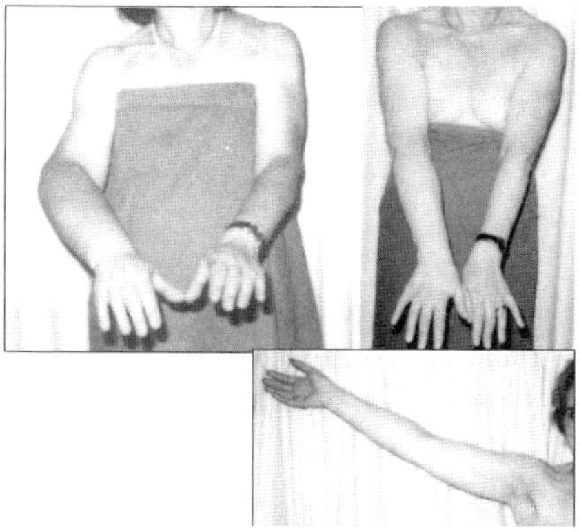

Fig. 9.

Discussion and Conclusions

Microsurgery has proved to supply positive results especially in the early stages of lymphedema till, in some very early cases[31,32], even the complete healing. In more advanced stages, microsurgery techniques may be helpful in obtaining a more rapid and significant edema reduction (with regard to its fluid component). Patient conditions remain stable over time and may even improve through medical-physical procedures aiming at an optimization of surgically performed drainage pathways.

Microsurgery can be carried out to treat not only secondary, but also primary lymphedemas, which, in the majority of cases, are due to congenital obstruction at the site of proximal (axillary or inguinal) lymph nodes due to fibrosclerosis. The lymphatics afferent to these lymph nodes are generally properly operating and often dilated and hypertrophic in the attempt to overcome the obstacle. Microsurgery techniques allow to create a shunting to lymphatic flow which is obstructed for congenital or acquired reasons, into the venous circulation or, alternatively, to reconstruct - at the level of the obstruction - all connections between lymphatics upstream and downstream the obstacle, through autologous venous segment interposition (lymphatic-venous-lymphatic plasty)[33].

In cases of more complex clinical lymphatic-chylous dysplasia with chyle reflux into the peritoneal cavity (chyloperitoneum) associated with chylothorax, chyledema of genitalia and/or lower limbs, chyluria etc., microsurgical techniques associated with CO_2 LASER[34], provides valuable and long-lasting solutions.

To conclude, microsurgery represents a therapeutic weapon which is at our disposal and that we use when adequately intensive cycles of combined physiotherapy allowed to obtain the maximum possible result in terms of reduction of edema and of its consistence, but in the moment in which keeping in using only physical treatment we can not obtain any further improvement of the situation. At this point, the surgical approach, thanks to microsurgical derivative or reconstructive methods, allows to obtain a further rapid and marked edema reduction within very few days after operation. After that, the use of physiotherapy again, with the newly manufactured lymphatic pathways, permits to reach the stabilization of the general outcome and even improve it. That is the summarized scheme of the therapeutical strategy that we use by our Unit: the proper combination of all the possible therapeutical means nowadays available, because this is the best evidence-based strategy that we can offer to the patient affected from lymphedema and correlated symptoms. Finally, we had already published an article on the assessment of quality of life in patients with lymphedema after treatment by microsurgical lymphatic operations and the conclusions were that microsurgery allows to bring about positive results also from the psycho-social point of view[35].

References

1. Wienert V.: Lower-limb chronic lymphedema and Stewart-Treves syndrome. Phlebolymphology 2000; 27: 13-16.
2. Földim.: The therapy of lymphedema. European Journal of Lymphology and Related Problems 1993-1994; 14: 43-49. 59.
3. Leduca.: Le drainage lymphatique. Théorie et pratique. Masson, 1980.
4. Charles R.H.: A system of treatment. Latham A. e English T.C. (eds.), Churchill, London, 1912, 3, 504.
5. Thompson N.: The surgical treatment of chronic lymphoedema of the extremities. Surg. Clin. North Am. 1967; 47:2.
6. Servelle M.: La lymphangiectomie superficielle totale. Traitement chirurgical de l'éléphantiasis. Rev. Chir. 1947, 294.
7. Battezzati M., Donini I.: Il sistema linfatico nella pratica clinica. Piccin: Padova, 1967.
8. Belardi P.: Terapia dei linfedemi. In: Casaccia M., Campisi C. (eds): Lymphology: Advances in Europe. Ecig, 1989; 215-220.
9. Olszewski W.L.: Four years observation of patients with secondary and primary lymphedema treated with lympho-venous shunt. III International Congress of Lymphology, Brussels, 1970.
10. Degnim.: New techniques of lymphatic-venous anastomosis for the treatment of lymphedema. Cardiovascular, Revista Brasileira, 1974, 10-15.
11. Clodius L.: Lymphedema. Stuttgart: Thieme-Verlag, 1977.
12. Clodius L.: Anastomosi linfatico-venose periferiche (nuova tecnica chirurgica). Minerva Chirurgica, 1978; 33: 1711-1718.
13. Campisi C.: Rational approach in the management of lymphedema. Lymphology 1991; 24: 48-53.
14. Campisi C.: Microchirurgia ricostruttiva dei linfatici. Archiviio ed Atti della Società Italiana di Chirurgia, Roma ott. 1992. Ed. Luigi Pozzi, vol.2, 218-223, 1992.
15. Campisi C., Boccardo F., Casaccia M. et al. Dibattiti su casi clinici di linfedema: microchirurgia derivativa o ricostruttiva? 96° Congr. SIC, Roma, Ed. Minerva Medica, 1467-1470, 1994.
16. Campisi C.: Lymphatic microsurgery: legend or reality?. Phlebolymphology 1994; 7: 11-15.
17. Campisi C., Boccardo F., Casaccia M.: Il linfedema dell'arto superiore secondario a linfoadenectomia e radioterapia

adiuvante per cancro della mammella. Ospedali d'Italia Chirurgia 1997; 3: 112-8.

18. Tosatti E.: Lymphatique profonds et lymphoedèmes chroniques des membres. Paris, Masson, 1974.
19. Kinmonth JB.: The Lymphatics. Surgery, lymphography and diseases of the chyle and lymph systems. London: Edward Arnold (Publishers) Ltd, 1982.
20. Campisi C.: Microchirurgia Applicata in Clinica Chirurgica Generale e d'Urgenza. Monografia, UTET, 1991.
21. Campisi C., Boccardo F.: Role of microsurgery in the management of lymphoedema. International Angiology 1999; 18, 1: 47-51.
22. Campisi C., Boccardo F.: Frontiers in Lymphatic Microsurgery. Microsurgery 1998; 18: 462-71.
23. Campisi C.: Use of autologous interposition vein graft in management of lymphedema. Lymphology 1991, 24, 71-76.
24. Campisi C., Olszewski W., Boccardo F.: Il gradiente pressorio linfo-venoso in microchirurgia linfatica. Minerva Angiologica, 1994, 19.
25. Witte C., McNeill G., Witte M. et al.: Whole-body lymphangioscintigraphy: making the invisible easily visible. Progress in Lymphology XII, Elsevier Science Publishers B.V. 1989; 123.
26. Campisi C.: Lymphoedema: modern diagnostic and therapeutic aspects. International Angiology 1999 March; 18,1: 14-24.
27. Papendieck C.M.: Temas de Angiologia Pediatrica. Editorial Medica Panamericana, Buenos Aires, 1992.
28. Badini A., Fulcheri E., Campisi C., Boccardo F.: A new approach in histopathological diagnosis of lymphedema: pathophysiological and therapeutic implications. Lymphology 1996; 29 (Suppl), 190-198.
29. Olszewski WL.: Recurrent bacterial dermatolymphan-gioadenitis (DLA) is responsible for progression of lymphoedema. Lymphology 1996; 29 (Suppl): 331.
30. Mariani G., Campisi C., Taddei G., Boccardo F.: The current role of lymphoscintigraphy in the diagnostic evaluation of patients with peripheral lymphedema. Lymphology 1998; 31 (Suppl): 316-9.
31. Campisi C., Boccardo F.: Prevention of secondary lymphedema: possible role of Microsurgery. Lymphology 29 (Suppl): 41-43, 1996.
32. Fulcherie, Dellachà A, Boccardo F, Campisi C. Latent disorders of lymphatic vessels and lymph nodes as substrate of chronic secondary lymphedema. The European Journal of Lymphology and related problems 2002; 10, 35-36: 10-15.
33. Campisi C, Boccardo F, Zilli A. Microsurgical treatment of peripheral lymphedema: an overview upon 25 years clinical experience. The European Journal of Lymphology and Related Problems 1999; 7 (26): 36-40.
34. Casaccia M., Campisi C.: Chyloedèmes. J Malad Vascul. Masson Ed, Paris, 1988; 13.
35. Azevedo WF Jr., Boccardo F, Zilli A, Maccio' A, De Melo Couto E, Stein C, Napoli F, Campisi C. A reliable and valid quality of life in patients with lymphedema – version of the SF-36. Lymphology 2002; 35 (Suppl): 177-180.

LYMPHATIC GRAFTING AND LYMPHOSCINTIGRAPHY

R.G.H. Baumeister*, M. Weiss, A. Frick ***

*Plastic -, Hand-, Microsurgical Department of Surgery
Klinikum University of Munich – Großhadern
**Clinic of Nuclear Medicine University of Munich

Treatment of lymphoedemas due to a local blockade by microsvascular grafts has shown impressive clinical results. Especially oedemas after surgical interventions are major candidates for such a bypass procedure (1,2)

For the scientific approval of a possible real benefit regarding the lymphatic outflow pre- and postoperative lymphoscintigraphies have been performed.

For lymphoscintigraphy 70 MBq Tc-99m-labeled nanocolloid has been injected into the subcutaneous/subdermal tissue of the first interdigital space. An intravascular administration had to be carefully avoided.

Sequential images (600 seconds) of the extremities were obtained using a large-field-of-view-gamma camera fitted with a low-energy, all-purpose collimator (3).

For semiquantitative evaluation of the lymphatic outflow a numeric index was used, which was described previously by our group (4).

The transport kinetics were evaluated according to 5 visually assessed criteria: lymphoedema, transport kinetics (k), distribution pattern of the radiopharmaceutical (d), time to appearance to lymph nodes (t, minutes), visualization of lymph nodes (n) and visualization of lymphvessels/grafts (v).

The transport index (TI) was calculated according to the formula:
$TI = k + d + 0{,}04\ t + n + v$
The calculation of the parameters was performed according to the following table

Transport Index	Kinetics	Distribution	Time	Node	Vessel
0	No delay	Normal		Clearly demonstrated	
↓	Low-grade delay	Partially diffuse	X 0 .04 (min)	Faint visualization	
↓	Extreme delay	Diffuse		Hardly recognizable	
9	Missing transport	Transport stop	No appearance	No visualization	

The resulting transport index ranged therefore from 0 (absolutely normal) to 45 (highest pathological).

The borderline between healthy extremities has been proven with transport indexes of 10.

A group of 20 patients with a minimal follow-up period of 7 years has been investigated.

A significant improvement of lymphatic transport after lymphatic grafting has been seen.

Locally blocked lymphatic system e.g. after removal of lymphglands in the axilla or at one side at the inguinal or pelvic region has been bypassed.

The patients own lymphatic vessels were used as grafts harvested from the ventromedial bundle of the healthy leg. There about 16 lymphatic vessels are running nearly parallel. 2 to 3 of them are used as grafts.

Under high power magnification lympholymphatic anastomoses are performed at the upper arm and the neck in cases of arm oedemas. In case of an unilateral leg oedema the graft remained attached to the inguinal lymph nodes at the healthy leg, a transport via the symphysis to the oedematous leg and are anastomosed to ascending lymphatics below the blocked inguinal or pelvic region.

In upper extremities the transport index improved from 30,2 to 17,1.

In lower extremities the transport index came down from 33,5 to 15,0.

In both groups several patients reached normal transport values beneath 10.

In the group of patients where the grafts could be visualized also the mean value of the transport index came with a TI of 10,4 into the range of healthy extremities.

Restorating a locally interrupted lymphatic system using the patients own lymphatic vessels can therefore reach normal values.

Secondary changes in oedematous limbs endanger the results. Therefore after a rigid conservative treatment regime the possibility of a reconstruction of a locally blockade lymphatic system should earnestly taken into consideration.

Literature

1. Baumeister RGH: Reconstructive Lymphatic Microsurgery European Journal of Lymphology (2001) 88
2. Baumeister RGH, Frick A: Die mikrochirurgische Lymphgefäß-transplantation Handchirurgie – Mikrochirurgie – Plastische Chirurgie 35 (2003) 202-209
3. Weiss Mayo, Ruediger Georg Hans Baumeister and Klaus Hahn: Post-therapeutic Lymphedema: Scintigraphy before and after autologous lymph vessel transplantation. 8 years of long-term follow-up Clinical Nuclear Medicine 27 (2002) 788-792
4. Kleinhans E, Baumeister RGH, Hahn D et al: Evaluation of transport kinetics in lymphoscintigraphy: follow-up study in patients with transplanted lymphatic vessels Eur J Nucl Med. 10:349, 1985

LYMPHOVENOUS MICROSURGICAL SHUNTS AFTER 40 YEARS - INDICATIONS, TECHNIQUES AND FOLLOW-UP EVALUATION METHODS

Olszewski W.L.

Department of Surgical Research & Transplantology, Medical Research Center, Polish Academy of Sciences, Warsaw, Poland

Over the last 40 above 1000 microsurgical lympho-venous shunts have been performed in our center in patients with lymphedema of lower limbs. The follow-up has been from 5 to 40 years. The indications for shunts were: postsurgical (after hysterectomy), postinflammatory, hyperplastic and idiopathic lymphedema. The 5-year follow-up results were dependent on the type of lymphedema. They were in postsurgical group 80% (in the survivals), 40-50% in postinflammatory, above 80% in hyperplastic, and 5-10% in the idiopathic group. Main problems: (i) establishing proper indications, (ii) postoperative evaluation of shunt patency, (iii) etiology of shunt obliteration, (iv) discrimination of effectiveness of shunts from elastic support, massage and antibiotic therapy effects. Basing on personal experience our present policy is as follows: (i) indications: lymphoscintigraphy of superficial and deep systems delineating at least one lymphatic and fragment of inguinal lymph node within 3h in all patients with obstructive edema, fast growing edema after hysterectomy or groin dissection not controlled by elastic support, hyperplastic lymphedema in children and teenagers, decompression of thigh lymph stasis before lower leg debulking. (ii) contraindications: lack of even rudimentary lymphatics on lymphoscintigraphy, inflammatory changes in skin and lymphatics, idiopathic lymphedema (previously hypoplastic, precox and tarda), (iii) immediate postoperative low molecular heparin for 6 weeks, long-lasting penicillin for one year and longer, elastic stockings, intensive walking and muscular exercises, foot hygiene (iv) postoperative evaluation: lymphoscintigraphy with liver scanning (time of appearance of tracer in blood circulation), measurement of tissue fluid pressure in standardized conditions, subsidence of DLA attacks, lack of increase of circumference or volume. Combined microsurgery, long-lasting penicillin and elastic support with intensive muscular exercise seem to have stopped progression of lymphedema in the majority of our patients.

Lympho-venous shunt between dog's mesenteric lymph node
and IVC (1966). Oily contrast medium in the vein

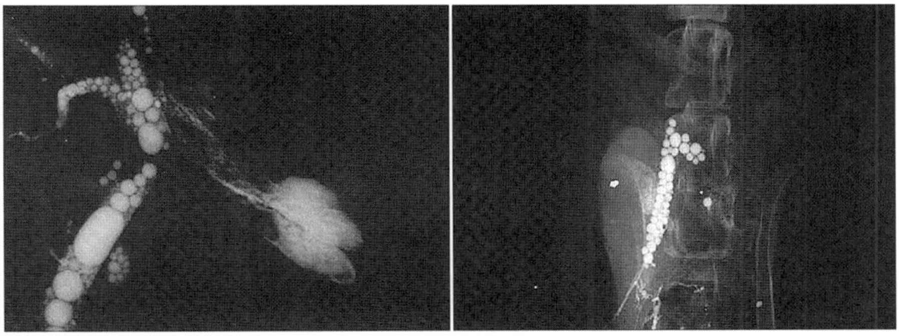

Table 1. Lower lymph lymphedema of various etiologies treated by a) lymphnode-vein, b) lymphatic-vein, c) inguinal node excision since 1966. Total number (n=774)

N° of Patients	Postinflammatory 520			Postsurgical 120			Idiopathic 110			Hyperplastic 24		
Stage	LNV	LVSV	EXC	LNV	LVSV	EXC	LNV	LVSV	EXC	LNV	LVSV	EXC
I	151	31	0	61	8	0	22	10	0			
II	119	20	0	21	0	10*	28	2	20			
III	20	6	84*	0	0	20*	0	0	28**	24	2	0
IV	0	0	80*									

* total fibrosis of groin lymphatics, nodes and subcutaneous tissues
** lack of lymph flow from fibrotic involuted nodes

Table 2. Lower lymph lymphedema of various etiologies treated by a) lymphnode-vein, and b) lymphatic-vein shunt. Results of follow-up for a minimum period of 5 years (n=522)

N° of Patients	Postinflammatory 520		Postsurgical 120		Idiopathic 110		Hyperplastic 24	
Stage	LNV	LVSV	LNV	LVSV	LNV	LVSV	LNV	LVSV
I	151(82)**	31(76)	61(86)	10(72)	22(32)	10(21)		
II	119(80)	20(66)	21(80)	0	28(11)	2(0)		
III	20(22)	6(12)	0	0	0	0	24(90)*	2(86)
IV	0	0						

* 6 patients above 25 years follow-up

** in parentheses percentage of improvement

Various types of lympho venous shunts in humans between the inguinal nodes (ILN) and femoral (FV) and saphenous vein (SV)

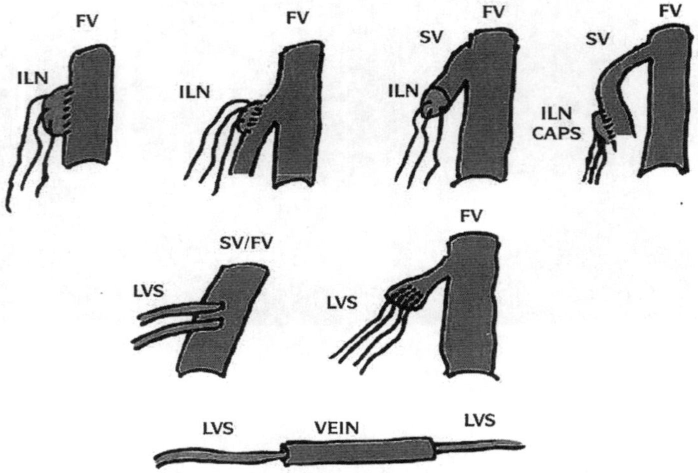

POSTOPERATIVE EVALUATION CRITERIA

1 Decreased leg circumference
2 Improved flexing in ankle and knee joints
3 Increase in softness of tissues
4 Subsidence of pain in long-lasting upright position
5 Decreased frequency of DLA attacks

FACTORS INFLUENCING RESULTS OF LYMPHO-VENOUS SHUNT OPERATIONS

1 Duration of lymphedema
2 Frequency of DLA (recent episodes)
3 Longterm antibiotic therapy
4 Elastic support

PROBLEMS WITH EVALUATION OF CLINICAL RESULTS

1 Lack of objective evaluation methods
2 Recurrent dermatolymphangioadenitis attacks (although decreased frequency)
3 Subjective judging by patient of limb movement freedom, decreased heaviness of leg, and softness of tissues
4 Inconsistency in using elastic support
5 Contemporary indications for lympho-venous shunts in lymphedema of lower limbs
6 Visualization of a thigh lymphatic and inguinal single lymph node on limb stress lymphoscintigraphy (irrespective of type of lymphedema)
7 Early stage of:
Post-surgical lymphedema (after cancer surgery), Hyperplastic lymphedema,
Post-inflammatory obstructive lymphedema
8 Introduction for debulking surgery

TYPES OF LYMPHEDEMA FOR LYMPHO-VENOUS SHUNT OPERATION

1966	2005
Postsurgical (post-hysterectomy) +	Postsurgical (post-hysterectomy) +
Hyperplastic +	Hyperplastic +
Postinflammatory (post- overt or occult dermatitis?) –	Postinflammatory (post- overt or occult dermatitis?) ++
Idiopathic ++	Idiopathic –

PRE- AND POSTOPERATIVE PHARMACOLOGY

Ciprofloxacin 1.0g daily for 3 days before 7 days after operation

Longterm penicillin 1200 000 u. weekly for 3 to 6 months (depending on previous DLA attacks)

Postoperative LMWH (low molecular weight heparin) daily fraxiparin 40mg for 2 weeks

INDICATIONS FOR LYMPHOVENOUS SHUNTS

9 visible node or lymphatic fragments in the groin on lymphoscintigraphy
10 early stage (I and II)
11 no frequent attacks of DLA
12 first step before debulking surgery

POSTOPERATIVE PHYSIOTHERAPY

Elastic stocking or pentahoses II degree pressure
or Elastic bandaging ca 40mm Hg
and Intensive walking

CAUSES OF OBLITERATION OF LV SHUNT

1. Local
(a) infection of the operative wound:
(b) damaging of the afferent vessels;
(c) chronic inflammatory reaction due to the presence of nonabsorbable sutures;
(d) formation of a parietal clot with subsequent organization;
(e) lack of union between lymphatic and venous endothelium.
2. Distant
(a) lack of lymph vessel contractility due to replacement of contractile elements with fibroblasts due to infective inflammatory changes
(b) inflammatory changes (lymphangitis) and progression of inflammation from distal lymphatics upwards to the anastomosis (immunohistochemical evidence);
(c) segmental or total obliteration of main collecting lymphatics with insufficient collateral circulation;
(d) major fibrotic changes in the lymph nodes with lymph flow obliteration.
(e) progression of tissue fibrotic changes.

OBJECTIVE INDIRECT METHODS FOR EVALUATION OF FUNCTION OF LV SHUNT

1 Time of appearance of radioactivity over liver after Nanocoll toeweb injection
2 Decrease of tissue fluid pressure in leg subcutaneous tissue measured under standard conditions
3 Increased volume of interstitial space (fluid volume infusion test)
4 Postoperative lymphoscintigraphy imaging of lymphatics (questionable)

REFERENCES

1. Olszewski, WL: Experimental lympho-venous anastomoses. Abstracts Congr Pol Surg Soc, Lodz, 1966.
2. Nielubowicz, J, Olszewski, WL: Surgical lympho-venous shunts in patients with secondary lymphedema. Brit J Surg 55 (1968), 440.
3. Olszewski, WL: Surgical lympho-venous shunts for the treatment of lymphedema. In: C1odius L, ed. Lymphedema. Thieme, 103, 1977

LIMB-SAVING SURGICAL PROCEDURES IN VERY ADVANCED LYMPHEDEMA OF LOWER LIMBS

Olszewski W. L.

Department of Surgery and Transplantation, Medical Research Center, Polish Academy of Sciences, Central Clinical Hospital, MIA, Warsaw, Poland and Norwegian Radium Hospital, Oslo

Very advanced stage IV lymphedema cases are not common in the Western hemisphere. They account for less than 1 percent of all lymphedema patients. However, they are quite frequent in the Asian and African countries. The morphological changes include: 1. Hyperkeratosis and fibrosis of skin, 2. Fibrosis of subcutis, 3. Lack of lymphatic channels with formation of numerous tissue fluid lakes, 4. Growth of fat tissue, 5. Very limited capillary filtration with total stop for immune cell extavasation, 6. Tissue fluid subepidermal blisters with leakage, 7. Superficial skin ulcer, 8. Bacterial colonization of deep tissues, 9. Doubling or tripling limb weight with destruction of hip and knee joint, 10. Frequent episodes of limb-origin septicemia. The number of advanced cases is estimated at a level of 10-15 million. The historical surgical procedures comprised total denuding of limb down to fascia and covering with epidermal grafts. The results were unsatisfactory because of acute infections of non-removed foot skin, epidermal ulcerations and plasma leakage from the uncovered surfaces. The contemporary knowledge of type and localization of infection as well as visualization of lymphatic pathways allowed to redesign the surgical procedures. The contemporary protocol includes: 1. Antibiotic preparation (ciprofloxacin 1.0 g daily for 3 months, 2. Daily disinfection of skin with antimicrobial soap containing phenol or similar chemical for 14 days before operation, 3. Two-week limb elevation in bed, 4. Surgery divided into 3 stages: a. removal of fibrotic inguinal lymph nodes and vessels, b. 3-4 weeks later surgical excision of fibrotic lymphatics down to knee level together with the neighboring fibrous infected tissues, c. debulking of calf and dorsum of foot in a bloodless limb (arterial tourniquet) and covering with pedunculated skin flaps, 4. bed -confined limb elevation and continuation of 0.5 g cipro for another month, 5. elastic support (pressure grade III). This modified approach can save limbs otherwise qualified for amputation when the stage of destruction of joints and frequent life-endangering septicemias is reached. The practitioners should possess the knowledge of this type of surgical procedure not to qualify limbs for amputation.

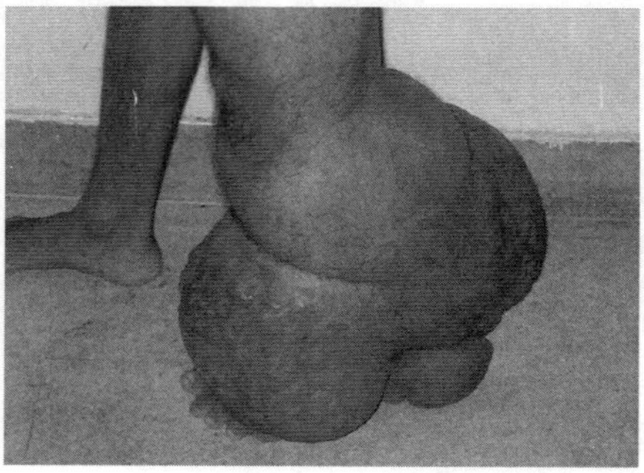

Long-lasting inflammatory processes in soft tissues of lower limbs bring about obliteration of lymphatics and fibrosis of lymph nodes with depletion of their lymphoid elements. The lymphatic system of the extremity looses its functional capacity in regulating the water and protein content of the tissue fluid and as a defence organization recognizing and eliminating the penetrating microorganisms.

The result is not only swelling of tissues but also a chronic inflammatory reaction with recurrent acute episodes. There is a large body of evidence that skin deprived of lymphatic outflow is prone to infections. The spectacular example is the remnants of infected foot skin after debulking operations.

Very advanced stage IV lymphedema cases are not common in the Western hemisphere. They account for less than 1 percent of all lymphedema patients. However, they are very frequent in the Asian and African countries.

The morphological changes of advanced lymphedema include:

1. Hyperkeratosis and fibrosis of skin,
2. Fibrosis of subcutis,
3. Lack of lymphatic channels with formation of numerous tissue fluid lakes,
4. Growth of fat tissue,
5. Limited capillary filtration with total stop for immune cell extravasation,
6. Tissue fluid subepidermal blisters with leakage,
7. Superficial skin ulcers,
8. Bacterial colonization of deep tissues,
9. Doubling or tripling limb weight with destruction of hip and knee joint,
10. Frequent episodes of limb-origin DLA attacks and sepsis.

Classic operations as total denuding of limb down to fascia and covering with epidermal grafts turned to be unsatisfactory because of acute infections of remaining foot skin, epidermal ulcerations and plasma leakage from the uncovered surfaces.

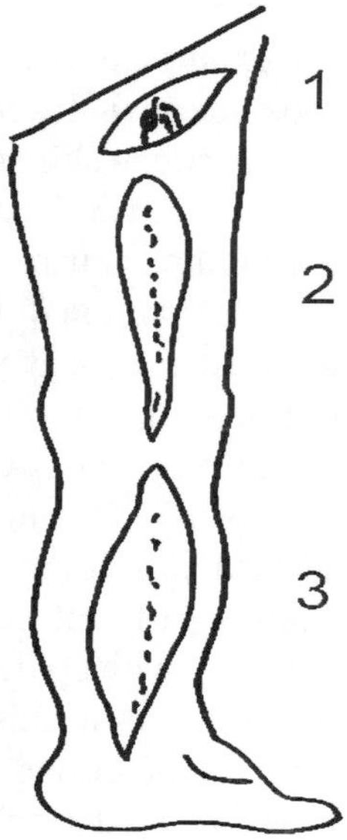

I redesigned the surgical procedures and the contemporary protocol includes:

1. Antibiotic preparation (ciprofloxacin 1.0 g daily for 3 months),
2. Daily disinfection of skin with antimicrobial soap containing phenol or similar chemical for 14 days before operation,
3. Two-week limb elevation in bed,
4. Surgery divided into 3 stages: a. removal of fibrotic inguinal lymph nodes and vessels, b. 3-4 weeks later surgical excision of fibrotic lymphatics down to knee level together with the neighboring fibrous infected tissues, c. debulking of calf and dorsum of foot in a bloodless limb (arterial tourniquet ?) and covering with pedunculated skin flaps,
5. bed-confined limb elevation and continuation of 0.5 g cipro for another month, later long-lasting penicillin,
6. elastic support (pressure grade III).

INDICATIONS FOR EXCISION OF INGUINAL LYMPAHTICS AND NODES

1. Lymphedema stage III and IV
2. Lack of lymphatics and nodes on lymphoscintigrams
3. Rapidly increasing size (volume) of the entire limb limiting movements
4. Frequent attacks of DLA (> 5 year)
5. Fibrotic nodes and lymphatics upon groin surgical revision

Operations is indicated only when all criteria are met

NEW ELEMENTS IN DEBULKING SURGERY

1. Long-term systemic antibiotic preparation (3 months)
2. Resection of redundant skin and subcutaneous tissue (with fibrotic lymphatics) and covering denuded surface with pedunculated flaps
3. Excision of fibrotic fascia

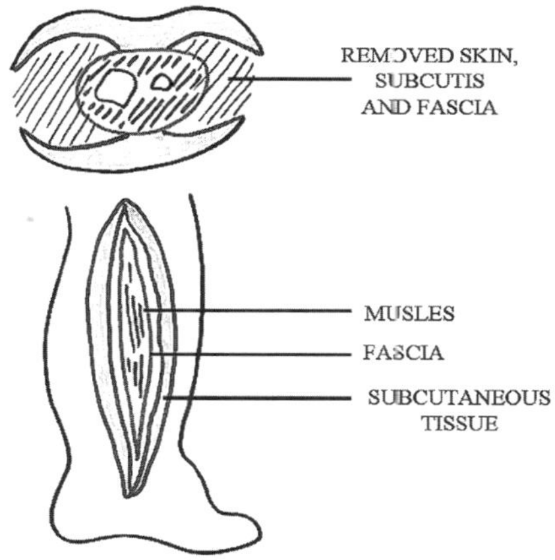

FOLLOW-UP 2005

1. Excision of fibrotic inguinal lymph nodes and vessels: 27 patients, stage IV, follow-up 24 mo, Soft thigh but not calf tissues
2. Calf debulking: 12 patients, stage IV, follow-up 12 mo, Fast uneventful healing ! Hard scar, no recurrent edema, no recurrent DLA

LIPOSUCTION OF LEG LYMPHEDEMA: PRELIMINARY TWO YEAR RESULTS

Håkan Brorson MD, PhD, Karin Ohlin OTR, Gaby Olsson PT, Barbro Svensson PT

The Lymphedema Unit, Department of Plastic and Reconstructive Surgery, Malmö University Hospital, SE-205 02 Malmö, Sweden

INTRODUCTION

Patients with long-standing pronounced non-pitting lymphedema do not respond to conservative treatment [CDT (complete decongestive therapy), CCT (controlled compression therapy), compression pumping (CP)] or microsurgical procedures (such as lympho-venous shunts or transplantation) because slow or absent lymph flow, as well as chronic inflammation, cause the formation of excess subcutaneous adipose tissue which cannot be removed by these methods. Previous surgical techniques utilizing either total excision with skin grafting or reduction seldom achieved acceptable, cosmetic and functional results. The swelling of chronic non-pitting arm lymphedema following breast cancer, can be completely reduced by liposuction and has not recurred during more than ten years' follow-up. Encouraged by this experience, we decided to test the effectiveness of liposuction on leg lymphedema.

PATIENTS AND METHODS

(median and ranges): 11 patients (7 women and 4 men) with an age of 55 years (21-73) and a duration of leg swelling of 18 years (6-50) underwent liposuction due to non-pitting, chronic lymphedema. There were 7 primary (PL), and 4 secondary lymphedemas (SL) following cancer therapy (cervix, penis, melanoma). One patent had PL, which was grossly aggravated by SL due to treatment of a seminoma. This patient was classified as a PL. In all 3 SL, regional lymph nodes were removed, and 2 received postoperative irradiation due to local glandular metastasis. All patients had received conservative treatment (CDT, CCT, and/or CP) before surgery without further reduction. All were wearing compression garments before surgery. Aspirate total volume, as well as the concentration of adipose tissue in the aspirate, removed under bloodless conditions, were measured.

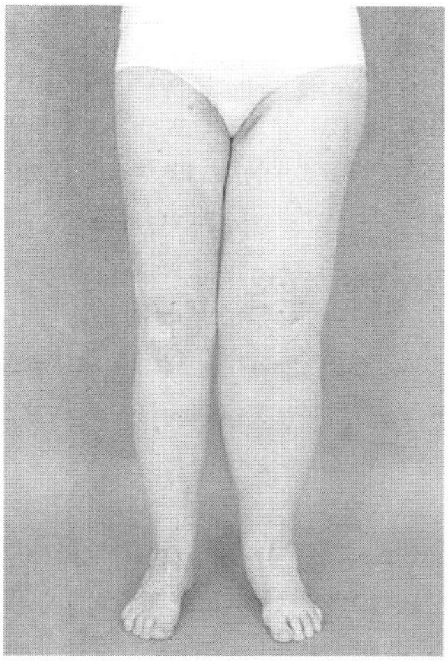

Fig. 1. 73-years-old woman with a non-pitting primary lymphedema since 50 years. Preoperative excess volume is 5790 ml. (© Håkan Brorson 2005)

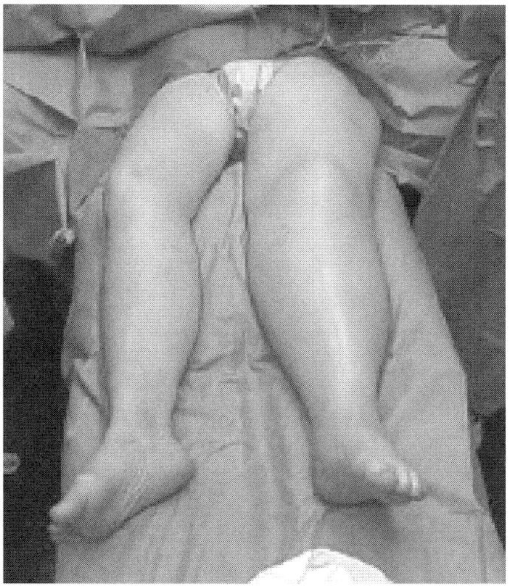

Fig. 2. Before surgery. (© Håkan Brorson 2005)

Pre- and postoperative leg volumes were recorded using water pletysmography. The decrease in the excess volume was calculated both as a percentage of the preoperative excess volume, as well as a ratio between the volumes of the swollen and healthy leg.

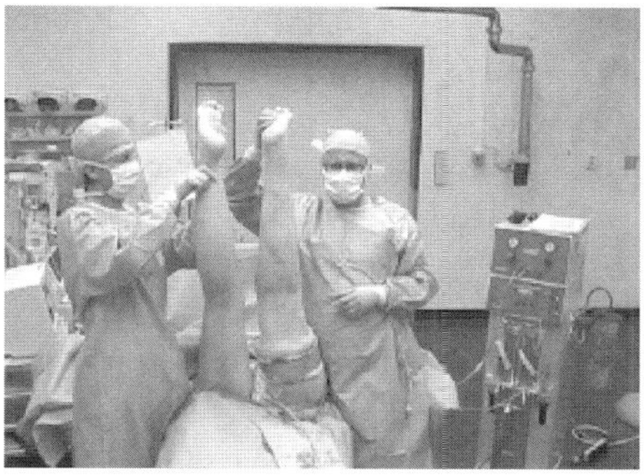

Fig. 3. 5930 ml adipose tissue removed. (© Håkan Brorson 2005)

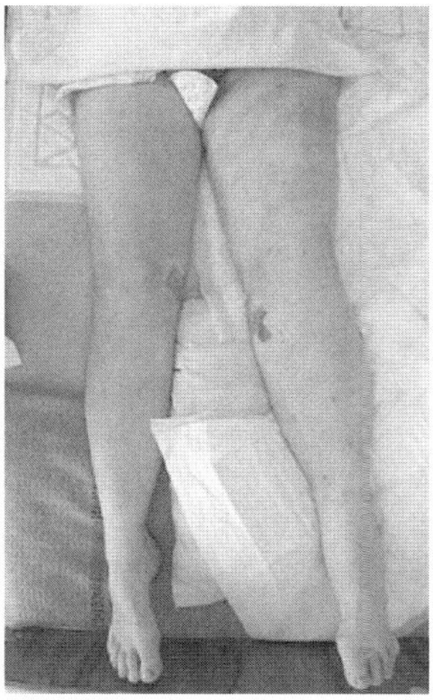

Fig. 4. Two days after surgery. (© Håkan Brorson 2005)

RESULTS

(median and ranges): Aspirate volume was 4060 ml (1360-7330), and the concentration of adipose tissue was 93% (40-100). Preoperative excess volume and ratio (swollen/healthy leg) were 4655 ml (1200-7190) and 1.4 (1.2-1.7) (n=11) respectively. Postoperative percentage reductions and ratios (swollen/healthy leg) were 43% (24-96) and 1.2 (1.0-1.4) at 2 weeks (n=11); 72% (13-96) and 1.1 (1.0-1.3) at 4 weeks (n=11); 79% (35-121) and 1.1 (1.0-1.2) at 3 months (n=8); 90% (15-100) and 1.1 (1.0-1.3) at 6 months (n=8); 113% (64-158) and 1.0 (1.0-1.1) at 1 year (n=5); and 99% (64-124) and 1.0 (0.9-1.1) (n=3) at 2 years.

CONCLUSIONS

These preliminary results demonstrate that liposuction is also effective for treating long standing chronic, non-pitting, leg lymphedema (Figure 1-4). Conservative methods and microsurgical procedures cannot remove the hypertrophied adipose tissue (induced by inflammation and the slow or absent lymph flow), which is a prerequisite to achieving complete reduction. Although lower extremity lymphedema has been refractory to treatment because of the combination of fat accumulation and dependency, liposuction provides reductions in volume of up to more than 90% that are maintained through constant use of compression garments post operatively for up to two years. The short term results are extremely encouraging and warrant continuing follow-up.

LONG TERM COSMETIC AND FUNCTIONAL RESULTS FOLLOWING LIPOSUCTION FOR ARM LYMPHEDEMA: AN ELEVEN YEAR STUDY

Håkan Brorson MD, PhD, Karin Ohlin OTR, Gaby Olsson PT, Barbro Svensson PT,

The Lymphedema Unit, Department of Plastic and Reconstructive Surgery, Malmö University Hospital, SE-205 02 Malmö, Sweden

INTRODUCTION

Breast cancer is the most common disease in women, and up to 38% develop lymphedema of the arm following mastectomy, standard axillary node dissection and postoperative irradiation. Limb reductions have been reported utilizing various conservative therapies such as manual lymph and compression therapies. Patients with longstanding, pronounced, non-pitting lymphedema do not respond to conservative treatment because diminished lymph flow and inflammation result in the formation of excess subcutaneous adipose tissue. Previous surgical treatments utilizing either total excision with skin grafting or reduction seldom achieved acceptable cosmetic and functional results. Microsurgical reconstruction involving lymphovenous shunts or transplantation of lymph vessels, although attractive as a physiological concept, cannot provide complete reduction in chronic non-pitting lymphedema because it does not eliminate newly formed, subcutaneous adipose tissue collections.

PATIENTS AND METHODS

87 women with non-pitting edema, a mean age of 64 years (41-89) and a mean duration of arm swelling of 9 years (1-38) underwent liposuction. Mean age at breast cancer operation and mean interval between breast cancer operation and lymphedema start were 53 years (34-80), and 3 years (0-32) respectively. The total volume of aspirate was measured. Pre- and postoperative arm volumes were recorded. The decrease in excess volume was also calculated both as a percentage of the preoperative excess volume, as well as a ratio between the volumes of the swollen and healthy arms (Figs. 1a, b).

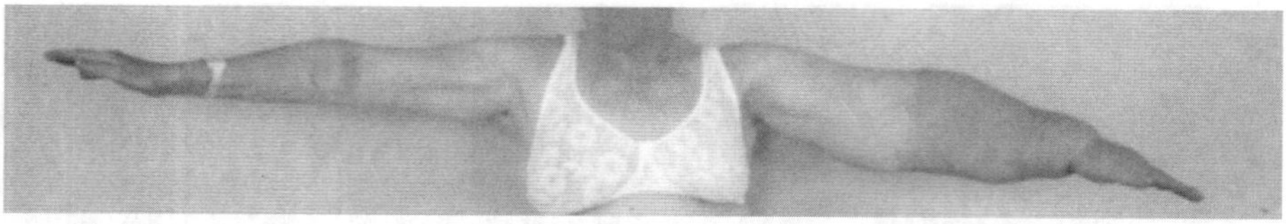

Fig. 1a. A 74-years-old woman with a non-pitting arm lymphedema of 15 years. Preoperative excess volume is 3090 ml. (© Håkan Brorson 2005).

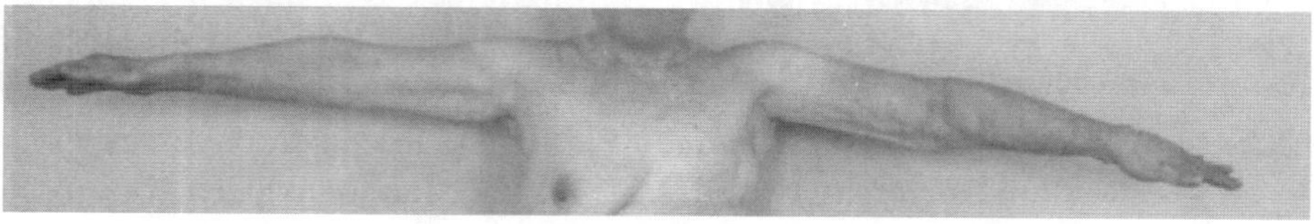

Fig. 1b. Postoperative result. (© Håkan Brorson 2005).

RESULTS

Aspirate mean volume was 1960 ml (845-3850). Preoperative mean excess volume was 1740 ml (570-3195) (Fig. 2). Postoperative mean reduction values were 95% at 3 months (n=84), 101 % at 6 months (n=82), 107% at 1 year (n=78), 110% at 2 years (n=75), 110 % at 3 years (n=75), 111% at 4 years (n=68), 111% at 5 years (n=58), 113% at 6 years (n=37), 114% at 7 years (n=33), 115% at 8 years (n=24), 115% at 9 years (n=20), 117% at 10 years (n=14), and 108% at 11 years (n=7), i.e. the lymphedematous arm was somewhat smaller than the healthy arm. The preoperative mean ratio between the volumes of the swollen and healthy arms was 1.54, rapidly declining to 1 at 6 months and less than 1 after 6 months.

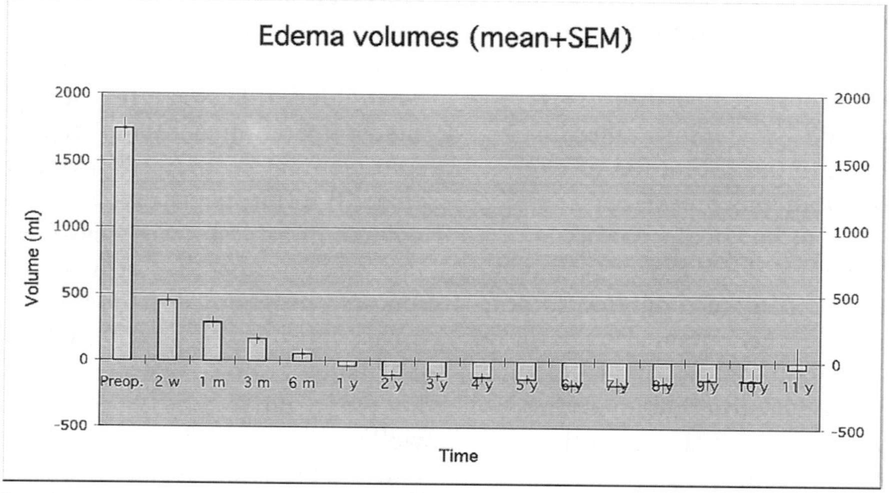

Fig. 2. Mean postoperative excess volume reduction.

CONCLUSIONS

These long-term results demonstrate that liposuctioning is an effective method for treatment of chronic, non-pitting arm lymphedema in patients who have failed conservative treatment. Because of adipose tissue hypertrophy, it is the only known method that completely reduces excess volume. The removal of hypertrophied adipose tissue, induced by inflammation and slow or absent lymph flow, is a prerequisite to complete reduction. The newly reduced volume is maintained through constant (24-hour) use of compression garments postoperatively.

REFERENCES

1. Brorson H, Svensson H. Skin blood flow of the lymphedematous arm before and after liposuction. Lymphology 1997; 30: 165-172.
2. Brorson H, Svensson H. Complete reduction of lymphoedema of the arm by liposuction after breast cancer. Scand J Plast Reconstr Surg Hand Surg 1997; 31: 137-143.
3. Brorson H, Svensson H. Liposuction combined with controlled compression therapy reduces arm lymphedema more effetively than controlled compression therapy alone. Plast Reconstr Surg 1998; 102: 1058-1067.
4. Brorson H, Svensson H, Norrgren K, Thorsson O. Liposuction reduces arm lymphedema without significantly altering the already impaired lymph transport. Lymphology 1998; 31: 156-172.
5. Brorson H. Fettabsaugung des Lymphödems am Arm. Handchir Mikrochir Plast Chir 2003; 35: 225-232.
6. Brorson H. Liposuction in arm lymphedema treatment. Scand J Surg 2003: 92: 287-295.

MANAGEMENT OF PRIMARY CHYLOUS ASCITES IN A YOUNG PATIENT

Andrade M, Carvalho Sobrinho AC, Martins ACP, Neves CB

Dept. Of Surgery, Univ. of São Paulo, Brazil

INTRODUCTION

Chylous ascites is the accumulation of chyle into the peritoneal cavity. It is an uncommon disorder usually caused by obstruction or rupture of peritoneal or retroperitoneal lymphatic ducts[1]. The management of this disorder is difficult because of the mechanical, nutritional and immunological consequences of continuous loss of protein and lymphocytes[1, 4, 13].

Besides congenital defects, many disorders can cause this condition, such as: tuberculosis, bacterial infections, filariasis, liver cirrhosis, malignant neoplasm, blunt abdominal trauma and surgical injury to lymphatic vessels[3, 6, 10, 12, 14, 15]. The increase in the incidence of chylous ascites diagnoses may be related to the more aggressive thoracic and retroperitoneal surgery and with the prolonged survival of cancer patients.

Treatment of this condition involves total parenteral nutrition (TPN); high protein and medium chain triglyceride (MCT) diet, somatostatin and repeated paracentesis, isolated or associated to each other. The surgical approach to the lymphatic fistula is only recommended when conservative treatment fails.

CASE REPORT

A 26 year-old male was referred to our institution because of the finding of chylous ascites during epigastric hernia repair. He had lost 10 Kg in the last four months. Oncological investigation was negative, the seven liters of bright white fluid with high triglyceride level were aspirated through paracentesis and the patient was kept under total parenteral nutrition.

After 20 days, no evident clinical sign of ascites remained and a medium-chain triglyceride diet was initiated and the patient was discharged. Two months after, voluminous ascites recurred, despite the rigorous diet control. Ten liters of ascites were evacuated this time, and it was decided for surgical approach to the lymphatic fistula, associated to somatostatin (Sandostatin™ at a dose of 100 mcg 3 times a day). Surgical procedure consisted in extended resection of dysplastic periaortic and pericaval lymphatic tissue from superior mesenteric artery down to iliac bifurcation (FIG.). Resection of a 20 cm segment of jejunum was also performed because chylous leakage was identified. At the end of operation there was no sign of chylous in the surgical field (Figs. 1 and 2).

Eight months after operation, the patient was under a normal fat diet and presented a new ascites recurrence. Conservative treatment with aspiration of seven liters of fluid, somatostatin, MCT diet was again initiated. After a follow-up period of 20 months, the patient shows no signs of recurrence.

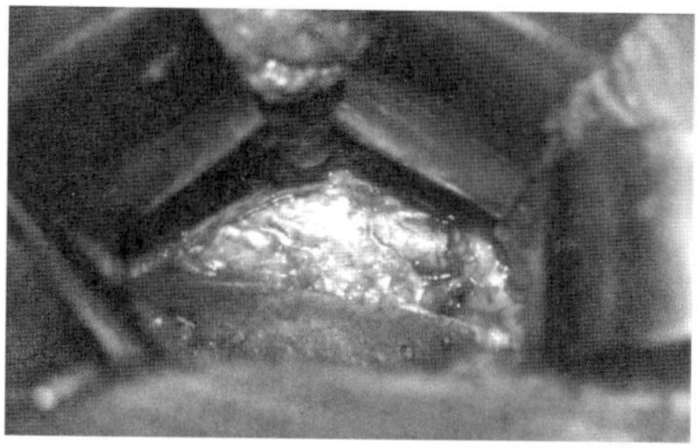

Fig. 1. Extensive retroperitoneal lymphatic dysplasia. Vessels identified after a fatty meal.

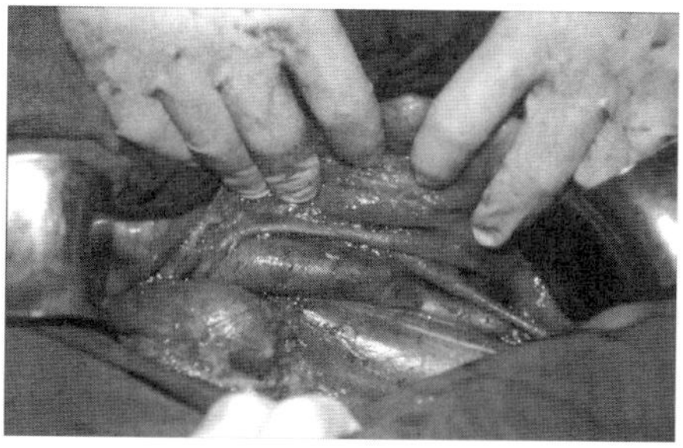

Fig. 2. Postoperative aspect. Complete resection of the dysplastic vessels from the superior mesenteric artery to the iliac bifurcation.

DISCUSSION

Many clinical conditions may be associated with the development of chylous ascites. The important nutritional deficit in association to the drop in lymphocyte counts and diaphragm compression (mechanical factor) lead to a higher risk of infectious complications, one of the most important causes of death.

Regardless the cause of this complex disorder, its initial management involves conservative measures such as medium chain triglyceride, high protein, low salt diet, associated to diuretics, total parenteral nutrition and use of somatostatin[2, 7, 9].

When conservative measures are not successful, surgical approach is indicated. Suture of the lymphatic fistulas, small bowel resection, extended retroperitoneal resection of dysplastic lymphatic pathways and peritoneal-venous are some possible surgical interventions. Some authors perform this ligatures trough a minimally invasive video assisted technique[8, 11]. This approach is helpful in visualization of any involvement of small bowel as a source of lymph leak. Campisi et al.[5] reported a series of 12 patients when the authors associated microsurgical lymphovenous shunts to removal of dysplastic retroperitoneal lymphatic in all patients, and observed recurrence in only one, who received a peritoneal-jugular shunt with good outcome.

In this case, extensive resection of dysplastic tissue with

ligature of all lymphatics of the leaking zone was performed; recurrence may indicate that even though surgical resection is considered complete, it is important to keep the patient under prolonged conservative treatment in order to reduce recurrence.

CONCLUSION

Management of chylous ascites is directed to ensure a decrease in intestinal lymphatic flow, associated with parenteral nutrition. As long as there is no sign of ascites it is possible to introduce medium chain triglyceride diet. Surgical approach is not the first choice of treatment, being reserved to patients with poor response to conservative treatment.

REFERENCES

1. Aalami, OO; Allen, DB; Organ, CH. Chylous ascites: A collective review. Surg, 2000; 128: 761-778.
2. Berzigotti, A; Magalotti, D; Cocci, C; Angeloni, L; Pironi, L; Zoli, M. Octreotide in the outpatient therapy of cirrhotic chylous ascites: A case report. Dig. Liver Dis., 2006; 38: 138-142.
3. Boran, N; Cil, AP; Tulunay, G; Ozgul, N; Kose, MF. Chylous ascites following para-aortic lymphadenectomy: a case report. Gynecol. Oncol., 2004; 93: 711-714.
4. Browse, NL; Wilson, NM; Russo, F; Al-Hassan,H; Allen,DR. Aetiology and treatment of chylous ascites. Br. J. Surg., 1992; 79: 1145-1150.
5. Campisi, C; Bellini, C; Eretta, C; Zilli, A; Rin, E; Davini, D; Bonioli, E; Boccardo, F. Diagnosis and management of primary chylous ascites. J. Vasc. Surg., 2006; 43: 1244-1248.
6. Caumartin, Y; Dujardin, T. Postoperative chylous ascites in urology. Prog. Urol., 2005; 15: 1046-1055.
7. Collard, JM; Laterre, PF; Boemer, F; Reynaert, M; Ponlot, R. Conservative Treatment of Postsurgical Lymphatic Leaks With Somatostatin-14. Chest, 2000; 117: 902-905.
8. Cristodoulou, M; Ris, HB; Pezetta, E. Vídeo-assisted right supradiaphragmatic thoracic duct ligation for non-traumatic recurrent chylothorax. Eur. J. Cardiothorac. Surg., 2006; 29: 810-814.
9. Giovannini, I; Giuliante, F; Chiarla, C; Ardito, F; Vellone, M; Nuzzo, G. Non-surgical management of a lymphatic fistula, after laparoscopic colorectal surgery, with total parenteral nutrition, octreotide, and somatostatin. Nutrition, 2005; 21: 1065-1067.
10. Gloviczki, P. Primary chylous ascites. J. Vasc. Surg., 2006; 43: 1297-1298.
11. Jensen, EH; Weiss, CA. Management of chylous ascites after laparoscopic cholecystectomy using minimally invasive techniques: a case report and literature review. Am. Surg., 2006; 72: 60-63.
12. Link, RE; Amin, N; Kavoussi, LR. Chylous ascites following retroperitoneal lymphadenectomy for testes cancer. Nat. Clin. Pact. Urol., 2006; 3: 226-232.
13. Noel, AA; Gloviczki, P; Bender, CE; Whitley, D; Stanson, AW; Deschamps, C. Treatment of symptomatic primary chylous disorders. J. Vasc. Surg., 2001; 34: 785-791.

14. Poux, JM; Benevent, D; Guiserix, J; Le Meur, Y; Lagarde, C; Leroux-Robert,C. Chylous ascites in 12 patients undergoing peritoneal dialysis. Nephrologie, 1994;15:201-205.

15. Takeuchi, S; Kinoshita, H; Terasawa, K; Minami, S. Chylous ascites following operation for para-aortic lymph node dissection in a patient with cervical cancer. Int. J. Gynecol. Cancer, 2006; 16 Suppl 1: 418-422.

EXERETIC SURGERIES – WHEN AND WHY

Walter Ferreira de Azevedo Júnior[1, 2], Robyson Uzeda[1], Gilberto Ferreira de Abreu Junior[1], Jose Amandio [2],Gustavo Barreiros, José Maria Martins Alves[1], Allan Maia[1], Fabio Maia[1], Mauricio Aquino[1], Paulo César Menezes Santos[1]

1- Angiology and Vascular Surgery Service of Santa Isabel Hospital
2- Plastic Surgery Service of Santa Isabel Hospital

Introduction

Lymphedema represents a not rare pathological clinical sign, characterized by incapacity for lymph transport, either caused by mechanical blocked of the semi lymphatic circle or by increase of the lymph flow. The most advance stage of lymphedema in fibroses, acantosis, verrucosis lymphostatic and member deformity is good indication for this kind of treatment. One important contribution for the long post operate of the Charles Operate Dermal – Epidermal Lipectomy of the limbs. The modification by Josias Freitas – Mayall by including the skin flap below the knee, to help the nutrition of the of the muscle and skin and tissue reimplanted after dermal –epidermal – lipectomy. The good Limphoscintilography is important for show present deep lymphatic and lymphnodes.

Materials and Methods

Lymphedema with angiodysplasic basic of non identified genetic origin patient with bilateral attack. Patient present bone dystrophy with total blindness. Laboratorial exams presented threshold normalcy results. The Lymphatic lymphoscintilographic showed that lymph took the deep route direction with apparition of poplitel Lymphonodes in the superficial circle there was no progression of the contrast.

The patient presented the right lower member in elephantiasic stage so was undertaken an ablative surgery by Charles modified by Josias de Freitas and Rubens Carlos Mayall, a dermo – epidermal lipectomy with maintenance of a nutritional flap under knee.

Conclusion

The patient evolved in post surgery stage with discreet anemia which was corrected by the infusion of a bag of hemacis concentred. There was no vast skin necrosis and 1 month there was total skin healing. At the hospital the patient was given direction to rehabilitative physical therapy and elastic contention.

The Surgical treatment Center of Lymphology and Microsurgery of Genoa University relates 5% of the patients operated on are operated by exeretic techniques.

However aiming a functional improvement of the member and the patients reintregation to social conviviality and labor activities.

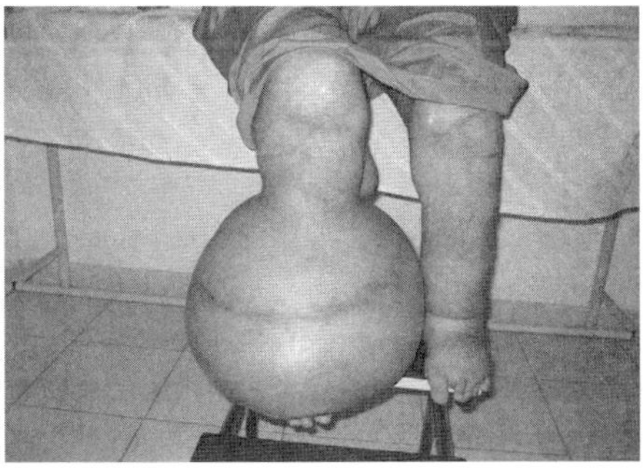

Fig. 1. Pre op patient with elephantiasis stage.

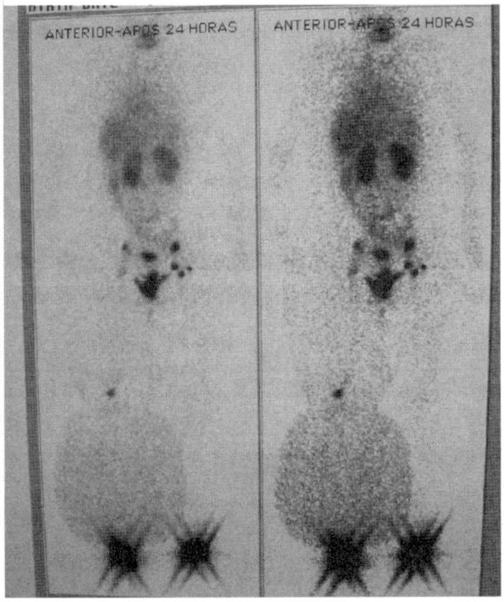

Fig. 2. Lymphoscintilography showed deep lymphati.

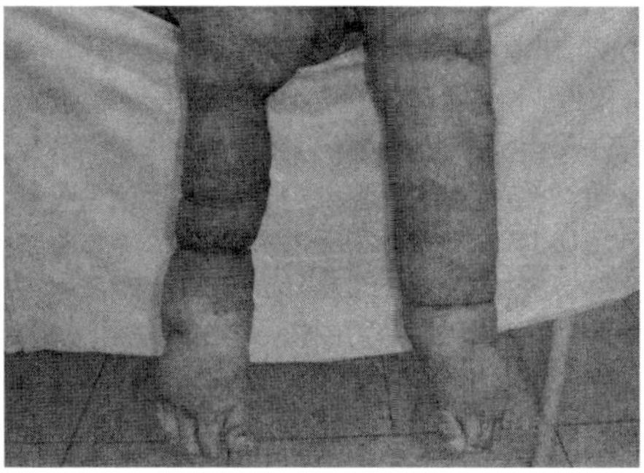

Fig. 3. Intra-operatory.

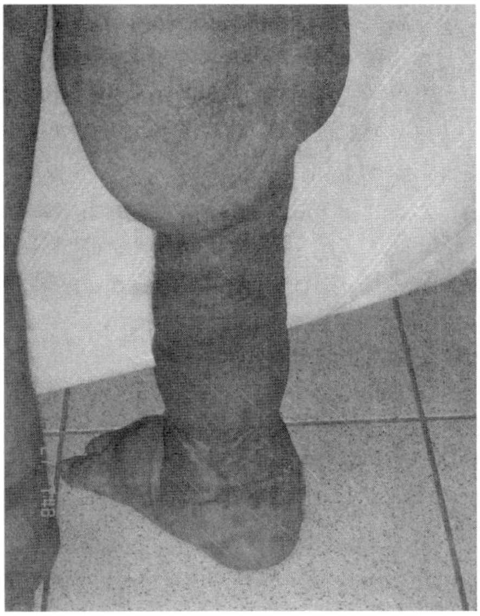

Fig. 4. One month of post operated.

References

1. Charles R H. A system cf treatment. Lathan and T C English. 1912 Vol 3 n 504
2. Mayall R C . Lymphology for Surgery. In Lymphology for Surgery. Campisi C Witte C L. Witte M H. Lymphology 2003 , 35 (Suppl 2). 1-472
3. Campisi C. Angiodysplasias and Lymphedema. Lymphology, 27 (Suppl) 893 p. 195.

LYMPHOSCINTILOGRAPHIC EVALUATION OF LOWER LIMBS AFTER LIPOSUCTION: PRELIMINARY RESULTS

Kafejian-Haddad, A. P.; Haddad Filho, D.; Perez, M. D. C. J.; Castiglioni, M.; Anger, M.; Alonso, N.; Marchetti, R. R.; Fukutake, M.F.

- Discipline of Vascular Surgery - Faculdade de Medicina do ABC
- Discipline of Plastic Surgery of Universidade de Santo Amaro - Medical School
- Discipline of Vascular Surgery - Escola Paulista de Medicina - Unifesp
- Departament of Image Diagnostic - Coordination of Nuclear Medicine-Escola Paulista de Medicina - Unifesp
- Service of Plastic Surgery of Hospital Brigadeiro

INTRODUCTION

Valuate the alterations of lymphatic system of the lower limbs after liposuction, pre and postopertative days, through radioisotopic lymphocyntilographie. METHODS: Three patients with diagnosis of lipodystrophy included lateral and medial side of upper third part of thighs, were submitted to two lymphoscintilography exams by injecting by thechnnetium-99m-labeled dextran (Tc ^{99m} Dx) in the intradermic space in the operated areas. The first examination was done in pre-operatory (lymphoscintilography control). After 90 days of surgery, another lymphoscyntilographie was done with the same methodology to do the comparison. The analisis was qualitative according to the calculus of medium time of acquisition´s curve of radiopharmacon and clearance of the interested areas, comparing the pre and post-operatory values. Surgical procedure: After pre-operatory lymphocyntilographie, the patients were submitted to classical liposuction, exclusively in lateral and medial side of upper third part of thighs.

RESULTS

Two patients had an increase of the medium time and clearance aggravated, suggesting a worse lymphatic drainage of region.

CONCLUSION

These results infer a decrease of the lymphatic drainage in the liposucted area, being necessary larger casuistics.

EARLY EXPERIENCE OF SURGICAL CORRECTION OF LYMPHOEDEMA USING LIPOSUCTION

M. Hough, S. Lundie, M. Finnegan, D.A. Munnoch

Department of Plastic Surgery, Ninewells Hospital, Dundee, United Kingdom

Introduction

The development of lymphoedema after mastectomy, axillary clearance and radiotherapy is not uncommon. The mainstay of management is non-surgical, combining a variety of massage and decongestive therapy techniques with compression garments. Surgical treatment may be necessary for those patients who fail to respond to conservative techniques or develop a progressive fatty hypertrophy. Debulking techniques can lead to significant scarring which is cosmetically unacceptable, whereas liposuction has been described as an effective means of removing the excess fatty tissue from the limb, while maintaining good cosmesis and controlling the lymphoedema (1-3).

Materials and Methods

Patients

Three patients have been referred from the lymphoedema service, all with upper limb lymphoedema following breast cancer surgery and radiotherapy. The lymphoedema had been present for between 12 & 80 months, and all patients had been treated with decongestive therapy and pressure garments. Two patients had suffered repeated episodes of cellulitis in the arm. Pitting oedema was excluded by performing a pressure test for one minute. Limb volume measurements were calculated using the conal volume technique which revealed an average excess of 1066mls in the affected limb.

Psychosocial assessment

In the absence of a good quality of life questionnaire for lymphoedema, it was decided to use the Hospital Anxiety & Depression Score (4) and the European Quality of Life EQ-5D (5) questionnaires. Both are simple to use and have been validated across a wide range of illnesses (6,7). Questionnaires have been completed preoperatively and at 3 months postoperatively.

Liposuction

Liposuction is performed under general anaesthesia with tourniquet control and antibiotic cover. Using cannulae designed by Dr Brorson, multiple stab incisions are made in the arm and liposuction carried out to remove the subcutaneous fat. A compression garment (Joebst Elvarex) is then applied, before the tourniquet is released. Should the upper arm require treatment, this area is infiltrated with dilute adrenaline to control bleeding. Once liposuction is completed, the pressure garment is advanced to cover the whole limb. The patient is returned to the ward with the limb elevated, and continues with postoperative antibiotics and analgesia as required.

Postoperative care

The patients remain on the ward and the dressings are removed at two days. There is usually minimal bruising at this stage and the wounds are healing well. The limb is cleaned, measured for a custom made garment and a fresh pressure garment applied. These first garments are standard 'off the shelf' garments with shoulder strap, having been measured from the opposite limb. The patients are discharged and return two days later for further wound check. The standard garments are used for two weeks, until the first custom garment is available. They are seen in the outpatient clinic at two and four weeks, and again at three months, with measurements taken and garment adjusted to maximise compression.

Results

Two patients sustained minor ulceration in the first webspace due to the pressure from the garments, which resolved very quickly. There have been no episodes of infection. The mean aspirate volume was 1242mls of fat (Fig. 1) and in two cases, this aspirate equalled the preoperative excess measurement, while in the third case it exceeded the excess measurement (Fig. 2). Over the three months, postoperative oedema has resolved completely in two patients, with a slower resolution in the third case, partly due to her active lifestyle.

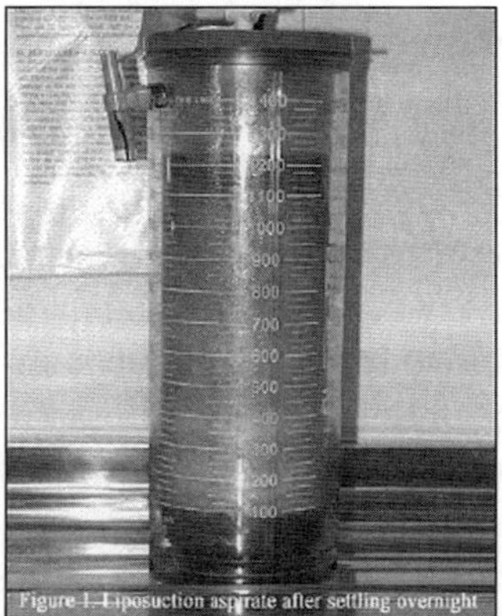

Figure 1. Liposuction aspirate after settling overnight

Figure 2. Volume reduction

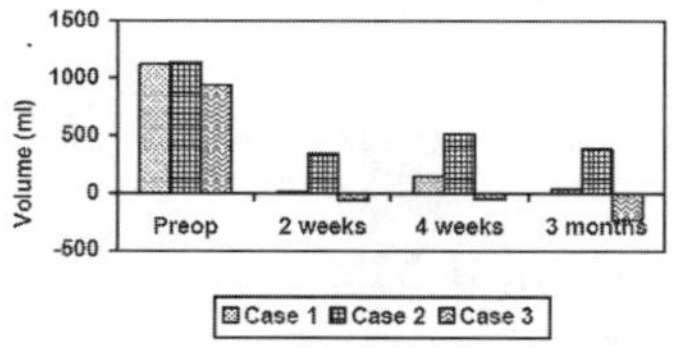

The patients' general well-being has improved as demonstrated by the reduction in anxiety and depression scores and the higher EQ-5D visual analogue scores. The patients have also expressed their

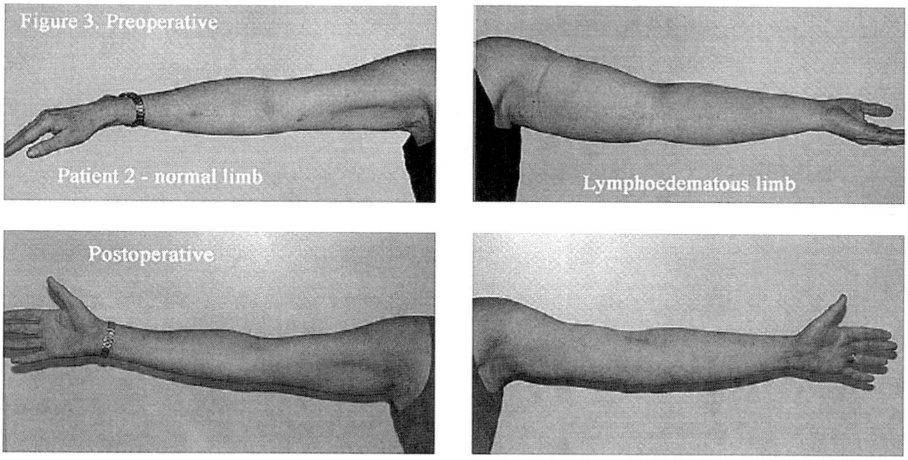

own opinions on this treatment. Non-compliance has been an issue with one patient, who visited Turkey for two weeks in the height of summer and did not wear her pressure garment. When she returned for her six month follow up, immediately after her holiday, she had 600mls of excess volume due to oedema. This is now being corrected with new pressure garments.

Conclusion

Liposuction combined with continuous compression therapy is effective in reducing, and maintaining, limb volume in chronic lymphoedema (Fig. 3). It is our intention to continue to offer this service.

References

1. O'Brien, BM, RK Khazanchi, PAV Kumar et al: Liposuction in the treatment of lymphoedema: A preliminary report. Br. J. Plast. Surg. 42 (1989), 530.
2. Brorson, H, H Svensson: Complete reduction of lymphoedema of the arm by liposuction after breast cancer. Scand. J. Plast. Reconstr. Surg. Hand Surg. 31 (1997), 137.
3. Brorson, H, H Svensson: Liposuction combined with controlled compression therapy reduces arm lymphedema more effectively than controlled compression therapy alone. Plast. Reconstr. Surg. 102(4) (1998), 1058.
4. Zigmond A, RP Snaith: The hospital anxiety and depression scale. Acta Psychiatrica Scandinavica. 67 (1983), 361.
5. EuroQol Group: EuroQol - A new facility for the measurement of health-related quality of life. Health Policy. 16 (1990), 199.
6. Bjelland I, A Dahl, T Haug et al: The validity of the Hospital Anxiety and Depression Scale. An updated literature review. J Psychosom Res. 52 (2002), 69.
7. Brooks R: EuroQol: the current state of play. Health Policy 37 (1996), 53.

MAYALL HIPERSTOMY SYNDROME, A SUCCESSFUL CASE

Walter Ferreira de Azevedo Júnior, Robyson Uzeda , Gilberto Ferreira de Abreu Junior, Mauricio Aquino, Allan Maia, Fabio Maia, Gustavo Barrreiros, Paulo César Menezes Santos

Cirurgia Vascular do Hospital Santa Izabel-Salvador-Bahia

Abstract

The presence of hyperstomy is properly investigated by high speed arteriography, which shows some indirect signs, such as praecox venous back flow and spots on the muscle tissue, that are considered typical findings of hiperstomy. Hiperstomy to avoid troubles in vascular pathology mainly arteries, venous and lymphatics, that have a very single treatment in most cases guided skeletization on aterioles branches, showed by arteriography.

Introduction

The hemodynamic alteration caused by arterioles venular micro shunt formation has clinical repercussion of difficult diagnoses [1].

Clinical aspect as varicose veins of limb, difference between long of limb at relation with contra lateral, cutaneous hypothermy, praecox venous back flow and ulcer with no healing with traditional treatment for venous insufficiency are sign and symptoms of this syndrome[7]

Amir-Jahed e Pratesi e cols characterized as particular clinical condition with simulation of ischemia without artery obstruction[5 6]. The etiopathogenesis, etiological factors, and the symptomatology are comum of many diseases that turns difficult the diagnosis.

In 1997, Campisi call attention in XVII Lymphology International Congress with new vision for phisiopatology that better define the participation lymphatic on process[11].

The ulcer has as etiological the appearance of abnormal arteriolar branches, with pathogeneses no objective artery obstruction.

Materials and Methods

This is the report of serious ulcers complicating and important venous insufficiency and also lymphedema after repeated crisis of erysipelas and lymphangitis, during 15 years treated by home care without physician.

This patient 32 years that to go at ambulatory of Department of Angiology and Vascular Surgery of Santa Isabel Hospital in Salvador – Bahia, With a big ulcerations in left leg. Repeated crisis of erysipelas and lymphangitis that no bettered whit antibiotic therapy and function aspect of limb were limited on evaluation of the ulcer.

The patient don't talks about traumatic and family history this disease.

Physical exam showed a big ulcer with pain type paresthesias, 0,5 of deep, bigger extension and infection.(Fig. 1). A inspection also showed varicose vein in the limb affected, more evident on the size of ulcer. The distal pulse with good expansion and intensity, no have local an machine murmurs are always present, as the Nicoladoni Branhham sign of bradycardia after local digital compression.

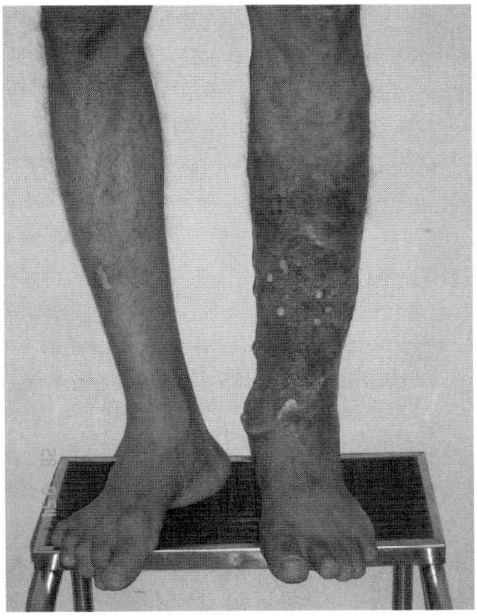

Fig. 1. Pre op.

Performed the color Doppler Ultra sonography of artery and venous system, where no were concluded critic artery disease, even though the superficial venous system showed reflux by all its extension.

After an good mapping biopsies too showed normal and culture were positive for pseudomonas sensitive the ciprofloxacin 400mg iv 2x day 12/ 12h.

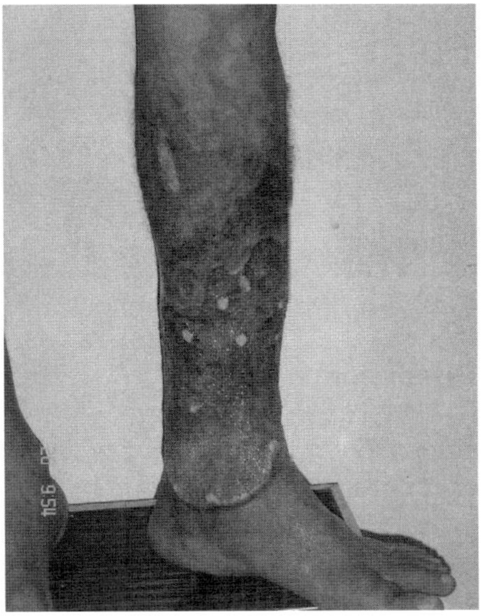

Fig. 2. Ulcer in patient with 15 years of evaluation.

The presence of hyperstomy was properly investigated by high-speed arteriography. It showed three abnormal branches in posterior tibial artery. This exam has a good accuracy, in this condition make possible diagnosis of Mayall Syndrome.

The operation to skeletize the abnormal branching off the calf arteries was followed by complete cure in one month. The follow up this patient is 2 years.

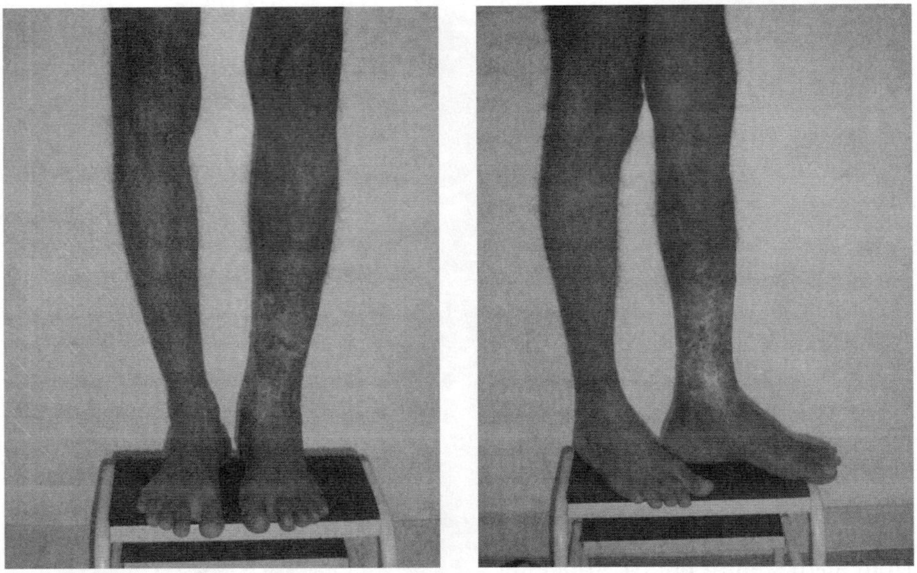

Figs. 3-4. Pos Operate 1 month after.

Discussion

The present study emphasize the importance of an exam of arterial circulation on disease with venous clinical aspect. The Hiperstomy Syndrome is a chronic disease and no has many reference in literature, only four on Medline. Even though this case call attention the necessity of avaliation this hypothesis.

Important Brazilian research dedicated part of your life emphasizing this syndrome. In present moment , with convinced and repeated argument present by him, Campisi, 1997 call attention that Rubens Carlos Mayall no has beneficed by vulgarization scientific and consideration on practical of angiology medicine and vascular surgical.

The arteriography aspect is simile the form that Mayall wrote. The injury of ulcer in Hiperstomy Syndrome has radical cure with long time follow up, after skeletization of all abnormal branches.

References

1. Mayall R C. Síndrome de Hiperostomia – Tese , Ed. Villani , Filhos , 1976 – Rio de Janeiro – R.J.
2. De Bakey, M E Burch G. Ray,T. Ochsner, A. The Borrowing – Lending hemodynamic phenomenon (Hemometakinesia) and therapeutic application in periphral vascular distubances. Ann , Surgery, 120 , 850 . 1947.
3. Malan E D. patologia delle communicazioni artero venose della planta del piede – Bolletino della societá Piemontese di chirurgia , XXV nº 3 ,1955.
4. Dramez C ., Gerson L. Natali J. Arteriovenous Thigh Shunts giving

rise to serious ischemic disorders of the extremities . treatment by ligaturing the the arteria profunda femoris in both sides. Angiology , vol. 1 ,2 ,3, 4,:147-195, Avril 1965.
5. Haimovici H. Steinman C. Caplan L.H. Angiographic Evaluation of arteriovenous Shuntings in peripheral vascular Diseases , Radiology . 87 pg 696-704 ,Oct. 1966.
5. Amir Jahed A K. Angiodyskinesia – Collective Reviews Surg. Gynec. Ostetric., 217-609 , 1968.
6. Pratesi F., Nuti A. Due Nueve Sindromi Vascolari di Hiperostomia Arteriovenosa della coscia . Acad. Médico Física Fiorentina, April 18 , 1957.
7. Mayall , R C. Mayall ACDG. Mayall JC. Freitas J. Kurten M O. Almeida , MF Gonzalez RR. Souza , WDP. Hyperstomy syndrome in lymphedema 31 (Suppl.) Lymphology, 1-621, 1998. Pg.385.
8. Campisi C. Boccardo, F. Casaccia Jr., Tacchella :Angiodyplasia and lymphedema .27 (Suppl .) Lymphology 1-893 , 1994 .Pg 155.
9. Kurten ,M O. Hyperstomy Syndrome in Lynphedema .29 (Suppl.) Lynphology , 1- 404 ,1996. Pg 352.
10. Campisi, C., Boccardo , F., Caro D.G., Ieracitano V.M. , Zilli A.: Angiodysplasia Peripheral Lymphedema and Tumorigenous Syndromes, Lymphology 31 (Suppl.) 1-621 .1998. Pg 379.
11. Campisi C. Mayall's Hyperstomy Syndrome. Book of Abstracts of XVII International Congress of Lymphology , Chennai , India , Sept. 19 – 25 , 1999 , pg.49.

POST-MASTECTOMIC LYMPHEDEMA TREATMENT WITH LIMPHATIC ANASTOMOSES MICROSURGERY TECHNIQUE: A PERIMETRIC ANALYSES

Walter Ferreira de Azevedo Júnior[1, 2], Robyson Uzeda[1], Gilberto Ferreira de Abreu Junior[1], Luise Lange[2], Lorena Meyer[2],Gustavo Barreiros, José Maria Martins Alves[1], Allan Maia[1], Fabio Maia[1],Mauricio Aquino[1], Paulo César Menezes Santos[1]

1- Angiology and Vascular Surgery Service of Santa Isabel Hospital
2- Venous and Lymphatic Rehabilitation Nucleon

Abstract

Lymphedema post-mastectomy is one of the complication on the breast cancer. Prophylactic procedures post-surgery is important, what one the precocious diagnoses is necessery[1], even though sometimes are not really efficient. The clinic avaliation associated with lymphoscintilography allowed the precocious diagnoses. Lymphoscintilography has been useful at the diagnose, treatment plain and the surgery and clinic treatment avaliation[2].

Until few times ago the lymphedema clinical treatment was the main treatment indication[3 9], however lymphatic microsurgery has been indicated for these patients. The results shows improve at the lymph drainage at the post-mastectomy lymphedema[2].

The aim of study is emphasize the surgical option into Brazilian reality.

Introduction

The incidence of secondary lymphedema on upper limb is between 20-25% at the women submitted to mastectomy or quadrantectomy and with axilar lymphadenectomy, even 35% when associated to radiotherapy[10].

With the increase of the lymphology studies and the technology, Tossati and Campisi (Italy) come to give a new vision on the lymphedema treatment. Improving the venous-lymphatic anastomosis for Degni and Cordeiro[8] (Brazil) and changing the conception about surgical treatment of lymphedema what were until the end of century XX.

The patients more indicated for this surgery are that one with secondary lymphedema, because of lymphatics ways block caused by traumatic section or exercise. On the primary cases with fibroses of lymphatics vessel, lymphangitis of repeated and radiotherapy, the indication depends of the injury grade of the lymphatics, subcutaneous and skin. The best results are those that the surgeries are realized precocious. After the orientation viewed at the Lymphology and Microsurgery Center of Genoa University and with the initial experience of two years at Angiology and Vascular Surgery Department of Santa Isabel Hospital, we concluded that is vital procedures lymphatic-venous anastomosis for patient's rehabilitation.

The aim of present study is avaliation the reduction perimetric of the limb accometed before and after microsurgery lymphatic. The hypotheses that is the microsurgery lymphatic reducts 80% of the patients limb on the first post-operated week[5].

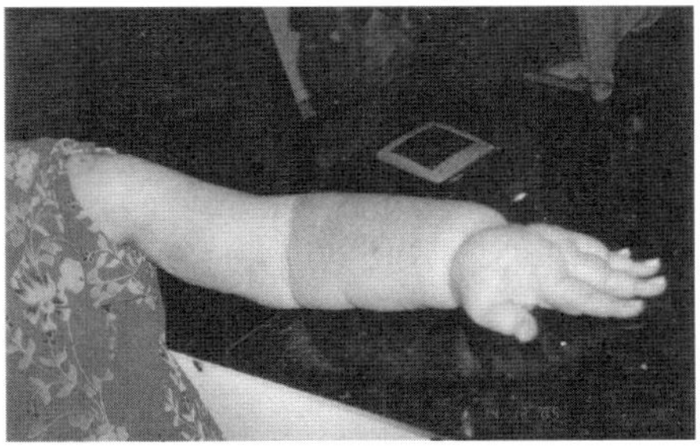

Fig. 1. Patient with lymphedema post mastectomy.

Materials and Methods

This research hasn't been submitted to the ethical committed on research, even though was respected the ethics principles of Helsinque 2000 declaration and the resolution 196/96 of the National Health Council.

The type of study of descriptive was done at the Angiology and Vascular Surgery Department of Santa Isabel Hospital and Venous and lymphatic rehabilitation Nucleon, Bahia Hospital.

Upper limb lymphedema Patients post-mastectomy with or without radiotherapy with the volumetric more than 200ml or the perimetry more 2 cm or 5 % of increase on the limb circumference than the contra lateral and confirmed by the scintilography were included at the study.

The Sample no probabilistic consecutive inclusion of patients with upper limb lymphedema post-mastectomy visited in the lymphology ambulatory of Santa Izabel Hospital and the Venous-lymph rehabilitation nucleon of Bahia Hospital.

Ten patients with lymphedema post-mastectomy were studied whose were done a documentation about pre-operative perimetry. The perimetry started on the metacarpi´s head increasing each 7 cm.

The patients were treated clinically. The lymphedema was treated using the Foldi-Leduc-Godoy technique, however didn't have satisfactory results. Than was done a lymphoscintilography to evaluated the possibility of a surgical treatment. The lymphatic microsurgery was chosen after the

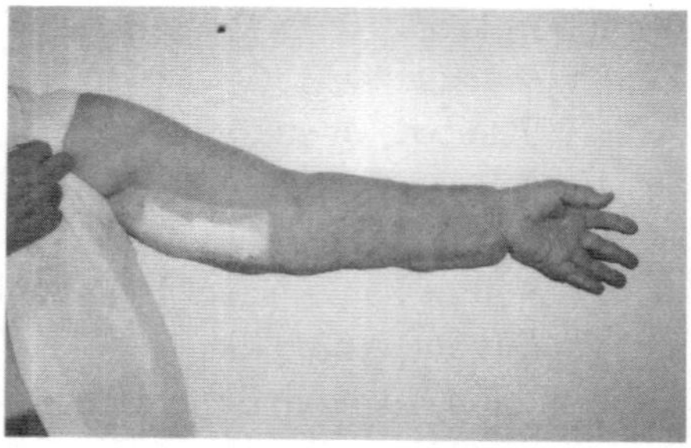

Fig. 2. Patient in DPO after microsurgery lymphaticy venous.

pre-operative exams, which one was done a derivation venous-lymphatic in the upper limb.

The surgical technique was done with the patient at dorsal position with 90°abdution of the right upper limb. The general anesthesia allowed a safe intervention during all procedure.

The lymphocromy was done by the kinmonth with Blue Patent injection in the dermal and subcutaneous space with the objective of color the lymphatic vessel.

Was done a longitudinal incision on the medial face of the upper limb, following the biceps medial board. Usually the incision is not bigger than 15 cm.

The braquial vein was isolated and choosen one of tributates, dissection and sectioned doing venous distal segment ligature. The lymphatic vessel just colored were dissected carefully avoiding the contact of the surgical material at the zone endothelial of vessel, manipulating just the peri-lymphatic tissue.

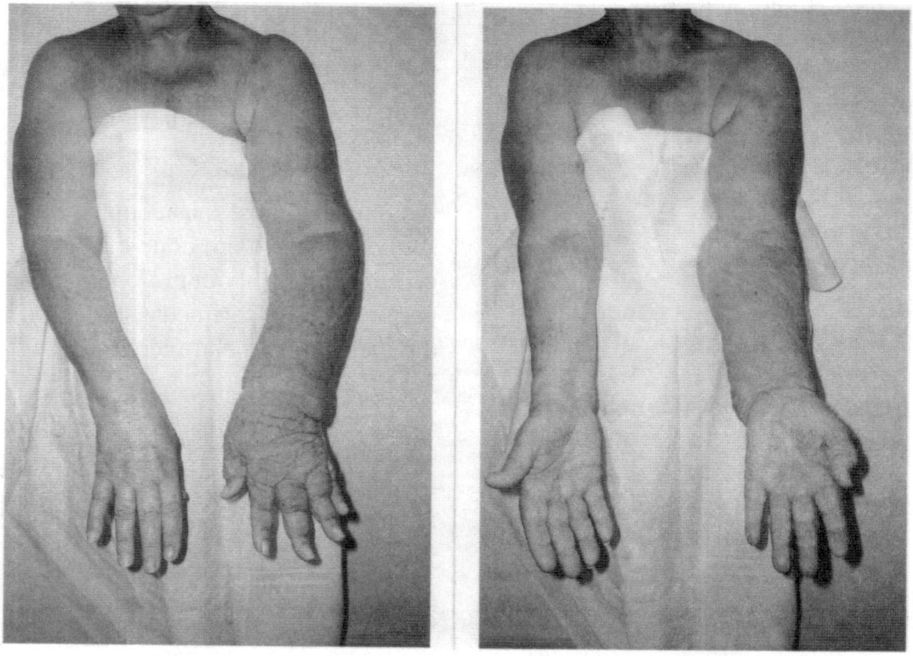

Fig. 3. Patient in DPO after microsurgery lymphaticy venous.

The operative microscopy allowed a increase of the operative field 25-40x. The telescopic technique allowed the introduction of the selected lymphatic vessels in the vein. The nylon used was mononylon 90. The vein was sutured at the subcutaneous tissue of side. For end was done the surgical sintese. The patient evaluated without claim and left the hospital 3 days after the surgery.

The statistical method was the Ficher test, admitted a error alpha 0,5 with a confiance de 95%.

Conclusion

We concluded that 90% of the studied patients reduced more than 80% with a p less than 0.001.

Discussion

The present study shows a surgical option at lymphedema post-mastectomy and emphasize this treatment to the Brazilian reality.

Many authors done study at national and international level, driving the lymphedema clinical treatment, however this technique came up during the last years. Even though, some important groups as Professor Campisi in Genova have been emphasized on the technique of lymphatic microsurgery with a large experience. Thanks these improvement was possible make better technique parameters and the clinical indication for the procedure. The present study describe one of these indication, with one the surgical treatment is more efficient than the conservative therapy what wasn't satisfactory and the patients were in great surgical conditions associated to great criteria like lymphedema post-mastectomy, fibrosis and previous infections less. These criteria come good possibilities of therapeutic success and results. All the cases should be analyzed individually, emphasizing the great conditions and contra-indication for the treatment.

The microsurgery is a reality during the years and appropriated indication come benefits to the patients.

References

1. C.Campisi,F. Boccardo, A.Zilli,A.Macciò,F.Napoli,Walter Ferriera de Azevedo Jr Linfedeema Secondario al Trattamento del Cancro Mammario- Possibillità di Prevenzione Diagnostica e Terapêu-tica Ann Ital Chir..,LXXIII,5,2002
2. Campisi C, Boccardo F, Casaccia M - Il linfedema dell'arto superiore secondario a linfoadenectomia e radioterapia adiuvante per cancro della mammella. Ospedali d'Italia Chirurgia 3:112-8,1997
3. Mayall, JC, ACDG Mayall: Standardization of methods of treatment of Lymphedema. Progress in Lymphology XI - Excerpta Medica (1988), 517.
4. Ciucci JL, Krapp JC, Soraccco JE, Ayguavella J, Marcovecchio JL, Salvia C, Gerez S, Gerez S, Felicia C, Belczak CEQ, Isola MC, Lamuedra I, Rosales S. Changes in clinical management and the evolution of an interdisciplinary therapeutic, in progress of lymphology.

5. C.Campisi,F. Boccardo,Walter Ferriera de Azevedo Jr, E. De Melo Couto, C. Stein Gomes Linfedemas dos Membros Superiores Secundários ao tratamento do câncer de mama. É possível preveni-lo? Revista Brasileira de Angiologia e Cirurgia Vascular- Volume 17 – Número 6 – dez 2001
6. Cossio J.A. Progresos en Linfologia I. Madrid, Jarpyo Editores SA, 1987.
7. Cossio J.A.: "Diagnostico y tratamiento de los linfedemas". Barcellone, Ed. Centro de Documentacio de Laboratorios Uriach, 1987.
8. Degni M. A new technique of lymphatico-venous anastomosis for the treatment of lymphedema of the limbs. *J Mal Vasc* 1988; 13: 131-135.
9. Földi M - The therapy of lymphoedema. Eur J Lymphol Rel Probl 4(14):43-9,1994.
10. Farrar WB, La Valle GJ, Kim JÁ - Breast cancer, in *Cancer Surgery*, Mc Kenna RJ, Murphy GP, JB Lippincott Company. Philadelphia 209:59,1994.
11. Ferrandez JC, Serin D, Bouges S - Frequency of lymphedema of the upper limb after treatment of breast cancer. Risk factors. A Propos of 683 cases. Bull Cancer 83(12):989-95,1996.
12. Witte CL - Breast Cancer - An Overview. Lymphology 27(Suppl):397-400,1994.
13. Witte CL, Witte MH - Consensus and dogma. Lymphology 31(3):98-100,1998.

Chapter 7
Management of Lymphedema

THE EFFECTIVENESS OF MACHINE-BASED MASSAGE (LPG ®) FOR TREATMENT OF POST-MASTECTOMY ARM LYMPHOEDEMA: 3 CASE STUDIES

Mariëlle A Esplin, Neil B Piller & Amanda L Moseley

Lymphoedema Assessment Clinic and Department of Surgery, Flinders University and Flinders Medical Centre, Bedford Park, South Australia

INTRODUCTION

Aim

To describe the effectiveness of the LPG® technique, a non-invasive treatment involving mechanical manipulation of tissues for post-mastectomy arm lymphoedema. It is anticipated that this might provide assistance with trial data interpretation for clinical practice.

Background

Arm lymphedema secondary to breast cancer therapy is a common complication that can have both functional and psychological impacts on the individual.[1] A 1998 review of seven large publications from five countries (United States, England, Italy, France and Germany) found the incidence of lymphoedema during 1991 to 1997 ranged from 6% to 30% among women with breast cancer following axillary treatment.[2] Recent research suggests that the evolution of less invasive breast cancer surgery may reduce the incidence of lymphoedema.[3] However, with the increasing survival of breast cancer patients, lymphoedema may possibly become more prevalent, suggesting further research in providing and evaluating the efficacy of therapeutic interventions.[1]

The LPG® device was developed in the 1970s by Louis Paul Guitay for trauma and burn scars, and since then the technique has been applied to other conditions, including cellulite and body contouring,[4,5] in combination with liposuction[6] and for secondary arm and leg lymphoedema to reduce oedema and soften fibrosis.[7] The LPG® technique (LPG Systems, France) delivers a mechanical treatment of the skin by lifting tissues with a mild continuous or intermittent suction, combined with motorised movement of two rollers.

The following case studies were part of a randomised trial conducted at the Lymphoedema Assessment Clinic, Flinders

University and Medical Centre, comparing machine-based massage (LPG®) with the Dr Vodder method of manual lymphatic drainage. The three patients described in the case studies below were selected to highlight the varied effectiveness of LPG® that can occur in management of secondary arm lymphoedema.

METHODS

Patients were recruited for clinically manifest chronic secondary unilateral arm lymphoedema associated with previous breast cancer treatment from May 2004 to February 2005. Ethics approval for the study was given by the Flinders Medical Centre Clinical Research Ethics Committee, Adelaide, Australia and each patient provided informed consent.

Participants received 25 minutes of LPG® technique to the upper body, upper arm and lower arm using a standardised treatment procedure, four times per week, for four weeks. Each treatment was followed by padded compression bandaging on the lymphoedematous arm.

Objective measurements were obtained through validated equipment, using bioimpedance (BioSpace®, Korea) for segmental limb and trunk fluid[8,9] and perometry[10,11] (Perosystems®, Germany) for arm volume. Subjective arm symptoms were rated on a previously validated 11 point scale[12,13] (0-10), where zero is no problem and 10 is the worst problem imaginable. Symptoms that were rated included arm heaviness, tightness, hardness, pain, cramps, pins and needles, and perceived temperature difference, size difference and range of movement compared to the unaffected arm. Measurements were taken over the four-week treatment regime, with a follow-up measurement one month after the final treatment.

Actual oedema was calculated according to the following calculation:[14]

$$\text{Actual oedema at time(x)} = \frac{\text{lymphoedema arm volume at time(x)} - \text{unaffected arm volume at time(x)}}{\text{unaffected arm volume at time(x)}}$$

The percentage change in actual oedema was then calculated as follows:

$$\text{\% oedema change at time(x)} = \frac{\text{actual oedema at time(1)} - \text{actual oedema at time(2)} \times 100}{\text{actual oedema at time(1)}}$$

Participants were encouraged to acquire a new compression garment after the final treatment. During the follow-up period no other treatment for lymphoedema was utilised by the patient, except where self-massage was part of a pre-existing self-management routine.

RESULTS

Case 1

A 79 year-old woman presented with right arm lymphoedema developed 12 months after a partial mastectomy and axillary clearance combined with radiotherapy conducted two years ago. Her last treatment was lymphatic massage six months prior, and she reported no history of wearing a compression garment but had been conducting daily self-massage for a month prior. Initial fluid difference between her two arms was 1000 ml.

The four-week LPG® program decreased fluid in the lymphoedematous arm by 350 ml (28.7% actual oedema) and volume by 221 ml (15.0% actual oedema) (see table 1a). Both of these reductions were maintained at the follow-up measurement. She reported subjective arm symptoms of tightness and a larger size difference with her unaffected arm (see table 1b). Arm tightness resolved after four weeks of treatment, which was maintained at follow-up. Her rating for a perceived larger affected arm, reduced from 5 to 3 after the course of treatment, but went back to baseline at the one-month follow-up. During the follow-up period she was completely compliant with wearing a compression garment and daily self-massage of her lymphoedematous arm.

Table 1a. Case 1- right arm fluid and volume changes from baseline

	Post-treatment (4 weeks)	**Follow-up (1 month)**
Fluid (ml)	-350	- 330
Actual oedema (%)	- 28.7%	-29.9%
Volume (ml)	-221	-201
Actual oedema (%)	-15.0%	-14.7%

Negative values indicate loss of fluid or reduction in volume.

Table 1b. Case 1 – right lymphoedematous arm subjective changes

	Pre-treatment (baseline)	**Post-treatment (4 weeks)**	**Follow-up (1 month)**
Subjective symptoms:			
Tightness	5	1	1
Size	5	3	5

Other measured symptoms were rated as no problem throughout trial.

Case 2

This 70 year-old woman had undergone a partial mastectomy with axillary clearance and radiotherapy 16 years ago, and had experienced lymphoedema of her right arm for the past 14 years. She had her last treatment of laser and lymphatic massage for her lymphoedematous arm 12 months earlier, with a history of daily self-massage and intermittent use of her compression garment. She presented initially with 450 ml fluid difference between her two arms.

After the four weeks of treatment, 140 ml (17.1% actual oedema) of fluid loss occurred from the affected arm, and 190.5 (11.3% actual oedema) ml volume reduction was recorded over this time (see table 2a). At follow-up, the fluid in the affected arm had increased by 30 ml, but was still 110 ml less than baseline. The actual oedema loss had decreased from 17.1% to 4.3%, because the unaffected arm had lost fluid over the follow-up period. The volume of the affected arm had increased over the one month follow-up, but was still 73.5 ml below baseline (9.1 % actual oedema loss).

She reported arm symptoms of pain, heaviness, tightness, hardness, and a temperature and larger size difference compared to the unaffected arm (see table 2b). All these symptoms reduced after four weeks treatment, of which arm pain,

Table 2a. Case 2 - right arm fluid and volume changes from baseline

	Post-treatment (4 weeks)	Follow-up (1 month)
Fluid (ml)	-140	-110
Actual oedema (%)	-17.1%	-4.3%
Volume (ml)	-190.5	-73.5
Actual oedema (%)	-11.3%	-9.1%

Negative values indicate loss of fluid or reduction in volume.

Table 2b. Case 2 – right lymphoedematous arm subjective changes

	Pre-treatment (baseline)	Post-treatment (4 weeks)	Follow-up (1 month)
Subjective symptoms:			
Pain	4	1	1
heaviness	8	3	5
tightness	5	1	5
arm hardness	4	1	6
arm temperature	3	1	1
Size	10	7	10

Other measured symptoms were rated as no problem throughout trial.

tightness, hardness, and temperature difference with the unaffected arm completely resolved. After the follow-up period, arm pain and temperature difference were still resolved, with reported arm tightness and size back to baseline, and a slight increase in reported hardness of the arm. She was moderately compliant with wearing her compression garment during the follow-up period, but conducted daily self-massage.

Case 3

A 63 year-old woman, with full mastectomy and axillary clearance combined with both chemotherapy and radiotherapy eight years prior, presented with 200 ml fluid difference between her two arms. She had experienced right arm lymphoedema for the past seven years, and her last treatment for this condition was laser and lymphatic massage four years ago. She had never used a compression garment. During the trial, she reported a history of sporadic occurrences of rashes on her arms of unknown origin, which started a few years ago.

Over the four-week treatment period, an increase in the lymphoedematous arm fluid (150ml; 16.4% actual oedema) and volume (28.5 ml; 25.8% actual oedema) occurred (see table 3a). There was also a 110 ml fluid increase in the unaffected arm. During the treatment period, she acquired mosquito bites as well as a rash on both forearms. The increase in fluid in both arms remained at follow-up measurement. According to perometry, the affected arm volume increased mainly in the forearm during the treatment period by 20 ml (location of rash/bites), but at follow-up the forearm volume had decreased by 27 ml, with an increase in the upper arm volume of 97 ml from baseline. She reported symptoms of arm hardness, and a larger size and range of movement difference compared to her unaffected arm (see table 3b). Subjectively, there was resolution of arm hardness over the treatment period, which was maintained at follow-up. She also reported relief of some arthritic symptoms in the lymphoedematous arm. At the end of the trial the patient obtained a compression garment that was too tight on the upper arm. She wore the garment moderately over the follow-up period and did not perform self-massage.

Table 3a. Case 3 - right arm fluid and volume changes from baseline

	Post-treatment (4 weeks)	**Follow-up (1 month)**
Fluid (ml)	+150	+180
Actual oedema (%)	+16.4%	+2.6%
Volume (ml)	+28.5	+88.5
Actual oedema (%)	+25.8%	+35.0%

Positive values indicate gain in fluid or increase in volume.

Table 3b. Case 3 – right lymphoedematous arm subjective changes

	Pre-treatment (baseline)	Post-treatment (4 weeks)	Follow-up (1 month)
Subjective symptoms:			
arm hardness	5	1	1
Size	5	5	5
Range of movement	5	5	5

Other measured symptoms were rated as no problem throughout trial.

DISCUSSION

The presented case studies demonstrate the varied effectiveness of LPG®, in terms of decreasing limb fluid and volume for secondary arm lymphoedema, ranging from 29% actual oedema fluid loss and 15% actual oedema volume loss to 16% actual oedema fluid increase and 26% actual oedema volume increase after four weeks of treatment. It highlights that mixed treatment outcomes can occur, that often are not discussed in larger trials when only general and not individual outcomes are considered.

The importance of the therapist motivating patients to care for themselves outside of treatment sessions to achieve best outcomes is often not divulged in studies. All patients were motivated by the therapist to wear compression bandages during the four weeks of treatment, maintain skin care and self-massage and obtain a proper fitting compression garment after the course of treatment. The best outcome occurred in Case 1, who was diligent in wearing the bandaging, self-massage, skin care and wearing her compression garment.

The least effective outcome was for Case 3, whom gained an increase in affected arm fluid and volume, as well as an increase in fluid of her unaffected arm, over the treatment period. The affected arm volume increased mainly in the forearm, which had decreased by follow-up. The volume change could be due to the mosquito bites she developed on both forearms, which were red and itchy. This inflammatory response could also account for the increase of fluid in the unaffected arm, which had resolved by follow-up. At the one month follow-up, she had an increase in upper arm volume, which could be due to her wearing a compression garment that was too tight on the upper arm.

Therefore patient-specific factors can occur outside the control of the researcher or therapist that can influence the effectiveness of treatment. Factors that occurred in these case studies included level of compliance with treatment, compression garment fit and insect bites. Issues related to the individual patient should be carefully considered when generalising the effectiveness of treatment from trial results into clinical practice. The motivation by the therapist to encourage patients to maintain with the treatment regime is believed to have played a role in achieving best outcomes.

REFERENCES

1. Erikson, VS, ML Pearson, PA Ganz, J Adams, KL Kahn: Arm edema in breast cancer patients. Journal of the National Cancer Institute 93(2) (2001), 96-111.
2. Petrek, JA, MC Heelan: Incidence of breast carcinoma-related lymphedema. Cancer 83(12) (1998), 2776-2781.
3. Goffman, TE, C Laronga, L Wilson, D Elkins: Lymphoedema of the arm and breast in irradiated breast cancer patients: risks in an era of dramatically changing axillary surgery. The Breast Journal 10(5) (2004), 405-411.
4. Watson, J, P Bela Fodor, B Cutliffe, D Sayah, W Shaw: Physiological Effects of Endermologie®: A Preliminary Report. Aesthetic Surgery Journal 19(1) (1999), 27-33.
5. Ersek, R, GE Mann II, S Salisbury, AV Salisbury: Noninvasive Mechanical Body Contouring: A Preliminary Clinical Outcome Study. Aesthetic Plastic Surgery 21 (1997), 61-67.
6. Bacci, PA, M Scarolini, S Leonardi, P Belardi, S Mancini: Vibroassisted Liposuction and Endermologie for Lipolymphedema: The European Journal of Lymphology and Related Problems 10(35-36) (2002), 16-21.
7. Campisi, C, F Boccardo, A Zilli, A Maccio, W Ferreira de Azevedo Jr, C Stein Gomes, E de Melocouto: LPG® Technique in the treatment of Peripheral Lymphedema: Clinical Preliminary Results and Prospectives. The European Journal of Lymphology and Related Problems 10(35-36) (2002), 22-23.
8. Watanabe, R, A Miura, K Inoue, M Haeno, K Sakamoto, H Kanai: Evaluation of leg edema using a multifrequency impedance meter in patients with lymphatic obstruction. Lymphology 22(2) (1989), 85-92.
9. Cornish, BH, M Chapman, C Hirst, B Mirolo, IH Bunce, LC Ward, BJ Thomas: Early diagnosis of lymphedema using multifrequency bioimpedance. Lymphology 34(1) (2001), 2-11.
10. Leduc O, P Klien, C Rasquin, P Demaret: Reliability of a volume measuring device (Volumeter®) for human limbs. European Journal of Lymphology and Related Problems 3(10) (1992), 53-56.
11. Stanton, AW, JW Northfield, B Holroyd, PS Mortimer, JR Levick: Validation of an optoelectronic limb volumeter (Perometer). Lymphology 30(2) (1997), 77-97.
12. Cohen, SR, BM Mount, E Bruera, M Provost, J Rowe, K Tong K: Validity of the McGill Quality of Life Questionnaire in the palliative care setting: a multi-centre Canadian study demonstrating the importance of the existential domain. Palliative Medicine 11 (1997), 3–20.
13. Lo, RS, J Woo, KC Zhoc, CY Li, W Yeo, P Johnson, Y Mak, J Lee: Cross-cultural validation of the McGill Quality of Life questionnaire in Hong Kong Chinese. Palliative Medicine 15(5) (2001), 387–397.
14. Swedborg, I: Effects of treatment with an elastic sleeve and intermittent pneumatic compression in post-mastectomy patients with lymphoedema of the arm. Scandinavian Journal of Rehabilitation Medicine 16 (1984), 35-41.

PARTIAL OXYGEN PRESSURE IN THE LYMPHEDEMATOUS SKIN BEFORE AND AFTER TREATMENT BY PHYSIOTHERAPY

Y. Tamai, A. Toudou, A. Imada and M. Ohkuma*

Department of Nephrology & Dialysis,* Department of Dermatology, Sakai Hospital, Kinki University, School of Medicine, Osaka, Japan

INTRODUCTION

Lymph contains less oxygen than blood. It is easy to suspect that the lymphedematous tissue has a lower partial oxygen pressure. Reisshauer et al has reported low PO2 pressure in the lymphedematous limbs (1).Tamai et al reported the similar result in the unilateral lymphedema (2). Mayrowitz et al insist PO2 pressure is different neither between the lymphedematous and uninvolved extremity nor between before and after the edema reduction due to treatment (3).

MATERIAL AND METHOD

Total 12 (6 before and 6 after the treatment) cases of unilateral secondary lymphedema with stage 2 were evaluated before and after the physiotherapy for partial oxygen tissue pressure checked at 4 points of lower extremity by FLEX 8000 (heating the skin to be 42°C, Kohka Medical, Co. Ltd., Japan). Advance Laser flowmeter was also used for evaluation of blood flow in the same way. Treatment was performed by a new physiotherapy by pulse magnetic fields, vibration and hyperthermia (4) after the 1-2 treatment courses (one course consists of daily 60 minutes' therapy for a month). After the treatment in all cases the difference between the lymphedematous and untreated extremity was less than 1 cm in circumference 10 cm above and beneath the patella edge.

RESULTS

The PO2 of the lymphedematous skin is low in all examined points of the extremity before the treatment (Fig. 1). It becomes elevated after the treatment with no statistical difference between the edematous and normal contralateral limbs (Fig. 2).The edematous skin shows increase in PO2 after the therapy, whereas the contralateral side does not. Laser flow meter value is variable after the points and the case before and after the treatment (Fig. 1,2).

DISCUSSION

If the tissue PO2 is low, immunological inflammatory reaction is intensified (5). Clinical case of

Result of before treatment

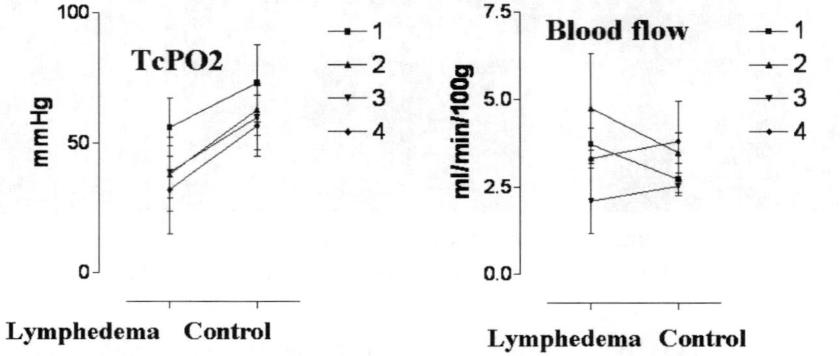

	lymphedema (mmHg)	Control (mmHg)	t test p value	lymphedema (ml/min/100g)	Control (ml/min/100g)	t test p value
1	56±11	73±15	p<0.01	3.7±0.5	2.7±0.5	N.S.
2	38±14	63±10	p<0.005	4.8±1.6	3.5±0.6	N.S.
3	39±10	60±12	p<0.05	2.1±0.9	2.5±0.2	N.S.
4	32±17	57±12	p<0.05	3.3±0.3	3.8±1.1	N.S.

Fig. 1

Result of after treatment

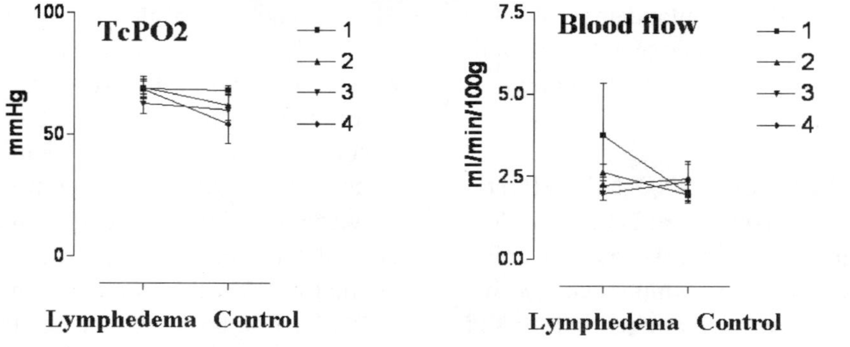

	lymphedema (mmHg)	Control (mmHg)	t test p value	lymphedema (ml/min/100g)	Control (ml/min/100g)	t test p value
1	69±8	68±5	N.S.	3.8±1.6	2.0±0.3	N.S.
2	69±11	62±16	N.S.	2.6±0.3	1.9±0.2	p<0.05
3	62±10	60±15	N.S.	2.0±0.2	2.4±0.6	N.S.
4	68±10	54±19	N.S.	2.2±0.3	2.4±0.5	N.S.

Fig. 2

spontaneous flare up shows it, because allergic inflammation is seen in the lymphedematous limb alone, although the contrast media are injected bilaterally.

A small amount of intradermally invaded bacteria may cause a strong immunological inflammation in the lymphedematous skin and lymphedema gets worse. This happens even without clinically recognized attack. That is why lymphedema, even without any inflammatory complication, gets worse. The reason why PO2 pressure of the upper extremity differs neither from the normal contralateral side nor after the massage treatment (3) is not understood. Flow meter should be examined at least at the multiple points, because it varies after the points of the extremity. PO2 value is influenced by blood flow, distance from the blood vessel, hyaluronic acid deposit, shape & number of the blood erythrocytes and convection. Nephrotic edema shows also a low PO2 in the skin. The epidermal thickness is no so different in edematous and uninvolved extremity of the 2 stage of lymphedema. All influencing factors except conviction can be ruled out in this investigation.

CONCLUSION

PO2 of the lymphedematous skin is lower than the uninvolved limb, which becomes increased after a new physiotherapy.

REFERENCES

1. Reisshauer A, A Bischoff, K Mathiske-Schmidt: Transcutaneous oxygen partial pressure before and after manual lymphatic drainage in patients with chronic lymphedema of the limbs. Europ. J. Lymphology 12(2004), 13.
2. Tamai Y, Toudou A, Imada A and M. Ohkuma: Transcutaneous partial oxygen pressure in unilateral lymphedema. 30th European Congress of Lymphology, Bruxelles, 2004.
3. Mayrovitz HN, N Sims, D Brown-Cross et al: Transcutaneous oxygen tension in arms of women with unilateral postmastectomy lymphedema.
4. Ohkuma M: A new treatment of lymphedema by magnetic fields, vibration and hyperthermia – The second report. Lymphology 35(Suppl.) (2002), 320
5. Moore T, PL Khimenko, and AE Taylor: Endothelial damage caused by I/R and perfusion and different ventilatory strategies in the lung. Chinese J Physiol. 39L1996), 65.

WHY IS MECHANICAL DRAINAGE OF LYMPHEDEMATOUS TISSUES NECESSARY?

Olszewski W. L.

Department of Surgery and Transplantation, Medical Research Center, Polish Academy of Sciences, Warsaw, Poland and Norwegian Radium Hospital, Oslo

Massage is not only useful for removal of excess of water. The most important is elimination of colonizing microorganisms, then infiltrating immune cells, cellular debris arising from senescent and traumatized cells and fragments of cellular membranes e.g. cholesterol released in the process of reverse cholesterol transport.

Lymphoscintigraphies clearly show in majority of cases lack of patent lymphatics. Thus, massage does not press stagnant tissue fluid into these obliterated structures. Tissue fluid has to find its way along tissue spaces. We showed on lymphoscintigraphies spread of tracer above the groin or in the pectoral or dorsal regions but not in the lymphatics which should bridge the surgically damaged areas. Moreover, we were not able to show lymphangiogenesis on tissue specimens using specific staining for lymphatic endothelium, its mitoses or production of VEGF C (cytokine specific for lymphatic growth). On the other hand, we showed formation of "new" lymph nodes along the deep lymphatics. This has been the effect of a continuous stimulation by bacterial antigen. Formation of new tissue fluid flow channels by a high pressure generating massage seems to be indicated. No histological changes were found in tissues after application of pressures above 100 mmHg. In our studies, tissue fluid pressures (wick method) produced by contraction of calf muscles in limbs with elastic stockings (grade II) during walking reach levels even above 200 mmHg. Reevaluation of the approach to the parameters of massage and drainage physics would be useful.

Manual or pneumatic massage of tissues with lymph stasis is an integral component of combined therapy comprising:

a) Mechanical evacuation of excess of tissue fluid
b) Elastic support
c) Anti-microbial and anti-inflammatory therapy
d) Microsurgery

Mechanical evacuation of excess of tissue fluid is not only removal of water, it is also elimination of:

a) cellular debris of senescent, apoptotic and traumatized cells
b) colonizing microorganisms

c) recirculating immune cells and their products as cytokines and chemokines
d) degradation products of extracellular matrix
e) fat tissue?

Pathways of tissue fluid flow from lymphedematous tissues

a) lymphatic trunks NO! lost contractility, obliterated
b) deviation of flow to deep vessels
c) collateral lymphatics YES! usually few vessels, low total cross section area
d) tissue spaces filled with loose connective tissue, perivascular sheats
e) water back to blood capillaries?

Contraindications for manual or pneumatic massage

Acute and subacute dermatitis
Inflammatory foci detected on lymphoscintigraphy
Venous thrombotic changes detected by color-doppler

Lack of new lymphatic pathways across the sites of obstruction after long-lasting massage

Lack of lymphangiogenesis in lymph-edematous tissues

Lack of: VEGF C in lymph vessel EC
BrdU incorporation into lymphatic EC (no mitoses)
LYVE 1 staining of lymphatic EC
Dilatation of preexisting lymphatic capillaries
Transparent specimens stained with Paris Blue

CONCLUSIONS

a. Mechanical massage (application of vertical forces) of tissues with lymph stasis is essential in therapy of lymphedema
b. Contraindications are inflammation and thrombosis
c. External pressure exerted upon skin is not necessarily transmitted to subcutaneous tissue (low skin compliance)
d. Theoretically each massaged limb region should have tissue fluid pressure measured
e. High tissue fluid pressures recorded during manual massage and walking in elastic stockings seem not to produce tissue changes
f. Mechanical massage moves excess of tissue fluid along tissue spaces but not through lymphatics

THE EFFECTIVENESS OF MANUAL LYMPH DRAINAGE (MLD ®) FOR TREATMENT OF POST-BREAST CANCER ARM LYMPHOEDEMA: FOUR CASE STUDIES ARISING FROM A CLINICAL TRIAL

Douglass J, Piller NB & Moseley AL

Lymphoedema Assessment Clinic and Department of Surgery, Flinders University and Flinders Medical Centre, Bedford Park, South Australia

BACKGROUND

The Dr. Vodder method of Manual Lymph Drainage (MLD®) is a proven technique for the treatment of lymphoedema[1] and can be a useful benchmark against which to assess new treatments. However application of the full scope of MLD and CDT is rarely used in clinical trials, where a standardised protocol with minimal variation is preferred in order to reduce confounders.

The following four case studies were drawn from a control group participating in a randomised trial to test the efficacy of a machine-based massage. This group was treated with a standardised protocol of the Dr Vodder method of MLD® and compression bandaging. Each of the cases presented illustrates some of the difficulties encountered when instigating treatment within a trial setting and highlights the necessity to assess and prescribe treatment on an individual basis. They also show that subjective gains, not fluid losses, are often the most important markers of success for a given individual.

METHODS

Participants who has unilateral, clinically manifest, secondary arm lymphoedema ($\geq$ 200mls) associated with previous breast cancer treatment were recruited. Ethics approval for the study was given by the Flinders Medical Centre Clinical Research Ethics Committee, Adelaide, Australia and each patient provided informed consent.

Treatment

Initially each participant was treated with MLD® and padded compression bandages 4 days per week for 4 weeks with follow up measures taken at 1 month. A standardised protocol of treatment was applied including

45 minutes of MLD® to the neck, unaffected chest, affected chest, back, arm and hand (if involved). Skeletal muscular techniques were not used and postural imbalance, breast oedema and scar contracture were not treated. Compression bandaging was applied after each treatment and when possible kept on overnight. Gauze bandage was applied to the fingers if indicated, followed by medium density foam to the hand and arm and then 2 – 3 layers of short stretch bandages. Exercises normally prescribed during bandaging were not given.

During the 3 days without treatment patients who had been previously wearing a compression sleeve were asked to continue to do so as usual, patients not already using a sleeve used no compression on the non treatment days. Similarly if self massage had been part of a self maintenance routine prior to commencement of the trial this could be continued on non treatment days, if not then no self massage was to be performed on these days. Participants were encouraged to purchase a new compression garment after the 4 weeks of treatment and this could be used during the one month follow up period.

The trial protocol did not allow for patient education or self treatment, however this was offered after the one month follow up period. Patient education included a self massage routine, Tai Chi breathing exercises and information about skin care, garment use, exercise and infection control.

A sub group of eight participants treated by a single therapist was then followed for up to 12 months. Of this group of eight, three were offered further treatment by the same therapist and all were remeasured at various intervals up to 12 month post trial.

Measurements

Objective measurements were obtained using validated equipment, including bioimpedance (BioSpace®, Korea) for segmental limb and trunk fluid[2,3] and perometry[4 5] (Perosystems®, Germany) for arm volume and tonometry for induration. Subjective arm symptoms were rated on a validated 10 point scale,[7,8] where 1 is no problem and 10 is the worst problem imaginable. Subjective symptoms included arm heaviness, tightness, hardness, pain, cramps, pins and needles, and perceived temperature difference, size difference and range of movement compared to the unaffected arm. Measurements were taken at prescribed intervals over the four-week treatment regime, with a follow-up measurement one month after the final treatment.

Actual oedema was calculated according to the following formula:

$$\text{Actual oedema at time(x)} = \frac{\text{lymphoedema arm volume at time(x)} - \text{unaffected arm volume at time(x)}}{\text{unaffected arm volume at time(x)}}$$

The percentage change in actual oedema was then calculated as follows:

$$\text{\% oedema change at time(x)} = \frac{\text{actual oedema at time(1)} - \text{actual oedema at time(2)} \times 100}{\text{actual oedema at time(1)}}$$

RESULTS

Case 1

This 60 year old woman presented with a very large and fibrotic oedema. She was unable to wear a garment and did not practice self massage. Eight and a half weeks prior to trial commencement she had had her remaining breast removed prophylactically. During the course of treatment he surgical wound became quite sore and sensitive as fluid were being moved towards it from the affected side. This adverse effect resolved well during the one month follow up period where no treatment was received.

An excellent result was achieved during the treatment period with reduction continuing in the month after the cessation of treatment. Percentage oedema changes during the trial and at one month follow up are summarised in Table 1.

By the 6 month follow up it was apparent that the reduction achieved during the trial was being lost. This was most likely due to the large amount of fibrotic induration in the arm, (which had not been properly addressed in the generalised trial protocol) as well as a lack of self treatment by the patient.

Long term

A further treatment period was offered and carried out on 3 alternate days per week for 4 weeks. The new protocol included addressing shoulder, neck and upper back pain with Dr. Vodder special

Table 1. Trial results, % actual oedema and % oedema change

Case 1 Trial protocol	Baseline (1) % actual oedema	% change after 4 weeks of treatment	At 1 month follow up (1)
Perometry	0.80% (1519ml)	36.11%	48.74%
Bioimpedence	1.18% (1770ml)	37.63%	47.46%

techniques, and the use of a foam chip muff to reduce fibrotic induration in the forearm. Padded bandages were applied after each session and kept on overnight. After 4 weeks good reduction had been achieved and this was maintained at the one month follow up. Tonometry showed some softening, particularly in the forearm. The percentage changes during the follow up treatment period and compared to the original baseline measurements are shown in Table 2.

Case 2

This 63 year old woman presented with a moderate, well established oedema. She had a compression garment but was not able to wear it. After the first week of treatment she asked to review her original scores on the subjective questionnaire as she was experiencing pain relief and increases in ROM which made her realise she had come to accept pain and arm restriction as 'normal'. The patient responded very well to treatment. Percentage actual oedema and percentage oedema changes are summarised in Table 3.

Whilst the figures do show a good result, they do not indicate the most useful aspects of treatment for this participant which included a change in perspective from believing nothing could be done to improve her arm, to knowing that she can manage the arm herself and access beneficial treatment if needed. She also reported an increase in ROM of the affected arm and an increased ability to undertake activities of daily living.

Table 2. Further treatment, % actual oedema and % oedema change

Case 1	Baseline (2) % actual oedema	% change after 4 weeks of treatment	At 1 month follow up (2)	% change Baseline (1) to follow up (2)
Perometry	0.77% (1404ml)	16.06%	22.07%	19.2%
Bioimpedence	1.00% (1470ml)	8.28%	14.5%	27.54%

Table 3. Case 2, % actual oedema and % oedema change

Case 2 Trial protocol	Baseline % actual oedema	% change after 4 weeks of treatment	At 1 month follow up	At 12 month follow up
Perometry	0.26% (479.5ml)	31.86%	27.29%	31.29%
Bioimpedence	0.37% (550ml)	41.49%	30.19%	27.59%

Long term

This participant continues to practice self massage daily and has excellent skin care and garment compliance. At the 12 month follow up all subjective gains had been maintained or improved with further reductions in pain and heaviness and improvement in ROM. She also had further reduction in the volume of the arm (as measured by perometry). This case highlights the importance of perceived gains, some of which were not objectively measured in the trial. It also demonstrates the importance of positive patient attitude and self maintenance to preserve long term the benefits gained through treatment.

Case 3

This 53 year old woman came into the trial 12 months after her breast surgery. There was swelling generally over the whole arm, forearm and dorsum of the hand but this was mild. Of greater concern to her was breast discomfort due to persistent breast inflammation and oedema. The breast was very pink, sore, quite hard and she found it difficult to wear a bra.

Her initial fluid losses during the trial were reasonable. In particular swelling of the dorsum of the hand resolved during treatment and has not returned. During the 1 month following treatment she developed an infected tooth which required oral surgery. The swelling in her arm increased as a result and this effect is reflected in her follow up measurements. Percentage actual oedema and percentage oedema changes are summarised in Table 4.

Further Treatment

During the intervening 9 months this patient experienced a further increase in arm fluid, mainly in the upper arm, possible due to a bout of cellulitis. A few subsequent treatments were given to address the breast oedema which then resolved completely and the arm volume has remained relatively stable since.

Despite the appearance of negative figures at follow up and at 9 months this patient was happy with the results of the treatment she received during the trial in particular she was very pleased about the resolution of oedema at the hand and wrist which has not returned. She now wears a garment whilst working

Table 4. Case 3, % actual oedema and % oedema change

Case 3 Trial protocol	Baseline % actual oedema	% change after 4 weeks of treatment	At 1 month follow up	At 9 month follow up
Perometry	0.15% (332ml)	10.74%	8.05%	-48.05%
Bioimpedence	0.10% (542ml)	-3.06%	-28.57%	-83.26%

and practices self massage most days. She also commented that her involvement in the trial had increased her sense of hope and control over her own life.

Case 4

This 78 year old woman had a very well established oedema with a large amount of fat accumulation. (This is illustrated by the difference in the volume as measure by perometry and bioimpedence.) The fibrotic induration in her forearm was her primary worry as she had a history of cellulitis infections. A warm rosy patch on the posterior/lateral aspect of the forearm was noted at commencement of the trial and worsening of this reddened area at the beginning of the fourth week meant that bandages could not be worn during this final treatment week. This is the most likely explanation for the poor result at the 1 month follow up compared to the initial losses achieved in the first 3 weeks. Percentage actual oedema and percentage oedema changes are summarised in Table 5. Figures for 3 weeks (instead of 4) are given.

Long Term

After the 1 month follow up, a more holistic treatment protocol which included treatment of a rotator cuff injury and additional fibrosis techniques to the forearm was implemented every fortnight for 7 treatments. Treatment ceased in the 6th month and at the 12 month follow up the forearm was still soft (as measured by tonometry), with volumetric measurements demonstrating a further reduction in fluid. She continues to practice daily self massage, tai chi breathing and is very compliant with use of her compression sleeve. This woman is now able to take better care of her oedematous arm the greatest advantage of which has been the prevention of previously recurrent cellulitis infections.

Remaining four cases

The remaining 4 participants in the subgroup followed long term all achieved initial fluid losses but by the one month follow up there was an increase in volume in each case. By 6 months post trial most of the women had returned to original baseline measurement or had further progression of the lymphoedema.

Table 5. Case 4, % actual oedema and % oedema change

Case 4 Trial protocol	Baseline % actual oedema	% change after 3 weeks of treatment	At 1 month follow up	At 12 month follow up
Perometry	0.64% (1472.5ml)	19.09%	-1.38%	3.62%
Bioimpedence	0.44% (770ml)	52.39%	-21.54%	26.80%

The cases which showed the greatest fluctuation in percentage oedema change also reported inconsistencies in garment use and self massage after the trial. In the case study group this trend of returning fluid is interrupted by the treatment periods and reinforcement of self maintenance with generally more positive results being maintained over time.

Conclusion

These cases highlight the importance of proper assessment and tailoring of the treatment strategy to the individual to achieve best outcomes. They also demonstrate that women often place a higher value on subjective gains in determining the significant successes of treatment indicating that it is not always about the size of the arm. The cases which appeared to have the best outcomes as measured objectively are not necessarily the most successful cases when viewed holistically. Whilst the need for evidence based research is important, it is equally important in clinical care to pay attention to subjective symptoms and develop treatment plans which take into consideration the expected outcomes and perceived benefits from the perspective of the patient.[10]

REFERENCES

1. Harris R. Piller N. Case studies indicating the effectiveness of Manual Lymphatic Drainage on patients with primary and secondary lymphedema using objective measurement tools J Bodywork and Movement Therapies 2003 7(4) 210-221
2. Watanabe, R, A Miura, K Inoue, M Haeno, K Sakamoto, H Kanai: Evaluation of leg edema using a multifrequency impedance meter in patients with lymphatic obstruction. Lymphology 22(2) (1989), 85-92.
3. Cornish, BH, M Chapman, C Hirst, B Mirolo, IH Bunce, LC Ward, BJ Thomas: Early diagnosis of lymphedema using multifrequency bioimpedance. Lymphology 34(1) (2001), 2-11.
4. Leduc O, P Klien, C Rasquin, P Demaret: Reliability of a volume measuring device (Volumeter®) for human limbs. European Journal of Lymphology and Related Problems 3(10) (1992), 53-56.
5. Stanton, AW, JW Northfield, B Holroyd, PS Mortimer, JR Levick: Validation of an optoelectronic limb volumeter (Perometer). Lymphology 30(2) (1997), 77-97.
6. Stanton, AWB, Badger C, Sitza J: Non invasive assessment of the lymphoedematous limb. Lymphology 33 (2000), 122-135
7. Cohen, SR, BM Mount, E Bruera, M Provost, J Rowe, K Tong K: Validity of the McGill Quality of Life Questionnaire in the palliative care setting: a multi-centre Canadian study demonstrating the importance of the existential domain. Palliative Medicine 11 (1997), 3–20.
8. Lo, RS, J Woo, KC Zhoc, CY Li, W Yeo, P Johnson, Y Mak, J Lee: Cross-cultural validation of the McGill Quality of Life questionnaire in Hong Kong Chinese. Palliative Medicine 15(5) (2001), 387–397.
9. Swedborg, I: Effects of treatment with an elastic sleeve and intermit-

tent pneumatic compression in post-mastectomy patients with lymphoedema of the arm. Scandinavian Journal of Rehabilitation Medicine 16 (1984), 35-41.

10 Piller, N When absence of controls can help in the gaining of control. Situations where findings are likely to be valuable for practitioners and patients. Lymphology 2004 37(2) 45-47

FOUR YEAR INTERNET SURVEY PROVIDES EVIDENCE FOR THE BENEFITS OF SELF-CARE PROGRAMS IN SECONDARY LYMPHEDEMA

Saskia R.J. Thiadens, RN; Mugur V. Geana, MD; Jane M. Armer, RN, PhD

National Lymphedema Network; Health Communication Research Center University of Missouri at Columbia; Sinclair School of Nursing;Ellis Fischel Cancer Center University of Missouri at Columbia

Lymphedema (LE) is a chronic condition in which protein-rich fluids accumulate in the interstitial spaces of an affected body part, most frequently in the extremities. It may (1) be present from birth or arise from no known external cause (primary lymphedema) or (2) it may arise from an identified external cause such as trauma or surgery (secondary lymphedema).

Study Design

Using both regular mail and an online administered questionnaire (www.lymphnet.org), the National Lymphedema Network (NLN) collected data on primary and secondary lymphedema over four years (between March 2001 and May 2005). The NLN-created survey was designed to explore understanding of characteristics and perceptions of LE by those who reported having the condition.

Sample Characteristics

Over the course of the four years, 3898 Americans responded to the survey.

Seventy-three percent (n=2851) of respondents reported secondary lymphedema, 21% (n=1038) reported primary lymphedema, and nine reported experiencing both types. The mean age of those with secondary lymphedema was 56 years old, whereas the mean age of those with primary lymphedema was 42 years. Ninety-one percent of respondents with secondary lymphedema were female, as were 81% of primary lymphedema respondents. The present analysis focuses on symptoms and self-care practices among American women with primary and secondary LE.

The mean age of onset for primary lymphedema was 25 years of age (range = 0-85 years). In both primary and secondary lymphedema, 63-65% of women with lymphedema (n=539 and n=1594, respectively) reported pain in their affected limbs.

Statistical Analysis of Self-Care Behaviors and LE Outcomes

A statistical analysis of the correlations between self care behaviors, such as Manual Lymphatic Drainage (MLD), bandaging, skin care, garment and exercise, and symptom report of infection and pain was conducted. Chi Square was used to test for the statistical significance of the observed differences in associations. The survey data suggests that the pain experience and symptoms are similar for those with primary and secondary lymphedema. Self-care behaviors, like exercise and garments, are significantly related to reported pain and infection only in the secondary lymphedema group. The relationships for secondary lymphedema that were statistically significant are summarized below. Levels of significance were set at 0.05 for all comparisons.

From all of the women with secondary lymphedema who reported having no pain, 584 reported wearing a garment compared to 427 who reported not using a garment (Chi Square 13.75, p=0.05). Of those who reported an infection, 574 reported not exercising, while 438 of them reported exercising (Chi Square 7.75, p=0.005). In the relationship between pain and exercise, fewer of those who reported exercising reported pain in the affected limb (n=785), as compared to those who did not report exercising (n=967) (Chi Square 5.53, p=0.021).

Because the current analysis was performed on self-reported data from a convenience sample, it is difficult to account for cause-effect relationships. Future research should use the exploratory value of these findings to conduct further inquiry into the links between self-care behaviors and lymphedema symptomatology.

Concomitantly, a longitudinal study that follows lymphedema onset should provide more detailed information on the evolution of symptoms and the effectiveness of treatment measures. Finally, the age of onset and developmental stage may be factors to be further explored in lymphedema self care management behaviors; these factors may shed insight into relationships among these constructs of interest (symptoms and self-care practices) in persons with primary lymphedema in comparison to those with secondary lymphedema. In future studies, comparisons of gender differences in relationship to symptoms and self-care can be examined, as well.

Bibliography

National Lymphedema Network (2005). Survey retrieved at www.lymphnet.org.

MUSCLE HYPERTROPHY AND INFLAMMATION IN THE LYMPHEDEMATOUS UPPER EXTREMITIES OF WOMEN FOLLOWING TREATMENT FOR BREAST CANCER

KP BonHomme[1], WH Williams[1] and MH Witte[2]

Departments of Radiology (Nuclear Medicine)[1] and Surgery[2] , University of Arizona, 1501 N. Campbell Ave. Tucson, AZ, USA

Abstract

The upper extremities of 17 patients with breast cancer related lymphedema (status post axillary dissection, chemotherapy and radiation therapy) were studied after the IV administration of 10 to17 mCi of 2-Fluoro Deoxyglucose (FDG) following a standard protocol. The patients were imaged on a Simens/ CTI ECAT EXACT Positron Emission Tomography (PET) scanner. Images were obtained from the orbits to the mid-thighs. Image sets were reconstructed with attenuation correction based on a transmission scan and displayed in multiple tomographic and 3 dimensional orientations.

Measurements of the diameters (D) of the FDG muscle uptake and Standard Uptake Values (SUV) were measured at the wrists, mid forearms, elbows, mid-humerus regions and at the shoulders. In addition, the distances (h) between regions were determined. The volumes of these regions were approximated by using the expression for the volume for a truncated cone; $V = \pi/12*h*(D_1^2 + D_2^2 + D_1 D_2)$.

The average arm SUV's in the 17 patients with edema was 1.2 in the edematous arm and 1.2 in the normal contralateral control. The SUV results are within normal limits and do not suggest inflammation or tumor. Increased relative muscle volume (volume of muscle plus bone in treated arm versus contralateral control) was noted in 8 of the 11 patients (17 to 63% relative difference in volume). No definite difference in volume was noted in 6 patients (0 to 5% relative difference). 3 patients had an increase in the relative volume of the contralateral (non-treated) arm (16 to 41%).

The results suggest that chronic lymphedema is often accompanied with musculature hypertrophy of the affected limb. Arm dominance was not assessed and may be a contributing factor and while bone volume contribution is included in the results we assumed equal bone contributions at each point from both sides. Interestingly, we have no evidence for inflammation in the involved upper extremity as indicated by normal FDG uptake.

Introduction

Increased glucose metabolism in cancer has been known for 70 years. The predominant radiotracer used in Positron Emission Tomography

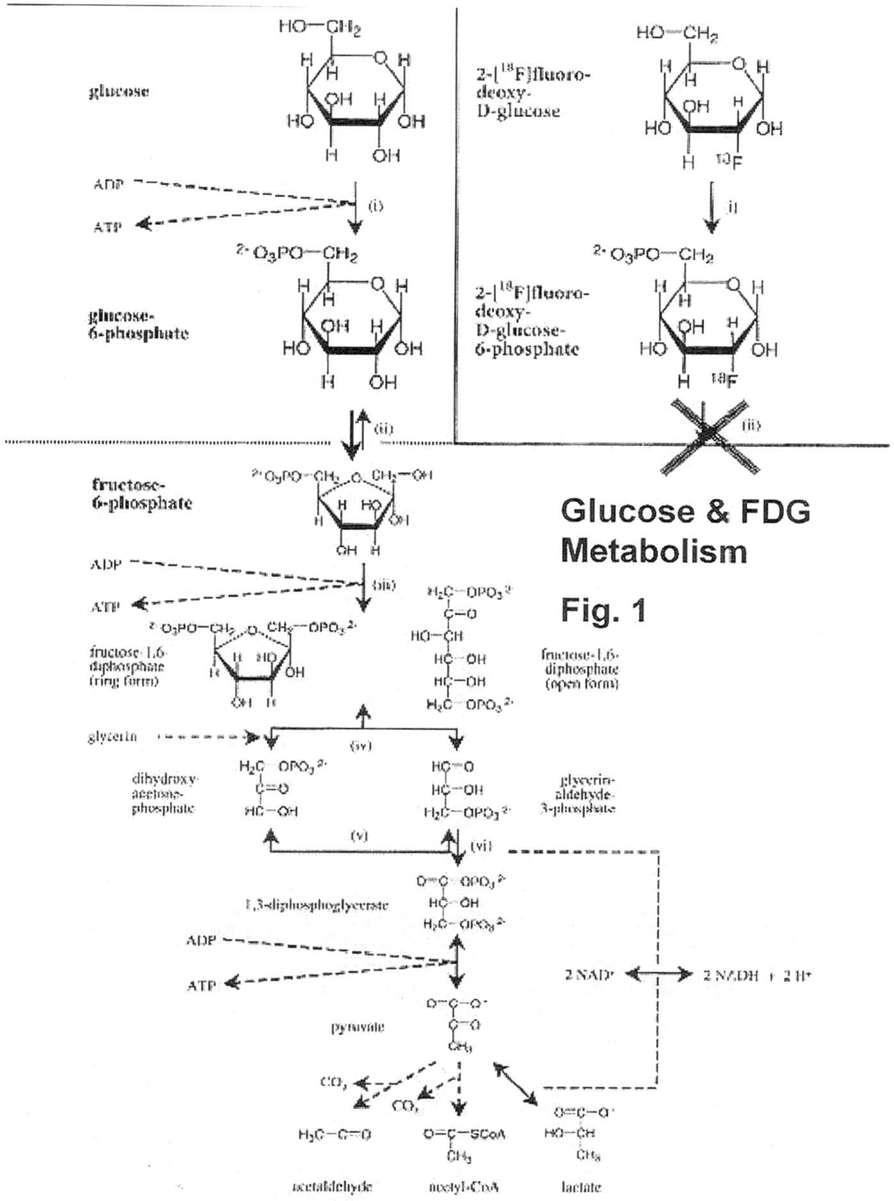

Glucose & FDG Metabolism

Fig. 1

(PET) is 2-(fluorine-18)-2-deoxy-D-glucose (18F-FDG) which was initially used by Phelps[1] in the brain. FDG follows the glucose pathway and is blocked at FDG-6-P, see Fig. 1. FDG is now routinely used to stage Breast CA.

Skeletal muscle shows increased FDG uptake during muscle contraction or glycogen depletion. Glycolytic metabolism increases in inflammatory process associated with leukocyte infiltration[2]. The FDG uptake in normal muscle is small.

Procedure

10 to 17 mCi of F-18, 2-Fluoro Deoxyglucose (FDG) was administered intravenously following a standard protocol. The patient fasted for greater than 6 hours and blood glucose was less 150 mg/dL prior to FDG administration. Following injection of FDG and an uptake period of 60 minutes, the patient was imaged on a Siemens/CTI ECAT EXACT PET scanner, Fig. 2. Images were obtained from the orbits to the mid thighs. Image sets were reconstructed with an attenuation correction based on a transmission scan and displayed in multiple tomographic (axial, coronal and sagittal) and 3-dimensional orientations.

Diameters (D) of the FDG muscle uptake (muscle + bone) and Standard Uptake

Values (SUV's) were measured at the wrists, mid forearms, elbows, mid-humeri and the shoulders, Fig. 3. The distances between the regions were also determined. The volumes for these regions were determined from the expression for the volume of a truncated cone: Fig. 1A.

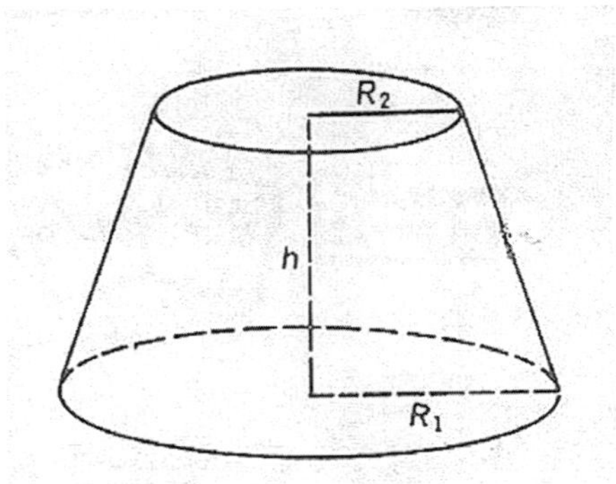

$$V = \pi/12*h*(D_1^{\,2} + D_2^{\,2} + D_1 D_2).$$

D=2r

Discussion

Standard Uptake Values (SUV) for glucose were taken on the upper extremities of each patient. A measure of the glucose metabolism can be approximated by using the SUV which is related to the injected dose per body mass. An attenuation scan must be used to correct the emission scan. In Positron Emission Tomography using F-18, 2-

ECAT

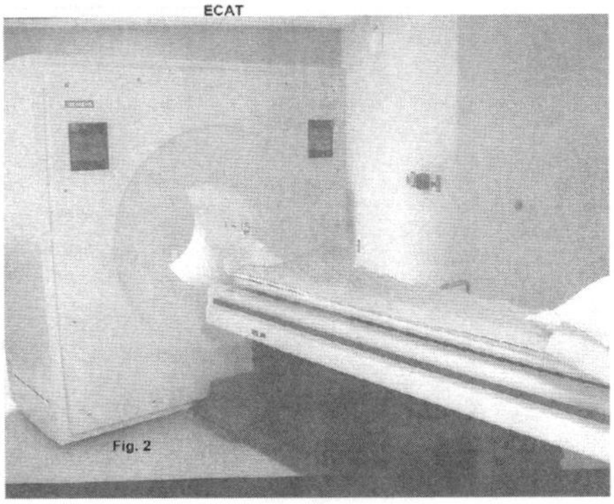

Fig. 2

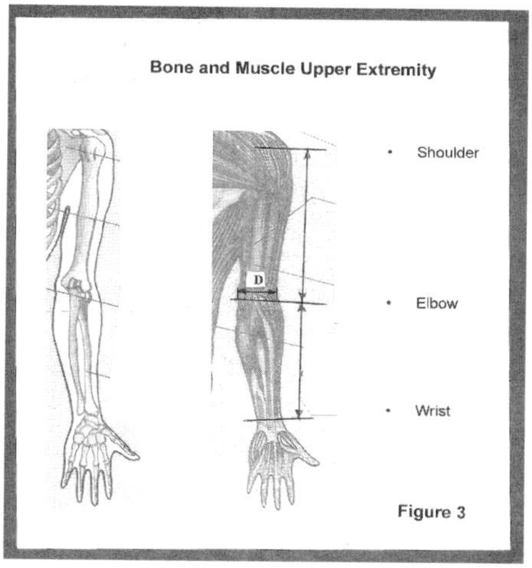

Figure 3

deoxyglucose (FDG) SUV values greater than 2.5 are considered suspicious for inflammation. A value greater than 3.5 may be consistent with tumor in the settting of a known primary tumor (e.g., Breast, Lung, Renal, Melanoma). An example of Breast CA. with right upper extremity edema is shown in Fig. 4 along with lymphangioscintigraphy. Examples of PET studies are shown in Figs. 5, 6, and 7.

Lymphangioscintigraphy

Secondary Lymphedema

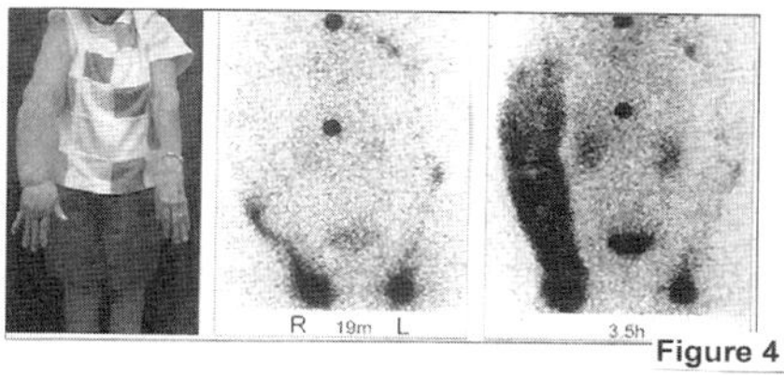

Figure 4

Positron Emission Tomography

Coronal Slices

- 49 year old female with history of right breast CA. The patient is status post mastectomy and chemotherapy.
- The patient complains of right upper extremity edema.
- The injection site is in the left upper extremity. There are two mediastinal lymph nodes seen and right upper extremity relative increase in muscle mass.

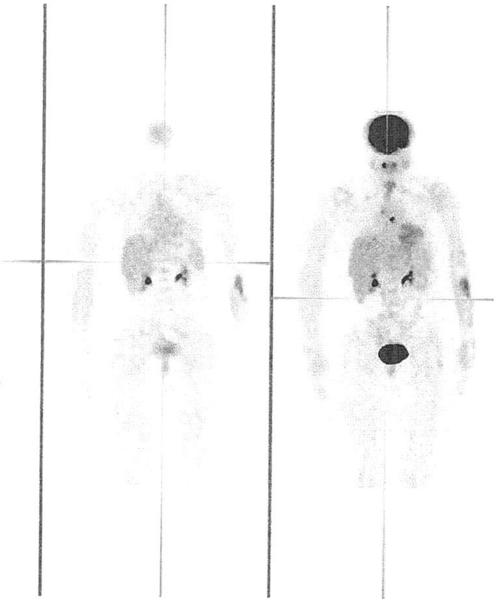

Fig. 5

Positron Emission Tomography

*

Coronal Slices

- 72 year old female with history of left breast CA. The patient is status post left mastectomy and chemotherapy.
- The patient complains of left upper extremity edema. The PET scan was performed for restaging.
- Metastases are seen in the posterior and anterior ribs, spinal column and pelvis. Metastatic disease is also seen in the proximal femurs. The patient has left upper extremity edema and increased muscle mass.

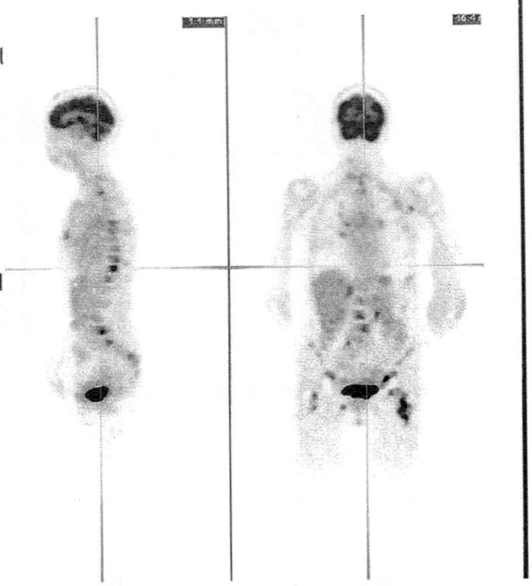

Fig. 6

Positron Emission Tomography

Axial Sagittal Coronal

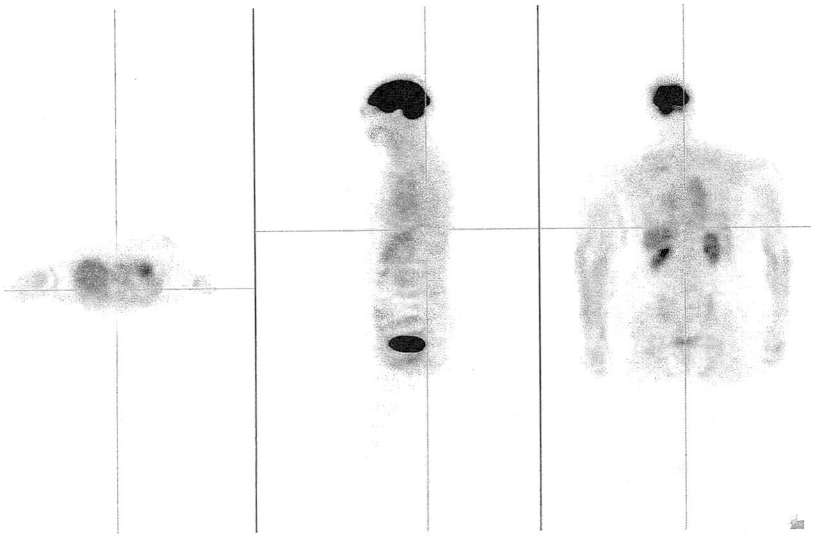

77 year old female with history of breast CA.
The patient is status post chemotherapy
and radiation treatment.

Fig. 7

In all cases reported here, SUV (Standard uptake value for FDG) values in the affected edematous arm and the contralateral arm were approximately: SUV's=1.2, which is within normal limits. The chronic process of muscle hypertrophy in the edematous arm appears to not be associated with significant long-term inflammation.

Increased relative muscle volume (volume of muscle plus bone in the edematous arm versus contralateral) was noted in 8 of the 11 patients (17 to 63% relative difference in volume). No definite difference in volume was noted in 6 patients (0 to5% relative difference). 3 patients had an increase in the relative volume of the contralateral arm (16 to 41%).

We did not investigate the effect of dominance (handedness) in the SUV uptakes. None of these patients had significantly increased uptake secondary to muscle usage or tension during the uptake phase of FDG.

Conclusions

The results suggest that chronic lymphedema is often accompanied with muscle hypertrophy of the affected limb. The relative muscle hypertrophy that we documented here is probably secondary to the extra work required to move an extremity with increased mass. Interestingly, there is no evidence for inflammation in the upper extremities. The FDG uptake in all cases was normal.

References

1. Phelps ME etal. Tomographic measurement of local cerebral glucose metabolic rate in humans with (18F) 2-fluoro-2-deoxy-D-glucose: Validation of method. Ann. Neurol 1979; 6(5): 371-388.
2. Weisdorf DJ etal. Glycogenolysis versus glucose transport in human granulocytes: Differential activation in phagocytosis and chemotaxis. Blood 1982; 60: 888-893.

EXERCISES WITH HEAVY WEIGHTS FOR PATIENTS WITH BREAST CANCER RELATED ARM LYMPHOEDEMA

Karin Johansson, RPT, PhD; Neil Piller, Prof.

Dept of Health Science, Div of Physiotherapy, Lund University Hospital, S-221 85 Sweden; Dept of Surgery, Lymphoedema Assessment Clinic, Flinders Medical Centre, Adelaide, South Australia

INTRODUCTION

Knowledge of the influence of exercise and work based activity on arm lymphoedema is very poor. A few pilot studies suggest moderate to heavy controlled physical activity, does not increase the -risk of developing or worsening lymphoedema (Harris & Niesen-Vertommen 2000, McKenzie & Kalda 2003). However, the influence of exercise and activity needs to be more carefully examined taking into account the nature of the training programs: the type of activity, its frequency, duration and intensity (Wilmore & Costhill, 1999), and measuring this objectively. Just as important is a -measure using validated instruments of the patients own experience of the programs.

OBJECTIVES

To evaluate the influence of physical loading, (subjectively experienced as exertion), on the amount of objectively measured arm lymphoedema.

SUBJECTS AND METHODS

Eighteen women with breast cancer related arm lymphedema were recruited into the study. Mean±SD age was 58±11 years, oedema duration 54±49 months and oedema volume– 25.6±18,0 %– They were recruited at the Lymphoedema Assessment Clinic, Flinders Medical Centre, Adelaide, South Australia. None of the patients had been wearing a compression sleeve on the affected arm for at least 6 months.

Arm fluids were measured by using multi frequency bioimpedance (MFBIA) with a 8 electrode system whose contact points were the fingers, the thumbs, the ball and the heel of the feet. (Bio-Space-Korea). **Arm volume** were measured using water displacement method (WDM). The patients' **subjective experiences** of heaviness and tension of the affected arm were scored on a 10-point Lichert scale and **perceived exertion** after physical exercise was rated on Borg´s scale, both of which have been previously validated.

Limb volume measurements were undertaken prior to the study , immediately post exertion, then after a further 30 mins and at 24 hours. Perceived exertion was also measured at the same times after each exertion session.

The exercise program design– Following baseline limb volume measurements, a specially designed *arm training program* (Fig. 1) derived from a clinically employed weight lifting program (Miller 1998) was initiated– Five different actions were each performed 10 times (50 movements in total) in the following order. Shoulder flexion and abduction in standing position,– adduction in the supine position with long lever-arm, (all starting with 0.5 kg weights in each hand), elbow extension in the supine position and flexion in sitting position with short lever-arm, (both starting with 1 kg weights in each hand). The patients' rating of perceived exertion following each session was measured). The modes were repeated with an increase of weights (maximum 2 kg for long lever-arm and 3 kg for short lever-arm at each new session (maximum 5 sessions) until the patients' rating exceed 15 (strenuous) or more on the Borg's scale.– Patients were free to stop the session at any time.

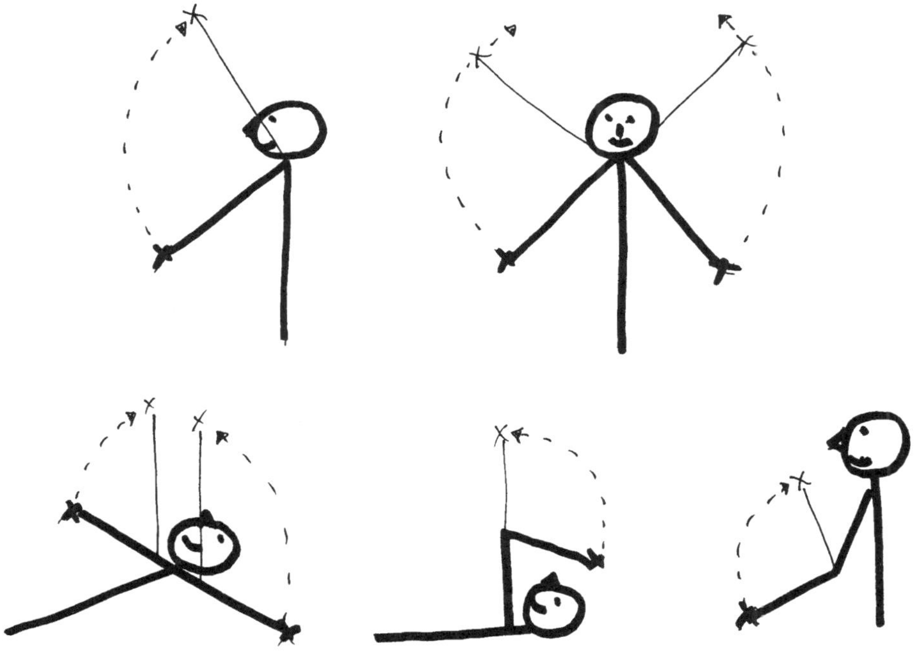

Fig. 1. Exercise programme with weights including shoulder flexion, abduction and horizontal adduction together with elbow extension and flexion.

RESULTS

Sixteen patients completed at least 3 sessions rating 17 (very hard) on Borg's scale and 5 patients completed all 5 sessions. An analysis of limb volumes was conducted immediately when patients indicated they could progress no further and then at the other times indicated in the Immediately after the exercise program an increase of 24 ml (1%) ($p=0.08$)–_of the total arm fluids measured with MFBIA was found. Twenty-four hours after training the total arm fluid– returned to the pre training level and total arm volume measured with WDM reduced ($p=0.1$) by 16 ml (0.5%). This reduction was supported by reductions in the patients' subjective experiences of heaviness ($p \leq 0.05$) and tension ($p \leq 0.01$) in the affected limb.

CONCLUSION

Exercises with heavy weights do not worsen breast cancer related arm lymphoedema.

REFERENCES

1. Harris, SR, SL Niesen-Vertommen. Challenging the myth of exercise-induced lymphedema following breast cancer: A series of case reports. J Surg Oncol 2000; 74; 95-9.
2. McKenzie DC, Kalda AL. Effect of upper extremity exercise on secondary lymphedema in breast cancer patients: A pilot study. J Clin Oncol 2003; 21: 463-466.
3. Wilmore JH, Costill DL. Physiology of sport and exercise. 2nd ed., Champaign, Ill.:Human Kinetics, 1999.
4. Miller LT. Exercise in the management of breast cancer-related lymphedema. Innovations in breast cancer care 1998; 3 (4): 101-106.

LYMPHOSCINTILOGRAPHIC EVALUATION OF THE EFFECT OF MANUAL LYMPHATIC DRAINAGE IN LOWER EXTREMITY LYMPHEDEMA

Kafejian-Haddad, A.P.; Perez, M.D.C.J.; Figueiredo L.F.P.; Castiglioni, M.L.V.; Haddad-Filho, D.; Miranda-Júnior, F.

Discipline of Vascular Surgery - Faculdade de Medicina do ABC
Discipline of Vascular Surgery - Escola Paulista de Medicina - Unifesp
Departament of Image Diagnostic – Coordination of Nuclear Medicine-Escola Paulista de Medicina - Unifesp

Purpouse

To evaluate the effect of manual lymphatic drainage in the technnetium-99m-labeled dextran ($Tc^{99m}Dx$) transport injected in the lower extremites of patients with lymphedema, evaluated by lymphoscintilography.

Methods

16 patients with lymphedema in the lower extremites were randomly selected and submitted to two lymphoscintilography exams by injecting of $Tc^{99m}Dx$ intradermal at the first interdigital space of the affected extremity. A control examination in rest and an examination including a manual lymphatic drainage session, after the injection of the $Tc^{99m}Dx$. Imagens were produced 45 minutes and three hours after the injection of the radioisotope, in the examinations without and with drainage. The extremites were also measured before and after the drainage session. The findings from the examinations were assessed in a quantitative, semiquantitative and qualitative manner, with the participation of three observers. Findings were compared without and with drainage, and submitted to statistical analyses.

Results

The analyses of the comparison of the extremites circumference before and after the drainage, by t-paired test revealed a significant decrease in them. The analysis of the quantitative, semiquantitative and qualitative evaluations evidenced no significant difference en any studies parameters, when submitted to a statistical study: wilcoxon test for the quantitative evaluation variation analysis for the semiquantitative evaluation and exat binomial test for the qualitative evaluation when comparing the results of exams without and with drainage, withim the 45 minutes and three hours periods.

Conclusion

The manual lymphatic drainage caused effective reduction in the circumference of the extremites, but didn't cause significant effect in the $Tc^{99m}Dx$ transportation through the evaluated by lymphoscintilography in the lower extremites of pacients with lymphedema.

KNOWLEDGE AND SELF-CARE IN RELATION TO LYMPHOEDEMA SCHOOL

Helene Lindquist

Karolinska Hospital, Stockholm, Sweden

Introduction

In lymphtherapy, guidances of self-care is one part of the treatment of lymphoedema (Henriksson,1996, Getz, 1985, Sunesson et al, 1995) and one of the challenges is to find pedagogic tools to influence the patients' possibilities to manage their lymphoedema related problems and perform self-care activities.

The rational behind the lymphoedema school is that deepend theoretical knowledge and support in self-care groups with the possibility to relate to others in the same situation, might help the participants to cope with their lymphoedema related troubles.

Knowledge can give the patients a feeling of safety and in control with their daily life (Antonofsky, 1993). The purpose with lymphoedema school is to motivate the participants to keep the lymphoedema on an acceptable level with self-care-actions and to adjust their situation in daily life and work.

The content in the lymphoedema school is based on the participants' own experiences and knowledge, theoretical knowledge and practical guidance in self-care (Lindquist, 2001).

Practical parts include practising special movements that stimulate the musclepump and the law of gravity, and to maintain functional joint movement. The participants learn deep breathing for relaxation and for making them more focused on the training programme. In the relaxation we use positive affirmations for the body awareness. Skincare is also important to prevent injuries and to maintain a normal pH-balance. They learn how to use pH-balanced lotions and while using these, the participants also touch the skin with long efflurage to stimulate the superficial lymph vessels. The participants also learn how to bandage the swollen arm and how to use the comprehession sleeve in the best way. With the bandages on they learn to feel differences between static and dynamic work and they also learn to do rhythmical movements near the center of the body.

The theory includes anatomical and physiological parts of lymphatic system, treatment of lymphoedema, complications, factors that worsen or improve the lymphoedema, adjustment to daily living and work, and how to cope with the "new body". The theoretical part also connects to the practical part.

The duration of the education is eight times two hours each, one hour for the theoretical part and one hour for the practical one. The follow-up is done after six months and after one year(Lindquist, 2001).

Knowledge could be seen from three aspects, the constructive, the contextual, and the functional aspects. Learning in a constructive way is to base the process on earlier experiences and intentions.

By putting earlier experiences to the current problem a contextual way of learning is produced, and if you use knowledge directly in your daily life, learning is functional (Madsen, 1994).

Self-care is in definition to Orem (Orem, 1995): *Self-care is an activity of mature and maturing persons who develop the abilities to take care of themselves in their environmental situations. It is the practice of activities that individuals initiate and do on their own behalf in maintaining health and well-being. When performed effectively, it contributes to human structural integrity, human functioning and human development.*

This study focused on describing the participants' knowledge, self-care and status of lymphoedema in relation to the interventional lymphoedema school.

Research method

The purpose of this study was to describe the status of lymphoedema, the knowledge and the self-care in a group of patients participated in the lymphoedema school.

The more specific questions that the study were focused on were as follow:

Did the participants' objective status change during the study period?

Did the participants' subjective problems change during the study period?

Did the participants' self-care agency change during the period of study period?

Did the participants' specific self-care related knowledge change during the study period?

The participants were breast cancer operated women from a small hospital in Sweden. They had over 10 % difference volume between the arms, a subjective feeling of having a swollen arm and no active malignancy. 30 women were asked to participate,10 women said no because of sickness and practical problems to participate. 20 women were at last included. The middle age was 60,9 years, the youngest 48 and the oldest 79.

Three separate groups attended the learning programme of lymphoedema school.

Status of lymphoedema was controlled before and six months after participating in the lymphoedema school.

The arm volume was measured with Archimedes' method (Kuhnke, 1979), and the circumference of the arm was measured with tape measure every fourth centimetres. The measures were compared with the healthy arm.

The active joint movement in shoulder, elbow, and hand, were measured while standing and lying with a goniometer.

Subjective arm problems were measured with visual analog scale (VAS) in a special questionnaire. Duration of the problems was noted as ordinaldata in the same questionnaire.

BMI (Body Mass Index) was recorded.

For general capacity of self-care we used the "Appraisal of Self-care Agency" scale (ASA) (Söderhamn, 1998, Söderhamn, Evers et al, 1996, Söderhamn, Lindencrona et al, 1996). ASA focuses on the subjetive experience of self-care activity. The questionnaire has 24 items with five possible answers (Orem, 1996). Measuring with ASA was done before, after, six months after and one year after the lymphoedema school. Eleven of the items were related to the lymphoedema school. A questionnaire of 41 questions was used at each occasion, the questions focusing on special lymhoedema related self-care and the effect of it. The questionnaire was tested on ten women before start of the study, and the opinion was that the questionnaire had good validity.

Tabel 3 The participants' self-estimated self-care capacity measured with ASA-A before and after lymphoedema school självskattade egenvårdskapacitet mätt med ASA

ASA-A points (0-120)			
Measureoccasions	**Before** **M (SD)**	**After** **M (SD)**	**p-value**
Before and/directly after (n=19)	90.6 (12.6)	94.4 (11.8)	<0.01
Before/after 6 months (n=17)	90.1 (13.2)	93.2 (10.5)	n.s.
Before/after 12 months (n=17)	90.1 (13.2)	91.4 (13.2)	n.s.

a) n.s.=non significant

Findings and discussion

On average, the participants had had problems with lymphoedema for 27,5 months. The objective and subjective status of lymphoedema did not change during the study period.

The self-care agency measured with ASA-scale, improved directly after the lymphoedema school (tabel 3), but only item 20 "take time to practise daily self-care" remained improved after six months and one year (tabel 4).

In the follow-up one year after the self-estimated frequency of performed self-care actions showed a significant difference in practising arm and shoulder movements, but no difference for the other self-care actions.

The follow-up after one year also showed a significant difference concerning practical knowledge, such as bandageing, skincare, practise of movements, and how to bring out relief of lymphoedema problems in weekday and work.

The lymphoedema related knowledge increased significantly during the study period, especially knowledge regarding of the lymphatic system, treatment and complications.

The women had knowledge about the cause of swelling, holding the arm high, the musclepump, how to avoid heavy lifts and injuries before the intervention started. During the study period the women developed and deepened the lym-

Tabel 4.Outcome of certain ASA-items before and after lymphoedema school

ASA-item	Before M (SD)	After M (SD)	P-value (0-5)
Before/directly after intervention			
2. Control of health actions	3.2 (0.8)	3.7 (1.0)	<0.05
14. Request of clearing health Infomation.	3.6 (1.2)	4.2 (0.9)	<0.05
Before/after six months			
20. Take time for daily self-care	3.1 (1.2)	3.5 (1.3)	<0.05
Before/after 12 months			
20. Take time for daily self-care	3.1 (1.2)	3.6 (1.2)	<0.05

phoedema related knowledge and the benefit of balance between activity and rest.

The validity had improved if a control group had been included, but the study base was to small. This reduces the possibility to generalise our conclusions. It can be worth questioning measuring of the joint movement and arm volume in this study since the women had good joint movement and small differences in arm volume from start. As in other studies the intervention showed improvements just after the intervention. It would be very interesting to analyse why in future studies. How can we maintain general self-care even after a long time? Or should we be satisfied with the fact that they "took time fore daily self-care" even one year after the school?

Conclusions

In this descriptive study, we focused on knowledge and self-care in relation to the lymphoedema school. There were no changes in the objective and subjective lymphoedema status in this group of women. The most obvious influence was the deepened knowledge of lymphoedema, but also the self-care actions with focus on "take time for daily self-care" remained improved one year after the intervention.

Future studies could focus even more on the pedagogic effects in controlled trials.

References

1. Antonofsky, A (1993). *Hälsans mysterium.* Stockholm, Natur och Kultur.
2. Getz, DH. (1995). The primary, secondary and tertiary nersing interventions of lymphoedema. *Cancer Nursing,* 8: 177-81.
3. Henriksson, T-G (1996). Bättre behandling lindrar lymfödem. Energisk egenvård fullbordar. *Läkartidningen*, 93(37): 3127-31.
4. Kuhnke, E (1979). Methodik der volumenbestimmung menschlicher Extrimitäten aus umfangsmessungen. *Physiotherapie,* 4:251.
5. Lindquist, H (2001). Kunskaper och egenvård i samband med lymfödemskola.
6. *Nordisk Fysioterapi,* 5:58-67.
7. Madsen, T (1994). *Lärares lärande.* Lund, studentlitteratur.
8. Orem, D (1995). *Nursing. Consepts of practice.* Fifth edition. Mosby Year Book Inc., St Louis. Missouri.
9. Sunesson, B-L, Lindholm, C, hamrin, E (1995). Clinical incidence of lymphoedema in breastcancer patinets In Jönköping County, Sweden. *European Journal of cancer care,* 5: 7-12.
10. Söderhamn, O (1998) *Potential of self-care. Assessing and describing self-care among elderly people* (Disertation). Department of medicine and care, Division of Nursing Science, faculty of health Sciences, Linköping University.
11. Söderhamn, O, Evers, G, Hamrin, E. A swedish version of the Apprasial of Self-care Agency (ASA) scale. *Scand J caring Sci*, 10:3-9.
12. Söderhamn O, Lindencrona C, Ek A-C. Validity of two self-care instruments fore the elderly. *Scand J Occup Ther*, 3:172-9.

COULD AN EARLY TREATMENT OF LIMB LYMPHEDEMA BE A CURATIVE TREATMENT?

Salvador Nieto, MD, FICA

Salvador Nieto Foundation

PURPOSE

Generally, specialists in Lymphedematology receive patients in advanced stages of their illness. The purpose of the study is to demonstrate the importance of early intervention on patients' outcomes after treatment with lymphedema of the upper and lower limbs.

MATERIAL AND METHODS

This study included 39 patients with primary and secondary upper and lower limb lymphedemas (27 upper limb lymphedemas and 12 lower limb lymphedemas). Requirements to be included in this study were: (1) a short elapsed time between the moment when lymphedema was observed and Földi Method performed, and (2) patient's lymphedema(s) have to be Stage I in the Grandval Classification (less than two centimeters of difference between affected and non-affected limb on symmetrical sections). The

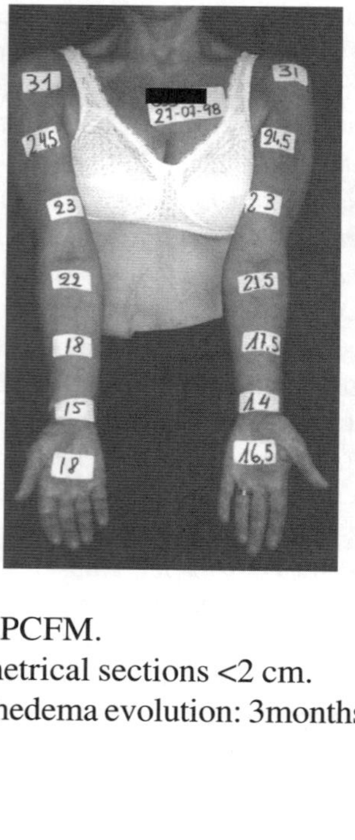

Pre DPCFM.
Symmetrical sections <2 cm.
Lymphedema evolution: 3months.

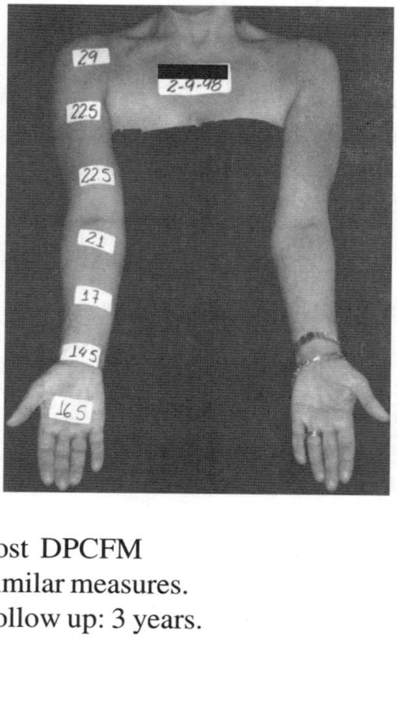

Post DPCFM
Similar measures.
Follow up: 3 years.

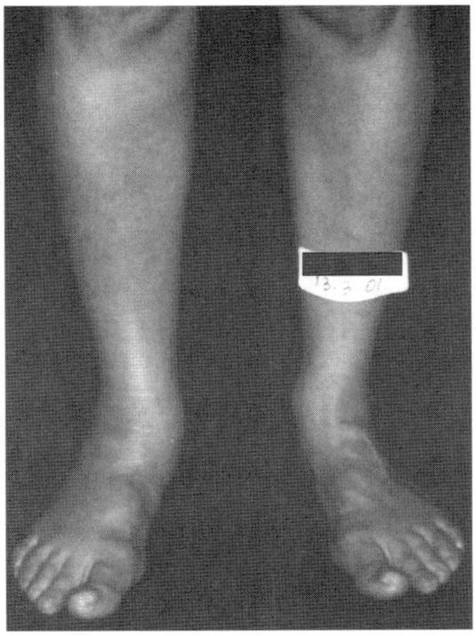

Pre DPCFM (limb bone metastasis)
Symmetrical sections <2 cm.
Lymphedema evolution: 1month.

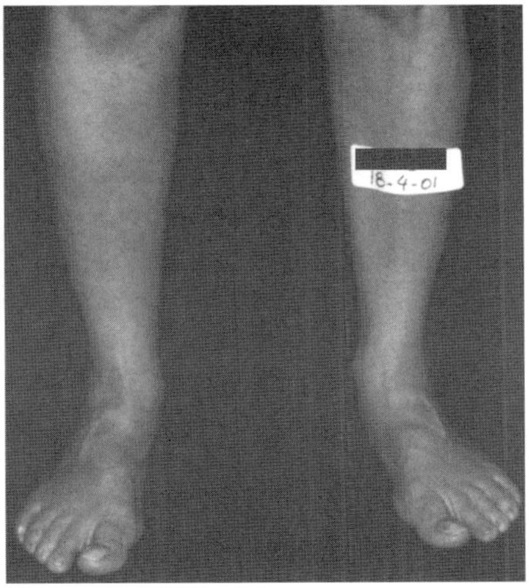

Post DPCFM
Similar measures.
Follow up: 4 months.

patients were treated and then observed first in the short-term and then in the long term. The follow-up period for the patients varied from two to fifteen years.

RESULTS

All patients involved in the study experienced between a 90/100% reduction in their limb lymphedema(s) after the "Intensive Phase" of their treatment and maintained this result during the follow-up period. To date, the longest follow-up period in this study is fifteen years.

CONCLUSION

Early treatment of patients with lymphedema experience drastic reductions of affected limbs that are consistently maintained throughout the follow-up period; these outcomes can be categorized as successful.

PREPUTIAL AND SCROTAL LYMPHEDEMA TREATED SUCCESSFULLY BY CDP FÖLDI METHOD

Salvador Nieto, MD, FICA

SALVADOR NIETO FOUNDATION

PURPOSE

To document a case of giant preputial and scrotal lymphedema, its treatment without surgery and the outcome.

MATERIAL AND METHODS

A 38 year old man presented a giant preputial and scrotal lymphedema characterized by the swelling of the prepuce and scrotum skin. Genital lymphedema is "a functionally disabling and emotionally incapacitating entity" which interferes with life activities and physiological performance. Further physical examination showed lymphatic vessels draining a large quantity of lymph. Many episodes of erysipelas occurred. Studies did not demonstrate chylous reflux. CDP Földi Method treatment was performed over a period of two weeks (Very Intensive Földi treatment, two sessions a day).

RESULTS

A non-surgical procedure on a case of giant preputial and scrotal lymphedema was performed successfully and a significant reduction was achieved.

CONCLUSION

Generally, surgery is considered the only valid therapy for preputial and scrotal lymphedema but CDP Földi has demonstrated to be an excellent therapeutic procedure for this kind of lymphedema.

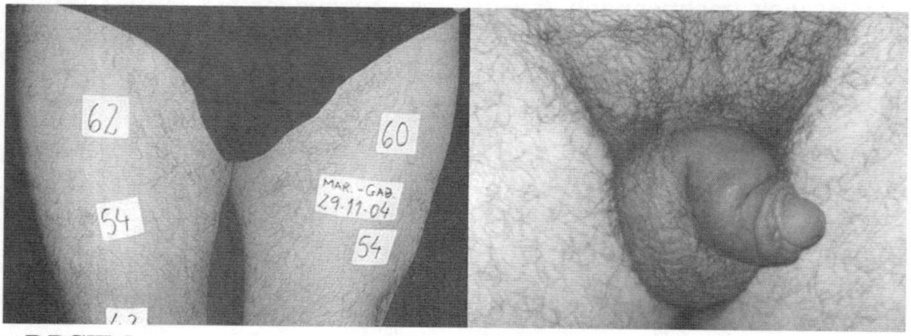

Pre DPCFM
29-11-2004

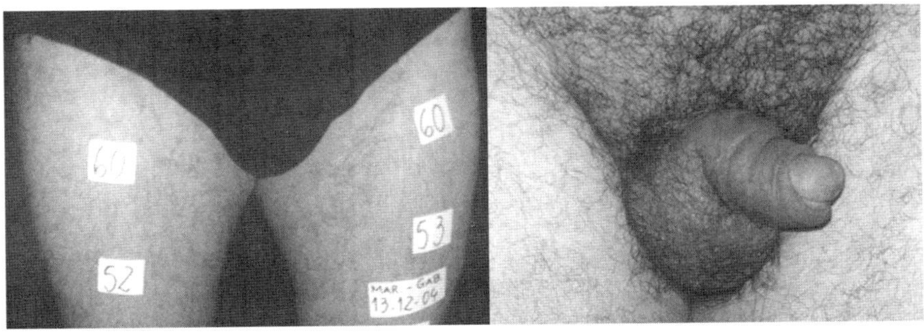

Post DPCFM
13-12-2004

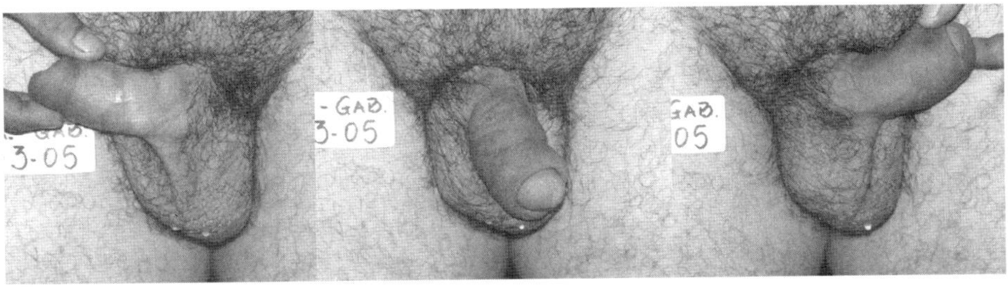

Follow up.
01-03-2005

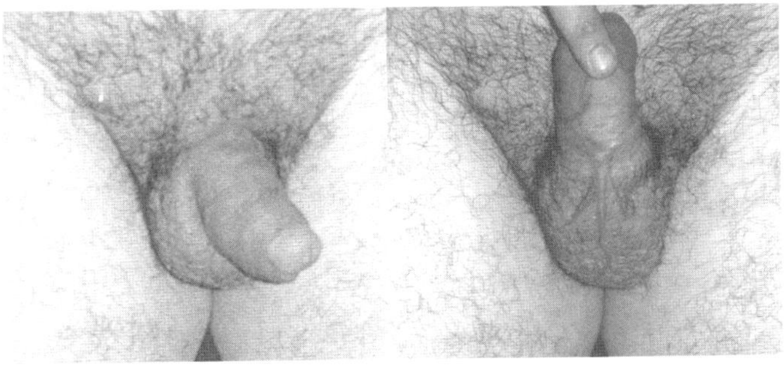

Follow up.
19-07-2005

Chapter 8
Adipose tissue and Lymphedema

ADIPOSE TISSUE AND LYMPHEDEMA – WHAT IS PROVED?

Robert Cluzan, Terence Ryan, Håkan Brorson

This session has been created due to the rising interest generated by the recognition of increased adipose tissue within the affected extremities and other tissues of patients with chronic lymphedema. One of the purposes of this panel is to disseminate knowledge about how this important finding will influence the clinical management of patients with lymphedema (1, 2).

REFERENCES

1. Brorson H. Adipose tissue in lymphedema: the ignorance of adipose tissue in lymphedema. Lymphology. 2004;37:175-7.
2. Brorson H. Liposuction and the consensus document: response to Prof. M. Foldi's remarks at the 19th International Congress of Lymphology. Lymphology. 2004;37:174.

ADIPOSE TISSUE: ONE OF THE OBSTACLES IN LYMPHEDEMA TREATMENT

Robert Cluzan, Scientific Advisor
Unité de Lymphologie, Hôpital Cognacq-Jay Paris

Since 1990 we have been interested by the tissue changes in relation to mechanical lymphatic insufficiency: edema, fibrosis, fundamental substances modifications and adipose tissue excess.

Clinically suspected and demonstrated, with the help of complementary examinations, an excess of fat tissue is one out of these tissue changes, which, like fibrosis, result in difficulties in the lymphedema treatment.

1 In upper limb secondary lymphedema post cancer of the breast treatment on 53 women the Dual X-ray Absorptiometry (DXA) demonstrated an excess of fat mass (range from 9 to 49%) compared with the contralateral limb (1).

2 In lower limb lymphedema there is also an increase of the adipose tissue component (2). On 29 patients examined with DXA, the mean of excess fat mass was 44% (range from 15 to 138%) compared with the contralateral limb. Post combined physiotherapy in this group, some patients had an increase, and some a decrease of this fat mass (3).

3 We had the opportunity to obtain an analysis of this fat component in lymphedema by using the High Resolution Nuclear Mag-

netic Imaging, which allows a resolution of about 70 micron. On 21 examined patients, at the level of the calf, presenting with lower limb lymphedema secondary or primary, the antero-posterior dimension of fat lobules was increased (relative mean increase of the thickness was 206%) (4–6).

4 The relations between adipose tissue and lymph circulation, observed in lymphedema, could also pose questions concerning the vast group of patients with an increase of fat mass, like obesity and lipedema (pathological entity which must be analyzed and more deeply with the actual techniques of explorations: demonstration of the reality of an edema in this condition, role played by some functional lymphatic abnormalities and weakness of the connective tissue as observed with the indirect microlymphangiography using a water soluble contrast medium).

5 The fat tissue excess is one of the cornerstones of any swelling treatment relative to an excess of adipose tissue. The different therapeutic approaches to this excess of fat must be carefully analyzed.

REFERENCES

1. Cluzan RV, Pecking AP, Ruiz JC, et al. Biphotonic absorbtiometry of the secondary upper limb lymphedema. In: Jimenez Cossio JA, A Farrajota A, Samaniego E, Witte MH, Witte CL, editors. Lymphology 1998;31 Suppl: 296-8.
2. Alliot F, Ruiz JC, Cluzan RV. Analysis of fat deposition in lymphedema and efficacy of Physiotherapy. The clinical and biphotonic evaluation. In: Witte M, Witte C, editors. Lymphology 1994;27 Suppl: 523-6.
3. Cluzan RV, Pecking AP. Treating lymphedema: from dream to reality. In: Földi E, Földi M, Witte MH, editors. Lymphology 2004; 37 Suppl: 621-8.
4. Cluzan RV, Idy Peretti I, Alliot AF, et al. Cutaneous and subcutaneous changes in lymphedema analysed with high resolution MR imaging, indirect lymphography and lymphscintigraphy. In: Witte M, Witte C, editors. Lymphology 1994; 27 Suppl: 305-8
5. Pecking AP, Idy-Pereti I, Bertrand Kermorgant F, et al, In vivo assessment of fluid an fat component in lymphedematous skin, In: Campisi C, Witte MH, Witte CL, editors. 2002;35 Suppl: 673-6.
6. Idy-Pereti I, Bittoun J, Alliot FA, Richard SB, Querleux BG, Cluzan RV, Lymphoedematous skin and subcutis: in vivo high resolution magnetic resonance imaging evaluation. Journal Invest Dermatol 1998;110:782-7.

ADIPOSE TISSUE AND LYMPHATIC FAILURE, IS THERE MORE TO THIS STORY?

Terence J. Ryan, Oxford University, Oxford, England

The excess of fat cells found in lymphoedema has long been recognised and was reviewed by

Curri and Ryan 1989 (1), and by Ryan 1995 (2).

Ryan was appalled by the brutality of liposuction when he first observed it, but now recognises that the removal of adipose tissue may be desirable and liposuction does it effectively. He suggests that little harm is done to the lymphatic system because it is excluded from adipose tissue and in the intervening septae lymphatic trunks are protected in the fibrotic sheaf that surrounds the neurovascular bundle of artery, vein and nerve along which the lymphatic exits from the skin.

Some reasons for the association with adipose tissue were proposed including a physiological imbalance of blood flow and lymphatic drainage favouring impaired clearance of lipid and its uptake by macrophages. There is however increasing support for the view that the fat cell is not simply a container of fat but that it is an endocrine organ and a cytokine activated cell. Further more as Catherine Pond and her colleagues have described (3-5) there may be a subtype of fat cell necessary for the metabolism of lymphocytes and dendritic cells in lymphoid tissue. In conditions of lymphatic failure, one must question whether the needs of sequestered lymphoid tissue in the skin stimulate a peripheral enlargement of the adipose tissue therein. The exceedingly fast growing hair bulb is endowed with a similar increase in adipose tissue surrounding it. Fat is a source of the fatty acids so necessary for the manufacture of specialised cell membranes.

Another intriguing possibility (6, 7) is that the worm of filariasis needs a similar source of fatty acids and prefers a location near the lymph nodes that have a direct metabolic relationship with the fat cells that surround them. The fat pad in the groin is more than a space occupying and passive filler of the flexures.

REFERENCES

1. Ryan TJ and Curri S. Cutaneous adipose tissue. In: Ryan TJ and Curri S. editors. Clinics in Dermatology, vol 7: Philadelphia: JB Lippincott; 1989. p. 1-163.
2. Ryan TJ. Lymphatics and adipose tissue. In: Ryan TJ, Mortimer PS, editors. The Cutaneous Lymphatic System. Clinics in Dermatology, vol 13: Amsterdam: Elsevier; 1995. p. 493-8.
3. Pond CM and Mattacks CA. Interactions between adipose tissue around lymph nodes and lymphoid cells in vitro. J Lipid Research 1995;36:2219-31.
4. Pond CM and Mattacks CA. The activation of adipose tissue associated with lymph nodes during the early stages of an immune response. Cytokine 2002;7:131-9.
5. Mattacks CA, Sadler D and Pond CM. The control of lipolysis in perinodal and other adipocytes by lymph node and adipose tissue-derived dendritic cells in rats. Adipocytes 2005,1:43-56.
6. Ryan TJ. Lymphatic filariasis and the International Society of Lymphology. Lymphology 2004;37:151-7.

7. Ryan TJ. Towards a strategic plan for research to support the global program to eliminate lymphatic filariasis. Summary of Immediate needs and opportunities for research on lymphatic filariasis. Philadelphia, Pennsylvania, USA, December 9-10, 2003. Am J Trop Med Hyg. 2004; 71(5 Suppl):iii. p. 1-46. [Consensus Development Conference]

ADIPOSE TISSUE AND LIPOSUCTION. CONFIRMATORY ANALYSES

Håkan Brorson, The Lymphedema Unit, Department of Plastic and Reconstructive Surgery, Malmö University Hospital, Lund University, SE-205 02 Malmö, Sweden

The first time I described my observation of increased adipose tissue content in the involved areas of patients with chronic non-pitting lymphedema was at the ISL meeting in Madrid in 1997. This occurrence has been evaluated in various papers (1-3, 4, 6) as well as my thesis, in which I discussed this specific finding (5). In 1987, when the first patient with post-mastectomy arm lymphedema underwent an operation at our hospital, we noted an excess of adipose tissue in the lymphedematous tissues and recommended a liposuction technique as the best method of treatment. New ideas and concepts of treatment, however, require evaluation, scrutiny, and confirmation by the scientific community treating these patients before they are accepted and become the standard of care.

Therefore it was necessary to further investigate this interesting phenomenon:

1. Consecutive analyzes of the content of the aspirate removed under bloodless conditions, using a tourniquet, showed a very high content of adipose tissue in 44 women (mean 90%, range: 58-100) was found (7).
2. Analyses with DXA in 18 women with postmastectomy arm lymphedema showed a significant increase of adipose tissue in the non-pitting swollen arm before surgery. Postoperative analyses showed normalization at 3 months. This effect was seen also at 12 months. These results paralleled the complete reduction of the excess volume ("edema volume") (8).
3. Investigation with VR-CR (Volume Rendering Computer Tomography) in 8 patients also showed a significant preoperative increase of adipose tissue in the swollen arm, followed by a normalization at 3 months paralleling the complete reduction of the excess volume (9).
4. Tonometry findings in 20 women with postmastectomy arm lymphedema showed postoperative changes in the upper arm, but not in the forearm, which also shoved significantly higher absolute values. Probably this is caused by the high adipose tissue content with

little or no free fluid; just like the situation in the normal arm. Perhaps also the thinner subcutaneous tissue in the forearm plays a part. Tonometry can distinguish if a lymphedematous arm is harder or softer than the normal one. If a lower tissue tonicity value is recorded in the edematous arm, it indicates that there is accumulated lymph fluid in the tissue, and these patients are candidates for conservative treatment methods. In contrast, patients with a harder arm compared to the healthy one has an adipose tissue excess that can successfully be removed by liposuction (10).

5. The findings of increased adipose tissue in intestinal segments in patients with Crohn's disease, known as "fat wrapping", have clearly shown that inflammation plays an important role (11-13).
6. In Graves´ ophthalmopathy a major problem is an increase in the intraorbital adipose tissue volume leading to exopthalmus. Adipocyte related IEGs (immediate early genes) are overexpressed in active ophthalmopathy and CYR61 (cysteine-rich, angiogenic inducer, 61) may have a role in both orbital inflammation and adipogenesis and serve as a marker of disease activity (14).
7. Could possibly anti-inflammatory medication decrease the formation of excess adipose tissue in lymphedema patients? This would be an interesting field for further research.

We now know that patients with chronic, non-pitting, lymphedema develop large amounts of newly formed subcutaneous adipose tissue, which precludes complete limb reduction utilizing microsurgical reconstruction or conservative treatment methods. Although incompletely understood, this adipocyte proliferation has important pathophysiologic and therapeutic implications.

Recent studies presented by Pond et al. suggest that inflammation may play a great role in the formation of excess adipose tissue (see Ryan).

Liposuction can be performed in patients who fail to respond to conservative management because the hypertrophy of the subcutaneous adipose tissue cannot be removed or reduced by the other techniques available. So far, after 11 years' experience, we have not had any complications with this technique, i.e. no deaths from fat embolism and no permanent damage to blood supply or nerves.

REFERENCES

1. Brorson H, Svensson H. Complete reduction of lymphoedema of the arm by liposuction after breast cancer. Scand J Plast Reconstr Surg Hand Surg 1997;31:137-43.
2. Brorson H, Svensson H. Skin blood flow of the lymphedematous arm before and after liposuction. Lymphology 1997;30:165-72.

3. Brorson H, Svensson H. Liposuction combined with controlled compression therapy reduces arm lymphedema more effetively than controlled compression therapy alone. Plast Reconstr Surg 1998;102:1058-67.
4. Brorson H, Svensson H, Norrgren K, Thorsson O. Liposuction reduces arm lymphedema without significantly altering the already impaired lymph transport. Lymphology 1998;31:156-72.
5. Brorson, H. Liposuction and Controlled Compression Therapy in the Treatment of Arm Lymphedema following Breast Cancer. Lund University 1998. [Thesis]
6. Brorson H. Liposuction in arm lymphedema treatment. Scand J Surg 2003:92:287-95.
7. Brorson H, Åberg M, Svensson H. Chronic lymphedema and adipocyte proliferation: Clinical therapeutic implications. Lymphology 37 Suppl 2004. p. 153-5.
8. Brorson H, Karlsson M. Dual X-ray absorptiometry (DXA) analysis of adipose tissue in patients with postmastectomy arm lymphedema treated with liposuction. [In preparation]
9. Brorson H, Nilsson M. Volume rendering computer tomography measurement of adipose tissue volume, before and after liposuction, in patients with postmastectomy arm lymphedema. [In preparation]
10. Bagheri S, Ohlin K, Olsson G, Brorson H. Tissue tonometry before and after liposuction of arm lymphedema following breast cancer. Lymphat Res Biol 2005; 3: 66-80.
11. Jones B, Fishman EK, Hamilton SR, Rubesin SE, Bayless TM, Cameron JC, Siegelman SS. Submucosal accumulation of fat in inflammatory bowel disease: CT/pathologic correlation. J Comput Assist Tomogr. 1986;10:759-63.
12. Sheehan AL, Warren BF, Gear MW, Shepherd NA. Fat-wrapping in Crohn's disease: pathological basis and relevance to surgical practice. Br J Surg. 1992;79:955-8.
13. Borley NR, Mortensen NJ, Jewell DP, Warren. BF. The relationship between inflammatory and serosal connective tissue changes in ileal Crohn's disease: evidence for a possible causative link. J Pathol 2000;190:196-202.
14. Lantz M, Vondrichova T, Parikh H, Frenander C, Ridderstråle M, Åsman P, Åberg M, Groop L, Hallengren B. Overexpression of immediate early genes in active Graves´ ophthalmopathy. J Clin Endocrinol & Metab. [In press].

ADIPOSE TISSUE AND LYMPHATIC SYSTEM

R.V.Cluzan

Tissue changes are the main difficult events, which limit the treatment's efficacy on Lymphedema (LO) Water and still mobile high molecular weight proteins can be eliminated more or less easily by the conservative measures or by derivative - reconstructive surgery (if the lymphatic vessels under the blockage are still functional). Unfortunately some tissue changes as fibrosis and excess of fat are much more difficult to eliminate and in some cases can represent the most important part of the swelling. When locking to Ct scam imaging of a LO we can demonstrate that the welling is mainly in relation to the epifascial compartment with probably a mixture of liquid, fibrosis and excess of fat

1 The analysis (personal data) of 55 Surgical Tissue removal (lymphangiectomy of primary lower limb LO performed by Dr. M.Servelle) (Fig. 1) allows to point out (when cutting the tissues: (right distal part near the ankle – left proximal part):

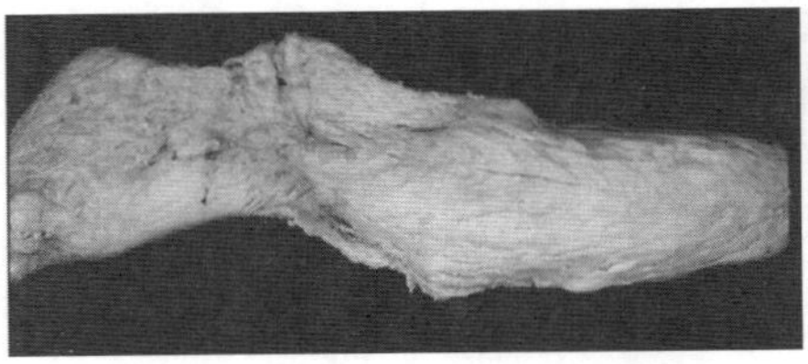

Fig. 1. Deep layer near fascia

1 Liquid flowing from the section
2 and in 33 cases (60%) fibrosis (Fig. 2) extended ± from the derma to the fascia and mainly into the septum. There is no relation between the extent of fibrosis and the lasting time of the LO. The connective tissue of the septum is surrounded by the adipocytes lobules.

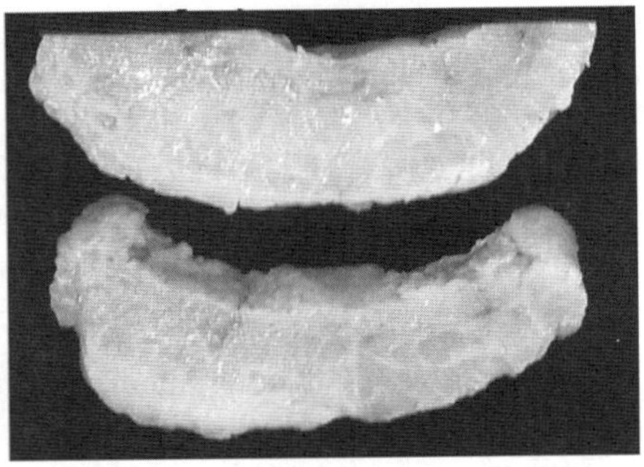

Fig. 2. Macroscopic view of fat and fibrosis. Section of a surgical specimen.

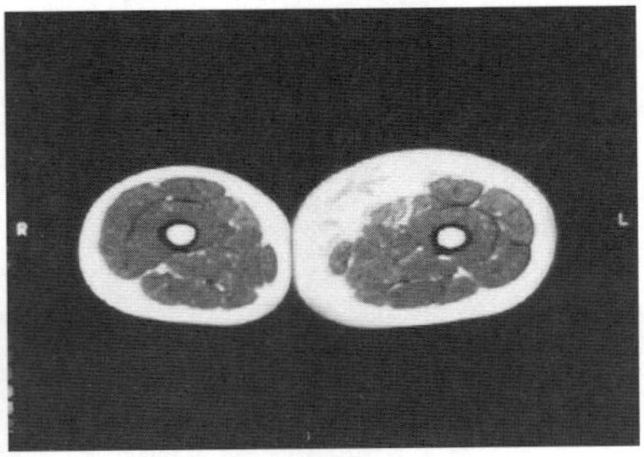

Fig. 3. Nuclear magnetic resonance imaging. Unilateral left lower limb LO. Increase of the fat component.

2 Oedema representing the mobile part of the swelling can be eliminated by any conservative measures or derivative surgery but old fibrosis and excess of fat are much more difficult to eliminate (and maybe it is doubtful)

As Huth (Ref1) underlined already in 1983 that fibrosis is responsible for fragmentations and separation of elastic fibres of the cutis but "*a rather high amount of cases with long persisting oedema do not lead to these alterations*"

3 Fat increased component of the lymphedematous tissue (Fig. 3) can be analysed with 2 different techniques

3-1 High resolution Magnetic Resonance Imaging

3-1-1. Iliana Idy Peretti et al. in 1998 into the **Journal of investigative dermatology** (2) shown that in 22 patients suffering from unilateral lower limb lymphedema (11 primary and 10 secondary) with a perfectly normal contralateral limb (Clinical examination, Lymph Scintigraphy, CT scan) that besides an increased content of liquid, there is a very important increased of the fat lobules size (Table 1) mainly into the superficial fat layer of the sub cutis.

3-1-2 Some exemples

First ex :Right Lower Limb LO post Lymph nodes biopsy 144 months (Fig. 4).

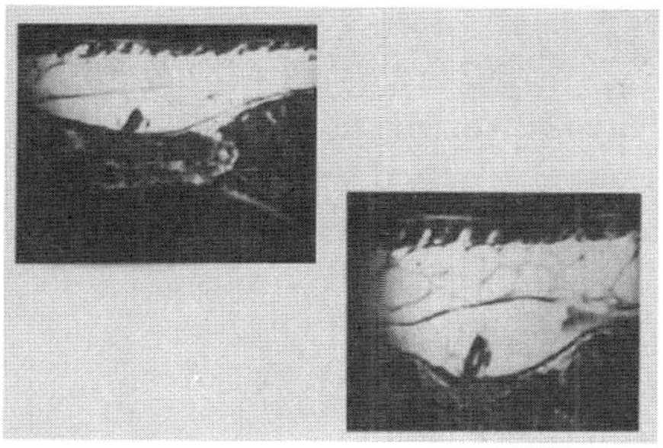

Calf at the level of small saphena
High resolution nuclear magnetic resonance imaging

Considerable increase of the fat tissue
Normal Calf LO

Table 1. Antero posterior size of the fat lobules between leg with LO and normal leg.

	Superficial Layer		Deep Layer	
	Mean Value	SD	Mean Value	SD
Lymphedema	4.67	1.43	5.44	1.68
Normal	2.99	1.50	3.85	1.58
P value	2.7×10^{-6}		1.1×10^{-4}	

Second ex : Right Calf .
LO post several Erisypelas (Fig. 5).

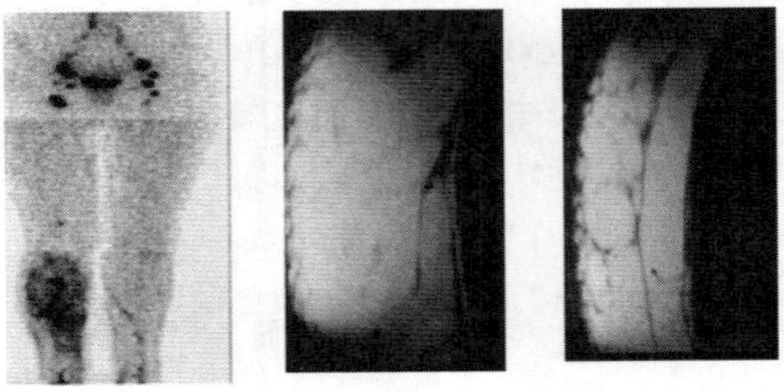

LO : 12 years old

Fig. 5. Increased fat component.

3-2 Analysis with Dual X Rays absorbtiometry.

Upper Limb. We published in 1998 (Ref 2) the results of the analysis of 53 upper limbs LO with DXA technique. (LO versus controlateral limb)

The mean calculated volume was +35.82 %. The mean Excess of fat mass was + 17.18% (Range: 2.41 – 60.64%) and the excess of Fat mass was + 18.19% (Range: 9.07 – 48.69%) This means that in some cases the tissue changes approaches 50% in weight of compared with the normal contralateral limb. There was no correlation between the excess of fat and the lasting time of LO.

Lower Limb. In 29 patients with lower limb Unilateral LO the same type of tissue changes can be observed without any relation between the excess of fat mass and the lasting time of the LO (personal data).

DXA and LO treatment

The analysis of 23 patients suffering of pure unilateral LO with DXA technique before any treatment and after decongestive therapy (Intensive courses of MLD + Bandaging - Mobilisation, Skin care + Elastic compression at the end of the treatment) allows to point out in:

7 / 23 cases: a decreased of the Total mass (Range of - 1.4 to - 31.7%) and an increase of fats Mass (Range of +1.4 to + 40%)

7 / 23 cases a decreased of Total mass (Range – 2.2% to – 53%) and of Fat Mass (Range – 6 ;9% to – 48%)

5 / 23 an increase of Total mass and Fat Mass (treatment failure)

4 / 23 an increase of Total Mass (Range +1.6% to + 28.4%) with a decrease of fat Mass (Range – 4.4% to – 11.7%).

4 Remarks The increase of fat tissue into a LO can be in some cases the main component of the swelling

4-1 The pathophysio-pathology of such changes is far to be clear

Some authors support the view exposed first by J.R.Casley Smith that the excess of fat is in relation to the activity of the macrophages.

This view is accepted by H.Brorson

« *The mechanism behind the adipose tissue hypertrophy is probably that macrophages and adipose cells take up lipids from the lymph which due to the interrupted lymph flow and can not be transported further* »(3)

But histologically it is difficult to accept such explanation. The differences between macrophages and adipocytes seems to be very important and we have never observed

by examining the surgical specimen of lymphangiectomies some macrophages at different level of absorption of lipids.

It is possible that the disorders into the regulation of tissue breakdown and remodelling process plays an important role in relation to the blokade of the circulations of immune cells or of some cytokines.

4-2 The fact that in some cases the Conservative treatment may play a role into the decrease of the fat mass have to be understood (this decrease of the fat component remaining limited)

5 The relations between fat tissue and lymphatic system represent an important factor in physiology and pathology.

The excess of fat can be responsible for microcilculatory disorders where the lymphatics can play an important role besides the blood microcirculatory unit. Speaking of lymphatic system means that all the components of this system must be taken in account. There is no doubt for instance that the prelymphatic pass-ways participate to the explanation of the disorders.

The indirect micro-clymphangiographies (Fig. 6) underline the change into the strength of the connective tissue .

This This aspect can be find into all the patient having an excess of fat in the distal part of their legs and not only in lipedema

Fig. 6. Indirect Micro lymphangiography with water soluble contrast media: flame like aspect underlining the weakness of the tissue.

The role of lymphatic dysfunctions in the physiopathology of abnormalities like the so-called Lipoedema is not clear. Into the term Lipoedema there is probably a lot of different pathological conditions. The presence of en excess of liquid (oedema) in such conditions must be verified with the new available techniques (like High resolution Nuclear Magnetic resonance Imaging). This examination has been able to demonstrate that in cellulite there is no excess of water into the adipocytes lobule (5). This technique could be useful in the exploration of Lipoedema in order to verify the excess of liquid as classically clinically describes. Also the possible hyper permeability in the so-called lipoedema must be verified with the isotopic Landis test.

Recently Haewood et al (6) expressed some doubt on lipoedema, which is for these authors much more a lipodystrophy than a direct consequence of venous or lymphatic insufficiency.

The relations between the so-called lipoedema and obesity are not clear. Nevertheless there is no doubt that some lymphatic abnormalities can be observed like dilatations of initial lymphatics in « lipoedema » (Ref 6) but are these dilatations causal factors or consequences?

It will be useful to practice the analysis of the initial lymphatics with this technique in order to explore other conditions like obesities.

Conclusions Excess of fat in LO is a reality demonstrated by several techniques. Sometimes this excess of fat being able to represent probably near the half of the swelling. This excess of fat can be a limiting factor when treating LO. The exact mechanism behind this tissue change is not known. The conservative treatment is able in some cases to reduce a little bit the fat mass; in others not at all or the reverse, the fat mass increases when the total mass reduces.

The links between Fat tissue and Lymphatic function seem to be a very important element in the equilibrium of the life of the tissues. Despite some excellent revues on Lymphatics and adipose tissue (7) the understanding concerning the relations between Lymphatics and Adipose Tissue is not completely understood. Much more researches have to be done in order to control this important tissues changes in LO and to clarify some pathological conditions and links between excess of fat and lymphatic dysfunction like in obesity or the so called lipoedema which have to be re-analyzed with the new available techniques.

References

1. Idy Pereti Iliana,J.Bitoun, F.Alliot, St Richard, B.Querleux, R.Cluzan Lymphoedematous skin and subcutis : In vivo High Resolution Magnetic Resonance. Imaging evaluation, The journal of investigative dermatology, Vol 110, N° 5, 1998,782-786.
2. A.P.Pecking, J.C.Ruiz, et al Biphotonic Absorbtiometry of the Secondary Upper Limb Lymphedema R.V.Cluzan, , Progress in Lymphology XVI, Ed J.A.Jimenez Cossio, A. Farrajota, E.Samaniego, M.H.Witte and C.L.Witte, Lymphology 31 (suppl) 1-621, 1998, 296-298
3. Brorson H,Chronic lymphedema and adipocytes proliferation : clinical therapeutic implication Progress in Lymphology XVIII, Lymphology 35 (suppl) 1:1-760, 2002,433.
4. Querleux B, Cornillon C, Jolivet O, Bittoun J Anatomy and physiology of subcutaneous adipose tissue by in vivo magnetic resonance imaging and spectroscopy: relationships with sex and presence of cellulite.Skin Res Technol. 2002 May;8 (2) :118
5. Haewood C.A, Bull RH, Evans J, Mortimer PS, Lymphatic and venous function in lipedema, Br.J. Dermatol, 1996, Jan 134, 1-6
6. Amann- Vesti B.R., U.K.Franzeck, A.Bollinger Microlymphatic aneurysms in patients with lipedema Lymphology 34, 2001, 170-175
7. Ryan T.J. Lymphatics and Adipose Tissue, Chronic in eramtology1995, 493-498.

CHRONIC LYMPHEDEMA AND ADIPOCYTE PROLIFERATION: CLINICAL IMPLICATIONS

Håkan Brorson MD, PhD, Karin Ohlin OTR, Gaby Olsson PT, Barbro Svensson PT

The Lymphedema Unit, Department of Plastic and Reconstructive Surgery, Malmö University Hospital Lund University, SE-205 02 Malmö, Sweden

INTRODUCTION

Adipocyte proliferation, not fluid collection, has been identified as a possible cause of limb enlargement in patients with chronic lymphedema. The rate of blood and lymph flow through adipose tissue is inversely proportional to tissue growth. Decreased flow, as well as chronic inflammation, is believed to stimulate lipogenesis and increase deposition of fat. Adipose tissue hypertrophy appears related to ingestion of lipids from the stagnant lymph by macrophages and adipose cells. Liposuction is a logical approach because it effectively removes hypertrophic adipose tissue.

PATIENTS AND METHODS

50 women with a mean age of 65 years (41-89) and a mean duration of the edema (non-pitting, grade II-III) of 11 years (1-38) underwent liposuction. Mean age at breast cancer operation and mean interval between breast cancer operation and lymphedema start were 51 years (34-77), and 14 years (1-44) respectively. All patients had failed conservative treatment prior to surgery. The amount of adipose tissue in both arms was analyzed, pre- and postoperatively, with DEXA (Dual Energy X-ray Absorptiometry) in one patient at 3 months, and with VR-CT (volume rendering computer tomograpy) in another at 12 months.

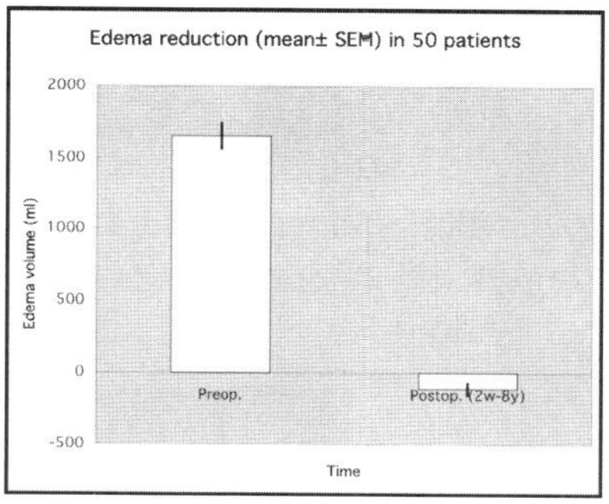

Fig. 1. Complete reduction in 50 patients with arm lymphedema.

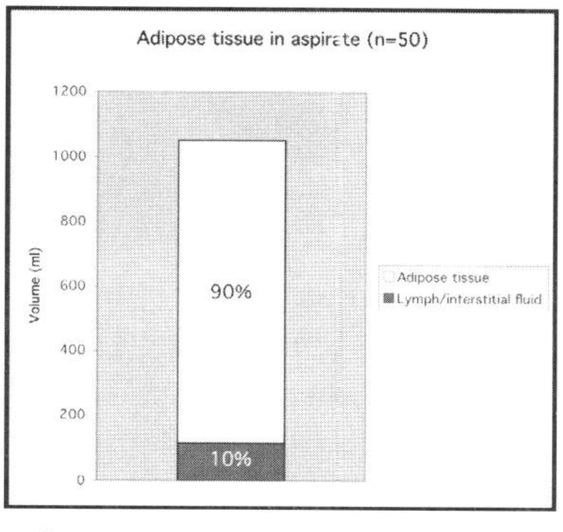

Fig. 2. 90 per cent of the aspirate representated adipose tissue.

RESULTS

Mean preoperative edema volume was 1650 ml (600-3755). Postoperative mean reduction was 112% at follow up 2 weeks to 8 years postoperatively (Fig. 1). Aspirate mean volume obtained under bloodless conditions was 1055 ml. Mean adipose tissue volume and lymph/interstitial fluid volume were 936 ml (90%) and 115 ml (10%) respectively (Fig. 2). Excess amount of adipose tissue in the edematous arm was found with both DEXA (510 grams) and VR-CT (1321 grams) preoperatively. Postoperative values were –138 grams (DEXA) and –180 grams (VR-CT), i.e. a slight overcorrection.

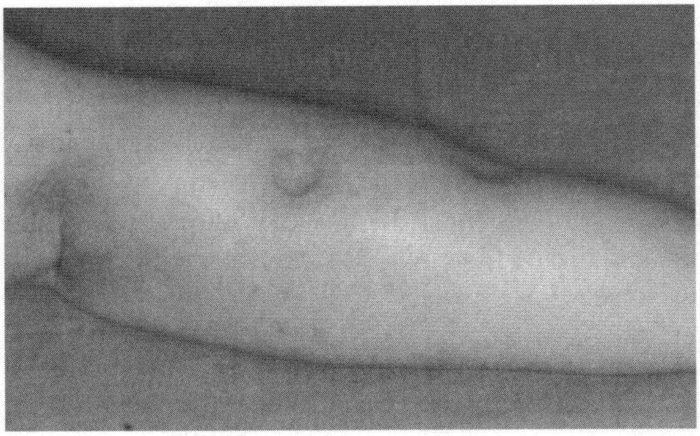

Fig. 3. Marked arm lymphedema after breast cancer treatment with deep pitting of several centimeters (grade I edema). The arm swelling is dominated by fluid, i.e. accumulation of lymph. (© Håkan Brorson 2005).

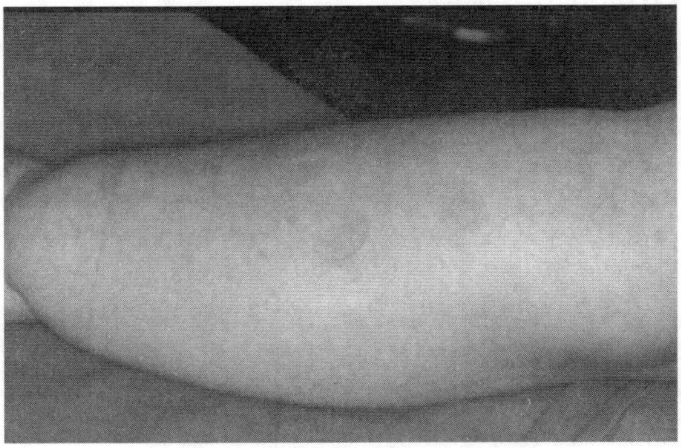

Fig. 4. Pronounced arm lymphedema after breast cancer treatment (grade II edema). There is no pitting is spite of hard pressure by the index finger during one minute. A slight reddening is seen at the two spots where pressure has been exerted. The 'edema' is completely dominated by adipose tissue. The term 'edema' is in this stage improper as the swelling is dominated by hypertrophied adipose tissue and nor lymph. In this stage the aspirate contains no or minimal amount of lymph. (© Håkan Brorson 2005).

CONCLUSIONS

Patients with chronic arm lymphedema after breast cancer treatment develop large amounts of newly formed subcutaneous adipose tissue, which preclude complete limb reduction by microsurgical reconstruction or conservative treatment methods. Although incompletely understood, this adipocyte proliferation has important pathophysiologic and therapeutic implications. Deep pitting in a lymphedematous arm implies excess lymph accumulation and warrants conservative treatment (Fig. 3). Absent or minimal pitting, found in grade II-III edema, indicates excess adipose tissue (Fig. 4). Liposuction is indicated in patients who fail to respond to conservative or microsurgical treatment because the hypertrophy of the subcutaneous adipose tissue is not removed with these methods. Biological study of the extracted materials may shed insight into the molecular mechanisms of the disease process.

REFERENCES

1. Brorson H, Svensson H. Skin blood flow of the lymphedematous arm before and after liposuction. Lymphology 1997; 30: 165-172.
2. Brorson H, Svensson H. Complete reduction of lymphoedema of the arm by liposuction after breast cancer. Scand J Plast Reconstr Surg Hand Surg 1997; 31: 137-143.
3. Brorson H, Svensson H. Liposuction combined with controlled compression therapy reduces arm lymphedema more effectively than controlled compression therapy alone. Plast Reconstr Surg 1998; 102: 1058-1067.
4. Brorson H, Svensson H, Norrgren K, Thorsson O. Liposuction reduces arm lymphedema without significantly altering the already impaired lymph transport. Lymphology 1998; 31: 156-172.
5. Brorson H. Fettabsaugung des Lymphödems am Arm. Handchir Mikrochir Plast Chir 2003; 35: 225-232.
6. Casley-Smith JR, Gaffney RM. Excess plasma proteins as a cause of chronic inflammation and lymphoedema: quantitative electron microscopy. J Pathol 1981; 133: 243-272.
7. Gaffney RM, Casley-Smith JR. Excess plasma proteins as a cause of chronic inflammation and lymphoedema: biochemical estimations. J Pathol 1981; 133: 229-242.
8. Larsen OA, Lassen NA, Quaade F. Blood flow through human adipose tissue determined with radioactive xenon. Acta Physiol Scand 1966; 66: 337-345.
9. Ryan TJ, Curri SB. Blood vessels and lymphatics. Clin Dermatol 1989; 7: 25-36.
10. Ryan TJ. Lymphatics and adipose tissue. Clin Dermatol 1995; 13, 493-498.
11. Smahel J. Adipose tissue in plastic surgery. Ann Plast Surg 1986; 16: 444-453.
12. Vague J, Fenasse R. Comparative anatomy of adipose tissue. In: Renold AE, Cahill GF Jr, editors. American Handbook of Physiology, Section 5. Washington DC: American Physiology Society; 1965. p. 25-36.

13. Jones B, Fishman EK, Hamilton SR, Rubesin SE, Bayless TM, Cameron JC, Siegelman SS. Submucosal accumulation of fat in inflammatory bowel disease: CT/ pathologic correlation. J Comput Assist Tomogr. 1986;10:759-63.
14. Sheehan AL, Warren BF, Gear MW, Shepherd NA. Fat-wrapping in Crohn's disease: pathological basis and relevance to surgical practice. Br J Surg. 1992;79:955-8.
15. Borley NR, Mortensen NJ, Jewell DP, Warren. BF. The relationship between inflammatory and serosal connective tissue changes in ileal Crohn's disease: evidence for a possible causative link. J Pathol 2000;190:196-202.
16. Lantz M, Vondrichova T, Parikh H, Frenander C, Ridderstråle M, Åsman P, Åberg M, Groop L, Hallengren B. Overexpression of immediate early genes in active Graves´ ophthalmopathy. J Clin Endocrinol & Metab. [In press].

Chapter 9
Oriental Medicine and Lymphatics

GENERAL VIEW ON ORIENTAL MEDICINE

M. Ohkuma

Department of Dermatology, Sakai Hospital, Kinki University, School of Medicine, Osaka, Japan

HISTORY

Oriental medicine is little known to Europe and Amerika and has never been discussed in the field of lymphology. The system originated in China in BC 97 and distributed in Korea, Vietnam and Japan. Lian wrote a famous book “Shen nong ben cao jing ji zhu” in AD 500 collecting 365 drugs. It was imported to Japan in the 7th century and Seishu Hanaoka developed to another direction in 17th century (Edo ara). The author has already reported clinical effects of Hochuuekkitoh and Juzendaihotou on volume reduction rate of the lymphedematous extremity (European Congress of Lymphology, Roma, 2005).

CLASSIFICATION AND SYMPTOMS

The diseases are classified by 6 concepts. The drugs are given not by diagnosis but by symptoms (Zuishoh touyo). There is another verified method of prescription; the drug is given after western pathological diagnosis (Byoumei tohyo).

CHARACTERISTICS

Characteristics are listed in the Table 1. The difference between the western and oriental medicine is shown in the Table 2.

DRUGS

They are made of plants (seed, leaf, stem, stalk and root). 300 drugs are commercially available after boiling, freeze dried and sugar added. All these procedures are done in sterile condition. Most of them are powdered and packed in colored & commonly numbered aluminium envelope and but some are capsulated. There are 20 companies which produce the drugs. 147 drugs are already admitted by the government and health insurance. 72 % of all medical doctors prescribe the oriental drugs (only doctors are allowed to prescribe). These are suitable for long time administration (Table 1).The adverse effects, if any, must be reported to the Ministry of Health which is obligatory. About 1/20,000 of incidence of drug eruption is known with the oriental drugs as compared with western drug.

Table 1. Characteristics of Oriental Drug

1. Multiple components: many pharmacological reactions are going on in a body at the same time influencing each other.
2. Rejections: if given drug contains only one substance, the tissue destroys, neutralizes, or produces antibody. However oriental drug contains many substances and this rejection occurs the less.
3. Adverse effects: if certain drug causes hepato-renal-hematological adverse effect or drug eruption, this combination of plants have been excluded from the collection. That is why the oriental drug has the least incidence of the above adverse effect and are suitable for a long period's administration.
4. History of prescription: after a long history of administration they know so and so symptoms fit so and so drugs (there is classical book of collection for it).
5. From a financial point of view, the oriental medicine is cheaper (1) (Table 3).
6. Some skin diseases such as acne, rosacea and senile pruritus are more effectively treated by oriental drug (2).

Table 2. Comparison of Oriental with Western Medicine

Western Medicine	Oriental Medicine
analyzing	synthesizing
etiology dependent	symptom dependent
synthesized drug	natural material (plant)
single substance	multiple components
treating the diseases	also for prophylaxis & high QOL
some adverse effects	seldom adverse effects (1/20,000)
expensive	less expensive (Table 3)

SOCIAL ACTIVITY

Two societies we have in Japan. 1. Jap. Society of Wkanyaku, which is mainly for research with 975 members and, 2. Japanese Society of Oriental Medicine which is for clinical medicine with 6,000 members. They both have annual meetings and their own journals. The latter society holds international congresses. 4,000 doctors have become specialists for oriental medicine for which they need to pass the oral and written qualifying examinations, a certain numbers of oral congress presentations as well

Table 3. Hospital Expense in Case of Flu Syndrome (1)

	Western drug	Oriental medicine
Cases evaluated	597	167
Age	40.5±26.6	34.2±25.3
Used drugs	2.9	1.2
Treated days	6.7	4.0
Expense/day	¥203.3	¥119.6
Total expense/patient	¥1,357.3	¥484.5

as written papers. This specialist is reevaluated every 5 years. Only medical doctors can prescribe the drug and this treatment is approved by health insurance. Generally speaking expense for the treatment is the less, if the patients are treated by oriental drugs (Table 3).

REFERENCES

1. Akase A: Hospital expense in flu syndrome. J Kampo Med. 50 (2000), 656 (in Japanese).
2. Ohkuma M: Treatment of acne by oriental drugs combined with external application J. Traditional Med. 10 (1993), 131 (in Japanese).

A NEW METHOD OF COMPRESSION IN SCLEROTHERAPY FOR VARICOSE VEIN

M. Ohkuma

Department of Dermatology, Sakai Hospital, Kinki University, School of Medicine, Osaka, Japan

INTRODUCTION

Complications such as erythema, bulla or intertrigo of the skin are often seen after sclerotherapy for varicose vein. A special compression sponge may prevent these complications. That is why this trial has been performed.

MATERIAL AND METHOD

Total 277 cases of varicose vein are divided into 4 groups; I. in 117 patients a rolled sponge (5-15 long, 3-4cm in diameter) is applied on the skin along the injected vein fixing by plaster. II. The sponge is fixed in the same as I. but leaving no space between the skin and the plaster in 26 cases. III. In 29 cases only the sponge is placed without plaster. IV. The sponge is attached by two parallel smaller & softer sponges fixed by the palster on one side is used in the same way in 102 patients. The sclerotherapy is performed by a unique method by injecting 5ml of hypertonic saline solution (23.4) into one vein at a time. After the injection the above sponge is placed on the skin and the less elastic bandage is put on. This compression is continued for 4 weeks. Skin condition is checked 1 to 4 weeks after the injection (Fig. 1).

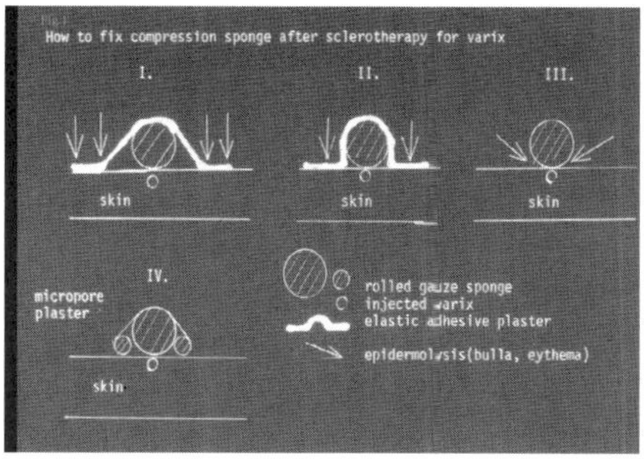

Fig. 1. A schematic demonstration of the various compression methods tried.

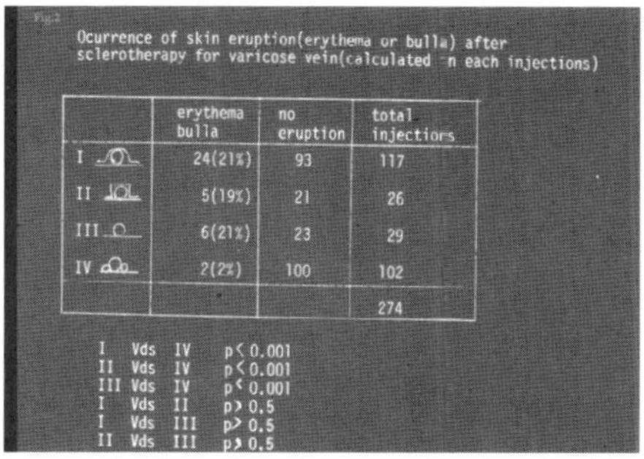

Ocurrence of skin eruption(erythema or bulla) after sclerotherapy for varicose vein(calculated in each injections)

	erythema bulla	no eruption	total injections
I	24(21%)	93	117
II	5(19%)	21	26
III	6(21%)	23	29
IV	2(2%)	100	102
			274

I Vds IV $p < 0.001$
II Vds IV $p < 0.001$
III Vds IV $p < 0.001$
I Vds II $p > 0.5$
I Vds III $p > 0.5$
II Vds III $p > 0.5$

Fig. 2. Results of the methods with skin eruptions.

RESULT

In group IV only 2 cases of skin erythema (Fig. 7) are observed which is statistics significantly less frequent than any other groups (Fig. 3-6). Later after some experience it is found that if the size and firmness of the main and parallel sponge as well as the compressing tightness is adequate, this skin complication never occurs.

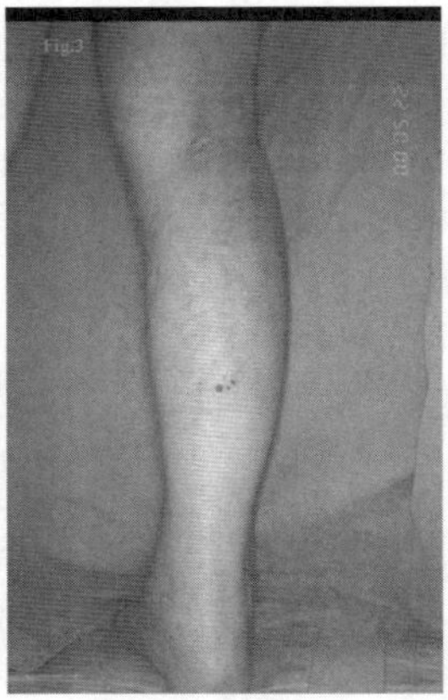

Fig. 3. Skin condition after sclerotherapy before the compression.

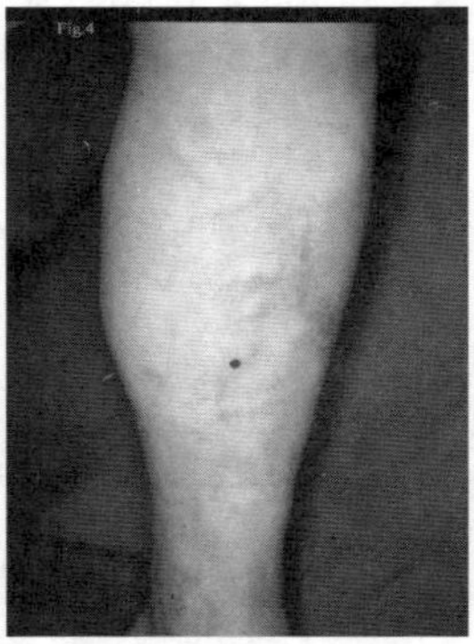

Fig. 4. Method I., i. e., the rolled sponge is fixed on the skin by plaster. Erythema is along the both sides of the rolled gauze

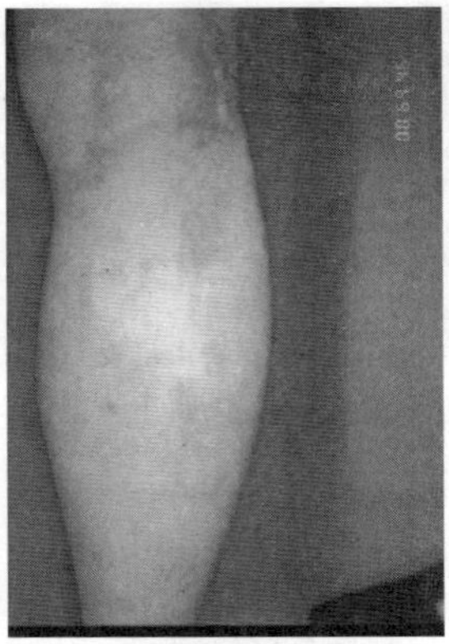

Fig. 5. Method II, the same as the method I but leaving no space between the plaster and the skin. A similar skin change as method I but less prominent.

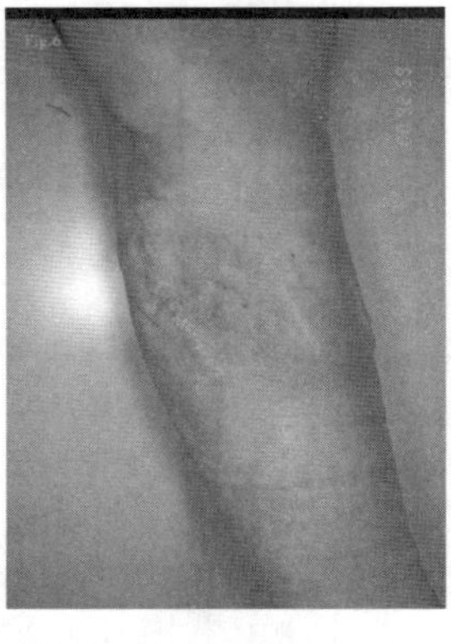

Fig. 6. Method III, only the sponge is placed without plaster applied on it. A remarkable blister formation is seen.

DISCUSSION

Compression after the sclerotherapy is extremely important because if it is incomplete, it leaves a space in the lumen of the injected vein which causes blood clot, recanalization and further recurrence of the varicose vein. On the contrary

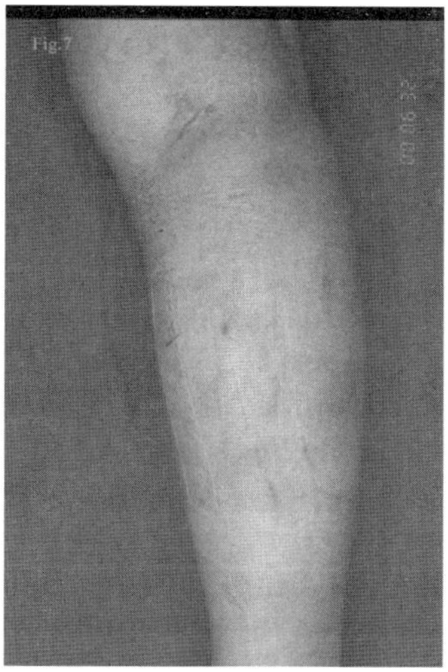

Fig. 7. Method IV., 3 parallel sponges are placed on the skin without plaster. No remarkable skin changes are noticed.

if the injected vein is compressed firm enough, there is no space for the blood clotting to occur and no recurrence to occur. Skin changes are mostly caused by epidermolysis by aspirating the epidermis by the fixed plaster to the other direction, it is well known that this change is obtained by aspirating the skin surface by a negative pressure in order to get epidermal skin specimen for transplantation.

CONCLUSION

If 3 rolled gauze sponges attached together are used for compression after sclerotherapy for varicose vein, it causes seldom skin complication.

A NEW TREATMENT OF HYPERKERATOSIS ASSOCIATED WITH LYMPHEDEMA BY EXTERNAL APPLICATION OF MAXACALCITOL (VITAMIN D3 ANALOGUE) OINTMENT

M. Ohkuma

Department of Dermatology, Sakai Hospital, Kinki University, School of Medicine, Osaka, Japan

INTRODUCTION

It is clinically well known that if lymphedema patients suffer from repeated episode of lymphedema-related acute dermatitis, they develop elephantiasis.The author has already reported clinical effect of oral and external retinoid for elephantiasis (1). However it causes serious hepatogenic and osteogenic disturbances. Maxacalcitol is a vitamin D3 analogue (Fig.1) which inhibits psoriatic lesion. Its ointment is safe and effective. Its mechanism how it works is not known but it is highly suspected that it inhibits inflammation of psoriasis. If so, it may inhibit inflammation in the lymphedematous tissue and further fibrosis & hyperkeratosis.

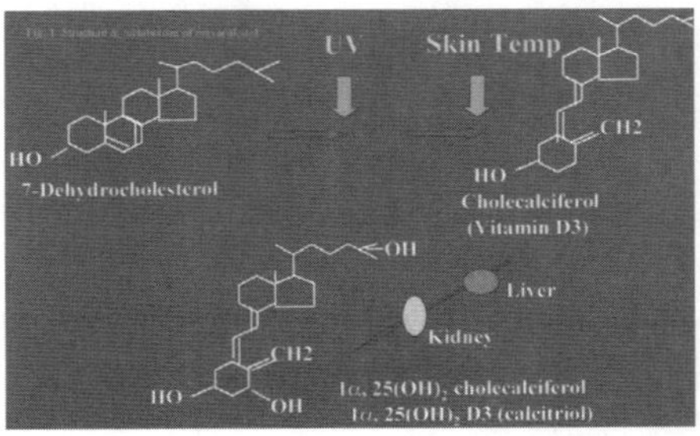

MATERIAL AND METHOD

Ten cases of lymphedema (2 primary and 8 secondary) are externally applied by maxacalcitol (25μg/g) ointment once in a day until the hyperkeratotic skin becomes diminished. Necessary length of the treatment is evaluated in each patient (Table 1). If the treatment becomes longer than 4 months, the patients are examined for serum calcium. Any clinical subjective and objective adverse effects are also evaluated.

RESULT

In all treated patients hyperkeratotic lesions have disappeared in 1 to 4 months of application (Fig. 2-4) (Table 1).There is neither subjective nor objective adverse effect observed. In two examined patients serum calcium level is within normal limit.

Table 1. Ten tried patients and results of the treatment

No.	name	sex	age	extremity	tinea	LERAD in past 3M	treated Tx part	duration	clinical effect	adverse effect
1.	SY	F	49	bil.lower	lt.foot	+	lt.foot	1M	+++	-
2.	TS	F	75	lt.lower	lt.groin	+	lt.foot	4M	+++	-
3.	TY*	M	41	bil.lower	feet	+	feet	3M	+++	-
4.	HN	F	50	rt.upper	-	+	rt.hand	3M	+++	-
5.	AT	F	72	rt.lower	rt.foot	+	rt.foot	1M	+++	-
6.	KI	F	48	rt.lower	rt.foot	+	rt.foot	2M	+++	-
7.	HD	M	76	bil.lower	feet	-	feet	4M	+++	-
8.	YH*	F	29	lt.lower	lt.foot	+	lt.foot	2M	+++	-
9.	KN	F	68	bil.lower	feet	+	feet	3M	+++	
10.	MN	F	74	rt.lower	rt.foot	+	rt.foot	1M	+++	-

*primary lymphedema; all others: secondary lymphedema; F: female, M: male; bil.: bilateral; lt.: left; rt.: right; M: month; LERAD: lymphedma-related acute dermatitis; + present; - absent; +++ very effective

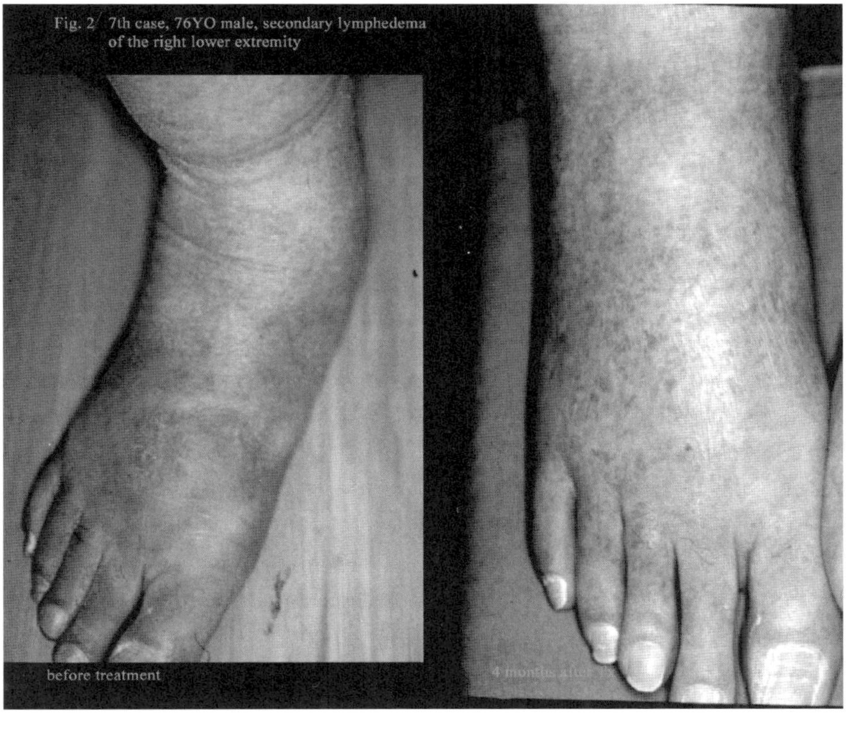
Fig. 2 7th case, 76YO male, secondary lymphedema of the right lower extremity
before treatment
4 months after

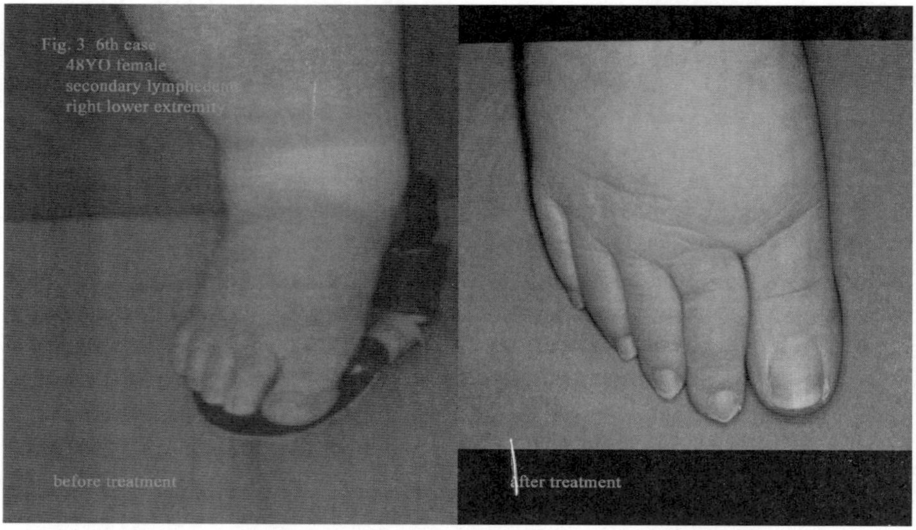
Fig. 3 6th case
48YO female
right lower extremity
before treatment
after treatment

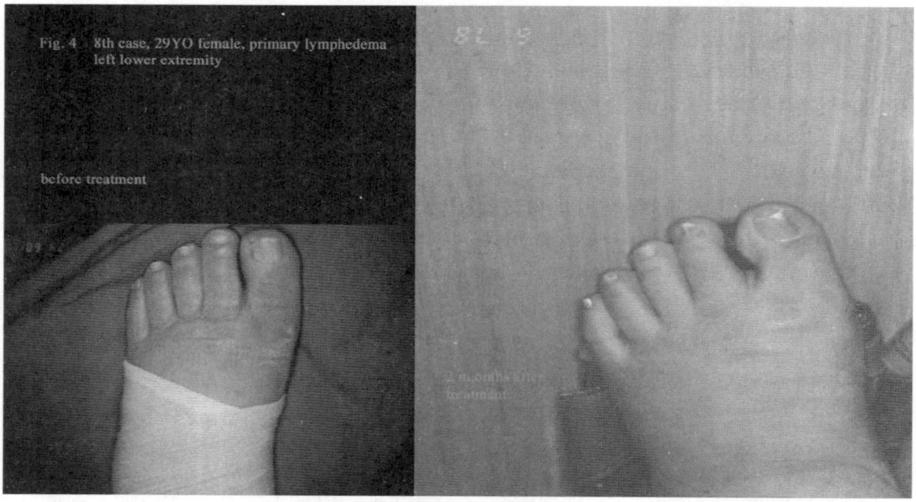
Fig. 4 8th case, 29YO female, primary lymphedema
left lower extremity
before treatment

DISCUSSION

The mechanism how the maxacalcitol works on hyperkeratosis is not known. After repeated episode of lymphedema-related acute dermatitis, the lymphedema develops to become elephantiasis with hyperkeratosis. In this complication inflammatory cytokines such as ICAM-1, VCAM-1 and ELAM-1 are elevated (2) and so are bFGF (3) and EGF (3). All these changes are responsible for epidermal changes with proliferation and hyperkeratosis. Maxacalcitol, vitamin D3 anlogue (Fig. 1) inhibits proliferation and differentiation of the keratinocyte (4), to which the effectiveness of this treatment is suspected to be attributed. Adverse effects are known in 6.6% of the treated patients with pruritus (4.1%), skin stimulation (3.2%), red skin (3%), etc. Laboratory adverse effects are known to be hyperpotassemia (2.5%), hyperphosphatemia (0.5%), elevated osteogenic alkaline phosphatase (0.5%), etc.

The both clinical and laboratory adverse effects are not found in this trial treatment, because the applied area is so small in size (hyperkeratosis is usually only a part of dorsal foot). It is very impressive that all patients except No.4 suffer from tinea which may cause intradermal invasion of responsible bacteria. No.9 case shows no episode of Lymphedema-related acute dermatitis. This case may have an insidious inflammation.

REFERENCES

1. Ohkuma M: Treatment of elephantiasis nostras by retinoid. Casley-Smith JR: Piller NB:. Progress in Lymphology, X. Univ. Adelaide Press, Adelaide, 1985.
2. Ohkuma M: Adhesion molecules in lymphedema before and after treatment as well as difference between those with and without complications. Lymphology37 (Suppl.) (2004), 289.
3. Ohkuma M: VEGF,c-GMP-&AMP,bFGF and EGF in lymphedema-related acute dermatitis. Lymphology 37 (Suppl.) (2004), 297.
4. Kmine M, Watanabe Y, Shimaba S et al: The action of a novel vitamin D3 analogue,OCT on immunomodulatory function of keratinocytes and lymphocytes. Archives Dermatol. Res. 291 (1999), 500.

IMMUNOLOGICAL EXAMINATION AFTER A NEW PHYSIOTHERAPY FOR LYMPHEDEMA COMBINED WITH ORIENTAL DRUGS HOCHUEKKITOU (TJ.41) AND JUZENDAIHOTOU (TJ.48)

M. Ohkuma

Department of Dermatology, Sakai Hospital, Kinki University, School of Medicine, Osaka, Japan

INTRODUCTION

In the past congress (31st European Congress of Lymphology, 2005), if it was combined with oral oriental drugs, a new physiotherapy (1) was more effective for treatment of lymphedema (Fig. 1). These drugs are suspected to stimulate immunological ability.

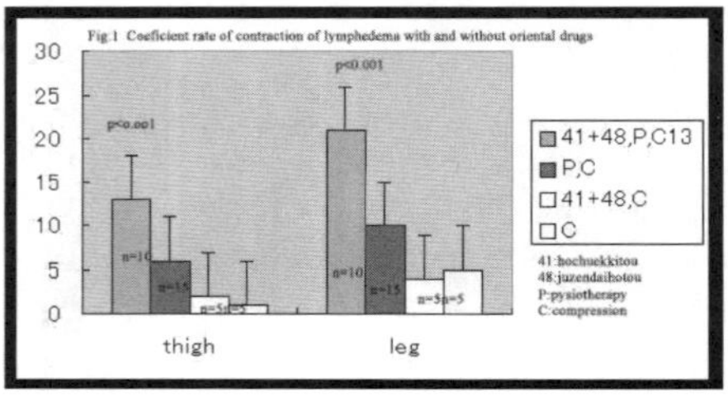

MATERIAL AND METHOD

I) 10 cases of secondary lymphedema (55-75 YO, mean 63 YO all females) of the lower extremity are treated by a new physiotherapy by magnetic fields, vibration and hyperthermia (1-5 treatment courses with mean 2) combined with oral oriental drugs, Tj. 41(Hochuekkitou) and Tj. 48 (Juhzendaihotou) 7.5g a day, respectively; II) 15 cases of secondary lymphedema (35-82 YO, mean 63 YO all females) of the lower extremity are treated by the same physiotherapy without oriental drugs (1-6 treatment courses, mean 3); III) 5 cases of the same patients receive the same oriental drugs alone. In all treatment groups, I-III, compression by less elastic and elastic bandages are applied. IV: 5 cases of the same patients have only the same compression bandages. Immunological examinations such as PHA, PPD skin test, peripheral leukocyte-, monocyte-, eosinophile-, T-cell, B-cell counts, CD 4/8 ratio, CH50, IgM, IgG, CRP and erythrocyte sedimentation rate are performed in each group.

RESULT

All the immunological examinations (Fig.3,4) are not different in I and II group except ESR (Fig. 2). All the

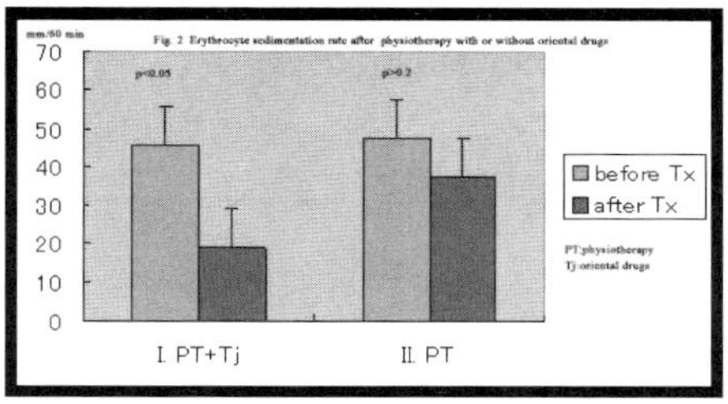

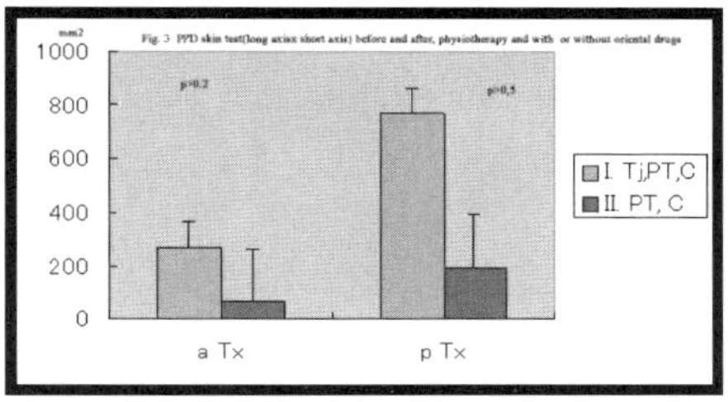

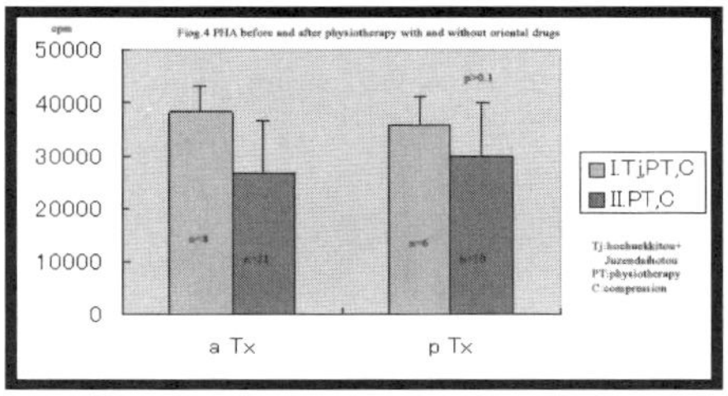

data of group III and IV have been dropped out.

DISCUSSION

After a treatment course of the new physiotherapy PHA and PPD skin tests were intensified (1). And Tj.41 and Tj.48 are known to stimulate immunological reactions and decrease inflammation (Table 1,2). The result is different from this data which may be due to the fact that these data are something obtained after several treatment courses. The lymphedematous tissue may get used to a new environment or new changes after several courses. The reason why ESR is more increased after the physiotherapy combined with oriental drugs is not known. However it is suspected to be due to an decreased inflammation in the

Table 1
Components of Tj.41, Hochuuekkitou and their pharmacological effects

	immunity	anti-tumor	anti-bact	anti-fungus	anti-virus	anti-inflam.	NO	vaso-dilitation	anti-thrombus
1. asteragali radix	RES ↑ IFN ↑	+				+	↑	+	
2. atractylpoides lanceae rhizome		+	+			+			
3. ginseng radix	steroid-like	+	+	+		+		+	+
4. augelicae radix	IFN ↑ complement ↑	+			+			+	+
5. bupleuri radix	antibody ↑	+				+	↓	+	
6. ziziphi fructus	allergy ↓								+
7. aurantil nobulis peric arpium	I type allergy ↓					+			
8. glycyrrhizae radix	NK cell ↑	+	+		+	+			+
9. cimiciguae rhizona	PHA ↓ IFN ↑					+		+	
10. zingiberis rhizoma						+		+	

The underlined: common in Tj41 and Tj.48; ↑: increased or stimulated; ↓: decreased or lowered; +: present; NO: nitrous oxide

Table 2
Components of Tj. 48, Juuzendaihotou and its pharmacological effects

	immunity	anti-tumor	anti-bact.	anti-fungus	anti-virus	anti-inflam.	NO	vaso-dilatation	anti-thrombus
1. <u>astragali radix</u>	RES ↑ IFN ↑					+	↑	+	
2. cinamoni Arthus	cortex reaction ↓	+	+			+		+	+
3. rehmanniae radix	lymphocyte ↑ macrophage ↑	+					↑	+	+
4. paeoniae radix	macrophage ↑		+				↑	+	+
5. cnidii rhizome	↑	+				+		+	+
6. <u>atocylodes lanceao rhizoma</u>			+			+			
7. <u>angelicae radix</u>	macrophage ↑ IFN↑ complement↑	+			+	+		+	+
8. <u>ginseng radix</u>	steroid ↑	+	+	+		+	↑	+	+
9. poria	lymphocyte ↑ complement ↑	+				+			+
10. <u>glyzzhizae radix</u>	NK cell ↑ IFN↓ complement ↑ chemical mediator ↓	+			+	+			

The underlined: common in Tj41 & Tj.48; ↑: increased or stimulated; ↓: decreased or lowered; +: present; NO: nitrous oxide

treated tissue combined with oriental drugs. It should be further investigated whether IFNγ is involved or not. The controls have been dropped out because they are not so effective and the patients did not wish the further treatment and examinations.

CONCLUSION

The more effective result by a new physiotherapy for lymphedema treatment combined with oral oriental drugs are not due to the more stimulated immunological reactions.

REFERENCES

1. Ohkuma M: A new treatment of lymphedema by magnetic fields, vibration and hyperthermia---the second report. Lymphology 35(Suppl) (2002), 320.
2. Ohkuma M: Immunological changes after a new lymphedema treatment by magnetic fields, vibration and hyperthermia. Lymphology 35 (Suppl) (2002), 690.

TAT AND D-DIMER CHANGES IN SCLEROTHERAPY FOR VARICOSE VEIN COMBINED WITH ORIENTAL DRUGS, KEISHI- BUKURYOU-GAN (TJ 25) AND OUREN-GEDOKU-TOH (TJ 15)

M. Ohkuma

Department of Dermatology, Sakai Hospital, Kinki University, School of Medicine, Osaka, Japan

INTRODUCTION

Since thrombosis of injected vein is inevitable, recurrence of varicose vein comes, if the injected and thrombosed vein is recanalized (Fig. 1). Tj 25 and Tj 15 are famous oriental drugs which inhibit an intravascular coagulation and increase intravascular microcirculation (Tables 1,2).Clinically recognized intravaricose thrombosis formation occurs in 36.9% of all sclerotherapy patients with varicose vein and deep vein thrombosis is recognized in 0.05% of the same patients (Survey of 2,065 cases in 126 Japanese hospitals, 199).

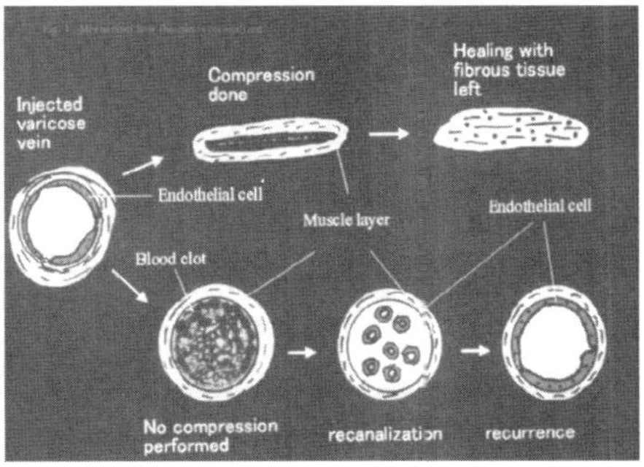

Table 1. Components and pharmacological effects of Keishibukuryougan (Tj.25)

Plant component	Pharmacological effect					
	anti-thrombotic	anti-allergic	vaso-dilatatoric	anti-bacteric	anti-inflammatoric	antalgic
1. cinamoni cortex	o	o	o	o	o	
2. hoelen	o					
3. moutan cortex	o	o		o	o	o
4. paeoniae radix		o	o	o	o	o
5. persicae semen	o	o			o	

Table 2. Components and pharmacological effects of Ourengedokutou (Tj.15)

Plant component	Pharmacological effect: anti inflammatory	anti allergic	anti-bacteric	anti-arteriosclerotic
1. scutellariae radix	o	o		o
2. phelldendri cortex	o		o	
3. coptidis rhizome	o		o	
4. asiasari radix		o		

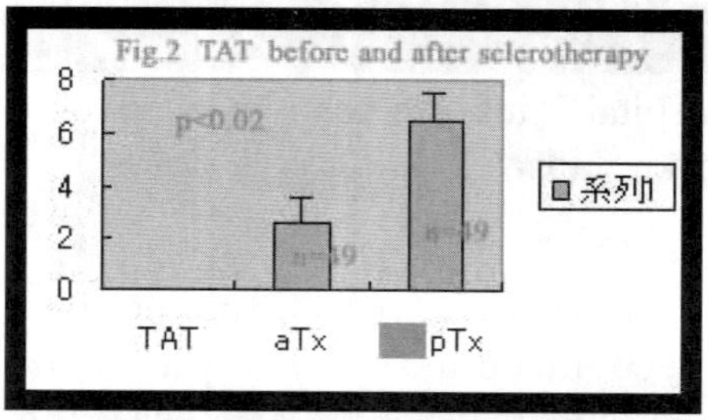

Fig.2 TAT before and after sclerotherapy

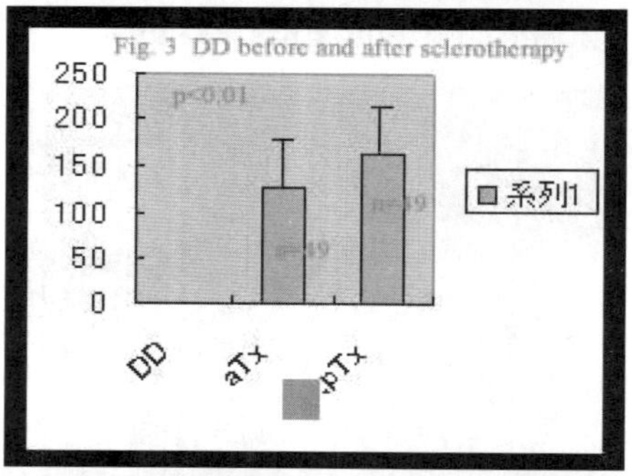

Fig. 3 DD before and after sclerotherapy

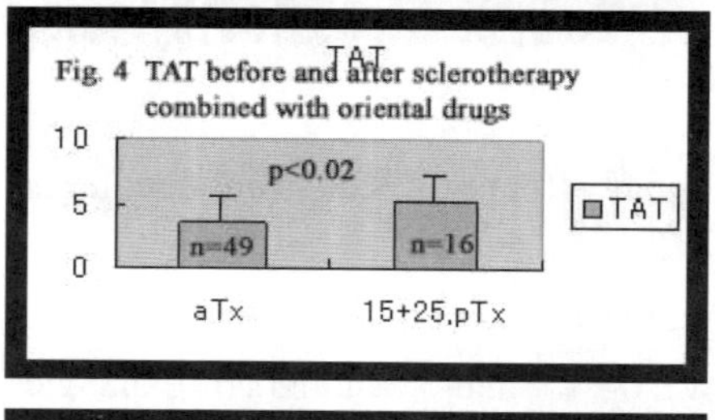

Fig. 4 TAT before and after sclerotherapy combined with oriental drugs

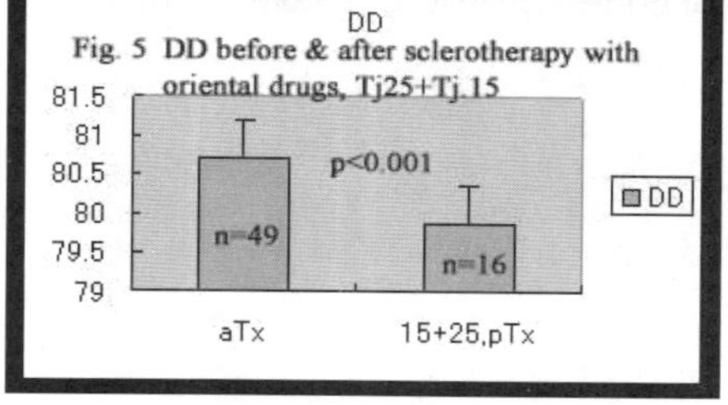

Fig. 5 DD before & after sclerotherapy with oriental drugs, Tj25+Tj.15

MATERIAL AND METHOD

TAT and D-dimer are evaluated after sclerotherapy for varicose vein in the following patients groups; I. 49 cases of varicose vein are evaluated before and 1 week after sclerotherapy. II. 16 patients are given the above oriental drugs, 7.5 g. a day, t.i.d. from 2 weeks before and up to 2 weeks after the therapy. TAT and D-dimer are examined 2 weeks before and 1 week after the treatment III. For the control 4 patients are given the same oriental drugs for 3 weeks and the same examinations are performed before and 3 weeks after the prescription.

RESULT

TAT becomes elevated after the sclerotherapy regardless of administration of the oriental drugs (Fig. 2,4). D-dimer is also elevated after the same therapy after sclerotherapy alone (Fig.3). However, it is rather decreased even after the sclerotherapy if the therapy is combined with oral oriental drugs (Fig. 5).When we compare the results, TAT is not different after the sclerotherapy regardless of administration of oriental drugs. On the contrary D-dimer is different if the drugs are given after the sclerotherapy. Deep vein thrombosis is not clinically observed after sclerotherapy in any case. There is no bleeding disturbance in the patients with oriental drugs administered. All cases of control have been dropped out.

DISCUSSION

Tj 25 contains 5 plant components which inhibit sialidase located in the outer membrane of the erythrocyte. That is why it inhibits intravascular coagulation (1). However, stop of bleeding in case of trauma is associated with sialidase located in the inner membrane of the red blood cells on which Tj 25 does not influence. That is why the stop of bleeding is not disturbed in the Tj 25 given patients.

Increased TAT as well as decreased D-dimer after the sclerotherapy combined with oral oriental drugs can be the result of the following;

1. Thrombus is formed but the secondary fibrinolysis is disturbed.
2. Thrombin is formed but polymerization of fibrin to become a stable fibrin is disturbed.

Any of the above two possibilities are favorable in case of sclerotherapy.

CONCLUSION

TAT is increased but D-dimer becomes decreased after sclerotherapy for varicose vein, if it is combined with oral oriental drugs; Tj.25 and Tj.15.

REFERENCES

1. Nagai T, Xiao-Guang C and Yamada H: Enhanced sialidase activity and sialic acid content of erythrocyte membrane from betamethazone-treated mice and their recovering effect of Keishi-bukuryo-gan. J of Traditional Med. 12 (1995), 195.

THE MECHANISM HOW THE LYMPHEDEMA BECOMES HEALED

M. Ohkuma

Department of Dermatology, Sakai Hospital, Kinki University, School of Medicine, Osaka, Japan

INTRODUCTION

Lymphedema has never been believed to become completely healed. A complete healing means edema free state continues even without compression. The author demonstrated 7 (now 9) cases with completely healing (1)

FACTORS INDUCING WORSENING OF LYMPHEDEMA

1. Lymphedema-related acute dermatitis: Tinea (2), intertrigo and microtrauma induces lymphedema-related acute dermatitis and further increases edema.
2. Unrecognized and insidious inflammation in lymphedema even without recognized dermatitis (Table 1) (Fig. 1,2).
3. Changed tissue with fibrosis (3), acanthosis and hyperkeratosis resulted from inflammation.

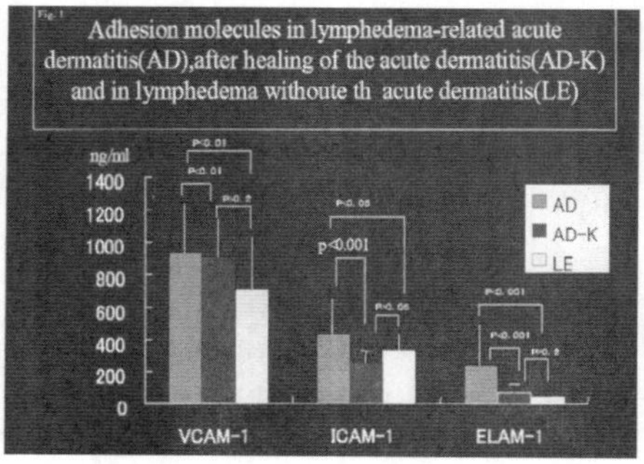

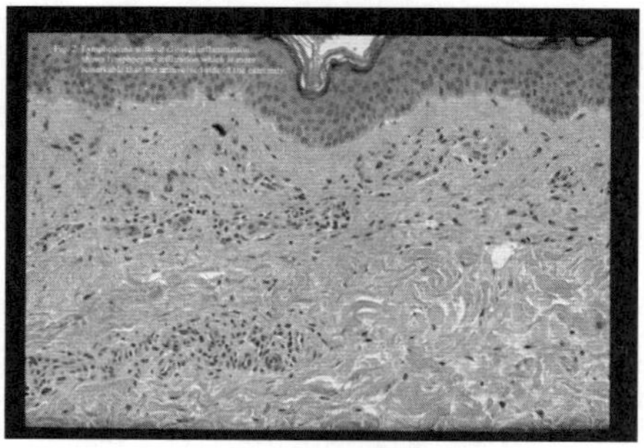

4. Low partial oxygen pressure in lymphedematous tissue with an intensified inflammatory reaction (4,5).
5. Blockade of the lymphatics in the proxymal area by infection, tumor, etc.
6. Insufficient compression therapy.

TO PREVENT WORSENING OF LYMPHEDEMA

1. External application of nadifloxacin lotion for prophylaxis of lymphedema-related acute dermatitis (6).Treat tinea, intertrigo and microtrauma.
2. The same as 1.
3. To give oral NSAID and steroid ointment during the attack of lymphedema-related acute dermatitis (7) in order to mini-

mize the inflammation and further tissue changes.

4. Treat lymphedema by physiotherapy to become edema free which shows normalized pO2 (8).
5. Treat the tumor by operation and infection by a proper drug.
6. Double layered compression by less elastic and elastic bandage (9).

A COMPLETE HEALING OF LYMPHEDEMA

Nine edema free lymphedema patients even without compression have been reported (10) (Fig. 3). They are characterized by all cases with secondary lymphedema, short period between its onset of edema and start of the treatment, strong positive PPD skin test which is intensified after treatment, rather slight or moderate extent of edema and absence of attack of lymphedema-related acute dermatitis after disappearance of the edema (1).

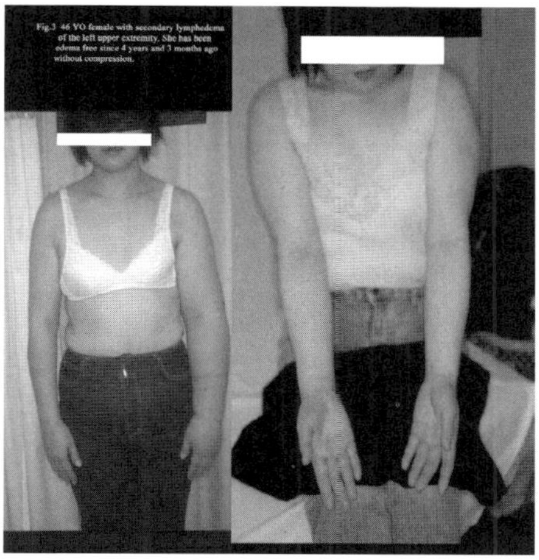
Fig.3 46 YO female with secondary lymphedema of the left upper extremity. She has been edema free since 4 years and 3 months ago without compression.

DISCUSSION

In the International Congress of Lymphology, 2005, Brazil the

Table 1. Lymphedema-related acute dermatitis (LAD) and its comparison with lymphedema with unrecognized inflammation (LUI)

	LAD	**LUI**
Eruption	erythema	unrecognized
Palpation	warm	normal
Systemic symptom	present	absent
EGF	high	normal
NO	iNOS	cNOS
Histology	T cell infiltration	T cell infiltration
Th1/Th2 balance	Th1 dominant	Th1 dominant
Adhesion molecule	high	slightly high
bFGF,VEGF	high	high
peripheral monocyte	high	high
ESR	high	slightly high
Skin resident bacteria	present	present
Mycosis, intertrigo	induces LAD	induces unrecognized inflammation
Edema	increased	increased?

author has shown the lymphedema patients in the second grade of staging are divided into two subgroups; in the one edema does not progress and stays as it its and in the other edema gets worse even without lymphedema-related acute dermatitis.The latter is suspected to be due to unrecognized moderate inflammatory process which changes the lymphedematous tissue and lymphatic system to worsen the edema (Table 1). The lymphedema without clinically recognized acute dermatitis shows a high erythrocyte sedimentation rate (10) and inflammatory cytokines such as VCAM-1, ICAM-1 and ELAM-1 (11). A patient with lymphedema (Fig.4) becomes reduced in edema after administration of oral steroid (Fig. 5). A patient with scrotal lymphedema shows a slow but remarkable reduction in edema after treated by external application of antimicrobiotics for 4 years (Fig. 6). All these facts supports the following hypothesis shown in Fig. 7. Even if

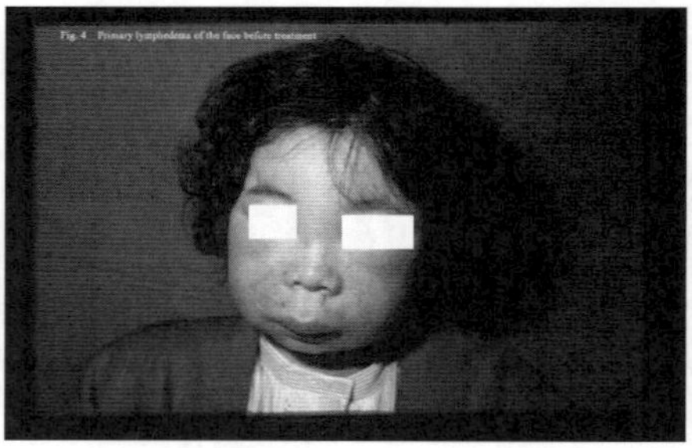

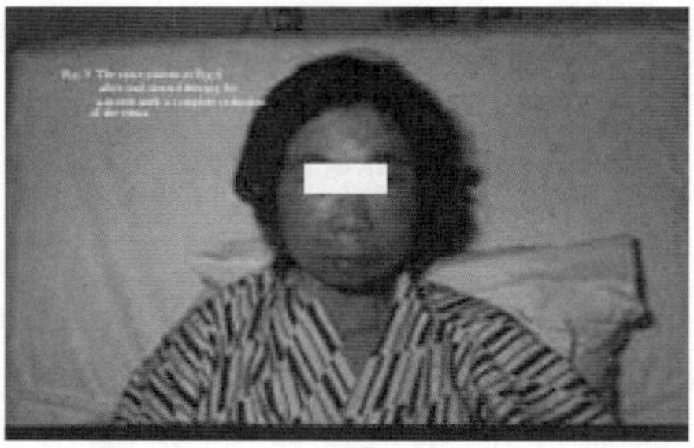

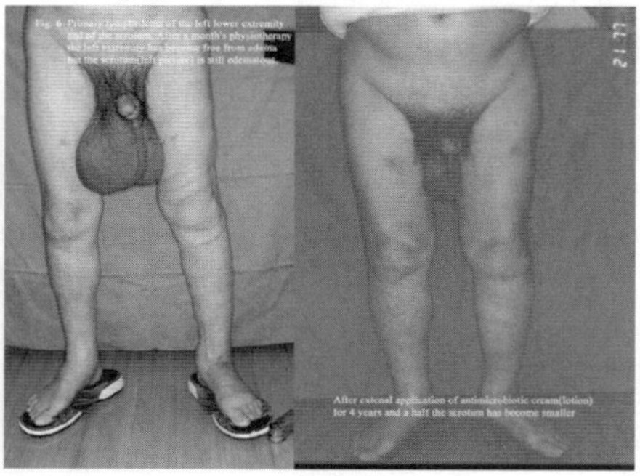

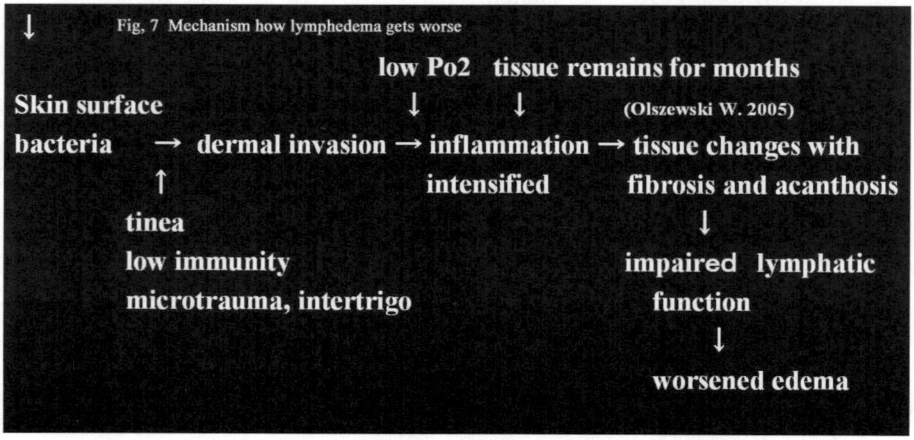

the lymphedema has been cleared by manual massage, the tissue changes remain for months (12). If the itssue is attacked by invading skin surface bacteria during this period, it will evoke the inflammation again and tissue pathological changes which induces recurrence of lymphedema.

CONCLUSION

The most important in treating lymphedema is not to increase lymph flow (by manual massage) but to avoid tissue changes caused by inflammation due to invaded bacteria. This is the shortest way to a complete healing.

REFERENCES

1. Ohkuma, M: What is healing of lymphedema and how to get it? Lymphology 37 (Suppl) (2004), 305.
2. Ohkuma M: Incidence of acute cellulitis in lymphedema,trial in its treatment dispensing antibiotics and its relation to mycotic skin infection—the second study. Lymphology 29 (Suppl) (1995), 313.
3. Ohkuma M: VEGF, c-GMP & AMP, bFGF, EGF in lymphedema-related acute dermatitis. Lymphology 37 (Suppl) (2004), 297.
4. Tamai Y, Toudou A, Iamda A et al: Transcutaneous oxygen partial pressure in unilateral lymphedema. Europ. J Lymphology 12 (2004), 41.
5. Moore T, Khimenko PL, Taylor AE: Endothelial damage caused by I/R and reperfusion and different ventilatory strategies in the lung. J. Chinese Physiol. 39 (1996), 65.
6. Ohkuma M: Prophylactic treatment of acute cellulitis in lymphedema by application of antimicrobiotic cream. Lymphology (Suppl) (1995), 317.
7. Ohkuma M: Acute cellulitis associated with lymphedema better treated by external application of steroid ointment. Lymphology(Suppl) (1995), 311.
8. Tamai Y, Shindou A, Imada A et al:Paritial oxygen pressure in the lymphedematous skin before and after treatment by physiotherapy. Abstract of 20th International Congress of Lymphology, Brazil (2005), 39.
9. Ohkuma M: Compression therapy of lymphedema by combination of elastic and less elastic bandage. Europ. J. Lymphology 8 (2000), 118.
10. Ohkuma M: Absence of adverse effects by a new physiotherapy for lymphedema. Lymphology 35 (Suppl) (2002), 324.
12. Ohkuma M: Adhesion molecules in lymphedema before and after treatment as well as difference between those with and without complications. Lymphology 37 (Suppl) (2004), 289.
13. Olszewski WL, Mosciska M, Zolich D: Reversal of immunohistopathological changes in lymphedematous skin transplanted to scid mice. Abstract of 30th International Congress of Lymphology, Brazil (2005), 50.

TREATMENT OF PSORIASIS BY A NEW PHYSIOTHERAPY BY PULSE MAGNETIC FIELDS, VIBRATION AND HYPERTHERMIA

M. Ohkuma

Department of Dermatology, Sakai Hospital, Kinki University, School of Medicine, Osaka, Japan

INTRODUCTION

A new physiotherapy for lymphedema has been introduced by the author with an excellent clinical result (1). Its working mechanism is thought to influence on inhibition of inflammation (2). Psoriasis vulgaris is a chronic disease of unknown etiology. Its pathogenesis and pathophysiology are associated with Th1dominant and type 1 cytotoxic T cell inflammatory reaction of the skin with rapid epidermal turn over with protein kinase C stimulated proliferation and hyperkeratosis. Wrons-Smith et al produced psoriasis like skin lesion by injecting bacterial antigen activated T cell into the uninvolved skin of the psoriatic patient (3). Lymphedema is suspected to be worsen by a chronic inflammatory Th1 dominant reaction (4) caused by resident skin surface bacteria invaded into the lymphedematous skin. There are many treatments tried for psoriasis such as oral and external applicational steroid, cyclosporine, retinoid, methotrexate, photochemotherapy and external application of vitamin D3 analogue. However these treatments show more or less adverse effects if they are given intensively. These similarities of the two pathological skin conditions have made me to try this trial treatment of psoriasis by the physiotherapy used for lymphedema treatment.

MATERIAL AND METHOD

Five cases of psoriasis vulgaris are treated by the new physiotherapy (1) for 30 minutes a day until all lesions disappear. If the lesions are numerous, they are divided into some areas and each are treated one by one. Clinical evaluation is done by macroscopic observation using PASI index as described in Table 1. Blood cell counts and biochemical examinations are performed before and after the therapy.

RESULT

In all patients the lesions are cleared away by the treatment.

Table 1
Material, Method and Result

No.	name	sex	age	PASI before Tx		PASI after Tx	duration	complication of Tx	length	effect	result adverse
1.	MS	M	59	18.0	→	0	1 year	arthropathy	6 months*	+++	none
2.	KM	M	62	0.6	→	0	10 years	none	2 months*	+++	none
3.	AY	F	16	1.0	→	0	2 months	none	3 months*	+++	none
4.	MO	M	58	3.6	→	0	28 years	none	5 months*	+++	none
5.	YK	M	55	13.0	→	0	5 years	none	5 months*	+++	none

*each lesion: 4-9 weeks; PASI: psoriasis area severity index=

Ah(Eh+Ih+Dh)x0.1+At(ET+It+Dt)x0.3+Au(Eu+Iu+Du)x0.2+Al(El+Il+Dl)x0.4

A: area involved; E: erythema; I: induration; D: desquamation; H: head; t: trunk; u: upper extremity; l: lower extremity; PASI>50:very severe; PASI>30: severe; PASI>10:moderate; PASI<10:slight; F: female; M: male; Tx: treatment; +++: excellent

Necessary length of the treatment is from 2 to 6 months with excellent result (Fig.1-3) (Table 1). There are adverse effects in neither blood cell count nor biochemistry examination.

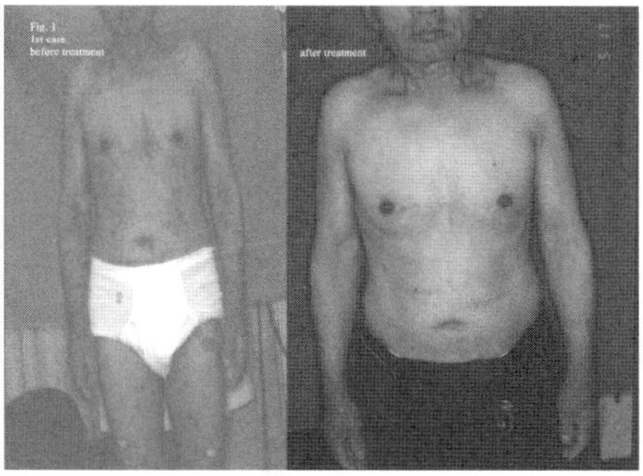

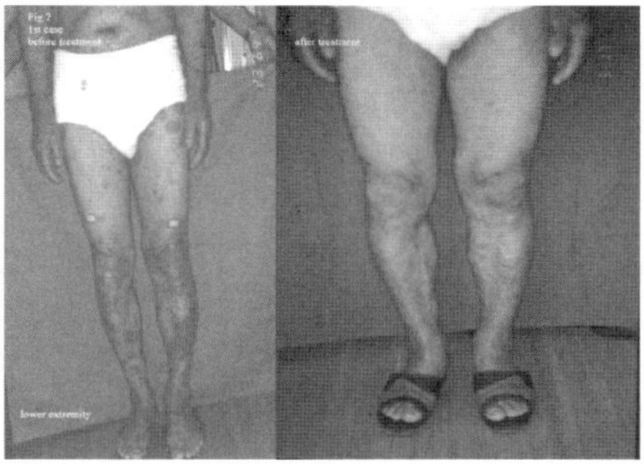

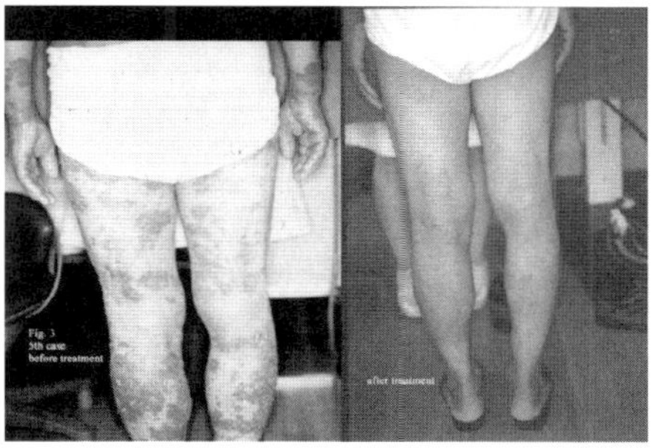

DISCUSSION

Inflammation seen in the patient, No.5 is Th1 dominant reaction (Fig. 4) and so is the one seen in lymphedema-related acute dermatitis as well as lymphedema (4). In the above 3 pathological

Fig. 4 Case 1 shows Th1 dominant inflammation

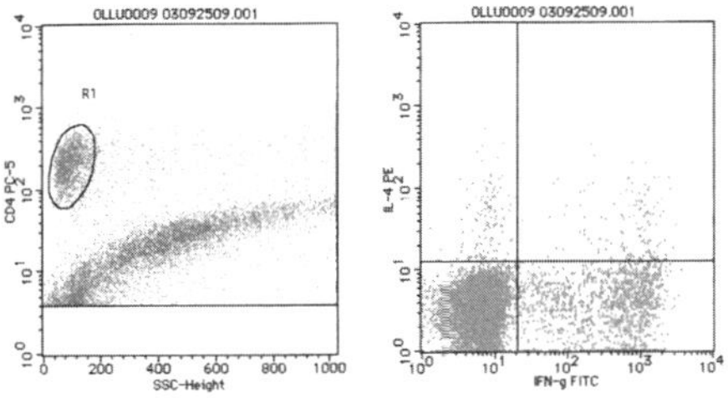

conditions the inflammation is Th1 dominant and infiltrated by T lymphocyte. The author suspects that the inflammation is inhibited by the physiotherapy in all tried psoriasis patients.

REFERENCES

1. Ohkuma M: A new physiotherapy for lymphedema by magnetic fields, vibration and hyperthermia. Lymphology 35(2002), 87.
2. Ohkuma M: Adhesion molecules in lymphedema before and after treatment as well as difference between those with and without complication. Lymphology 37 (Suppl.) (2004), 289.
3. Wrong-Smith T and Nickoloff: Dermal injection of inmates induces psoriasis. J Clin. Investigation 98 (1996), 78.
4. Ohkuma M: Th1 and Th2 cytokines and Th1/ Th2 balance in lymphedema-related acute dermatitis. Lymphology 37(Suppl.) (2004), 301.

HEALTH AND TENDERNESS ON TENDER POINT SITES

Akinobu Shoji

Department of Dermatology, Osaka Kaisei Hospital

Introduction

An investigation protocol for lymph node examination is presented here based on a clinical methodology developed by physicians more than 60 years ago. The principle involved application of digital pressure to the lymph nodes in the neck, armpit, and groin, as the author recalls from his childhood experience of frequent attacks of fever. In fact, once, the author fell asleep while in a fever and woke up with intense tenderness in the groin. He immediately underwent a visual oral examination that confirmed swollen tonsils. The physician then effectively treated the tonsillitis with an antibiotic. Thirty years later, when the author became a physician, he wondered as to the rationale for the diagnosis of tonsillitis based on intense tenderness in the groin, which is located at quite a distance from the tonsils, if indeed the diagnosis was accurate, then, the intense tenderness was in a lymph node that is located behind the jaw bone, would be far more intense than that in the groin. The author has now confirmed the observation in a patient with a dermatological disease presenting with complaints of a sore throat. The patient had no other subjective pain. Mild palpations were applied to the lymph nodes behind the jaw bone, elicited surprisingly intense tenderness. Following further evaluation based on patient response, a questionnaire was prepared and a statistical analysis carried out. The results are briefly discussed in this paper.

Methods

<Patients>

Atopic dermatitis: Five hundred and sixty two patients (male 233, age range 6-74 years, average 23.7, female 329, age range 5-65 years, average 25.6)

Chronic contact dermatitis: Thirty two (male 8, age range 19-62 years, average 34.5, female 24, age 19-70 average 42.8). Discoid eczema: Forty one patients (male 19, age range 14-78 years, average 46.8, female 22, age range 15-67years, average 36.7).

Urticaria: Twenty five patients (male 2, age range 47-61

years, average 54.0, female 23, age range 17-70 years, average 40.8)

Acne: Twenty three(male 4, age range18-63 years, 32.5, female 19, age range 15-61 years, average 29.1)

Palmo-plantal pustulosis and psoriasis: Fifteen (male 11, age range 22-80 years, average 49.6, female 4, age range 21-51years, average 31.5)

<Degree of tenderness on tender point sites> (1, 2, 3)

Digital pressure of approximately 5 kg was applied with fingers at the following 8 tender point sites: outer side of both right and left elbows (LE), axillary regions of both right and left arms (Ax), median aspect of right and left supra-clavicular regions(MSC) and right and left submandibular regions on right and left sides of face(SM). Degree of tenderness was determined and categorized into 7 grades as follows: "violent" (score 5) for spontaneous or violent pain, "very" (score 4) for very strong pain, "strong" (score 3), "moderate" (score 2), "mild" (score 1), "weak" (score 0.5) and no tenderness (score 0). When tenderness scores were different between right and left, the higher score was used for the statistical calculation. Tenderness score (TS) was calculated as follows:

TS=LE+Ax+MSC+SM.

<Skin symptoms> (3, 4)

Skin symptoms score (SS) of patients was determined at 10 levels (10: the clinical manifestation at the first visit, 0: complete recovery) (3, 4).

<Therapy> (3, 4)

Patients were treated with ordinary medicine and life style modification, especially with sleep and diet.

(1) Sleep: In order to improve the sleep cycle, a continuous wave beam at a wavelength of 830 nm was applied for two minutes to the neck around the stellate ganglion – minute each on right and left(SG-L), – using a diode laser system(Leuketron, Medilaser Soft 1000, Mastushita) once or more per week to control their sympathetic activity.

(2) Diet: Patients were advised normal breakfast, lunch and supper but to limit between-meal snack and to substitute fruits for dessert.

<Statistics>

1) All patients' TS and SS during the first visit were compared with the value at the next visit. Parallel changes were observed when TS showed decrease(↓) and no change(→), while SS showed improvement(↓) and no change(→) respectively, except during increase(↑), when SS showed an aggravation (↑). Although the method does not indicate a specific therapeutic option, patients with decreasing TS manifested improving of their skin symptoms. Non-parallel changes were noted when TS showed an increase(↑), decrease(↓) and no change(→) were noted while SS showed improvement(↓) or no

change(→), an aggravation(↑) or no change(→) and improvement(↓) or aggravation(↑) respectively.

2) TS and SS of the current visit were compared with value of the previous visit if the patients had already visited in 3 times or more. We calculated the ratio of parallel of each patient and the number of patients who showed 50% and more such parallel value in order to determine the correlation between TS and SS.

Results

Of patients who visited twice, the number showing decreased, increased or both unchanged (parallel) SS and TS values was 426 out of 562 (75.8%) in atopic dermatitis group, 25 out of 32 (78.1%) in chronic contact dermatitis group, 48 out 64 (75.0%) in disc eczema and urticaria group and 33 out of 38 (86.8%) in acne, psoriasis and palmo-plantal pustulosis group (Fig. 1). No statistically significant differences were found in any pair. Of the patients who visited three times or more, the number of SS and TS values that were both increased or both decreased from their previous visit was 246 out of 305 (80.7%) in atopic dermatitis group, 12 out of 15 (80.0%) in chronic contact dermatitis group, 32 out 38 (84.2%) in disc eczema and urticaria group and 16 out of 20 (80.0%) in acne, psoriasis and palmo-plantal pustulosis group (Fig. 2). No statistically significant differences were found in any pair.

Case: Eosinophilic pustular folliculitis

A 26-year-old Japanese female visited to the Department of Dermatology, Osaka Kaisei Hospital

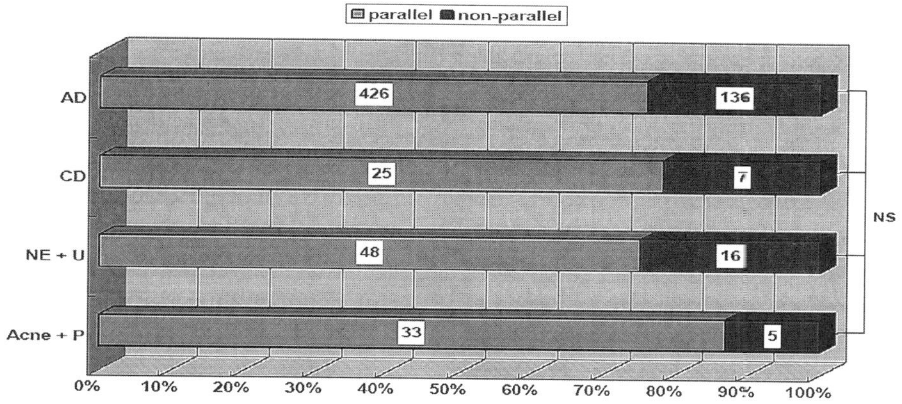

Fig. 1. Comparison of TS and SS between the first visit and the second visit in the atopic dermatitis group, chronic contact dermatitis group, disc eczema and urticaria group and acne, psoriasis and palmo-plantal pustulosis groups. No statistically significant differences were found between any pair.

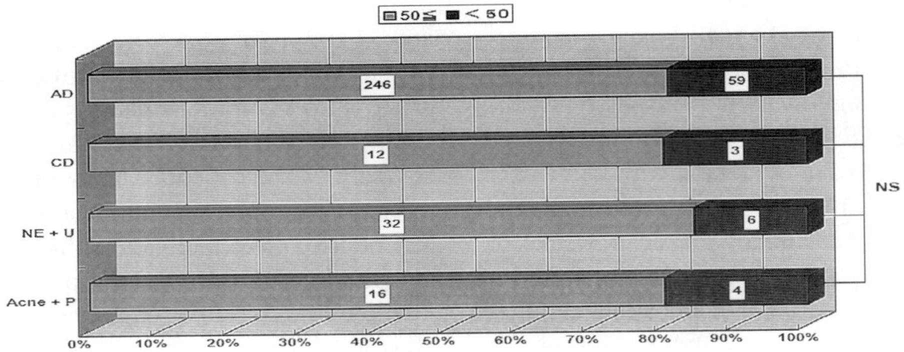

Fig. 2. The ratio of parallel for each patient and the number of patients who showed •† of such parallel values were calculated for the atopic dermatitis group, chronic contact dermatitis group, disc eczema and urticaria group and acne, psoriasis and palmo-plantal pustulosis groups in order to determine the correlation between TS and SS. No statistically significant differences were found between any pair.

on May 26, 2005, with an approximately two-month history of slightly pruritic eruptions on face, refractory to treatment with oral and topical anti-fungal agents (Fig. 3: Right upper). She was HIV negative. Symptoms improved following treatment with a suppository of indometacin 25 mg and SG-L for improvement in their life style (Fig. 3: Right lower). This patient with decreasing TS manifested improving of their skin symptoms (Fig. 3: Left)

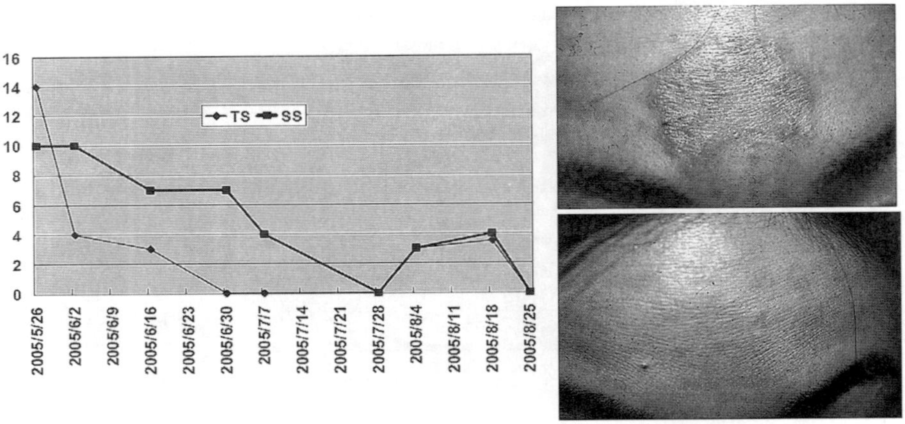

Fig. 3. Relationship between TS and SS in the patient (HIV negative) with eosinophilic pustular folliculitis.
Right upper: At first visit (TS 14 SS 10). Right lower: Two months later (TS 0 SS 0).

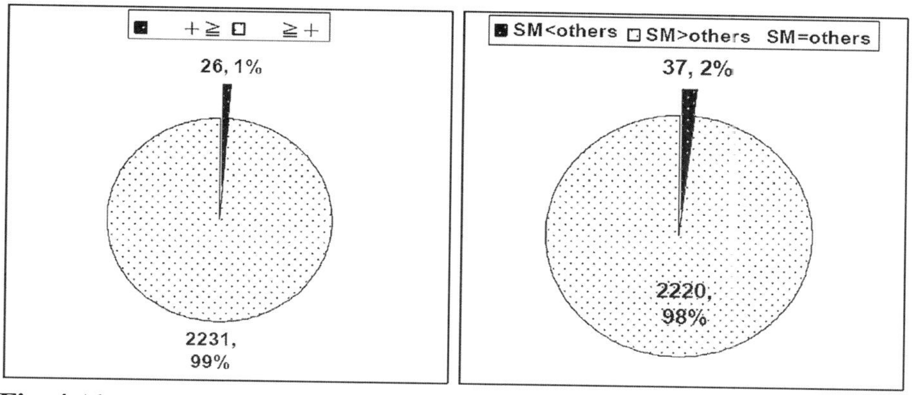

Fig. 4 Almost all the patients and healthy subjects complained of the pain (TS •†+) on submandibular lymph nodes and most severe pain on the submandibular lymph nodes (SM>others & SM=others).

Discussion

It is important to determine the origin of tenderness associated with digital palpation of the eight tender point sites. Submandibular and axillary lymph nodes can be felt as small nodules often causing severe pain even on gentle palpation, regardless of the person's disease status (5, 6, 7). Almost all patients and healthy subjects complained of intense pain at submandibular lymph nodes (TS •†+) (Fig. 3) (5).

Patients with diverse and recalcitrant skin diseases showed the same high rate of improvement with life style changes. In fact, diet remedies were effective with patients and healthy subjects alike, – decreased TS value or tenderness in lymph nodes during health recovery. WHO defines Health as follows: "Health is a state of complete physical, mental, and social well-being and merely the absence of disease or infirmity." This definition has not been amended since 1948, though recently a new definition was proposed at the 101st session of the WHO Executive Board. Toward that end, it is imperative to address human ailments comprehensively. Indeed symptoms of skin diseases can be alleviated through lifestyle interventions.

References

1. Shoji A: Tender spots in patients with atopic dermatitis. Lymphology 35(Suppl):703-705,2002.
2. Shoji A: Tender spots in patients with atopic dermatitis. – The effect of systemic steroid therapy – Jap J Lymphology 25:21-28,2002.
3. Shoji A: Relationship between tenderness on tender point sites and skin symptoms.– Prurigo and bullous diseases – Jap J Laser Therapy, 2:17-22, 2004.
4. Shoji A: LLLT in Dermatological disorders. – An Efficacy and Adverse effect – Jap J Laser Therapy, 3:18-22, 2005.

5. Shoji A: Tender Spots in Patients with and without Atopic Dermatitis (P262), the XXth World Congress of Dermatology, 2002.
6. Shoji A: Tenderness on tender points. Jap J Lymphology in press.
7. Bannister LH, Berry MM, Collins P et al: Gray's Anatomy 38th ed. Churchll Livingstone, London, 1995.

RELATIONSHIP BETWEEN THE DEGREE OF TENDERNESS AT TENDER POINT SITES AND SKIN SYMPTOMS IN PATIENTS WITH SKIN DISEASES (ACNE, PPP AND PSORIASIS)

Akinobu Shoji

Department of Dermatology, Osaka Kaisei Hospital

Introduction

Patients with recalcitrant skin diseases have often consulted several dermatologists and have a lot of knowledge about their condition. However, most of these patients who rely on text books are not satisfied with conventional treatments, and many complain that, “the result is the same no matter which dermatologist is consulted”, and so they use herbal medicines as a folk remedy without the supervision of a dermatologist. Patients such as these tend to prefer an examination which investigates the overall condition of their body, rather than a normal dermatological examination. This paper suggests a method for examining such patients. In this method, palpation of the tender point sites is performed at eight sites in four areas, and instructions to patients about daily activities are developed based on the results of this investigation.

Methods

<Patients>

Twenty-three patients afflicted with acne (age range 15-63, average 29.7) — male 4, age range 8-63, 32.5, female 19, age range 15-61, average 29.

Fifteen-five patients afflicted with palmo-plantal pustulosis and psoriasis (age range 21-80, average 44.8)—male 11, age range 22-80, average 49.6, female 4, age range 21-51 average 31.5

<Tender point sites>

Digital pressure of approximately 5 kg was applied at the following 8 tender point sites including outer aspect of right and left elbows (LE), axillary regions of both right and left arms (Ax), median side of right and left supra-clavicular regions (MSC) and right and left submandibular (SM) (1,2).

<Degree of tenderness>

Degree of tenderness was determined and categorized into 7 grades as follows: “violent” (score 5) for spontaneous pain or violent pain, “very” (score 4) indicating very strong pain, “strong” (score 3), “moderate” (score 2), “mild” (score 1), “weak” (score 0.5), and no tenderness(score 0). When scores were different between right and left, the higher value was used for the statistical calculation (1, 2). Tenderness score (TS) was calculated as follows:

TS=LE+Ax+MSC+SM.

<Skin symptoms>

Skin symptoms (SS) was marked by patients using 10 levels (10: the clinical manifestation at first visit, 0: complete recovery).

<Statistics>

1) All patient's TS and SS of two consecutive visits were subjected to differential analysis. Correlations of the score were determined on the following criteria: changes were parallel if there was a TS increase (↑), no change (→) and decrease (↓), when there was a concomitant SS aggravation (↑), no change (→) and improvement (↓), non-parallel changes were noted during TS increase (↑), no change (→) and decrease (↓), with SS decrease or improvement (↓) or no change (→), aggravation (↑) or improvement (↓) and aggravation (↑) or no change (→) respectively (Table 2).
2) TS and SS of the current visit were compared with those of the previous visit if the patients had already visited in 3 times or more. We calculate the ratio of parallel of each patient and the number of patients who showed 50% and more parallel in order to determine the correlation between TS and SS.

Results

The total number of the patients whose SS and TS both decreased or whose SS and TS both increased was 31 out of 38 patients (81.6%). The ratio of parallel of each patient and the number of patients who showed 50% and more was 16 out of 20 (85.7%), which was larger than that of the patients whose SS decreased while TS increased or whose SS increased while TS decreased.

Discussion

Though lymph nodes were touched on SM and Ax in many patients, no lymph nodes were touched on MSC and LE (6). We can find a part of the chain of deep

Table 1 Criteria for determining if there is a correlation between TS and SS
↑: increase or aggravation ↓: decrease or improvement →: no change

Change in TS	Change in SS
Parallel	
↑	↑
→	→
↓	↓
Non-parallel	
↑	↓ →
→	↑ ↓
↓	↑ →

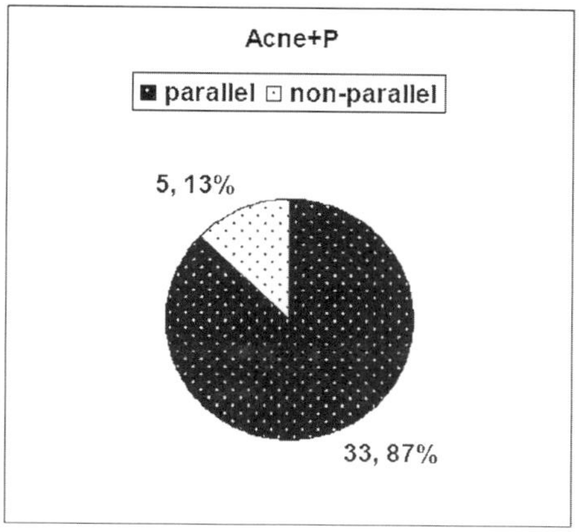

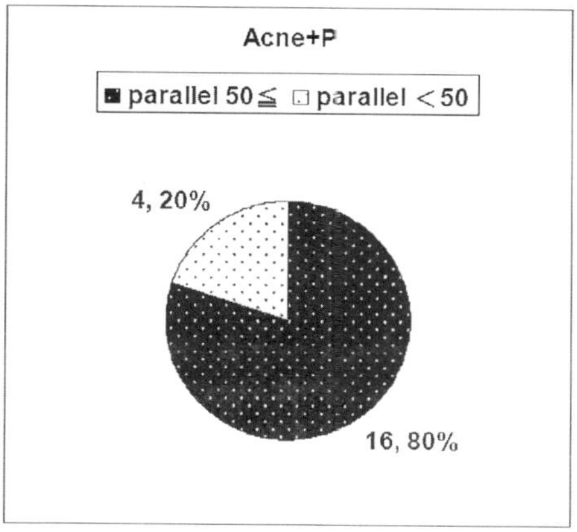

Fig. 1. Left: Comparison between the first visit and the second visit in TS and SS. The number of patients with parallel changes in TS and SS was 33 out of 38 patients.
Right: Comparison between 50% and more and <50 of parallel changes. The number of patients with 50% and more in parallel changes in 3time visits and more was 16 out of 20 patients.

cervical lymph nodes on the reverse side of the median side of the clavicle (3). No tumors and nodules like lymph nodes were, however, never palpable on MSC, because many muscles such as sternocleidomastoid, sternohyoid and sternothyroid are barrier against supraclavicular and deep cervical lymph nodes (7). Therefore, tenderness or pain in pressure with fingers may originate from muscles, lymph nodes and/or thymus of which cause inflammation by unknown. We could not be also palpable tumors and/or nodules on LE. One of our tender point sites or LE is close to one of the tender point sites on fibromyalgia or lateral epicondyle (7, 8). That is, both LE of our tender point sites are around epicondyle and both lateral epicondyles of fibromyalgia's tender point sites are 2 cm distal to the external epicondyle of humerus. Anatomically, there are no lymph nodes around lateral epicondyle (Fig. 2).

After palpation of the tender point sites, patients with a "TS= >15" were asked about the status of problems with daily activities such as "become sleepy during the daytime (particularly after a meal)", "have difficulty waking up in the morning", "have difficulty falling asleep at night", and "become irritated". Most of these patients stated that "such problems are present". From this finding, it could be suggested that intense tenderness at the tender point sites results in sleep disorder, and that insomnia, sleep disorder, and intense tenderness at the lymph nodes are involved in the aggravation of dermatological symptoms.

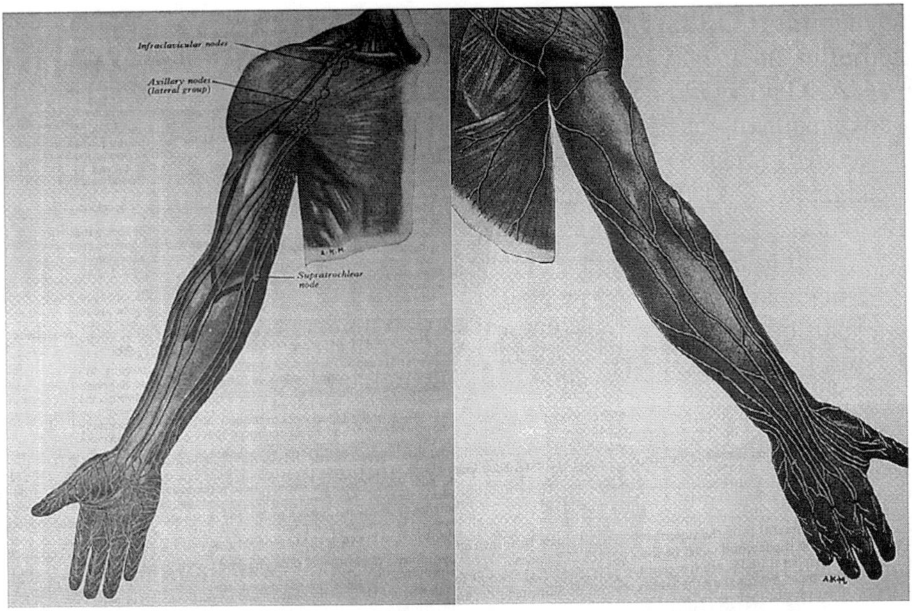

Fig. 2. Many patients feel tenderness pain on outer part of the elbow in pressure with fingers, though no lymph nodes can be found on this area. Acknowledgment: Reprinted from Publication Gray's Anatomy 38th ed., William PL, section author: Bannister L: Haemolymphoid system, p1614, p1615, 1995, with permiss on from Elsevier.

Furthermore, most dermatological patients "when they feel sleepy", "when they feel stressed", and "when they want to let loose from tension" will (depending on the patient): increase their intake of coffee or tea; eat sweets; have an increased appetite for sweet food; increase the number of cigarettes smoked (if they are smokers); and increase alcohol consumption. Although there are slight differences between these responses, all of these situations can be improved by having adequate sleep. From this finding it can be seen that, provided daily activities permit, it is

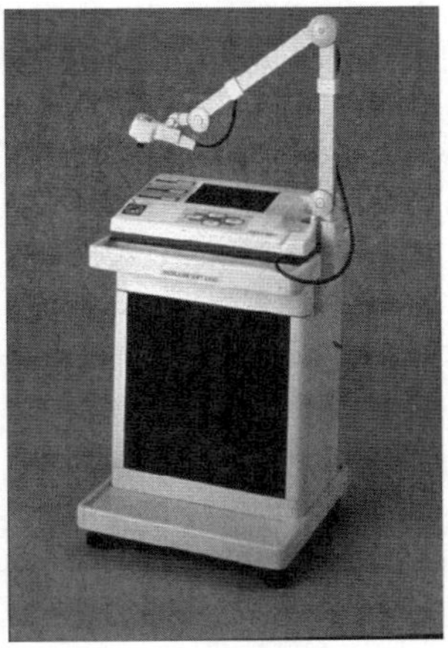

Fig. 3. GaAlAs 830 nm diode laser system LUKETRON, Matsusita co., Osaka SG-L: LLLT in the vicinity of the stellate sympathetic ganglion.

important to make “sleep a priority”. As a temporary measure, it is acceptable to use sleeping pills but the author suggests that it is more beneficial to perform LLLT (LLLT: low reactive level laser therapy or, in a series of researches, therapy by GaAlAs 830 nm diode laser system LUKETRON, Matsusita co., Osaka) in the vicinity of the stellate sympathetic ganglion (SG-L) (Fig. 3).

References

1. Shoji A: Tender spots in patients with atopic dermatitis. Lymphology 35(Suppl):703-705, 2002.
2. Shoji A: Tender spots in patients with atopic dermatitis. – The effect of systemic steroid therapy – Jap J Lymphology 25:21-28,2002.
3. Bannister LH, Berry MM, Collins P et al: Gray’s Anatomy 38th ed. Churchll Livingstone, London, 1995.
4. Shoji A: Relationship between tenderness on tender point sites and skin symptoms.– Prurigo and bullous diseases – Jap J Laser Therapy, 2:17-22, 2004.
5. Shoji A: LLLT in Dermatological disorders. – An Efficacy and Adverse effect – Jap J Laser Therapy, 3:18-22, 2005.
6. Shoji A: Tenderness on tender points. Jap J Lymphology in press.
7. Platzer W(Translated by Harry Monsen): Pernkopf Anatomy 3rd ed. Volume ‡T Head and Neck. Urban & Schwarzenberg, Baltimore-Munich, 1989, pp 236-7, 281, 305.
8. Wolfe F, Smythe HA, Yunus MB, et al: The american college of rheumatology 1990 criteria for the classification of fibromyalgia. Arthritis Rheum 33:160-172, 1990.

RELATIONSHIP BETWEEN THE DEGREE OF TENDERNESS AT TENDER POINT SITES AND SKIN SYMPTOMS IN PATIENTS WITH DISCOID ECZEMA AND URTICARIA

Akinobu Shoji

Department of Dermatology, Osaka Kaisei Hospital

Introduction

Patients with recalcitrant skin disease have often consulted several dermatologists and have a lot of knowledge about their condition. However, most of these patients who rely on text books are not satisfied with conventional treatment, and many complain that, "the result is the same no matter which dermatologist is consulted", and so they use herbal medicines as a folk remedy without the supervision of a dermatologist. Patients such as these tend to prefer an examination which investigates the overall condition of their body, rather than a normal dermatological examination. This paper suggests a method for examining such patients. In this method, palpation of the tender point sites is performed at eight sites in four areas, and instructions to patients about daily activities are developed based on the results of this investigation.

Methods

<Patients>

Number of patients with discoid eczema and urticaria:

Discoid eczema male 19 (age range 14-78 average 46.8)

female 22 (age range 15-67 average 36.7)

total 41 (age range 14-78, average 41.3)

Urticaria male 2 (age range 47-61, average 54.0)

female 23 (age range 17-70, average 40.8)

total 25 (age range 17-70, average 41.9)

Total 66 (age range 14-78, average 41.6)

<Tender point site sites>

Digital pressure of approximately 5 kg was applied at the following 8 tender point sites including outer aspect of right and left elbows (LE), axillary regions of both right and left arms (Ax), median side of right and left supra-clavicular regions (MSC) and right and left submandibular (SM) (1,2).

<Degree of tenderness>

Degree of tenderness was determined and categorized into 7 grades as follows: "violent" (score 5) for spontaneous pain or violent pain, "very" (score 4) indicating very strong pain, "strong" (score 3), "moderate" (score 2), "mild" (score 1), "weak" (score 0.5), and no tenderness (score 0). When scores were different between right and left, the higher value was used for the statistical calculation (1, 2). Tenderness score (TS) was calculated as follows:

TS=LE+Ax+MSC+SM.

<Skin symptoms>

Skin symptoms (SS) were recorded by patients using a 10-scale (10: the clinical manifestation at first visit, 0: complete recovery).

<Therapy>(4, 5)

Patients were treated and advised life style changes for better sleep and diet. (1) Sleep: In order to improve the sleep cycle, a continuous wave beam at a wavelength of 830 nm was applied using a diode laser system (Leuketron, Matsusita) for two minutes to the neck around the stellate ganglion•\\hichfor one minute each on right and left(SG-L), once or more per week to control their sympathetic activity. (2) Diet: Instructions for normal meals but limited snacks in between and substitution of fruits for dessert were offered.

<Statistics>

1) TS and SS value during two consecutive visits were analyzed. Correlation between the scores were derived from changed observed: parallel with TS increase (↑), no change(→) and decrease (↓), SS changed aggravation(↑), no change(→) and improvement(↓) respectively and non-parallel is that when TS changes show increase (↑), no change(→) and decrease (↓), with SS changes showing improvement(↓) or no change(→), aggravation (↑) or improvement(↓) and aggravation(↑) or no change(→) respectively.
2) TS and SS of the current visit were compared with value of the previous visit if the patient had already visited 3 times or more. We calculated the ratio of parallel for each patients and the number of patients who showed 50% and more such parallel value in order to determine the correlation between TS and SS.

Results (Fig. 1)

Forty-eight out of 64 patients (75.0%) had both the SS and TS value either decreased, no change or increased. The ratio of parallel for each patients and the number of patients who showed 50% and more was thirty-two out of 38 (84.2%). They were more than the number of patients whose SS decreased while TS increased or whose SS increased while TS decreased.

Case report: Chronic urticaria

A 55-years old Japanese women, housewife, visited our clinic on January 23, 2002. She had been a pollinosis. Since about 2 months ago, she had been suffering from pruritic skin eruptions on torso. She went to

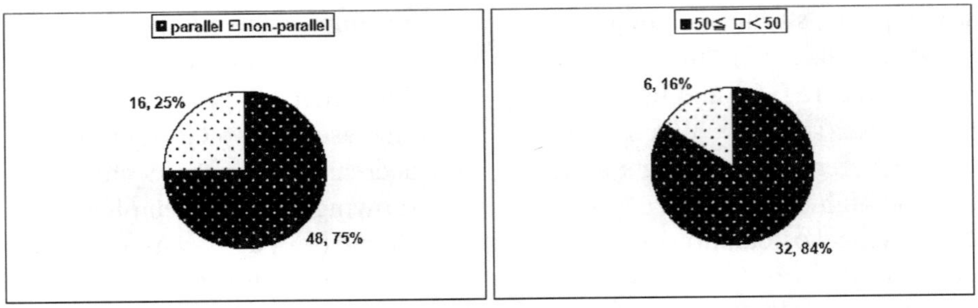

Fig. 1. Left: Comparison between the first visit and the second visit in TS and SS. The number of patients with parallel changes in TS and SS was 48 out of 64 patients.
Right: Comparison between 50% and more and <50 of parallel changes. The number of patients with 50% and more in parallel changes in 3times and more visits was 32 out of 38 patients.

a nearby dermatology clinic, and treated with oral antihistamines and oral steroids. However, the skin manifestations did not improve (Figs. 2, 3). She was treated with anti-allergic agents, intravenous drip injection (KN3B 200ml+Stronger Neo-Minophagen C 40ml <monoammoniumglycyr-rhizinate13.25mg/5ml

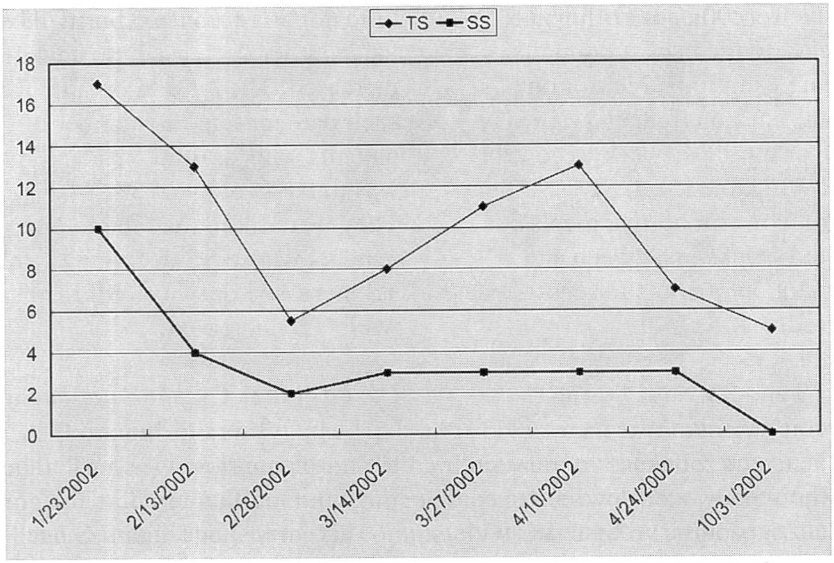

Fig. 2. Relationship between total tenderness (TS) and skin symptoms(SS) in one of the patients with chronic urticaria.

(glycyrrhizin 10mg) glycine 100mg L-cysteine 5mg> and SG-L for improvement in their life style. Three weeks later, we added ethyl loflazepate 1mg/day for improving sleep disturbance. About six months later, oral steroid, antihistamines and antibiotics were added for frequency of urticaria increasing and TS elevation. Nine months later, urticarial lesions disappeared completely (Figs. 2, 3).

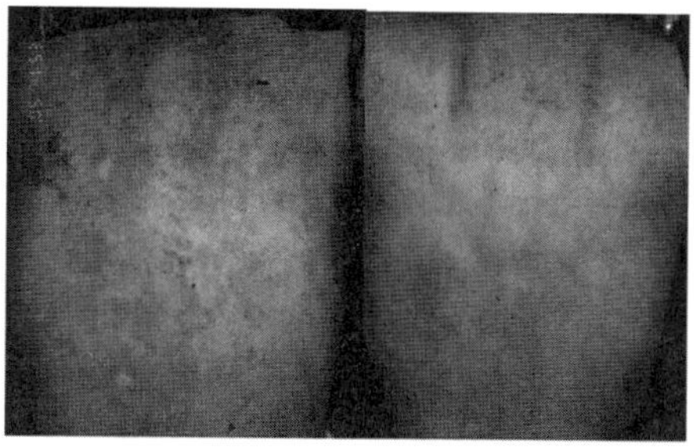

Fig. 3. Left: at first visit (TS 17, SS 10) Right: 9 months later, urticarial lesions were disappeared completely leaving post-inflammatory pigmentations (TS 5, SS 0)

Discussion

For patients who have been on long-term steroid treatment or have such a history, even when most of the skin symptoms are not improved, tenderness of the tender point sites may have been eliminated so caution is required (2). If palpation of SM is first performed on patients with dermatological diseases, tenderness of SM is extremely intense, and so patients would reject palpation of subsequent areas such as MSC, Ax or LE (7). Therefore, it is better to perform palpations in the order (1) LE, (2) Ax, (3) MSC, and (4) SM. Details of palpation of the tender point sites are presented below. Successful palpation by site (LE, Ax, MSC and SM) when the performer is right-handed is described below (1, 2).

LE: for both the left and right sides, support the forearm with the left hand, and while supporting the inner part of the elbow with fingers II~IV of the right hand, perform the palpation while moving the outer part of the elbow (Lateral humeral epicondyle) backward and forward with r-thumb (8).

Ax: in the case of the right armpit, place your right hand on the left shoulder of the subject, if you need to touch the lymph nodes, palpate the lymph nodes using fingers II~III of the left hand. If you do not need to touch the lymph nodes, press the rib in the deep part of the armpit. Do the reverse in the case of the left armpit.

MSC: for both the left and right sides, perform the palpation from up to down using fingers II~III of the right hand behind the median side of right and left supra-clavicular regions.

SM: normally, 2~3 submandibular lymph nodes are present behind the jaw bone. As they are attached to the jaw bone, perform the palpation from the inside towards the outside. In other words, to palpate the right submandibular lymph nodes of the subject, place your right palm on top of the left part of the subjects head and hold the side of the head to make the head stationery. Then place left finger I on the outside of the right jawbone, and position left fingers II~IV from the inside to the outside as if to sandwich the jaw bone and perform the palpation while searching for the lymph nodes. When you touch a lymph node, palpate that area. Do the reverse for the left jaw.

References

1. Shoji A: Tender spots in patients with atopic dermatitis. Lymphology 35(Suppl):703-705, 2002.
2. Shoji A: Tender spots in patients with atopic dermatitis. •\\hichThe effect of systemic steroid therapy – Jap J Lymphology 25:21-28,2002.
3. Bannister LH, Berry MM, Collins P et al: Gray's Anatomy 38th ed. Churchll Livingstone, London, 1995.
4. Shoji A: Relationship between tenderness on tender point sites and skin symptoms. – Prurigo and bullous diseases – Jap J Laser Therapy, 2:17-22, 2004.
5. Shoji A: LLLT in Dermatological disorders. – An Efficacy and Adverse effect – Jap J Laser Therapy, 3:18-22, 2005.
6. Shoji A: Tenderness on tender points. Jap J Lymphology in press.
7. Shoji A: Tender Spots in Patients with and without Atopic Dermatitis (P262), the XXth World Congress of Dermatology, 2002.
8. Platzer W(Translated by Harry Monsen): Pernkopf Anatomy 3rd ed. Volume ‡T Head and Neck. Urban & Schwarzenberg, Baltimore-Munich, 1989, pp 138-152.

RELATIONSHIP BETWEEN THE DEGREE OF TENDERNESS AT TENDER POINT SITES AND SKIN SYMPTOMS IN PATIENTS WITH ATOPIC DERMATITIS

Akinobu Shoji

Department of Dermatology, Osaka Kaisei Hospital

Introduction

Digital pressure of approximately 5 kg was applied at the following 8 tender point sites: outer aspect of the right and left elbows (LE), axillary regions of both right and left arms (Ax), median side of right and left supra-clavicular regions (MSC) and right and left submandibular regions(SM). The severest tenderness was observed on SM in most of the patients with skin disease and in healthy people (98.4%)(1,2). However significant changes in the degree of tenderness on LE, Ax, MSC and SM warranted an examination of the relationship between lymph node tenderness and skin symptoms.

Methods

<Patients>

Five hundred and sixty two patients afflicted with atopic dermatitis (male 233, range 6-74, average 23.7, female 329, range 5-65, average 25.6) were enrolled in this study. Number of patients with varying degrees of atopic dermatitis is shown in Table 1.

<Degree of tenderness on tender points>(1,2,3)

A digital pressure of approximately 5 kg was applied with fingers at the following 8 tender points: LE, Ax, MSC and SM. Degree of tenderness was determined and categorized into 7 grades as follows: "violent"(score 5) for spontaneous or violent pain,

Table 1. Number of the patients with serious, moderate and mild of atopic dermatitis

	Male			Female			Total		
	range	average	no. of patients	range	average	no. of patients	range	average	no. of patients
Serious	15-41	25.3	53	9-63	27.4	49	9-63	26.3	102
Moderate	12-74	24.5	122	12-57	25.1	159	12-74	24.8	281
Mild	6-36	20.6	58	5-65	25.5	121	5-65	23.9	179
Total	6-74	23.7	233	5-65	25.6	329	5-74	24.8	562

"very" (score 4) for very strong pain, "strong" (score 3), "moderate" (score 2), "mild" (score 1), "weak" (score 0.5) and no tenderness (score 0). When tenderness scores were different between right and left, the higher score was used for the statistical calculation. Tenderness score(TS) was calculated as follows:

TS=LE+Ax+MSC+SM.

<Skin symptoms>

Skin symptoms score (SS) was determined by patients using a 10 point scale (10: the clinical manifestation at the first visit, 0: complete recovery) (3,4).

<Therapy> (3,4)

Patients were treated and advised life style changes for better sleep and diet. (1) Sleep: In order to improve the sleep cycle, a continuous wave beam at a wavelength of 830 nm was applied using a diode laser system (Leuketron, Matsusita) for two minutes to the neck around the stellate ganglion – for one minute each on right and left(SG-L), once or more per week to control their sympathetic activity. (2) Diet: Instructions for normal meals but limited snacks in between and substitution of fruits for dessert were offered.

<Statistics>

1) All patient's TS and SS of two consecutive visits were subjected to differential analysis. Correlations of the score were determined on the following criteria: changes were parallel if there was a TS increase (↑), no change (→) and decrease (↓), when there was a concomitant SS aggravation (↑), no change (→) and improvement (↓), non-parallel changes were noted during TS increase (↑), no change (→) and decrease (↓), with SS improvement(↓) or no change(→), aggravation (↑) or improvement (↓) and aggravation(↑) or no change(→) respectively (Table 2).
2) TS and SS of the current visit were compared with those of the previous visit if the patients had already visited in 3 times or more. We calculate the ratio of parallel of each patient and the number of patients who showed 50% and more parallel in order to determine the correlation between TS and SS.

Table 2. Criteria for determining the status of correlation between TS and SS.

↑: increase or aggravation ↓: decrease or improvement →: no change

	Change in TS	Change in SS
Parallel		
	↑	↑
	→	→
	↓	↓
Non-parallel		
	↑	↓ →
	→	↑ ↓
	↓	↑ →

Results

Of those who visited the hospital twice, the total number of those with both decreases, increases or both unchanged (parallel) SS and TS values was 426 out of 562 patients (75.8%) (Table 3). Of the patients who visited three times or more, the ratio of parallel of each patient and the number of patients who showed 50% and more parallel was 266 out of 322 (82.6%) (Table 4) – this was larger than that of the patients whose SS decreased while TS increased or whose SS increased while TS decreased.

Case: Serious atopic dermatitis

A 26-year-old Japanese female visited to the Department of

Table 3. Number and ratio of patients who visited two times to our hospital twice

	Parallel	Non-parallel	Total	TS↑&SS↑
Serious M	40(5.5%)	13	53	0
F	38(77.6%)	11	49	2
Moderate M	92(75.4%)	30	122	5
F	128(80.5%)	31	159	9
Mild M	41(70.7%)	17	58	3
F	87(71.9%)	34	121	12
Total	426(75.8%)	136	562	31

Table 4. Number and ratio of patients with a change to parallel in TS and SS and who made three or more hospital visits

Numbers in parentheses show the total number and ratio of the patients who showed a correlation of •†50% between TS and SS.

Ratio of parallel	Male	Female	Total
A 100%	38	56	94
B 50%<	27	69	96
C 50%	37(102: 79.7%)	39(164: 84.5%)	76(266: 82.6%)
D 50%>	20	24	44
E 0%	6	6	12
Total	128	194	322

Dermatology, Osaka Kaisei Hospital on May 13, 1999, with an approximately 20-year history of recalcitrant pruritic eruptions of almost the entire body with more than 30% surface inflammation, diagnosed as serious atopic dermatitis. She was treated with antibiotics and anti-septic, anti-inflammatory, anti-fungal and anti-allergic agents as well as SG-L for life style improvement. After tonsillectomy was performed on August 1, 1999, her skin symptoms almost improved for a short time (Fig.1). However, the skin symptoms aggravated on December 1, 1999 as she returned to her ordinary life style in the middle of November. She retired from company for her personal reasons and moved to her parent's house in March 2000. Her TS had changed almost in parallel with her SS (Figs. 1, 2).

Discussion

Acute infectious diseases lead to tender and asymmetrically enlarged lymph nodes. In chronic infectious and immunologic diseases, and in malignancy, lymph nodes become enlarged without any tenderness (5). Submandibular and axillary lymph nodes can be felt as small nodules (5, 6) often causing intense pain on gentle palpation, regardless of the person's disease status (1-4). No acute infections were found around the lymph nodes underlying such tenderness (1-4). However, for patients who have been on long-term steroid treatment or have such a history, even when most of the skin symptoms are not improved, tenderness of the tender point sites may have been eliminated so caution is required (2).

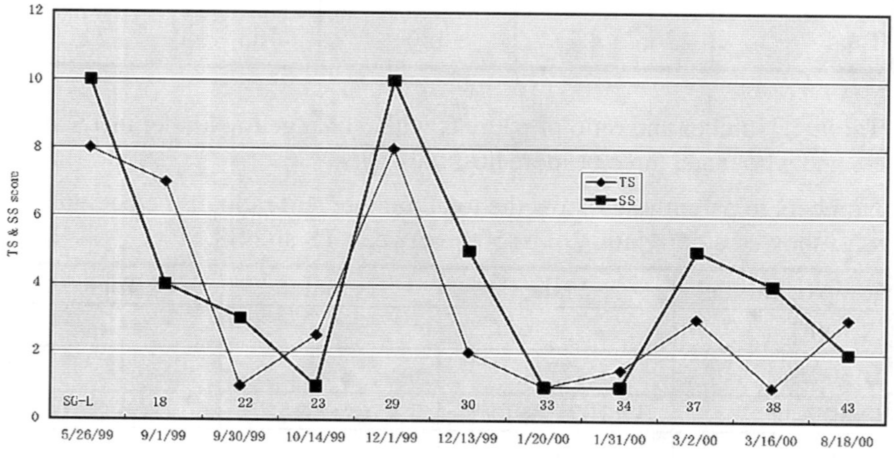

Fig. 1. Relationship between total tenderness(TS) and skin symptoms(SS) in one of the patient with atopic dermatitis (serious).

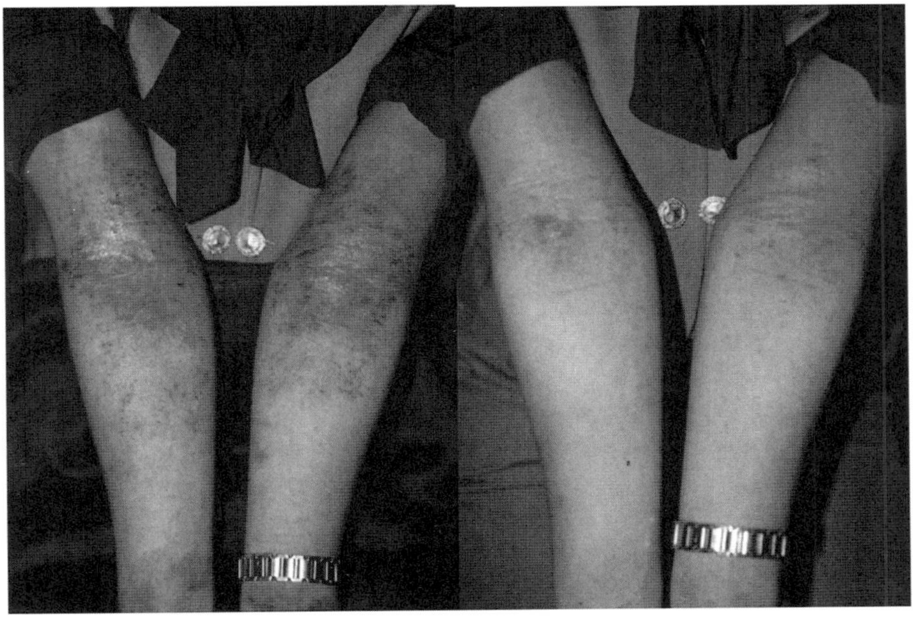

Fig.2. Skin manifestation Left: at first visit (TS 8, SS 10). Right: about 4 months later (TS 2.5, SS 1).

References

1. Shoji A: Tender spots in patients with atopic dermatitis. Lymphology 35 (Suppl): 703-705, 2002.
2. Shoji A: Tender spots in patients with atopic dermatitis. – The effect of systemic steroid therapy – Jap J Lymphology 25:21-28,2002.
3. Shoji A: Relationship between tenderness on tender point sites and skin symptoms.– Prurigo and bullous diseases – Jap J Laser Therapy, 2:17-22, 2004.
4. Shoji A: LLLT in Dermatological disorders. – An Efficacy and Adverse effect – Jap J Laser Therapy, 3:18-22, 2005.
5. Bannister LH, Berry MM, Collins P et al: Gray's Anatomy 38th ed. Churchll Livingstone, London, 1995.
6. Platzer W(Translated by Harry Monsen): Pernkopf Anatomy 3rd ed. Volume ‡T Head and Neck. Urban & Schwarzenberg, Baltimore-Munich, 1989, pp 236-7, 281, 305.

RELATIONSHIP BETWEEN THE DEGREE OF TENDERNESS AT TENDER POINT SITES AND SKIN SYMPTOMS IN PATIENTS WITH CHRONIC CONTACT DERMATITIS

Akinobu Shoji

Department of Dermatology, Osaka Kaisei Hospital

Introduction

Digital pressure of approximately 5 kg was applied at the following 8 tender point sites including outer aspect of right and left elbows (LE), axillary regions of both right and left arms(Ax), median side of right and left supra-clavicular regions(MSC) and right and left submandibular (SM). In most patients with skin diseases and in healthy people (98.4%), it elicits the severest tenderness on SM (1,2). In view of significant changes in degree of tenderness on LE, Ax and MSC during hospital visits, the relationship between the lymph node tenderness and skin symptoms was examined.

Methods

<Patients>

A total of 32 patients (age range 19-70, average 40.7) – 8 male (age range 19-62 average 34.5) and 24 female (age range 19-70 average 42.8) – with idiopathic chronic dermatitis.

<Tender point sites>

Digital pressure of approximately 5 kg was applied with fingers at the following 8 tender point sites: LE, Ax, MSC and SM. When I looked for some tumors and/ or nodules in submandibular and axillar regions, I pressed them with fingers (Figs.1, 2, 3)(1,2,3).

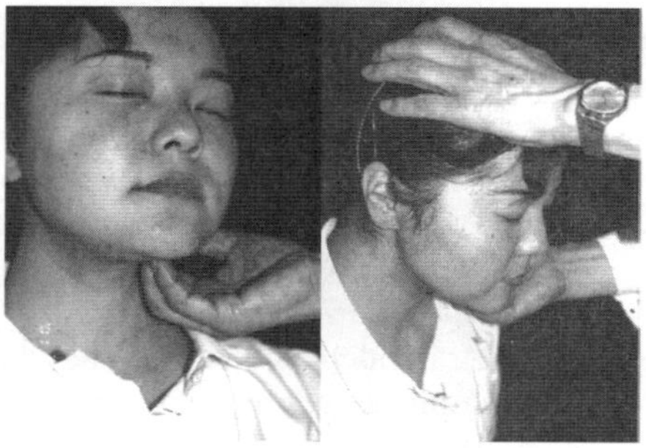

Fig. 1. Submandibular regions(SM) were pressed with the r-thumb outside and the r-2, 3, 4 fingers inside of the patient's left submandibular to deeply pinch the body of mandible (jaw bone) deeply while supporting the patient's head by putting the left hand on the r-side of the patient's scalp.

<Degree of tenderness>

Degree of tenderness was determined and categorized into 7 grades as follows: "violent" (score 5) for spontaneous pain or violent pain, "very" (score 4) indicating very strong pain, "strong" (score 3), "moderate" (score 2), "mild" (score 1), "weak" (score 0.5), and no tenderness (score 0). When scores were different between right and left, the higher value was used for the statistical calculation (1, 2). Tenderness score (TS) was calculated as follows:

TS=LE+Ax+MSC+SM.

<Therapy>

Patients were treated with general medicine and suggestions for lifestyle changes for better sleep and dietary regimens (2, 4, 5).

<Skin symptoms>

Skin symptoms (SS) were recorded by patients using a 10-scale (10: the clinical manifestation at first visit, 0: complete recovery).

<Statistics>

1) TS and SS values during two consecutive visits were analyzed. Correlation between the scores were derived from changes observed: parallel with TS increase (↑), no change (→) and decrease (↓), with SS changed aggravation (↑), no change (→) and improvement (↓) respectively and non-parallel when TS changes show increase (↑), no change (→) and decrease (↓), with SS changes showing improvement (↓) or no change (→), aggravation (↑) or improvement (↓) and aggravation (↑) or no change (→) respectively (Table 1).
2) TS and SS of the current visit were compared with values of the previous visit if the patients had already visited in 3 times or more. We calculated the ratio of parallel for each patient and the number of patients who showed 50% and more such parallel value in order to determine the correlation between TS and SS.

Results (Fig. 4)

Twenty-five out of 32 patients (78.1%) had both the SS and TS values either decreased, no change or increased. The ratio of parallel for each patient and the number of patients who showed 50% and more was 12 out of 15 (80.0%) – this was larger than that of the patients whose SS decreased while TS increased or whose SS increased while TS decreased.

Table 1. Criteria for determining if there is a correlation between TS and SS.

↑: increase or aggravation ↓: decrease or improvement →: no change

	Change in TS	Change in SS
Parallel		
	↑	↑
	→	→
	↓	↓
Non-parallel		
	↑	↓ →
	→	↑ ↓
	↓	↑ →

Discussion

Gentle palpation of patient lymph nodes can reveal tumors or nodules, although manipulating these tender point sites with 5 kg pressure does elicit tenderness or pain (1, 2). Digital examination did not reveal any tumors or nodules on the outer aspect of the right and left elbows or median side of right and left supra-clavicle. However, we could find several different lymph nodes as tumors or suspicious nodules in axillary and submandibular regions (3) (Figs. 2, 3) varying between males and females. Statistically the number of male patients was significantly more than females with palpable tumors and/or nodules on SM ($p<0.05$) and was highly significantly in Ax ($p<0.0005$) (7). The number of male patients with palpable tumors and/or nodules was highly significantly more in SM than Ax ($p<0.000005$)(7).

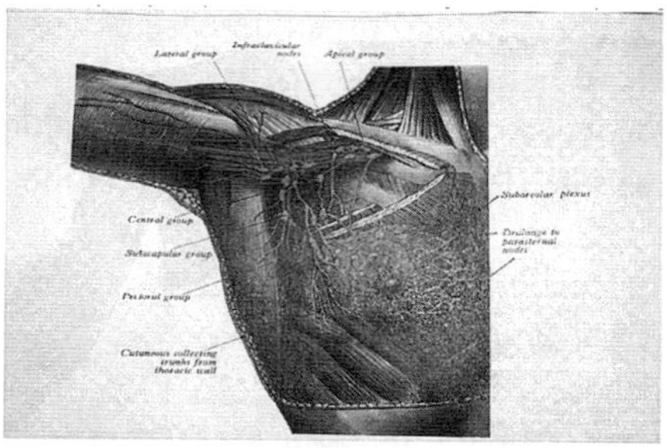

Fig. 3. Axillary lymph nodes are large, verying from 20 to 30 in number and may be divided into five not wholly distinct groups. Acknowledgment: Reprinted from Publication Gray's Anatomy 38th ed., William PL, section author: Bannister L: Haemolymphoid system, p1611, p1612, p1616, 1995, with permission from Elsevier.

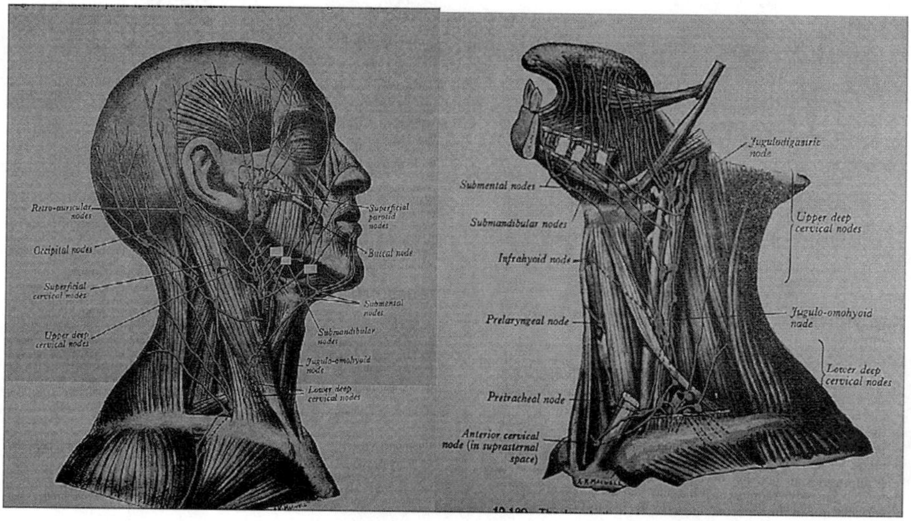

Fig. 2. In order to touch these lymph nodes, use your fingers to press from the inside to the outside towards the body of mandible, because submandibular lymph nodes (white square) are present behind the body of mandible (lower jaw bone).

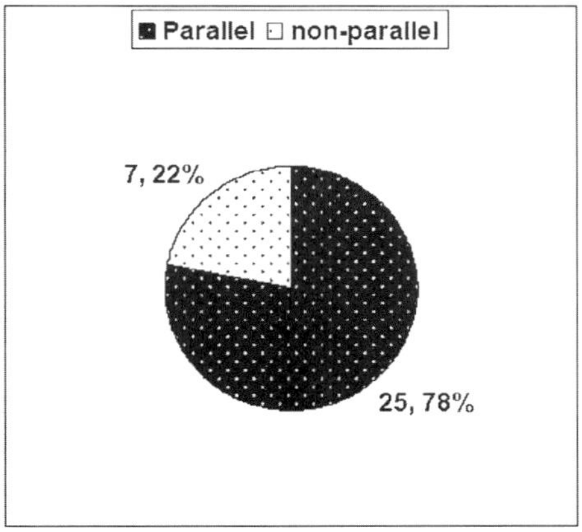

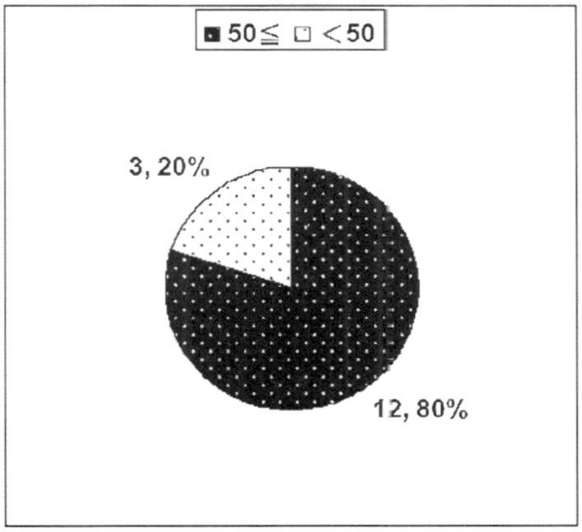

Fig. 4. Left: Comparison between the first visit and the second visit in TS and SS.
Right: Comparison between 50% and more and <50 of parallel changes.

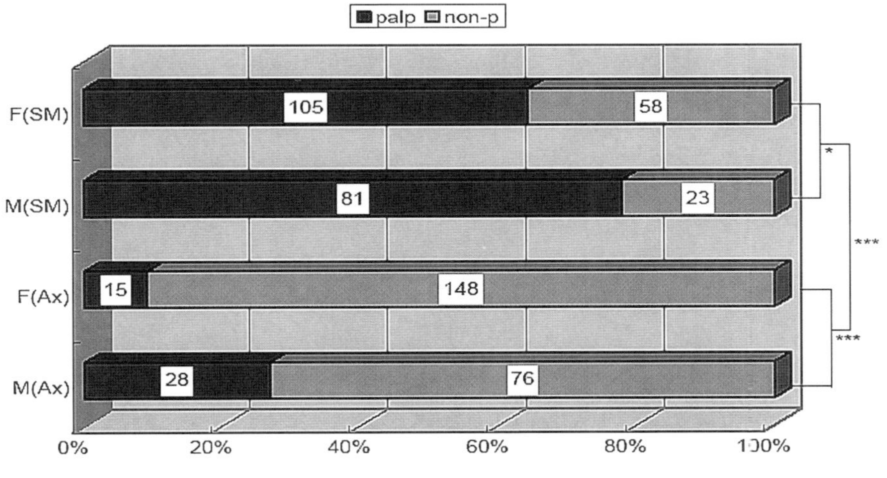

Fig. 5. The difference between male (M) and female (F) in the number of patients with palpable tumors and/or nodules on the submandibular (SM) and axillary (Ax) regions
The number of male patients exceeds that of the of females with palpable tumors and/or nodules statistically on SM ($p<0.05$) and highly statistically on Ax ($p<0.0005$).

References

1. Shoji A: Tender spots in patients with atopic dermatitis. Lymphology 35(Suppl):703-705, 2002.
2. Shoji A: Tender spots in patients with atopic dermatitis. – The effect of systemic steroid therapy – Jap J Lymphology 25:21-28,2002.
3. Bannister LH, Berry MM, Collins P et al: Gray's Anatomy 38th ed. Churchll Livingstone, London, 1995.
4. Shoji A: Relationship between tenderness on tender point sites and skin symptoms. – Prurigo and bullous diseases – Jap J Laser Therapy, 2:17-22, 2004.
5. Shoji A: LLLT in Dermatological disorders. – An Efficacy and Adverse effect – Jap J Laser Therapy, 3:18-22, 2005.
6. Platzer W(Translated by Harry Monsen): Pernkopf Anatomy 3rd ed. Volume | Head and Neck. Urban & Schwarzenberg, Baltimore-Munich, 1989, pp 236-7, 281, 305.
7. Shoji A: Tenderness on tender points. Jap J Lymphology in press.

COMPARISON OF TENDERNESS IN PATIENTS WITH FIBROMYALGIA, IN PATIENTS WITH SKIN DISEASES AND HEALTHY CONTROLS

Akinobu Shoji[1], Masao Yukioka[2]

1) Department of Dermatology, Osaka Kaisei Hospital
2) Department of Rheumatism, Yukioka Hospital

Introduction

Fibromyalgia (FM) is diagnosed on the basis of the presence of widespread pain in combination with musculoskeletal tenderness at 11 or more of the 18 specific tender point sites (1). We have compared the tenderness at 8 specific tender point sites: outer side of both right and left elbows (LE), axillary regions of both right and left arms (Ax), median side of right and left supra-clavicular regions (MSC) and submandibular regions on right and left sides of face (SM) (2), in patients with skin diseases and FM along with healthy controls.

Methods

<Patients>

Patients with FM: Forty nine patients (age range 23-73 years, average 48.6)

Patients with skin diseases: Two thousand and forty eight patients (age range 5-93 years, average 31.6) Healthy controls: Two hundred and nine persons (age range 22-82 years, average 43.5)

<Tenderness on tender point sites>

We applied digital pressure of about 5 kg on both sides of LE, Ax, MSC and SM. If the patient responded with severe tenderness or excessive pain, the pressure decreased to about 1-2kg. Degree of tenderness was decided as follows: “violent”, “very”, “strong”, “moderate”, “mild”, “weak” and no tenderness. In the event of a difference in tenderness on either side, we used the high score (2).

Table 1 Number of patients based on degree of tenderness on submandibular regions (SM), median side of supra-clavicular regions (MSC), axillary regions of (Ax) and outer side of elbows (LE) FM: fibromyalgia

SM	violent	very	strong	moderate	Mild	weak	No tenderness
FM	41	5	2	0	0	0	1
Skin Diseases	231	944	586	226	39	16	6
Health controls	26	67	60	44	8	16	6
MSC	violent	very	strong	moderate	Mild	weak	No tenderness
FM	32	10	5	2	0	0	0
Skin Diseases	10	150	621	553	345	189	177
Health controls	2	17	48	48	43	29	22
Ax	violent	very	strong	moderate	Mild	weak	No tenderness
FM	25	10	8	1	1	1	3
Skin Diseases	7	81	381	385	377	332	477
Health controls	1	6	26	25	30	42	79
LE	violent	very	strong	moderate	Mild	weak	No tenderness
FM	21	11	5	9	1	0	2
Skin Diseases	7	59	256	331	410	465	513
Health controls	1	4	22	19	37	50	76

Results

Patients with as "violent" response on SM were 41 in FM group, 231 in skin disease group and 26 in healthy control group. Patients showing "violent" with MSC included: 32 in FM group, 10 in the skin disease group and 2 in the healthy control group. The number of patients with "violent" response on Ax was: 25 in FM group, 7 in the skin disease group and 1 in the healthy control group. The number of patients determined as violent on LE included: 21 in the FM group, 7 in the skin diseases group and 1 in the healthy control group.

Patients with FM were divided into two groups: violent and non-violent, and then compared with the skin disease group and the healthy controls using ?2 test with Yates' correction for 2×2 tables. Compared to the skin disease group or the healthy controls, the increase "violent" response of FM group was highly statistically significant ($p<0.0001$).

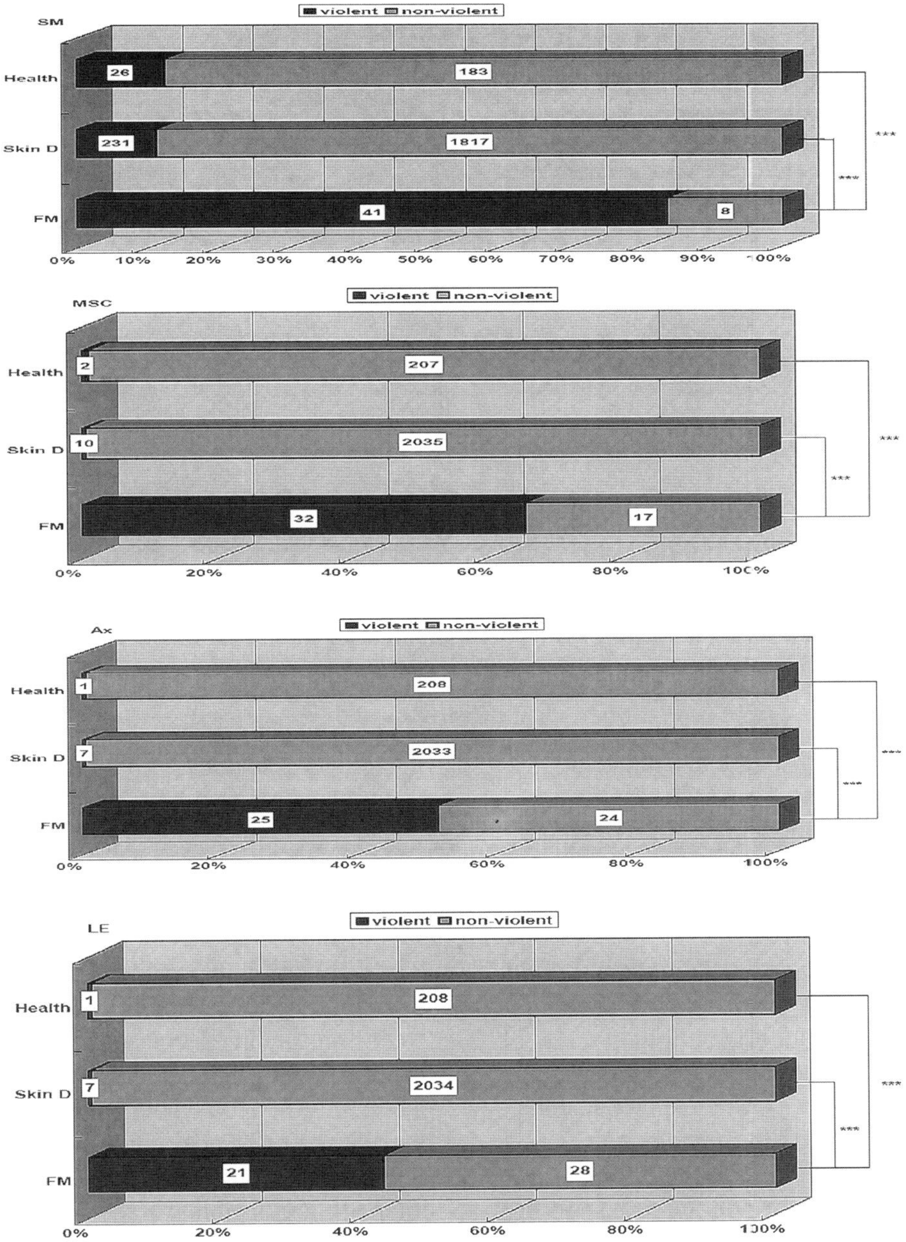

Fig. 1. Comparison of patients with a "violent" response and those with a "non-violent" response between FM group and the skin disease group (Skin D) or the healthy control group (Health) using $x2$ test with Yates' correction for 2×2 tables. FM group was found to have a highly statistically significant number of patients with a "violent" response compared to that in the Skin D or in Health ($p<0.0001$).

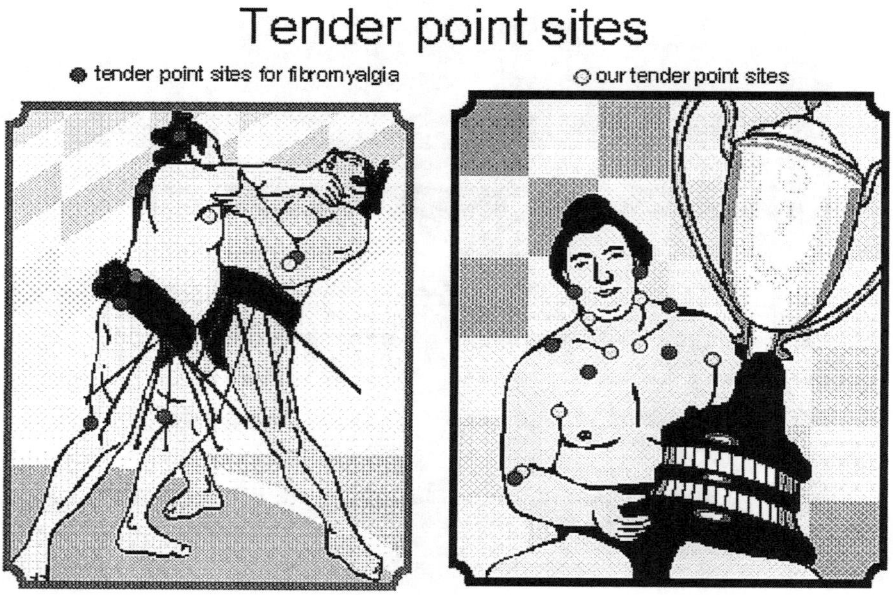

Fig. 2 Tender point sites for fibromyalgia and our tender point sites

Discussion

The American College of Rheumatology (ACR) diagnostic criteria are pain in 11 of 18 tender point sites on digital palpation (1). The eighteen tender point sites are as follows: occiput @ (2 sites): bilateral, at the suboccipital muscle insertions, Low cervical (2 sites) : bilateral, at the anterior aspect of the intertransverse spaces at C5-C7, Trapezius (2 sites): bilateral, at the midpoint of the upper border, Supraspinatus (2 sites) : bilateral, at origins, above the scapula spine near the medial border, Second rib (2 sites): bilateral, at the second costochondral junctions, just lateral to the junctions on upper surfaces, Lateral epicondyle (2 sites): bilateral, 2cm distal to the epicondyles, Gluteal (2 sites): bilateral, in upper outer quandrants of buttocks in anterior fold of muscle, Greater trochanter (2 sites): bilateral, posterior to the trochanteric prominence, Knee (2 Sites): bilateral, at the media fat pad proximal to the joint line (1) (Fig. 2). A few patients with prolonged treatment for fibromyalgia elicited "very", or "slightly decreasing" tenderness with digital palpation on our digital palpation on our tender point sites on 18 tender point sites established by the ACR diagnostic criteria. It is plausible that the tenderness in patients with FM may originate from lymph nodes based on the number of patients with "violent" response in fibromyalgia group more than that of the skin disease group or the healthy controls ($p<0.0001$).

FM is associated with various complications such as sleep disturbance, depression, rheumatic arthritis, systemic lupus erythematosus, drug eruption and systemic sclerosis. Of those complications, sleep disturbance is most characteristic of FM. Most of the patients with intense lymph node tenderness when asked about their daily activities, responded "yes" to sleep disturbance rather than to inflammatory diseases of the head and neck—upper respiratory tract disease and dental disease—or dietary problems that worsen them. When the level of tenderness becomes mild, the number of patients that respond "yes" to these problems tended to decrease. This observation should be investigated further. FM patients with sleep disturbance do not respond to sleep medications and require combined use of antidepressants, etc. When LLLT was performed in the proximity of the stellate ganglion in these patients, the so-called "laser sickness" such as nausea and vomiting occurred. The patients felt intense pain in areas irradiated with 1000mW of GaAlAs 830 nm diode laser system (Luketron, Medilaser Soft 1000, Mastushita). The findings in this study demonstrated the possibility of lymph node inflammation as a major factor underlying tenderness in the tender point sites. Therefore, improved lifestyle that would decrease the tenderness on tender point sites will likely decrease FM related symptoms.

References

1. Wolfe F, Smythe HA, Yunus MB, et al: The american college of rheumatology 1990 criteria for the classification of fibromyalgia. Arthritis Rheum 33:160-172, 1990.
2. Shoji A: Tender spots in patients with atopic dermatitis. – The effect of systemic steroid therapy – Jap J Lymphology 25:21-28,2002.
3. Bannister LH, Berry MM, Collins P et al: Gray's Anatomy 38th ed. Churchll Livingstone, London, 1995.
4. Platzer W(Translated by Harry Monsen): Pernkopf Anatomy 3rd ed. Volume | Head and Neck. Urban & Schwarzenberg, Baltimore-Munich, 1989, pp 236-7, 281, 305.

AUTHOR INDEX